DATABASE DECISIONS

Briefings on the Management of Technology

Bart O'Brien

Learning P

DATABASE DECISIONS
Briefings on the Management of Technology

How can you know what is worth knowing about technology? Often it is next to impossible to get the briefing you need about the facts of information technology, without being overwhelmed by confusing detail.

Database Decisions takes a new approach to this problem: it deliberately selects those facts and concepts that will assist decision-making. Time and again it asks:

Why is this particular fact worth the attention of non-specialists?

Why does this distinction between different varieties of technology matter?

How can you get a sense of direction in this confused area of technology?

What would be a simple example of an organisation using this knowledge to identify options and arrive at decisions?

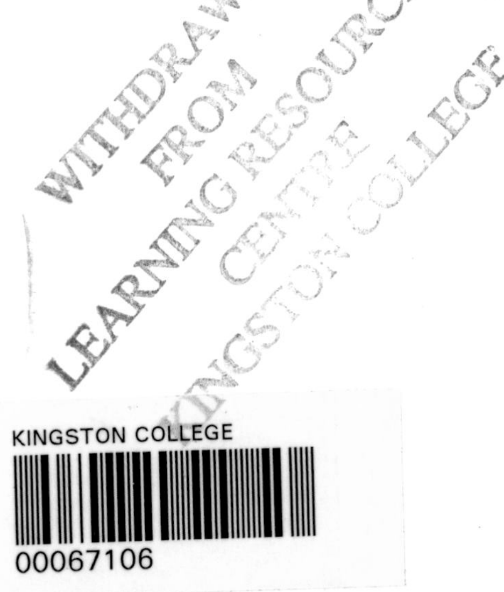

PITMAN PUBLISHING
128 Long Acre, London WC2E 9AN

A Division of Longman Group Limited

First published in Great Britain 1994

A CIP catalogue record for this book can be obtained fom the British Library.

ISBN 0 273 60289 6

Printed and bound in Great Britain by
Biddles Ltd, Guildford and King's Lynn

The Publishers' policy is to use paper manufactured from sustainable forests.

Contents

Acknowledgements

Credits are due to the following for assistance in the production of the book:

Henk and Walter Baghuis of Compubest BV, Rotterdam, the Netherlands, for PostScript printing facilities and image-editing expertise;

Cognitive Applications Ltd, Brighton, UK, for enabling reproduction of the images in Briefing 23;

and John Cushion of Pitman for enthusiasm and efficiency.

How to Use This Guide

A book that organises knowledge into a consistent format needs to start by defining conventions. The 'How to Use This Guide' section of a Michelin handbook states that two stars will mean 'worth a detour' and chevrons have a special meaning: «harbour» stands for 'a particularly attractive feature of this place is the harbour'.

The organisation of a book strongly depends on the *kind* of knowledge to be presented — something self-evident with a travel guide, but not with a guide to a technology.

What Knowledge is Worth Knowing?

Many people who are not database specialists need some knowledge of the technology. Many items of knowledge may plausibly seem to be worth knowing — concepts and explanations, general facts and product-specific facts. Far too many. The question arises: What is the most sensible approach to acquiring and using knowledge about this technology?[1]

It seems safe to avoid such topics from the textbook as 'transformation of universal to existential quantifiers' and 'heuristic algebraic query optimisation algorithms', but the relevance of many others is less easy to assess. Is it worth knowing about the main varieties of hypertext organisation or the criteria for a true distributed database system or typical problems of integrity with a geographic information system or the significance of the ANSI/SPARC three-schema architecture? This last may sound arcane but is at least as important as the others.

A plausible brief definition of the knowledge worth knowing is 'that which helps you participate in major decisions about the use of database technology in an organisation'. The notion of a major decision needs to be firmed up. Making a decision generally entails choosing between possibilities; with major decisions the possibilities available for choice have widely different implications. With this understanding, a plausible set of criteria can be given: It is worth possessing knowledge about database technology that helps you to:

- explore the range of **options** for using the technology to help the organisation;
- get some impression of the **complexity, risk** and other implications of possible options;

• ask the right **questions** to check that technical options with different business implications are noticed and considered;
• form a judgement of the competence and common sense of the **technology specialists** you discuss things with;
• *and thus* ensure that decisions are reached on a basis of **reason** rather than enthusiasm alone.

The material in this book is chosen and organised to meet these criteria. Applied to other sources of knowledge — magazine articles, suppliers' brochures, project proposals, consultants' reports and the like — the criteria can help you assess technology knowledge critically rather than passively to let it flow around you.

Another way of putting the above is to say that the knowledge in this book is meant to equip you to *participate* in decision-making about database technology, even if you are not a specialist. Of course, that does not mean that you should *take over* decision-making and banish database specialists from any position of influence. On the contrary, the better briefed you are, the better you can appreciate the contributions of experts.

Briefing Format

Textbook-like description, explanation and exercises are not the best means of meeting this book's aims. To link the *general* facts and concepts of technology to the decisions required in *specific* cases, the book's material is organised in 31 briefings, based on a standard five-segment format: *BEARINGS, POSSIBLE CONTEXT, WARRANTS, POSSIBLE DECISION-MAKING, CONNECTIONS*.

The middle segment, *WARRANTS*, is always much the largest and contains the bulk of the general knowledge about technology, organised in a form to promote well-warranted decisions in specific cases.[2] One warrant may be a comparison ('recognise three important varieties of X, each with the following pros and cons . . .'); another may set out aspects (eg 'with Y, the details are best assessed from the following six aspects . . .'); another may expose distinctions. . . and so on.[3]

WARRANTS is surrounded by two briefer segments, providing examples to justify the claim that the knowledge in the warrants can have practical relevance. *POSSIBLE CONTEXT* outlines a fabricated but nonetheless representative case where decisions are required.[4] *POSSIBLE DECISION-MAKING* describes how the analysis of technology in the briefing's main segment can provide good warrants for decisions in the representative case.

These middle three segments are cocooned within two segments whose purpose is orientation. *BEARINGS* locates the topics covered by the briefing in the picture of database technology as a whole. *CONNECTIONS* contains pointers to briefings elsewhere in the book, sometimes dealing with an interlocking topic, sometimes presenting parallel ideas in an unexpected area.

'Untangling' Briefings

Certain briefings are named 'Untangling . . .' As this suggests, they are mainly concerned with imposing order on some broad and complicated regions of technology.

Not all have *POSSIBLE CONTEXT* and *POSSIBLE DECISION-MAKING* segments, since it is often evident without this that untangling a certain area will assist decision-making.

In these briefings the *CONNECTIONS* segment shows how each of the main divisions of the subject area just identified are covered by subsequent briefings.

1. Untangling Database Technology

BEARINGS

Many books decompose a subject neatly into parts, chapters, sections and sub-sections. The breakdown may seem impeccable to somebody who possesses most of the knowledge already, but often it isn't a good means of *developing* an understanding of the whole subject.

A better approach may be to start off with an outline mental chart of the subject's main elements and their interactions. Then new insights and facts can be added gradually within the areas marked out by the chart.[1]

Samuelson's famous economics textbook begins with an outline chart, relating together taxes, labour, real GNP and so on. It helps the reader maintain a sense of direction as the elements and their interactions are gradually explored in more detail. This briefing follows an analogous approach by charting out database technology.

POSSIBLE CONTEXT

As a thought experiment, take the case of Pink Gum Products, a typical company using database technology in typical ways. You watch the system in operation, study its documentation and talk to its users and the technologists. You endeavour to summarise the main characteristics of Pink Gum's system in a way that will depict the main features of the whole forest rather than its trees, shrubs, bushes and ferns. Any description should minimise incidental detail specific to this particular company's system, but be sufficiently acute to expose its significant features in a comparison with a hundred other database systems from other companies and industries. How should such a description be organised?

WARRANTS

The thought experiment leads to a ten-element chart of the topics in database technology that are worth knowing about. This main chart is prepared by two simpler, though fundamental, charts.

Chart of Basic Concepts

First, separate out three things:

- **Database**: a body of related data, eg data about the customers, suppliers, outstanding works orders, material requirements plans etc of a manufacturing company.
- **DBMS** (database management system — but this full form is best ignored): a software product providing general-purpose facilities for setting up and using a database.
- **Database system**: the whole system by which the database of (say) a manufacturing company is used together with various hardware and software components to process customer orders, work out requirements for orders from suppliers and so on.

The software components of a database system will include both a DBMS — a general-purpose software product, Informix or Ingres or Sybase, say — and application software specially written for the particular application.

These terms and distinctions are widely accepted. They may seem straightforward, but even textbooks occasionally drift away from them.[2]

One possible false impression needs to be avoided. To say that a certain company has a *database system* may seem to imply that numerous other types of system exist and that many sensibly managed companies have no need for database systems at all. In reality, almost every organisation needs computer systems that store data, and database technology is the normal means of storing and accessing data. Whether to have a database system at all is rarely a serious issue in decisions about new developments; the main decisions concern the characteristics the database system should have.[3]

Charting the Factors of Supply and Demand

In understanding a complete database system (as opposed to a database or DBMS) one particular organising principle is fundamental. The description of a system might include some notes such as 'customer orders are keyed in and shown on a screen that is formatted rather like a paper form' or 'the system records links between similar products, so that if one is out of stock, another can be automatically suggested'. But other points about the system seem rather different in character: 'the system uses optimistic locking techniques to enable several people to access the same data concurrently' and 'data relevant to credit control for customers with multiple branches is stored using a special form of indexing, so that, though complex, it can be retrieved and updated far quicker than most other data'. What is the essential difference?

- Matters such as the order-input screen and the links between products are non-technical **demands** raised by the non-computer managers and staff of an organisation. They will surely care very much about any changes to these things. It would be absurd for somebody with a purely technical responsibility to decide that in future data about new orders would be collected in an entirely different way, or that from now on there was no purpose in the system suggesting alternative products.
- But locking and indexing are **supply** matters; they are technical devices intended to supply the demands placed on the system by the business. If the database administrator decides to alter the detail of these things, the line managers will probably have no strong feelings — provided, of course, that they have faith in the general competence of the database administrator.

A good first step towards thinking clearly about any technology is to see how certain matters are essentially demand for which supply is required, and others essentially supply that meets certain demands.

The second step is to see how supply and demand matters are often *intertwined* in complex ways. Take another possible observation: 'Each individual PC holds its own small database of current discount rates, but also accesses the main database that is held by a mainframe computer.' Any discussion of why this was done and whether some other setup might be better would probably raise issues on both sides of any supply-demand border. It is true that an essentially technical arrangement is being described; but to justify it as better than some other arrangement you would have to go into questions such as how complex the company's discount procedures were, how often the discount rates changed, what kind of override possibilities were desired and so on.[4]

Chart of Elements of Database Technology

The diagram suggests how any database system can be described within ten main topics, and, somewhat impressionistically, locates these topics along a supply-demand axis. The scope of the chart's elements is best suggested by brief example questions:

• **Kind of data.** What kind of material has to be stored in the database: numeric fields, texts, images etc?

• **Structure of data.** How is the data structured from a logical, as opposed to technical, point of view? What kind of links between different items does the database record?

• **Access to data.** What kind of interface (eg form-like screen) helps you get at data? How simple is it to extract and bring together items of information from different parts of the database?

• **Integrity**. How does the system ensure that different parts of the database remain consistent? What controls are there on complicated updates and how automatically are they enforced?

• **CRS (concurrency control, recovery, security)** — an acronym, devised for this book. What about the special problems posed by several people accessing and perhaps updating an item of data at the same time? How is recovery from hardware failure handled? What security arrangements, such as passwords, are there? These are rather like everyday infrastructure services such as electricity, fresh water, rubbish collection and so on. If handled successfully, most people will scarcely be aware of the challenges they pose. Only when they break down does their importance become clear.

• **Deep design.** What indexing and similar technical tricks are used to store the database for speedy access and update without excessive indulgence in hardware resources?

• **Database system architecture.** How do the main components of the system — pieces of hardware, pieces of database, pieces of software — fit together?

• **Data modelling.** What techniques are used to model information and database structure? Are there automatic features to draw diagrams and to control design consistency?

• **Software development.** What kind of programming languages and related facilities are used to develop the application software?

• **Database system control.** What facilities co-ordinate the work of modelling, design and development, document the operational system and allow it to evolve?

These elements differ in important ways:

• The first six elements — **kind of data** to **deep design** — each describe a certain database system as it is at a certain time. For instance, a substantial part of the system's current demand can be described under structure, while part of the supply that currently meets the system's demand can be described under deep design.

Charting the Elements of Database Technology

SUPPLY ⟷ DEMAND

Describing a certain database system at a certain time

Describing a system, but also its flexibility for change

Describing activities and processes

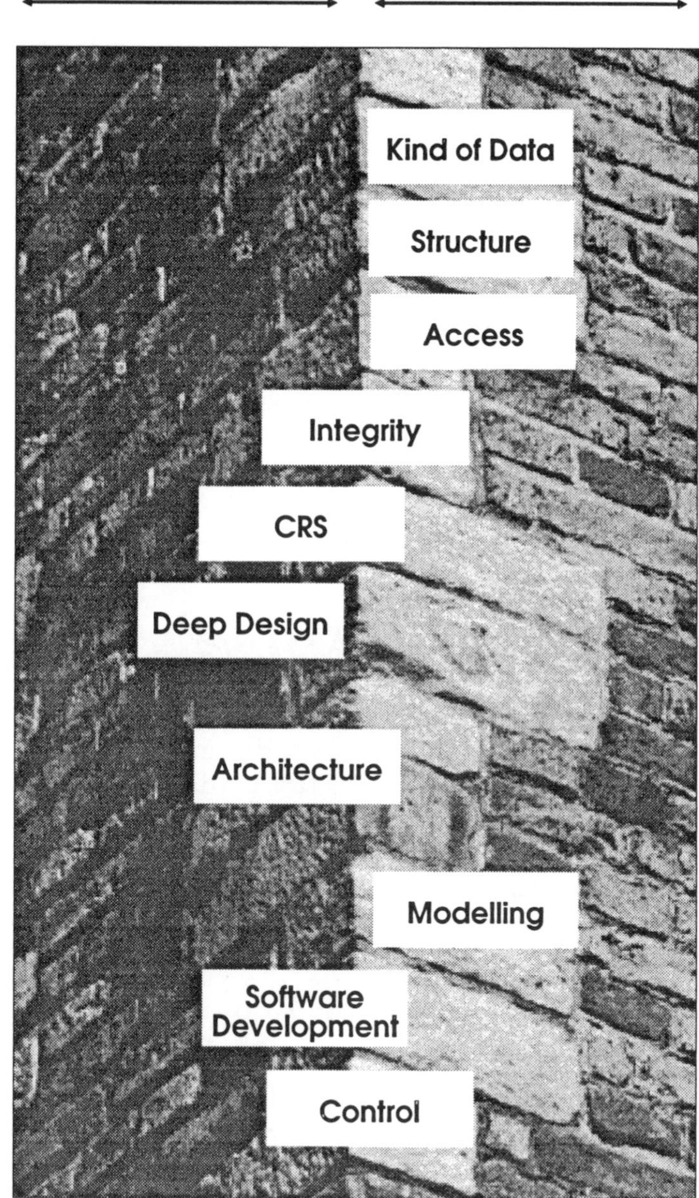

SUMMARY OF WARRANTS

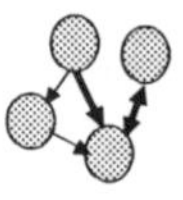

Chart connecting Top-level Concepts in Database Technology:
Database; DBMS; Database system

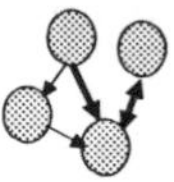

Chart of Interplay of Fundamental Factors:
Supply and demand

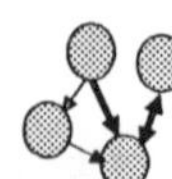

Chart of Ten Elements of Database Technology:
Kind of data; Structure of data; Access to data; Integrity; CRS (concurrency control, recovery, security); Deep design; Database system architecture; Data modelling; Software development; Database system control

- The next element — **architecture** — is about two things: how things fit together as a whole, in a certain system at a certain time and also, how much flexibility there is to change some parts of the system over time without disturbing others.
- The last three — **modelling to control** — are mainly concerned with the activities and processes of developing and controlling a database system. For instance, modelling is work that develops demand, while software development activities both develop demand in detail and also make the software to supply it.

POSSIBLE DECISION-MAKING

What do you gain by charting database technology in this way? The rest of the book uses the chart to organise its facts and concepts. Therefore the real test is whether the chart does provide a sense of direction in this complicated field. If it does, then it will promote more effective decision-making.[5] But imagine that the chart is explained to the board of Pink Gum Products. What awkward questions might they pose?

The Relevance of Supply Knowledge

At first glance it may seem that for most people involved in decision-making only demand-side knowledge is worth acquiring, since knowledge of supply matters is relevant only to technology specialists. But that is seriously over-simple.

For good decisions demand and supply possibilities should interact. Suppose you pose demands with no awareness whatsoever of their supply implications; you may well get what you ask for, without ever realising that for half the price you could have had a system meeting 90% of the demands — perhaps a better buy. Moreover, if you have some awareness of supply possibilities it may well stimulate you to identify certain demands you might otherwise not have noticed. And awareness of supply constraints may even be a spur to conceiving resourceful demands.[6]

How then do you equip yourself with knowledge to participate in decision-making about database technology? Here are some general principles:

- On a pure **demand** topic, aim for a clear analysis of demand options — not all options theoretically conceivable, but the main distinct options typically found in the current state of technology. Of course, in any particular case, you may decide to articulate some demand outside this range of options, but if so, it is surely best at least to know that you are being bold or eccentric.
- On a pure **supply** topic, it isn't worthwhile to try to know all the main options. You need a broad awareness of how the supply can interact with demand. This can be partly rational (eg 'This supply option is plainly more extravagant than this other one, but it is inescapable if certain demands are to be met . . .') and partly impressionistic (eg 'Here is a representative example of the kind of difficulty the supply-side designer faces in meeting certain demands . . .')
- Many topics straddle the **supply-demand border**. Temper the above principles accordingly, and above all see how supply and demand factors interact.

The Chart and DBMSs

The chart is a useful means of structuring the description of a *database system* in any particular organisation. The other two elements identified early on were *database* and *DBMS*. How do they fit in?

A description of any particular database system based on the elements given necessarily includes an account of the particular database(s) that exist. But a particular database system, such as Pink Gum's, uses a certain DBMS — a standard software product, such as DB2 or Allbase or Supra, which hundreds of other organisations use in their own database systems.

Thus the chart can also be used for a different job: its elements help focus on the characteristics of the database systems that *any particular DBMS software product* is good at supporting.

DBMSs are sometimes compared in matrices where each column is a product and each row one of the hundreds of possible features a product may have. But this makes it difficult to see the lawns for the blades of grass. By contrast, the ten-element chart makes useful generalisation possible:

'DBMS A is very appropriate for systems dominated by the demand to store different kinds of data, such as text and graphics.'

'If integrity is a big issue for the proposed system, DBMS B has an exceptionally sophisticated set of features.'

'DBMSs C and D are both strong in deep design, even though they offer different features.'

'The great selling-point of DBMS E is its software development features.'

'This selection process would be easier if we grouped our list of 300 possible features under ten headings, from kind of data through to control.'

Chart Status

General charts and models can be powerful but dangerous. Unless their status is clear, misunderstandings easily arise. Does this chart describe objectively how things are or does it recommend how things ought to be? Is the chart built of elements that actually do exist separately or does it suggest aspects or themes of one complex entity? If different people make different assumptions about such matters a chart's value may even be negative.

This chart claims to identify and relate *elements that are useful for describing database systems* — primitive as well as sophisticated systems and foolish as well as sensible ones:

- It doesn't imply that a system should have any particular feature for one-off enquiries — merely that this issue is best seen as part of a certain broader issue, access to data.
- It doesn't recommend that a system should have a separate software module for its password arrangements — only that the convenient place to discuss passwords is within CRS, rather than anywhere else.
- It doesn't propose ways of designing the architecture of a system —just that this should be treated as a separate element in describing any system.

Wouldn't an existing, established chart serve just as well? Some of the database textbooks do present lists of central database themes early on, but most are unsatisfactory. One lists four characteristics that distinguish the database approach from file processing, seven capabilities that an ideal DBMS would include and five additional advantages of the database approach over traditional methods.[7] The sixteen items overlap and some have a hazy status, but, most important, they have little to do with decision-making. Imagine saying to someone who knew nothing about cars: 'To enter this field of knowledge you need this list of the advantages of a car over a horse and carriage, and a specification of the capabilities of the ideal car.' That would scarcely provide any understanding of how elements such as fuel economy, reliability, style and so on interact to affect any decision about the best choice of car for a particular case.

CONNECTIONS

1. Untangling Database Technology	This briefing; establishing three-item chart: database, DBMS and database system — also ten-element chart to describe database systems
2. Untangling Kinds of Data	Distinguishing mainstream from other kinds of data

Briefings 3-16 Database systems (mainstream data) — most briefings about just one of the chart elements

17. Mainstream Software Products	DBMS and other products (mainstream)

Briefings 18-27 Database systems (non-mainstream and hybrid with mainstream) — most briefings about a particular type of system, concentrating on one or a few elements that expose particularly characteristic issues

28. Non-Mainstream Software Products	DBMS and other products (non-mainstream)

Briefings 29-31 Topics that transcend above distinctions or range further afield

2. Untangling Kinds of Data

BEARINGS

The kind of data to be stored in the database is the first element on the chart of database technology.

In the final analysis, many of the ten elements are inter-related in complex ways, but the kind of data has a cardinal importance. If (say) photos and texts are to be stored in a database rather than maps and tables of figures, this will have far-reaching effects on considerations of access, deep design, architecture and practically everything else.

Therefore a clear view of the various kinds of data that can be kept in a database is an essential step towards making sense of this technology and taking rational decisions about its use.

POSSIBLE CONTEXT

Imagine an agency for office staff called (say) Casuarina. The directors of Casuarina are ambitious to go far beyond their present business of supplying temporary typists and clerks. They have plans to move upmarket to place other kinds of staff, and on a permanent basis too. It seems an attractive prospect to offer prestigious new services for higher-level appointments: placing university lecturers, management consultants, financial controllers, publishers' acquisition editors and so on. This, it is hoped, will change the company's image as a supplier of mere office staff, and in the very long run be profitable too.

Casuarina is also considering other types of service beyond matching people to vacancies: counselling executives with career problems, for instance. In fact, Casuarina's provisional business strategy is to offer practically every kind of human resources service, both to employers and to candidates.

This strategy is still provisional for the following reasons:

- Casuarina doesn't intend to offer services that are utterly new. Other companies already offer services for higher-level appointments, counselling and so on.
- Rather, the idea is to offer services that are *better* than those of competitors. The key to this, so it is thought, is imaginative use of information technology.
- Therefore, the Casuarina directors need to make realistic judgements on just how new service opportunities and new technology possibilities should be matched together. Until they are at least this far, they can't claim to have a credible strategy, only fine aspirations.

During the brain-storming sessions it soon becomes clear that different types of service call for *different kinds of data* to be stored in a database. As a trivial example, any service will involve storing data such as the candidate's name and address, but if there is an extra facility to display a digitised photo of a candidate and print it out on documents sent to employers then this clearly entails storing a different kind of data altogether.

For Casuarina, a clear breakdown of the main different kinds of data that might be stored in a database will help in maintaining a sense of proportion about possible new services and their implications.

WARRANTS

It used to be reasonable to make broad, unspoken assumptions about the kind of data that could be kept in a computer database. Any data other than this mainstream kind of data, if considered at all, could be seen as relevant only to narrow, unusual applications. That is no longer a reliable assumption. It is now essential to make a conscious distinction between mainstream and other kinds of data, and have a reasonable grasp of the main kinds of data other than mainstream.

The natural approach for this briefing is to describe mainstream data as briskly as possible and then sketch out the ways in which other kinds of data differ.

Aspects of Mainstream Data

The majority of current database systems store and work with **mainstream data**, with, in crude summary, four main aspects:

- The whole body of data consists of many **small, individual items** of data, that may be called fields or data elements or something of the sort.

- The data items are related to each other in **patterns**, called records or segments or tables or something similar.
- The data items within each pattern are subject to **definable constraints** on their size in characters or on the values they may contain.
- The patterns may be complex but they are definable and **consistently repeated**.

To see how this abstract definition fits a typical system consider a straightforward database at an employment agency:

- The *surname* of each person seeking a job is one data item; *date-of-birth, sex* and *phone-number* are others. A *status-code* showing whether the person is currently employed or unemployed is another.
- These, together with various other data items, make up a *Candidate* record. If there are ten thousand candidates, there will be ten thousand such records, each storing the data in this format.
- There are other records, whose format contains other data items: *Vacancy* records and *Employer* records and *Salesperson-commission* records and *Government-subsidy-scheme* records.

Thus, the whole body of data is organised in definable, consistently repeated patterns. This way of thinking of data is relevant to computer applications in a thousand industries. Data items may be grouped together in quite complicated records, or perhaps arranged in rather simple records, that are related to each other in complex ways. Nevertheless, the basic idea remains: a database is a body of data items arranged in clearly definable, repeated patterns.

Most of the best-known database technology is concerned with managing this mainstream data. Many systems analysts and information analysts could define almost their whole job as translating the rather vague or convoluted demands of their organisations into the familiar mainstream form that can be readily supplied by database technology. This approach works well in very many systems found in business and government, but it doesn't fit every single case. To see why not, consider a related but different kind of data.

Comparison between Text and Mainstream Data

A database of job-seeking university lecturers would need to store data about each person's field of knowledge. The mainstream approach would have a *doctoral-thesis-code* within each *Candidate record.* In a code value of (say) 2467963, the 7 in the fourth digit might mean 'languages', the 9 in the fifth digit 'linguistic history', the 6 after that 'Romance' (rather than Germanic etc)' and the final

3 'Italian'. Then if a university needed a lecturer on the history of the Italian language, the database system could use the code to make a match. If another vacancy was for a lecturer on the history of *any* Romance language, or another was for a lecturer on any aspect of *Italian*, the coding system could handle that too, because each of the seven digits has its meaning.

However neat this may seem, there are grave disadvantages. Working out the detail of a comprehensive coding system might require years of work by highly paid experts before the system could even start. Then suppose that, once the system was live, one of the first unemployed academics to come into a branch office was the author of 'The account books of Florentine bankers as evidence for medieval Tuscan'. Staff at any branch would have to be skilled enough to judge that the *doctoral-thesis-code* here should indicate the history of the Italian language rather than accountancy. Other drawbacks could be spelt out but the essential point is that the mainstream approach to data, no matter how cleverly applied, doesn't suit this case. Moreover, this is just an example of quite a wide problem. Mainstream data is just as inappropriate in describing the skills of people in the law, medicine, publishing, computers, advertising or practically everything commonly regarded as a profession.

Fortunately there is a simpler, non-mainstream approach to this kind of problem: ask each candidate to write a summary of expertise in up to 300 words, and store that in the database. These texts in the database could then be searched for words like 'Italian', 'Tuscan'. 'Romance' and so on. The need for intricate coding systems disappears.

This **text data** is very different from mainstream data. There the seventh data item in every *Candidate* record always has the same well-defined significance (eg *last-salary*). Here, within a 300-word text it is impossible to say that the seventh or any other word always means anything in particular. It could be 'the' or 'Florentine' or 'paradoxical' etc.

Keyword Data

Text is closely associated with another kind of non-mainstream data. A *Candidate* record in a database might contain **keywords** (or key phrases — this rider will be dropped from now on): 'historical linguistics', 'Italian', 'socio-semantics', 'transformational grammar' etc. Each of these is a term included in the record to help convey the candidate's knowledge, skills and experience.

At first sight, keywords resemble mainstream data in that

individual data items have a fixed format and can be arranged into consistent, larger patterns. But there are important differences, making keyword data a special case, lying between mainstream and text data:

- If up to (say) ten keywords in arbitrary order are allowed in a record, the **consistent pattern** of mainstream data is undermined. Were it possible to lay down that *keyword-1* (and only *keyword-1*) always described (say) a person's profession, while *keyword-2* was always the person's main skill and so on, then the data would be normal mainstream and each field could be given a descriptive name. But that degree of structuring isn't usually possible with keywords.
- Unlike a code, a keyword has the advantages of the richness of **text** and the disadvantages of its imprecision. Take the key phrases: 'history of language', 'linguistic history', 'historical linguistics'. One person might regard all three as synonymous while another might consider them to have subtly different meanings.

Though different from mainstream, keyword data is less radically distinct than text. It is very prominent in one particular application — the cataloguing of literature, either the contents of libraries or newly published books and journal articles. In these cases, the keywords are often thought of as secondary or indicative information — as opposed to the primary texts of the books and articles themselves. However, keywords can be applied to describe any objects or beings, whose qualities are too diverse for reduction to mainstream data.

Rules Data

For a career-counselling service the expert system is a plausible technology. A computer system storing the expertise of a whole pool of counsellors could identify questions to pose to candidates and suggest avenues to explore. **Rules data** would be stored; eg 'If the whole career of this accountant has been with an accountancy practice, then consider ways of getting some commercial management experience' or 'If the candidate speaks a foreign language, then consider emigrating.'

A quite different application might help employers maximise government grants — for employing certain categories of worker, for various kinds of training schemes and so on. Finding a way through the bureaucratic labyrinth involves storing rules too. At the heart of such a system would be rules such as: 'If the company meets the conditions of paragraph 4a under the 1987 Act, and if it has already received a PQF certificate, and if it has a turnover of less than

Vector Graphics

A piece of Vector Graphics is stored in the database as a set of lines, geometric shapes and shading

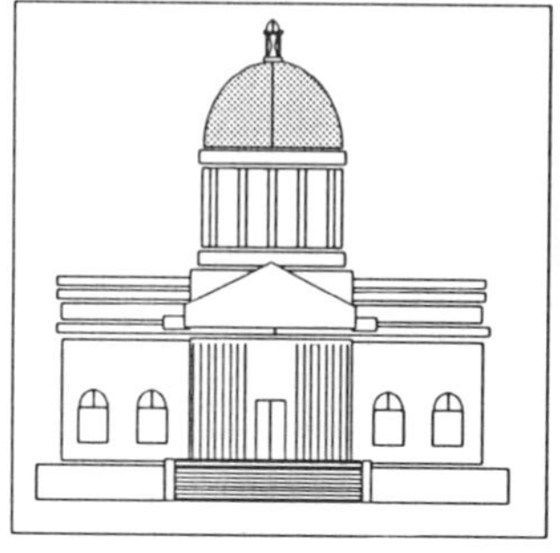

They can easily be manipulated

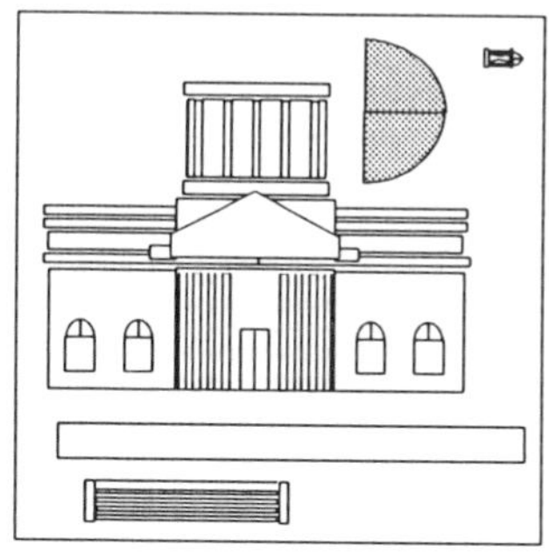

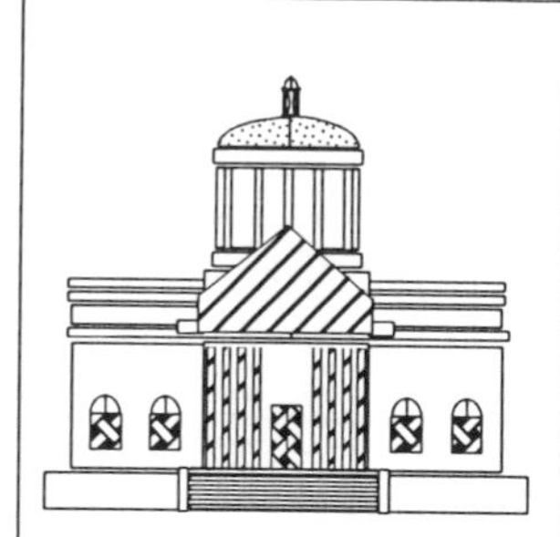

$500m, then the next step is to apply to the ministry for a form 1689A.'

These rules can be stored in a database. Though expressed in English, rules data is really closer to mainstream data than to text, because the English can be readily decomposed into discrete data items. Each rule consists of one or more 'if' limbs, followed by a 'then' limb. Each of these limbs consists of a subject (eg 'the person being counselled') and some quality possessed by the subject (eg 'being an accountant'). That isn't a precise or complete account, but with sufficient patience, a skilled analyst could break down a set of rules into very many units arranged in a consistent format.

Nevertheless, it is worth putting rules data in a separate category from mainstream data. Mainstream data stores information about candidates (eg 'Harold is an accountant') or about jobs or other things, without drawing conclusions, while rules data consists of statements about how to draw conclusions (eg 'If X is an accountant, then . .).

Bit-mapped Graphics, Vector Graphics, Spatial Data

So far, the kinds of data discussed have all shared one characteristic: they are characters (numbers, letters and so on) rather than graphics.

As the illustrations show, there are two main ways of storing **graphics data**:

Bit-mapped Graphics

A piece of Bit-mapped Graphics is stored in the database as an assembly of thousands of bits

There is no easy way
to change the proportions of the dome
or make the statue smaller relative to the building
or colour the horse white

- **Bit-mapped graphics.** To store a photo of (say) a person or building, a computer would store many thousands of bits, which, when assembled together, made up the whole picture.
- **Vector graphics.** But for some kinds of graphics (eg an architect's drawing of a building or a map of the streets of a town), the data can be held in a more clever way. Take a simple case: if a road goes in a straight line across a map, this information can be stored as the co-ordinates of the point at which the road starts, the co-ordinates of the point at which it ends, and the road's thickness. With this information, a system can generate the line representing the road, every time the map has to be shown on screen or printout.

This basic principle of vector graphics can be used to store the shape of any road; no matter what the twists and turns, they can be reduced to a set of lines and curves. Using circles and polygons as well as lines and curves, the shapes of rivers and buildings and other features can all be defined. The map and the colour photo may each be a graphic image on the screen, but the map is actually stored as an intricately fitting pattern of separate shapes.

A map stored as vector graphics has a very important property: as the diagram suggests, the data defining its shapes can be used in other ways besides just reproducing the image. A branch of an employment agency might store maps of the region in a database; then a candidate could be shown the location of a potential employer on a map on the screen. But the data about lines, shapes and the

Spatial Data: Dual Roles

Many thousands of pieces of Spatial Data

Item-type	road
Name	Langemarck Avenue
From Co-ordinates	3779630, 12243002
To Co-ordinates	3779638, 12243017
Width (metres)	11

are stored in the database for use:

constructing maps

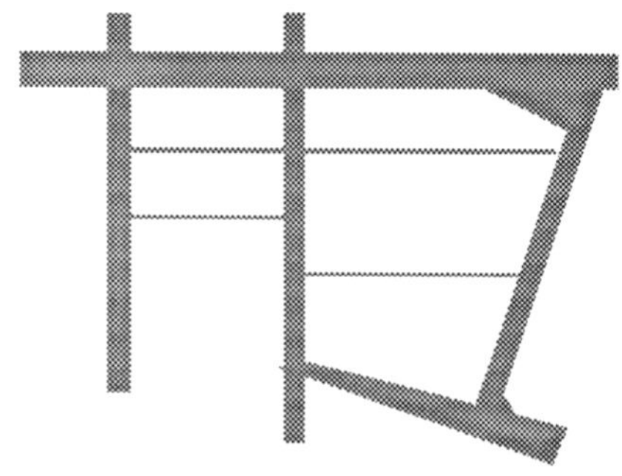

performing calculations:

to work out the distance from a certain house to a certain factory:
first, get the co-ordinates of the house; then co-ordinates of . . etc

to work out the travel time by public transport from a house to a factory:
first, use the co-ordinates of the house to establish where the nearest tram stop is . . . etc

rest stored in the database to reproduce the map might also be used by the system to *calculate* the distance between a candidate's home and workplace, and thus rule out jobs further away than some limit. Going further, the data underlying the map could be used to work out perhaps the time for travel between home and work by public transport.

Such things are possible if the map data is held as vector graphics rather than bit-mapped graphics. The spatial calculations could still be done, even if nobody ever bothered to produce the actual map on screen or printout. Data held for both the production of vector graphics and calculation is called **spatial data**.

Less Tractable Data

Databases can store many other varieties of data too. Esoteric though some may seem, they can be run through fairly briskly. Here are some examples of graphics data held in **bit-mapped** form:

- the **images of documents**; eg certificates of a candidate's

qualifications, containing various signatures, logos, university seals and so on;
- the **photos** of candidates accompanying their CVs; or photos of different jobs and workplaces, perhaps submitted by large employers to be shown to school-leavers;
- **sophisticated graphic design:** unemployed graphics designers might be allowed to store their favourite work (advertisements or book covers, perhaps) for perusal by employers.

These are just three examples marking out a spectrum of bit-mapped graphics possibilities. The further along the spectrum, the more desirable colour rather than monochrome is likely to be and the more important quality of reproduction. The image of a document needs to be easily legible, but there is little point devoting resources to raise quality above that level; with a sophisticated book cover, the higher the quality of reproduction, the better its creator will be pleased.

Before discussing the place of these kinds of data in database technology, it is best to mention briefly certain other possibilities:
- **motion video**: eg a company's video marketing itself to potential employees;
- **voice data**: an unemployed salesman might be allowed a thirty-second personal salespitch in the database;
- **audio data**: examples of the work of unemployed musicians, say.

From a *database* point of view all bit-mapped graphics, motion video, voice and audio data have much in common. They can be put together under the heading of **less tractable data**.

Characteristics of Less Tractable Data

Many issues arising with the less tractable kinds of data are humdrum practical matters such as how to go about capturing and storing data with adequate quality but without being too extravagant in resources. It may be quite feasible to store high-quality, full-colour motion video material, but pointless if the storage requirement is so great that no more than two minutes can be stored on one huge disk. If another technique makes it easy to store three hours of video on a disk, then the quality may be too poor for practical use. These are issues of technology practicality rather than authentic issues of database technology. Subtle questions of the structure, access and integrity of such data don't really arise: a bit-mapped image of a colour advertisement is simply one large item.

For this less tractable data, there is little scope for sophisticated organisation and searching of content, analogous to that of mainstream, text and spatial databases. A text database might be

SUMMARY OF WARRANTS

Aspects of Mainstream Data: Individual items of data; Related to each other in patterns; Definable constraints on size and values; Complex patterns definable and repeated

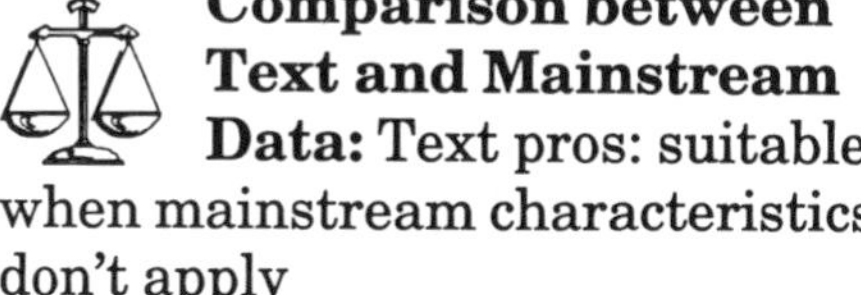

Comparison between Text and Mainstream Data: Text pros: suitable when mainstream characteristics don't apply

Distinctions between Keyword and Text or Mainstream Data: Keyword midway between the two

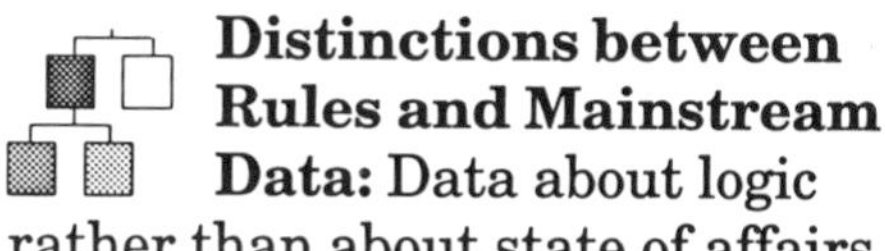

Distinctions between Rules and Mainstream Data: Data about logic rather than about state of affairs

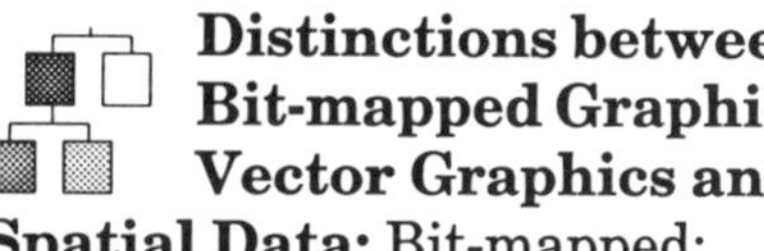

Distinctions between Bit-mapped Graphics, Vector Graphics and Spatial Data: Bit-mapped: straightforward assembly of dots; Vector: more subtle and flexible; Spatial: vector used for both maps and calculations

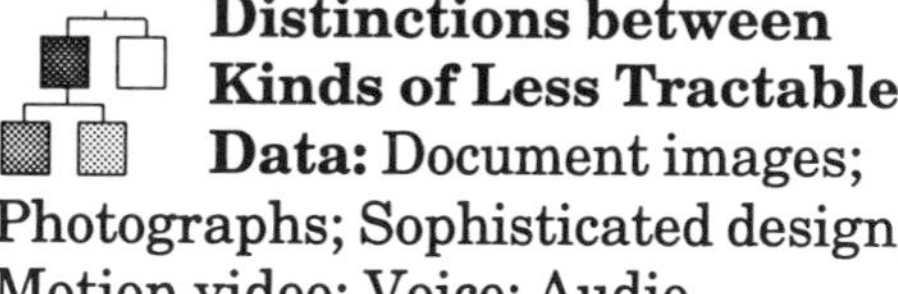

Distinctions between Kinds of Less Tractable Data: Document images; Photographs; Sophisticated design; Motion video; Voice; Audio

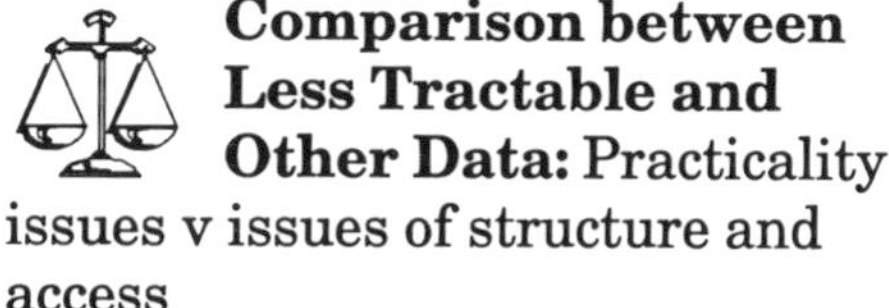

Comparison between Less Tractable and Other Data: Practicality issues v issues of structure and access

organised to handle the search: Find all academics using the words 'Italian' and 'medieval' but not 'glottochronology' in the text describing their interests. The hypothetical equivalent in a database of bit-mapped images might be: Find all graphic designs based on the image of a musical instrument, other than a guitar. At the moment, technology for that kind of task remains specialised or experimental.

Since less tractable data is difficult to organise usefully by itself, it frequently exists in **hybrid databases** — that is, in databases that combine several kinds of data. Thus a database of CVs of candidates might be a combination of mainstream data, keyword data, bit-mapped graphics (candidates' photos) and voice (for those wishing to record a message).

POSSIBLE DECISION-MAKING

It may seem self-evident that everybody involved in decisions about databases — directors as well as IT experts — should have a rough idea of the main kinds of data. Otherwise how can well-informed choices be reached? But as a thought experiment, suppose that the directors of Casuarina say that they have no interest in such matters: they will just define whatever data their business plans demand, as clearly as they can; if the technologists charged with supplying this demand find it helpful to their art to work out that the database will be (say) 90% mainstream data, 7% text and 3% spatial, then that is their affair; it is of no interest to demand-determining management.

Even if you don't find this viewpoint very compelling, it is as well to be clear why not. One day you may need cogent arguments against others who do favour it.[2]

The Responsibility Argument

First of all, a general argument of *responsibility* might be put:

- If, as at Casuarina, the business strategy of the organisation is bound up with extensive and innovative use of IT, then it follows that unwise decisions about IT may seriously damage the organisation.
- If that is so, then at least some of the directors surely need to know enough about IT to make judgements about the scope of system investments. Not to do so would be to bet the organisation on the judgement of the technical people.
- Even if you had great faith in the technical people it would be irresponsible to depend on their judgement entirely; but how can you even assess the quality of their judgement if you prefer to know nothing about their subject?
- Once you do accept that you need to know enough about IT to make *some* sensible judgements yourself, then, whatever technical details you may *exclude*, you must surely *include* enough to be able to distinguish one broad category of data from another. Otherwise how can you have any understanding at all of the scope of systems you are debating?

Sensible Proportions

This argument may seem valid but vague. How *specifically* might distinguishing broad categories of data be useful?

- Suppose that Casuarina determines a demand amounting to 99.8% mainstream, 0.1% text, 0.1% spatial data. (To talk in percentages begs several questions; but for this particular argument they can safely be left on one side.)
- Then it may well be that the *marginal* cost of having small

quantities of the two minority kinds of data is substantial. This cost is not purely financial; it embraces elapsed development time, risk of failure, need for skilled staff and so on.

- In other words, perhaps it would be a better buy to sacrifice the two minority kinds of data and stick to mainstream. Casuarina might lose very little benefit, but save a great deal of investment — financial and psychic.
- But perhaps there is some very strong reason for crossing the threshold into text and spatial data, accepting the risk and the need for skilled staff and so on. If so, might it be sensible to extract more benefit from that extra cost and (using figures impressionistically) have 92% mainstream, 6% text and 2% spatial data?

The mere expression of issues in these terms may stimulate more ideas for innovative services or better ways of doing things. Clearly all sorts of different balances and options can be hypothesised. Perhaps the choice of almost entirely mainstream data, with some tiny but important traces of textual and spatial data, really is on balance the wisest out of all the possibilities. The important thing is that the debate should take place. That can't possibly happen unless everyone concerned feels at home with the idea of recognising different kinds of data within the discussion of demand options.

Mixing Kinds of Data

Quantification of data in percentages caricatures the issues in order to make some simple points. Any realistic appreciation of options must also examine the degree to which different kinds of data may be *mixed up* together.

Suppose Casuarina directors are debating an idea for a substantial database of mainstream data that includes bit-mapped colour photos of candidates. In this scheme the two bodies of data would depend on each other only loosely. Even if some catastrophe occurred with the colour photos, the main part of the system could continue functioning quite smoothly.

But another plan might call for a substantial database of mainstream data with an admixture of rules data, and these two kinds of data might be fitted together very closely. Perhaps the rules part would govern the processing of practically every transaction that used the mainstream data. Here both components would have to work correctly and fit together perfectly if the system was to function at all. Other things being equal, this sounds a more ambitious and risky proposal than that of holding candidates' photos.

This doesn't mean that it is always best to minimise risk by coupling different kinds together of data as loosely as possible. 'Taking the risk of attempting something sophisticated but hazardous' may simply be another form of words for the positive-sounding notion of 'trying to gain competitive advantage by using technology more imaginatively'.

These matters call for judgements about tradeoffs. Unless the directors of Casuarina accept the notion of defining demand in terms of different kinds of data they won't even understand what the tradeoff factors are that need to be judged. If they do, then they will be able to give the claims and schemes of their colleagues the intelligent scrutiny they deserve.

CONNECTIONS

ALL KINDS OF DATA

Briefings 1-2 This and the previous briefing

MAINSTREAM

3. Untangling Mainstream Systems	*Overview:* the six elements from structure through to architecture

Briefings 4-10 *Detail:* mainstream topics

11. Untangling Models, Tools and Control	*Overview:* the three elements, modelling, software development and control

Briefings 12-17 *Detail:* mainstream topics

NON-MAINSTREAM AND HYBRID

18. Untangling Text Systems	*Overview:* varieties of text database system

Briefings 19-21 *Detail:* text topics

22. Untangling Hybrid Systems	*Overview:* varieties of hybrid database system

Briefings 23-28
Detail: hybrid and non-mainstream topics

ALL KINDS OF DATA

29. Object-oriented Topics	*Detail:* an approach applicable to all kinds of data
30. Untangling Adjacent Technologies	*Overview:* data and systems adjacent to database technology — not within it
31. Untangling Database and Wider Issues	*Overview:* beyond kinds of data to wider issues

3. Untangling Mainstream Systems

BEARINGS

This briefing focuses on mainstream database systems alone, and then only the six elements of the unifying chart from structure through to architecture. They all describe the *state* of a database system at a certain moment — as opposed to the *activities* represented by the last three elements.

This is still quite an extensive field. The briefing draws some distinctions and sketches out more charts to show how the six elements are related together. These untangling operations set the agenda for Briefings 4 to 10.

WARRANTS

The warrant sections of this briefing offer a variety of tools for maintaining a sense of direction among the different elements of mainstream database technology.

Distinctions between Structure and Access

It is well worth making a distinction between structure and access:

- **Structure** of data is concerned with the essential nature of the organisation of the data in database, without going into the matter of how easy it is to get at or how it may be used. Thus, the question *whether or not* the database system is inherently capable of telling you which salesperson was responsible for a certain order for a certain customer three years ago is a matter of structure.
- **Access** to data is concerned with the practicalities of getting at the data and making use of whatever structure it has. Questions such as *how easy* it is to pose ad hoc requests for information about salespersons and orders, or how pleasantly the system presents the information it extracts are questions of access.

The distinction can be a useful aid to clear thinking: 'We've taken great care to ensure that our database is *structured* in quite subtle ways. The failure of the system results from badly designed software that makes it so laborious to *access* useful data. We can probably rescue the system by adding new software to provide a mouse-based, graphic user interface without changing the database itself at all.'

'The *structure* of this database is just too crude. It is a hopeless basis for handling customer enquiries. No matter how much we spend on software development or new hardware to improve *access*, nothing can change the basic fact that this database doesn't record the links between data items with the subtlety that we need.'

Within structure of data, the classic discussion is about the logical form that a mainstream database may be given — hierarchical-network or relational. But since relational is now predominant, a more relevant issue is: How religiously or pragmatically should you follow the detailed conventions for this kind of structure?

Important! Throughout the book, unless the context clearly shows otherwise, the assumption is made that any *mainstream* database or DBMS is a *relational* one, or at least one in general relational style.

The topic of access to data can be sub-divided into four issues: the criteria that can be used for selection and combination; the degree of initiative allowed for accessing data in ways not completely defined beforehand; the interface style for formulating commands; the presentation of data on screen.

Distinctions between and within Integrity, CRS and Deep Design

First, a rough distinction can be made:

- **Integrity and CRS**. How are the special functions of integrity, concurrency control, recovery and security handled?
- **Deep design.** What technology design choices are taken to store and access the database in order to supply the complete set of demands efficiently; ie the obvious demands of the application system (being able to search and update a database that has a certain structure), in combination with the demands of integrity, concurrency control, recovery and security?

Thus, deep design is about the supply arrangements that underlie everything else: 'Bearing in mind all the updating and enquiries and concurrency control and security and other requirements of this particular system, it seems that the most effective design choices for indexes and hashing algorithms etc are as follows . . .'

But perhaps: 'No matter how cunning the deep design, we can't meet your stringent requirements on response-time in normal operation and on recovery-time after a hardware failure. We need to discuss tradeoffs; for instance, providing good response time, without quite the speed of recovery that would be ideal.'

There is no real purpose in breaking deep design down in great detail. The important thing is to possess an *impression* of what happens in this area, not to understand it in any depth.

But the other topics are well worth separating out. Here is how they typically apply in a substantial database system:

- **Integrity control**. There must be built-in safeguards that the content of the database is consistent; eg (presumably) there should be no orders in the orders part of the database for products that don't exist in the products part. Mechanisms are needed to ensure that such inconsistency can't arise.
- **Concurrency control.** The system has to make sure that if several people need to work on the same piece of data from the database simultaneously, this doesn't result in chaotic, inconsistent updating.
- **Recovery**. If some technical hitch occurs (extreme case: somebody accidentally switches off the main computer) there must be a way of restoring the database to an up-to-date, consistent state. This may be highly automatic or may require some data to be re-entered, but however it is done, the arrangements need to leave the administrator of the system sure of what has been processed and what (if any) transactions or updates have been lost and need to re-entered.
- **Security**. There must be some arrangements (eg passwords) to ensure that the whole database can't be viewed and updated by just anybody.

Integrity control and concurrency control are easily confused. The crucial difference is this:

- **Integrity control** ensures that one individual transaction (even a transaction that updates a number of different parts of the database) cannot update the database wrongly.
- **Concurrency control** ensures that two or more separate transactions, each in itself passing all checks of integrity control, but happening to occur *at the same time*, cannot thereby cause wrong updates to the database.

The difference between these two and recovery also needs to be kept clear:

- **Integrity control** ensures that an individual transaction cannot update the database wrongly *under normal circumstances*, but it can't exercise control in a case where (say) a certain transaction has to update four different parts of the database and the computer is switched off half-way through.

• Similarly, **concurrency control** prevents overlapping transactions updating the database wrongly *under normal circumstances*.
• **Recovery** is concerned with getting the system back fully operational after some technical mishap. One of the principal challenges is to ensure that the recovery procedure does not cause any of the system's normal integrity and concurrency controls to be by-passed.

The subject of recovery includes not only the actual procedure of *recovery* after a mishap, but also whatever things are done during normal *operations*, just in case there should be a mishap and recovery should be needed: keeping a log of transactions; enforcing complicated update rules so that, if necessary, some updates can be 'rolled back' during recovery; etc. Plainly, to discuss these operational arrangements, you need to take account of the recovery procedure and vice versa.[1]

Distinctions within Architecture

Architecture is the arrangement of the main components of the whole system: pieces of hardware (terminals, PCs, minicomputers etc), pieces of software (DBMS, application software, operating system and communications software), pieces of database (perhaps stored in different locations). The interest is in the way things fit together, rather than in the things themselves.

This element has two main angles: first, how effectively the architecture supplies the demands of the system at present; second, how much flexibility and scope it gives for smooth, uncomplicated growth and change. These are different things: a system might be super-efficient for today's needs, but so intricately constructed that it was inflexible; conversely, the design might be beautifully neat and amendable, because no attempt had been made to optimise its performance technically.

Here is an outline of the main architecture options:
• **Stand-alone PC.** One PC stores a database that is not shared. In all the other cases below, the architecture allows people at terminals or PCs to share data.
• **Host.** A mainframe computer or minicomputer looks after processing and storage. Access is through simple terminals.
• **File-server.** PCs are linked together in a network. Each can perform processing and can access data stored at another PC — but only in a primitive way. Complications inherent in a more sophisticated split of storage and processing are avoided.
• **Client-server.** PCs are linked together in a network. The main database is stored at a server PC. The work of accessing and processing the data is split between the server and its client PCs in

a sophisticated way, to reduce the transmission of data across the network or to gain other advantages.

- **Distributed database.** The database itself is split and stored on several computers at different locations, that also perform processing and control terminals or PCs.
- **Database machine.** The access and processing work at the hub (host or server) are split between several computers (or portions of computers) in a sophisticated way to achieve high efficiency.
- **Data warehouse.** While all the above are (roughly speaking) architectures to support update-transactions and related functions within one system, the data warehouse option segregates the system into two parts: one for transactions, and one with historical data for decision support systems.

Chart Relating Architecture to Other Elements

These architecture options interact in interesting ways with the options within the other chart elements. First, a charting of architecture, structure and access:

- **Architecture**. The three most prominent architectures are: stand-alone PC; host; client-server.
- **Structure and architecture.** With the host architecture there is a choice of structure between the relational and the hierarchical-network forms. But this is steadily becoming a side-issue; relational is the normal choice. The more important issue is the *degree* to which strict relational theory is followed.

With stand-alone PC, hierarchical-network is even less of an option. Though a structure in relational style is invariably used, the system usually scores low by the standards of relational theory.

A client-server architecture may well use a long-established database of hierarchical-network structure at the server. But most development of new software products to provide server DBMSs rests on relational assumptions.

- **Access and architecture.** A graphic, colour, multi-window, mouse etc interface is usually better than a plain green-on-black terminal screen showing just numbers and letters. (How much better is more problematical.) This is intrinsically far easier to provide at a reasonable cost with a stand-alone PC or with client-server architecture than with host architecture.

This chart can be extended further to show how some mainly-supply elements are related to the host and client-server architectures. (With stand-alone PC these issues scarcely arise.)

- **Concurrency control and architecture**. The system has to make sure that several people don't work on the same piece of data

SUMMARY OF WARRANTS

Distinctions between and within Structure and Access: Different structure patterns; Rigour in following structure rules; Access criteria; User initiative; Interface style; Data presentation

Distinctions between and within Supply Elements: Integrity control; Concurrency control; Recovery; Security; Deep design

Distinctions within Architecture: Stand-alone PC; Host; File-server; Client-server; Distributed database; Database machine; Data warehouse

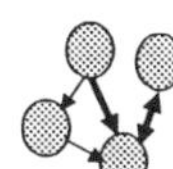

Chart relating Architecture to other Elements: Architecture (host; stand-alone PC; client-server); Structure (relational; hierarchical-network); Access (user interface); CRS (concurrency control, recovery); Deep design

---

from the database simultaneously, or if they do, to guarantee that chaos doesn't ensue. It is intrinsically easier to design reliable, efficient software to do this with a host architecture than with client-server.

- **Recovery and architecture**. If some technical hitch occurs there must be a fool-proof way of restoring the database to an up-to-date, consistent state. With client-server the range of failure situations is greater and the recovery arrangements are more complex than with host architecture.
- **Deep design and architecture**. Client-server architecture may permit a more efficient technical design than a host architecture — if the right technical design choices are made. But it may be more difficult to find the best choices, because the range of possibilities is greater. Moreover the problems of deep design in host architecture have been studied by computer scientists for decades and DBMS software products have developed appropriate techniques by trial and error. Client-server software, by comparison, is immature.

CONNECTIONS

4. Conceptual Schemas	Deals with structure element from the unifying chart — with respect to mainstream systems
5. Accessing the Database	Ditto access
6. Database Integrity	Ditto integrity
7. Concurrency, Recovery, Security	Ditto CRS
8. Internal Schema Design	Ditto deep design
9. Client-server Architecture	Mainly client-server, but with comparisons to host and file-server architectures
10. Special Architectures	The distributed database, database machine and data warehouse architectures
16. Mix, Match, Amend	Relation between architecture and issues such as flexibility for a system to change over time

4. Conceptual Schemas

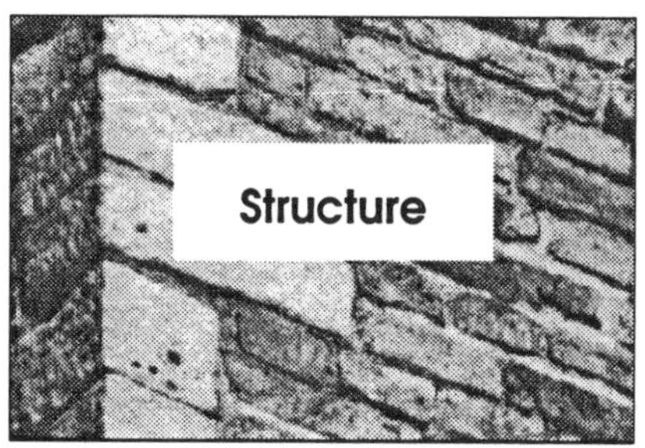

BEARINGS

One of the main themes of modern database technology is that a database should be considered from two different viewpoints:

- The data items and their structure should be defined in a way that is precise, but still non-technical. This definition in demand terms is usually called the **conceptual schema** of the database.
- The supply-side details required to implement the conceptual schema technically should be contained in a separate **internal schema** document.

This briefing is about the conceptual schema; the internal schema is left to Briefing 8. The question of what the conceptual schema of an operational system should be like — discussed in this briefing — is closely related to the question of how data modelling work preceding the full definition of the schema should be done — the subject of Briefing 12.

Within the briefing the relational form of conceptual schema is distinguished from the somewhat discredited hierarchical and network approaches. This clears the ground for the assumption made in subsequent briefings that a *mainstream* database or DBMS is normally a *relational* database or DBMS.

POSSIBLE CONTEXT

The hypothetical Sycamore Supplies is a wholesaler of office equipment with a network of depots around the country. Everyone agrees that the present computer arrangements need radical improvement.

A task force is set up to make plans. It soon produces the judgements that the most important thing is to get the logical, non-technical structure of the database right, and that, for Sycamore, the database to support a new generation of operational systems should be structured along *relational* lines.

This prompts questions from Sycamore board members: If the decision is taken that the database should be in relational form, what kind of decision is that? What options are being rejected? What other forms for a structure exist besides the relational one and what are the main differences? Does choice of a relational structure for the database close off any possibilities for the application systems that some other structure would provide? Is relational a clear concept or a vague one covering several different possibilities? Or are there perhaps other, more difficult issues of database structure than whether the database should be relational or not?

Without some idea of the answers to such questions, it is difficult for anyone to claim to know what it means to say that any database is structured in relational form. Discussion of such basic questions need not be particularly technical. A well informed choice to cross the Atlantic by liner entails being aware of the option of travel by air and rejecting it; but that doesn't call for a detailed knowledge of aviation or marine technology. Similarly, to participate in decisions of principle (as opposed to detail) about an organisation's database structure, a person needs to grasp what kind of thing database structure is and what options and related issues may arise. The trick is to be well briefed on these things and avoid the trap of confusing the sky with the clouds or the sea with the waves.

WARRANTS

Books on database rightly devote a good deal of attention to the structuring of data, but there is a question whether this detail is relevant to decision-making. The warrant sections in this briefing aim to expose the kind of issues and options that arise and decisions to be made.

Chart of Conceptual Schema Concepts

To start with, several associated concepts need charting out:

• **Database structure and conceptual schema.** Data in a mainstream database is arranged in an orderly pattern. Thus, *customer-name* and *customer-address* and various other items belong together in the part of the database devoted to *Customer* data. Elsewhere items of *Customer-order* data are held together. For every customer there will be one lot of fairly static data (such as name and address), but any number of groups of data about customer orders; *customer-number* is a link showing which orders belong to which customers. Statements like these are about the structure of the database, and the conceptual schema is the document containing them.

- **Conceptual schema and access.** The conceptual schema may show that all the data for one customer — address, orders and other things — can be brought together, but it says nothing about how easy or tricky this may be. Maybe touching a customer number on the screen will do it or maybe ten lines of keyed instructions are needed; the conceptual schema isn't concerned with such access arrangements.
- **Conceptual schema, deep design and internal schema.** The conceptual schema describes the database in a logical, non-technical way. To design it, you need to raise questions, such as 'can there be some customers who never place an order?', and draw inferences, such as 'presumably one order can't be for two customers'. For that, you don't need to know technical facts, such as whether 25 milliseconds or 25 microseconds is a respectable time for a disk access. A decision of deep design, by contrast, might be that, in order to provide reasonably swift access to customer data, the database should have multiple levels of indexes. Thus, the internal schema describes a database in the same structure as the conceptual schema, but furnished with additional technical details.[1]
- **Conceptual schema forms.** It might seem natural to approach each new case with an open mind and draw up the conceptual schema neatly as required, just as an artist begins painting on an empty canvas or a writer starts with a blank sheet. But in practice database design isn't done that way. The fine detail of the conceptual schema of any database is likely to be unique, just as the words of any poem are unique. But a poem is cast in a form (sonnet, limerick etc) used by thousands of other poems too. Similarly, there are some general forms and conventions for conceptual schemas. A database designer wondering which established form to use for a new conceptual schema is rather like a poet choosing between sonnet, terza rima and limerick.

Example of Conceptual Schema in Hierarchical-Network Form

The analogy with poetic forms raises questions: How, in a little more detail, does the analogy work out? What are the actual conceptual schema equivalents of sonnet, terza rima and so on?

As the first diagram shows, a conceptual schema expressed in the **hierarchical** form rests on the plausible idea of decomposing data into segments of items at different levels in a hierarchy. One segment is about a customer; segments of data about customer-or-

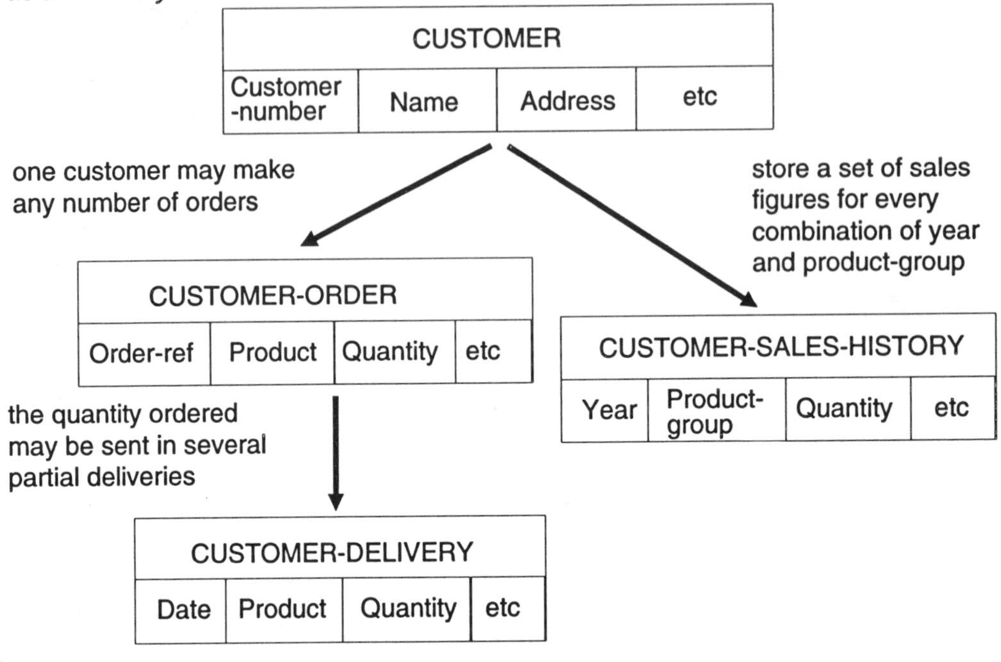
Hierarchical Data Structure
It seems plausible to arrange information about customers, their orders and sales history as a hierarchy
CUSTOMER
Customer -number
Name
Address
etc
one customer may make any number of orders
store a set of sales figures for every combination of year and product-group
CUSTOMER-ORDER
Order-ref
Product
Quantity
etc
CUSTOMER-SALES-HISTORY
Year
Product-group
Quantity
etc
the quantity ordered may be sent in several partial deliveries
CUSTOMER-DELIVERY
Date
Product
Quantity
etc

ders come a level lower, data about multiple deliveries another level down, sales history data on another branch and so on.

But as the second diagram shows, real-life data rarely fits this simple scheme well; data about part-deliveries is needed within the part of the hierarchy concerned with customers and also that concerned with distribution. As soon as those links are drawn in, there is no longer a pure hierarchy.

Moreover the example shown is unrealistically simple: it assumes that a customer-order is for one and only one product; it also leaves out the complication that a lorry might make *one trip* to a customer but delivering goods corresponding to *several orders*. Then, suppose a delivery is made of a product different from that originally ordered (eg the ordered product is out of stock, but the customer is prepared to accept a substitute). Structuring such data within the constraints of a pure hierarchy is practically out of the question.

The **network** form of conceptual schema gives far more scope; it allows a natural hierarchy structure, but with extra connections drawn in where needed. This accommodates the structure of data

Hierarchy becomes Network

Information about distribution operations can be hierarchical too

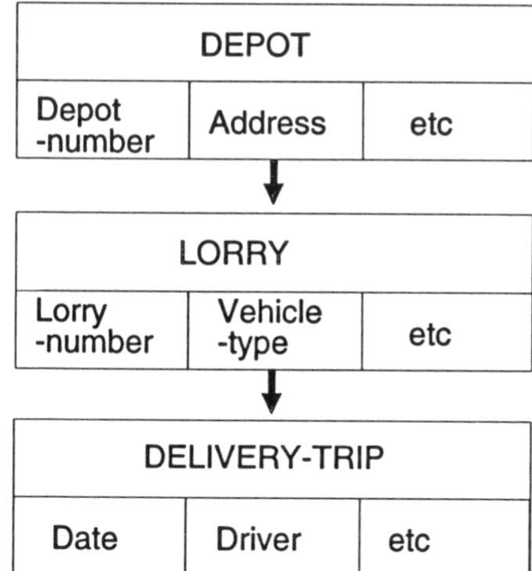

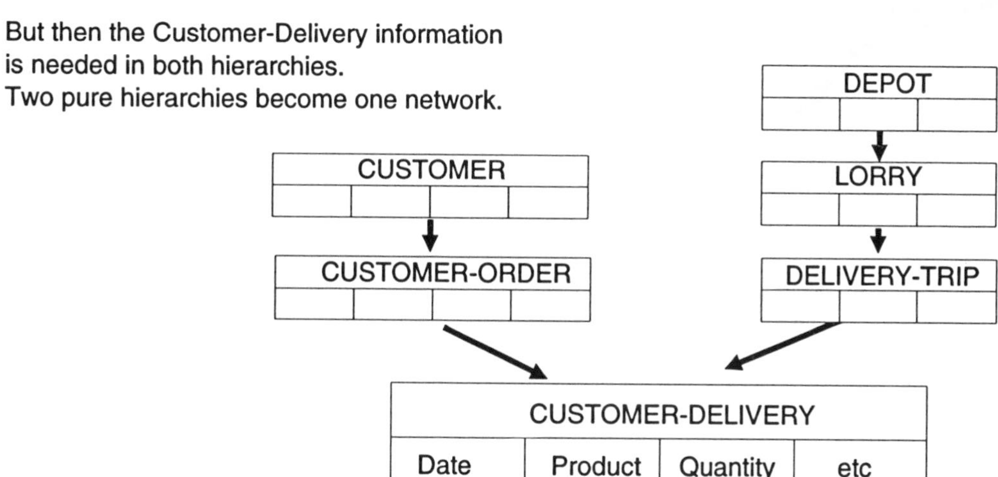

found in practice fairly readily. Since a pure hierarchy is really a simple form of network with extra constraints, it is clearest to talk from now on of a hierarchical-network form of conceptual schema.[2]

Aspects of Conceptual Schema in Any Generic Form

Given superhuman ingenuity, it might be possible to find some way of getting round the difficulties sketched above to structure data as a pure hierarchy, but the result would be intolerably awkward and unnatural. Moreover, as with Heath Robinson (aka Rube Goldberg) designs in any field, the construction would fall apart as soon as any tiny adjustment had to be made. With the full hierarchical-network form you could get much further, but still (though it would take too long here) cases could be described where its conventions seemed too restrictive to permit a clear, neat, natural design.

Certain general points apply to a conceptual schema in hierarchic-network or any other generic form for structuring data:

- **Logical connections**. The conceptual schema provides a fairly rigorous definition of the inherent structure of a database, showing from a logical point of view what connections may be made between data items and thus what may not.
- **DBMS**. The generic form provides a basis for DBMS software products. If thousands of organisations make conceptual schemas in the hierarchical-network form or any other, software companies can invest in development of powerful DBMS software products to manage such databases. There is an important corollary. The conceptual schema is non-technical, but it is not completely idealised; its description of the database is still constrained by the data structures that DBMS software can handle.[3]
- **Awkward structures.** There are bound to be some kinds of structures that real data may take which the generic form doesn't handle particularly well.
- **Analysis framework.** The typical mode of working is for an analyst fluent in the conventions of a certain form to fit the complicated, awkward features of the actual case into the framework of the conventions — exercising ingenuity and perhaps accepting compromises. This is less work than thinking everything out anew from first principles, but there is an accompanying drawback: important subtleties that don't fit easily into the generic form may be missed or brushed aside.[4]

Distinctions between Relational and Hierarchical-Network Forms

The main conventions of the **relational** form of conceptual schema can be sketched out quickly, if roughly:[5]

- The conceptual schema consists of a number of separate **tables**; eg the *Customer* table, *Customer-order* table etc.
- A table consists of **records**, which consist of **fields** of fixed length; eg in the *Customer* table, there is one record about each customer; within each of these records one field is *customer-number*, another is *customer-name* etc.[6]
- In any table all records have the **same format**: there can't be extra fields applying only to special customers within the table; to store

that extra data a separate table for special customers would be required.

- Each record of a table must possess a **unique key**. For instance, every record in the *Customer* table contains the field *customer-number*, which is different for every record of this table. A table's unique key can be defined if necessary as a combination, eg in the *Delivery* table *order-ref* together with *delivery-date.*

On the account so far, a record in a relational table may seem much the same as an individual segment in a hierarchical-network schema. But there are vital differences:

- There is no concept of tables being on **specific levels** in a hierarchy or specific nodes of a network; the database is simply a collection of (say) 28 or 15 or 192 different tables. Put another way, no explicit links are drawn between tables as they are for hierarchical-network. It might seem from the names that the table named *Customer* had much to do with the one named *Customer-order*, but that would be a mere guess. The schema itself does not link them together.
- However, the relational schema does show **links** in a more subtle way. Suppose *order-ref* is the unique key of the *Customer-order* table and this field *order-ref* is to be found also in other tables, eg *Delivery*. If all these tables of data were not in a database but simply written down on paper, you could ask a clerk to find the one record of data for a certain customer order and bring it together with perhaps several records of data for that order from the *Delivery* table. The schema shows that this and other such connections are logically possible. It doesn't say whether they will ever happen, nor that the database should ensure that this connection, if made, can be done within two seconds or two hours.
- The relational schema doesn't use the concept of **order** within a table. The records in the database may in fact be stored in some order, but this order is not supposed to convey any meaning. With the hierarchical-network form, by contrast, you can define that the data segments corresponding to individual deliveries within a lorry's delivery trip are actually stored in the order they occurred. Since the relational form abstains from the possibility of attaching meaning to order of storage, sequence has to be denoted in some other way, eg through fields such as *sequence-number* or *time-of-delivery*.

Distinctions between Types of Key

Relational theory can seem like monetarism or Darwinian evolution: confusingly simple, at first.

In summary, the relational form draws a firmer boundary than the hierarchical-network between the structure of *what* the database stores and *how* it does so. How data items can be linked together *efficiently* (eg how indexing or other techniques can speed up searching for records with particular keys) is a matter irrelevant to the relational conceptual schema. But this point is not as straightforward as it first appears. For instance, the key as *unique identifier* of a record may become confused with two other senses of key — as *access method* and as *basis for indexing*.

• **Uniqueness.** If *customer-number* is the key guaranteeing the uniqueness of each *Customer* record in the conceptual schema, that is a purely logical fact; it may well *influence* the way the database is used and designed technically, but it won't *determine* these things directly.

• **Access.** If information about outstanding orders is frequently *accessed* in a system by use of *customer-number* as the search-key, that doesn't necessarily mean that each order is identified uniquely by *customer-number*. Quite possibly, the typical access is for *all* orders with a certain *customer-number*. Neither are there necessary implications for the way the database is designed technically; the designers may set up special indexes for this type of access, but then again they may not.

• **Indexing.** The technical design of the database may include indexes allowing any searches using *customer-number* for access to be done particularly fast. If so, this presumably has some rationale: eg to optimise performance on some very common transaction, or on some search request that, though uncommon, would otherwise take far too long. This choice of indexing is *pragmatic*; it is not a *necessary* consequence of the conceptual schema or of typical access requirements.

In summary, the key as unique identifier has a rather fundamental character in defining the logic of the database structure. Arrangements for access and indexing, by contrast, are more contingent on changeable circumstances such as the way the database is used and its volumes of data.

Comparing Relational with Hierarchical-Network

How do you decide whether to draw up a conceptual schema in relational or in hierarchical-network form? This is usually not a very difficult decision, because relational has practically swept hierarchical-network aside as the normal style of database technology. Relational is the natural choice, unless there are special circumstances. Though many hierarchical-network databases survive, it is becoming more and more common for 'relational database' and 'database' to be used as synonyms.[7]

There is a more tricky type of decision: If a hierarchical-network database is already in operation, should it be converted to relational, and if so how urgently? Here is an outline of the main issues that come up in this debate:

- **Flexible access.** Suppose you wanted to set up a database and only after that decide how its data might be used, what pieces of data to bring together for what processing, what accesses to make and so on. A relational database leaves far more options open than hierarchical-network. On the other hand, if you already knew precisely how you wanted to use the data and were certain those requirements would never change, then this advantage of relational design would be nugatory. Real-life cases invariably lie somewhere between these wild extremes, but the more of this kind of flexibility you need, the more valuable is a relational design.
- **Robustness**. The more elaborate a database structure the more chance of awkward discrepancies arising in one of two ways: updates to data causing inconsistencies that are not trapped by validation software; amendment of the system's data or functions later on that has unforeseen repercussions. The relational approach, used properly, does reduce the chances of these things happening. Of course, for a database with very simple structures (though perhaps enormous volumes), the hierarchical-network approach may seem quite robust enough.
- **Naturalness**. A collection of data for a real application may be fitted into a certain form of conceptual schema somehow, but does the result seem natural or awkward? Relational normally wins on this criterion, since its conventions are general enough to provide a reasonable analysis of a great many different cases. But there can be times when hierarchical-network seems neater; eg tall, complicated hierarchies of parts making up a product, or data where order plays a large role, such as in the scheduling of lorry deliveries. Naturalness is important for its impact on matters such as flexibility, robustness and performance, but also because it helps people who design and use the system to understand it better.
- **Performance**. There is one particular scenario where hierarchical-network is generally the more efficient. The three conditions of this scenario are: the data fits the hierarchical-network form very naturally; transaction volumes are large; data access and update processing are simple, ie to process one transaction there is no need to access data from several different regions of the database.

Good and Bad Design - Representative Examples

Sycamore Supplies needs to store the addresses of customers.

- The address for deliveries may not be the same as the address for billing, since some large customers have many delivery addresses (their branches), but only one billing address (their head office accounts dept)
- No customer has more than one billing address.

Should you have one table (Option A) or two (Option B)?

A

Customer-No	Customer Branch-No	Billing-Address	Delivery-Address

i.e. for every Customer-No/Customer Branch-No combination, there is a record storing the two items Billing-Address and Delivery-Address

B

Customer-No	Billing-Address

i.e. for every Customer-No, one record; and . . .

Customer-No	Customer Branch-No	Delivery-Address

i.e. for every Customer-No/Customer Branch-No combination, one record

Option B is the better by far.

Examples of Design: Good, Bad and Normal Forms

Though the choice in favour of relational is often straightforward, a more difficult issue lurks. The relational approach has its purists, who lay down stringent conventions of some abstraction. How strictly should your conceptual schema conform to relational theory?

To discuss this start with a simple example. There are always different ways of structuring a collection of data, but it is often easy to sense that one way is better than another. In the case illustrated, it is easy to sense instinctively that Option B is much neater, more natural and more accurate than Option A.

Just as it would never even occur to a skillful author to use certain clichés of vocabulary or make certain errors of grammar, so a competent analyst would probably never need to sketch out Option A as a serious possibility for evaluation. But can the instinct that Option B is the better design be supported by reasons? Here are two:

- Option A is misleading and messy because it seems to suggest that different branches can have different billing-addresses — which, according to the information given, is not true. That kind of imprecision is undesirable. If the database design contained other tables with similar defects, there would be too much scope for misunderstanding and confusion. Option B, by contrast, is neat, clear and accurate.
- If a customer has (say) 15 branches, Option A will provide 15 records, each containing the same billing-address. Suppose the customer's billing-address changes. Then all 15 instances of it will have to be changed. If one is missed, the database will be inconsistent. True, some automatic device could be built into the software of the system to ensure that all or none of the addresses were always updated, but with Option B the need for such a thing simply doesn't arise. Surely, if you can avoid extra complications, you should.

A relational theorist could use more abstract language to show that Option A breaks certain generic rules of correct design. These rules are associated with the so-called **normal forms**. It is less important to know the definition of each normal form than to understand what *kinds* of things they are. The higher the normal form, the stricter the criteria met by a design. Thus:

- Option A is in **first normal form (1NF)**. That is, it does succeed in looking something like a relational schema, but that is about all.
- Option A is not good enough to count as **second normal form (2NF)**, because it breaks a rather important rule. To be more precise: 'The second normal form is based on the concept of a full functional dependency. A functional dependency X→Y is a full functional dependency if removal of any attribute A from X means that the dependency does not hold any more; that is, for any attribute A ∈ X, (X—{A})x→Y.' Or, in somewhat more approachable terms: 'Second normal form requires that all fields be dependent upon the *entire* primary key expression rather than upon any part thereof'.[8] Option A fails this test: the field *billing-address* is dependent on *customer-no* alone; no matter what the value of *customer-branch-no* (the other part of the key) may be or how it may change, *billing-address* will be the same.
- **Third** normal form (3NF) and normal forms beyond that (eg 4NF, 5NF, BCNF, DKNF etc) set further generic criteria that can lead to more elegant designs. Option B is a neat enough design to meet the criteria of 3NF. In practice, 3NF is widely regarded as a kind of minimum quality standard to be reached. (The whole question of

attitudes to these normal forms is discussed in the next section). Of course, for a real-life database, this will be much harder to achieve than for the artificially simple example.

- Relational theory isn't confined to the definition of normal forms. Much of its point is that, if certain general rules for structuring data are followed, then certain **other general concepts** associated with the manipulation of data in relational tables can be applied. Hence the body of theory about tuples, intension and extension, union and intersection, theta joins, Cartesian products and so on.

Charting the Topic of Relational Strictness

But why should you bother with the abstractions of relational theory if the difference between a neat and a messy design is plain without them? Before tackling this provocative question, look at two useful guidelines for conceptual schema design that are *not* part of relational theory:

- If possible, avoid using as primary key a field that is outside your own control, eg postcode or social security number. If (say) the post office reallocated or merged postcodes, that could cause chaos in the database. It is only common sense to try to avoid being vulnerable in that way.
- Avoid meaning-laden identifiers, as far as possible. It may seem attractive to have the first two digits of every product-number indicate the product-group, and the third digit the target market; but experience shows that this leads to problems. First, if the nature of the thing itself changes, eg the product is now directed at a different market, you have to introduce a new product-number, even though there is no new product. Second, if you ever wanted to reclassify things, eg have a different product-group breakdown, you might have to change thousands of product-identifiers. All this is avoided if each product has an identifying number with no inherent meaning and the genuine information is stored in other fields within the record.

These and some other common-sense guidelines do not belong to relational theory, and are generally subject to disclaimers such as 'as far as possible' and 'other things being equal'. A competent designer may use a field that includes some meaning for an identifier, without incurring criticism for it, because in some circumstances that is unquestionably the least-bad choice available.

Now the earlier question can be refined: Probably it is worth knowing at least *something* about the theory of relational design, but should it be treated as a set of useful guidelines, like those about identifiers, or should it be applied much more strictly than that?

To progress with this question, untwist two different strands. One is how the database schema *actually is*: a certain database might be assessed as being in 3NF (or BCNF, or perhaps 3NF, except for one table etc). But the *attitude* of the people who made it is a different thing altogether; perhaps they set themselves the deliberate goal of 3NF and always discussed it in those terms, but maybe they just designed it as seemed most logical and they don't care whether it is 3NF or not. Now, some facts:

- Consider the body of databases that currently exist in the world, excepting only those whose design is so poor that no theory is needed to condemn them. These **actual databases** are largely in 3NF, ie either completely in 3NF, or in 3NF with a few parts that only meet 2NF standards, and/or with a few parts that meet higher standards such as BCNF.
- But among the designers of those databases, a great range of **attitudes** can be found. Some think of 3NF as a useful guideline like the guidelines for identifiers; some insist firmly on 3NF but go no further; some have mastered all the theory far beyond 3NF, and are strict about it; some know all the theory, but regard it all as guidelines that may be broken; etc. There is no simple correlation between the actual databases and their designers' attitudes. People who don't care much for theory may still produce database designs that, a theorist would tell them, are in BCNF or 4NF.
- As might be expected, among the onlookers in the academic world, attitudes vary too but with some bias towards the theoretical.
- Some representative quotes from magazine articles: 'I guess we could build jets and bridges without theory, but I sure wouldn't want to use them. The same goes for databases.' *but* 'Dig into the thicket of arcane arguments, and you may detect the distinct odor of medieval theology' *and* 'Talking about database theory is like talking about religion or politics: You're sure to have an argument.'

Comparison of Strict and Less Strict Relational Design

The above is meant as a neutral report on the way things are in the world, to help clarify the questions rather than give the answers. One large question is outstanding: Since the higher normal forms are the neater and more elegant, why should anybody, whether conscious of theory or not, ever prefer a design in one of the lower forms — unless it be through incompetence? In fact, there can be tradeoffs:

- **Logical clarity.** The higher the normal form, the nearer the schema gets to breaking things down as naturally as possible. The

SUMMARY OF WARRANTS

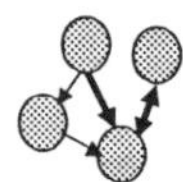

Chart of Conceptual Schema Concepts: Database structure; Conceptual schema; Access; Deep design; Internal schema; Established forms

Example of Conceptual Schema in Hierarchical-Network Form: Hierarchy clashing with reality, turning to network

Aspects of Conceptual Schema in any Generic Form: Logical connections; Awkward structures; DBMS; Analysis framework

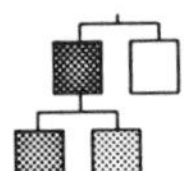

Distinctions between Relational and Hierarchy-Network Forms: No levels of tables or explicit links between them; Implicit links through data keys; No order

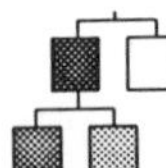

Distinctions between Types of Key: Identity; Access; Indexing

Comparison of Hierarchical-Network and Relational: Flexible access; Robustness; Naturalness; Performance

Examples of Design and Normal Forms: Avoiding repetition of billing-address for every branch; normal forms

Charting the Topic of Relational Strictness: Guidelines and rules; Actual databases; People's attitudes

Comparison of Strict and Less Strict Relational Design: Logical clarity; Future use and modification; Comprehension; Performance

---

more that is done, the easier it is to recognise and guard against all the possible ways in which the database may lose integrity through different parts becoming inconsistent with each other. Of course, the cost of such potential problems is difficult to quantify, but they are certainly worth avoiding if the price to be paid is not excessive.

• **Future use and modification.** The other main advantage of rigorous relational design is flexibility — in a certain sense. The higher the normal form, the more atomic the data, and thus the more options to combine different data items through quite simple instructions — even in combinations that have never been used or envisaged before. This kind of flexibility is more valuable in some systems than others. The more you need it, the greater the benefits of relational rigour.

• **Comprehension.** But, on the other hand, the higher your aspirations to meet abstract and rigorous relational criteria, the more difficult it will be to use the conceptual schema for communication — with non-technical people who are involved in the design process and with people who use the operational database system. Not everyone feels at home with the niceties of relational algebra.

- **Performance**. As the example suggests, higher normal forms make for more tables with simpler content, lower forms for fewer tables, but more complicated records. It is generally more efficient for a computer system to extract many fields from the records of one table than to bring together the records of (say) three different tables in order to extract the same number of fields. Thus, a high normal form may mean that more hardware resources will be needed to achieve adequate performance. As one authority puts it, 'It is as though you took your car apart to put it into the garage and had to reassemble it before driving it out'.[9]

This analysis may seem to favour the conclusion that you should treat third normal form as a desirable guideline to follow, subject to the way certain tradeoffs work out in the particular case. But a different attitude might be that the balance of tradeoffs *can never* justify anything slacker than third normal form, since logical clarity *should always* outweigh everything else.

POSSIBLE DECISION-MAKING

Some of Sycamore's directors wonder whether a decision to make a conceptual schema in relational form will lead inevitably to the choice of DBMS software based on relational, as opposed to hierarchical-network, principles. Whatever disclaimers and caveats are offered, it seems that in practice the answer is 'yes'.

One party within the board asserts that this is bad practice, because demand, eg non-technical database design, should ideally be defined in a way that leaves supply, eg DBMS software, open. The counter-argument is that, however desirable that may be in theory, it isn't realistic in this particular area of technology — any more than it would be possible to write the words of a poem first and decide on its metre afterwards.

Moreover, the decision between a relational and a hierarchical-network conceptual schema probably isn't the most important decision anyway. Perhaps some work should be done to show that Sycamore's is *not* one of those exceptional cases where hierarchical-network is appropriate, but after the assumption of relational form has been sanctioned, a more tricky issue arises: relational rigour. Which of the following three policies should Sycamore follow?

- *Either* the conceptual schema is entirely in third normal form as a matter of principle;
- *or* the conceptual schema is in third normal form — except that exceptions are allowed, if they are deliberate and the justification for each deviation is explicitly documented by good arguments;
- *or* the conceptual schema is built in a natural way in the broad relational style by bright, clear-thinking analysts, who regard third normal form as a useful guideline, but don't really care which parts are in which normal form.

Since the task force hasn't agreed a position on this issue, they are asked to go away and do so. That debate is likely to raise taxing questions about what Sycamore is really trying to achieve. To give exaggerated but not absurd extremes:

- Suppose the database is intended to support extensive new systems, most of which are only vaguely apprehended at present. Then there is a strong case for following relational theory strictly, and benefiting from the flexibility this brings, even at the expense of possible inefficiency in the short term.
- Suppose the intention is to have database systems that are particularly cost-effective at handling the essential needs of the business, whose main scope is known or can be readily defined. Then the balance tilts towards pragmatism rather than theory as the dominant factor in database structure.

CONNECTIONS

5. Accessing the Database	Relation between conceptual schema and access to data
8. Internal Schema Design	Making the internal schema and perhaps altering the normal form of the conceptual schema
12. Data Modelling Method and Process	Relation of conceptual schema to data model
16. Mix, Match, Amend	Degrees of independence between the schemas, Codd's rules and relational authenticity
17. Mainstream Software Products	DBMS software products for different forms of conceptual schema
29. Object-oriented Topics	An important new style for a database conceptual schema

5. Accessing the Database

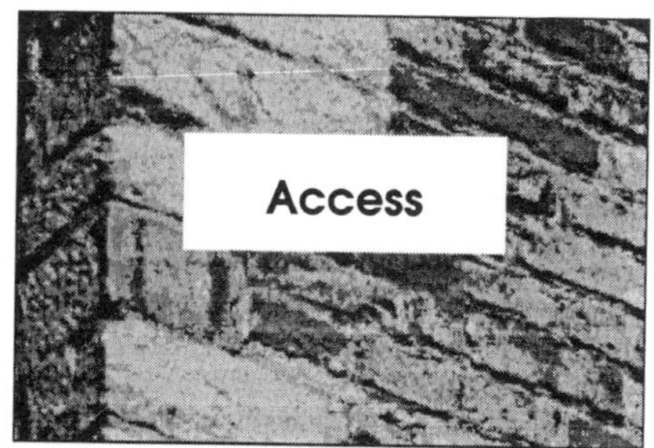

BEARINGS

This briefing concentrates on one element of the chart of database technology — access to data — for mainstream database systems. The rather vague term 'access' brings together matters such as the criteria that a user of the system can set for selection and combination of data items from the database, the scope for initiative in devising new access routes to data, the style of interface for interacting with the system and the way data is presented to the user.

This briefing is closely associated with one other. Examination of ever more flexible and sophisticated means of access that an operational system may offer leads towards another element, the development of new software for accessing the database. This is the subject of Briefing 15.

POSSIBLE CONTEXT

Forest Oak Energy is a utility company, responsible for the supply of gas, electricity, cable television and a variety of other things to buildings in its region.

Forest Oak's database system keeps records of customers, showing which services they take, generating bills and maintaining records of payments. This isn't the whole story; the database also holds technical data about cables and equipment operated by the utility, particularly in order to schedule inspection, maintenance and repair. The two bodies of data — customer and technical — can't be kept completely distinct. For example, scheduling a visit for repairs at a customer site has to take account of other technical commitments, and the charge for the repairs is included in the customer's quarterly bill.

Forest Oak has a steering committee to review in an Olympian way any IT matters of a fundamental, far-reaching character. Here is a synopsis of one of their debates:

- When a customer rings or comes into a branch with some complaint or request, it is desirable to offer a really impressive response: eg providing information to clear up disputes about outstanding bills, but also about when it will possible for someone to call and fix up a television cable.
- A necessary, though not sufficient, condition is that the structure of the database make it *possible* for a desk clerk to access and bring together different pieces of data, eg relating the locality of a customer with the schedule of an installation engineer. The database conceptual schema may show clearly that items of data can be accessed and combined in many ways, but some of these will be more demanding of technical resources than others. For a technically *efficient* system, judgements have to be made about which items of data will often be brought together and which rarely or never.
- This question of expected and unexpected accesses has further implications. The DBMS at the heart of the system provides many different means of accessing database information: 4GL, SQL, query-by-forms, query-by-example and so on. This is all very well, but at some point choices have to be made. If a front-line complaints clerk rings to ask how to access certain data, it is no use the database administrator saying: 'Well, there are at least four possible ways of finding the data you want . . .' A better response is: 'Page 41 of the user handbook will show you exactly what to do in step-by-step fashion.'
- But there are bound to be times when somebody needs to access some combination of data that has not been specifically foreseen, technically optimised and documented in step-by-step fashion. After all, one of the main characteristics of database technology in general is that it permits flexibility in accessing a pool of information. Surely this is only possible if there are *general-purpose* access facilities, whose use calls for initiative and judgement, rather than carefully following a defined procedure.

There is a possible tension between two desirable aims: providing users of a system with ready-made access mechanisms and encouraging them to master general-purpose access techniques. To get to grips with these and related matters the steering committee needs a briefing on the subject of access possibilities in mainstream database systems.

Query by Forms - Representative Examples

Customer Table

Account-No	Type	Status	Name	District	Address

Each customer has a unique account number.
The Types of customer are: H (household), C (commercial, eg shops and offices), I (industrial, eg factories), S (special, eg embassies, consulates)
The Status of a customer can be: V (VIP), N (normal)
There are 30 Districts in the region

Screen Displays (in outline concept)

Data Entry
To add a new customer record to the database, call up this blank form and key in the data

Account-No	Type	Status	Name	District	Address
52148356	C	N	*and*	*so on*	

Standard Enquiry
Key in an account number on the blank form and the system will retrieve the other five items in the record, and display them across the form

Account-No	Type	Status	Name	District	Address
52148116					

One-off Enquiry
Fill in (say) three values on the blank form; the system will retrieve all records that contain all three values and display their contents in the columns of the form

Account-No	Type	Status	Name	District	Address
	H	V		13	

Representative Access Requests in the SQL Language

```
SELECT  *
FROM    CUSTOMER
WHERE   ACCOUNT-NO = 52148116;
```

That is: From the *Customer* table pick out the record with account number 52148116 and give us all its fields. (* stands for all fields.)

```
SELECT  *
FROM    CUSTOMER
WHERE   TYPE = 'H'
        AND     STATUS = 'V'
        AND     DISTRICT = 13;
```

That is: From the *Customer* table pick out all records for a VIP household in district 13 and give us all the fields in each record.

```
SELECT  ACCOUNT-NO, NAME
FROM    CUSTOMER
WHERE   STATUS = 'V'
        OR      ACCOUNT-NO < 2000000
        OR      (TYPE = 'C' AND DISTRICT > 22)
        OR      (TYPE = 'I' AND DISTRICT = 1);
```

That is: From the *Customer* table pick out all records meeting any one of four conditions: VIP status *or* account number lower than 2000000 *or* commercial, outer suburban (district greater than 22) *or* industrial, inner city (district 1). For each, give us just account number and name.

WARRANTS

The access features of an operational database system enable its users to get at the database; these features are built in by the people who design and supply the system. Techniques of accessing an operational system are thus a different topic from techniques of developing the software of the system in the first place, or extending it with improved versions from time to time.

That may sound obvious but there is an awkward overlap. Many software products and techniques are applicable to both contexts; eg part of the application system may be coded in the SQL language, and this code may be executed thousands of times every day during the life of the system. But the SQL language can also be used to

Representative SQL Access, Joining Two Tables

```
SELECT  CUSTOMER.ACCOUNT-NO, CUSTOMER.NAME,
        MAINTENANCE.VISIT-DATE
FROM    CUSTOMER, MAINTENANCE
WHERE   MAINTENANCE.ENGINEER = 'BRANDT'
        AND   MAINTENANCE.DATE = '??.??.93'
        AND   MAINTENANCE.ACCOUNT-NO =
              CUSTOMER.ACCOUNT-NO
        AND   CUSTOMER.DISTRICT = 19
        AND   CUSTOMER.TYPE = 'H';
```

That is: From the *Maintenance* table (which has a record for each maintenance visit by an engineer over the last five years) pick out all visits by engineer Brandt any time in 1993.
Use the account number of the customer visited to search the *Customer* table for further data on all those customers.
Knock out any that are not in district 19; also any that are not households. For those that remain, give us account number, customer name and date of maintenance visit.

Note: The explanations describe the selection *logic* — not necessarily the exact *sequence* in which the computer does the steps of its work.

---

request *ad hoc* accesses, eg to display data of any maintenance visit by a certain engineer to a certain customer — just once, for some special reason, not as a regular procedure in the system.

Therefore this briefing is based on an arbitrary but necessary cutoff that captures issues relevant to *accessing the operational database* and leaves aside those more relevant to *setting up the database and application software.*

Examples of Query-by-forms and SQL

Examples generate an *impression* of what is at stake in discussing different styles of access. The first example of the briefing shows the **query-by-forms (QBF)** style of updating and enquiring about data. It ignores tedious (but soluble) practicalities; eg the data per customer will be too wide for one line on the screen; the screen will also need to display error messages for any invalid entries etc. More sophisticated accesses are possible too; eg key in different values to one or more fields on *several lines* of the form to define a search with alternative criteria.

The two SQL examples show a completely different style of

interface based on the concept of keying **instructions in a language** onto a blank screen. SQL is important because it is both powerful and widespread.

As the examples suggest, the two styles of interface are useful in different ways:

- You can add a record for a new customer by keying instructions in SQL or a similar language onto a blank screen, but this is so laborious and error-prone that almost nobody would prefer it over QBF.
- You can frame straightforward requests for information, whether standard or one-off, either way. Most people prefer QBF or other non-language approaches, but personal taste does play a part.
- The last SQL example shows a fairly complex access bringing together data stored in two different tables, *Customer* and *Maintenance*. As access gets more complex, it becomes steadily more convenient to work with a language, rather than with QBF.

Aspects of Database Access

Discussion of the *structure* of the database is about its essential patterns and connections, irrespective of the practicalities of getting at the data. The topic of *access* is concerned with ways of making use of whatever structure the database has. A database's structure might be subtle and yet the system might be a failure, if its access features were too laborious or counter-intuitive or very feeble compared to the richness of the database structure. Access really has four main aspects:

- **Access criteria:** Data items that meet certain criteria can be selected, but how subtle or complex can the criteria be? To what extent can the access criteria operate on data items brought together from different parts of the database?
- **User initiative**: How much opportunity for initiative is left to the user of the system to access data in ways that are not spelt out literally in advance?
- **Interface style:** How are commands to access data formulated? As program-like instructions or in QBF style, by filling in requests on form-like screens, or some other way?
- **Data presentation:** How varied and impressive is the way of presenting the data accessed? All in characters of exactly the same size, colour and font, or with different fonts, sizes and colours for a clearer, more pleasant effect?

Gradations of Access Criteria

As the opening examples show, different accesses can be based on access criteria of differing grades of complexity. There is a useful five-gradation scale:

- **Single record**. Example: Given a certain *account-number*, what are the rest of the details for that record in the *Customer* table?
- **Set of records from single table**. Given certain field values for use as criteria, extract all the records from the *Customer* table (however few or many) that meet these criteria.
- **Processed set of records from single table**. This isn't illustrated in the examples, but an artificial example might be: Given certain field values for use as criteria, extract all the records from the *Customer* table that meet these criteria, but then display only those that have the lowest *district-code* (ie the lowest *district-code* found among that set of records).
- **Set of records from multiple table**s. As in the last SQL example, present information based on search criteria that can only be applied by 'joining' two tables together through a common key (in this example *account-no* is the key common to both the *Customer* and *Maintenance* tables). There are actually two different types of join. The usual 'inner' join would join together all records from *Customer* and *Maintenance* tables sharing a common *account-no*. The 'outer' join would extract all *Customer* records and all *Maintenance* records, ie including those that could not be joined to any record in the other table, because there was no common *account-no*.
- **Processed set of records from multiple table**s. As with the previous gradation, but then apply further criteria to the chosen set of records; eg display only those with the earliest *visit-date* and with the latest *visit-date*.

Gradations of User Initiative

Once a system is delivered, how much opportunity for initiative do you want to leave to the user? Do you want to supply a handbook with the promise that everything the user ever needs to do is defined precisely there? If not, why not?

This question of user initiative is mixed up with the two aspects of access criteria and interface style. Again, a set of gradations is the clearest analysis:

- Gradation 1. Users use the **delivered system** to carry out specific functions in specific ways, exactly as laid down in the handbook that comes with the system; eg 'in order to see the details of a customer account, key in the following. . .'

- Gradation 2. Users employ a **simple general-purpose, one-off** access feature; eg 'you can search on *any* combination of data fields; if you wanted to search on (say) *type-status-district*, then. . .'
- Gradation 3. Users have a **sophisticated general-purpose, one-off** access feature; eg 'once you understand how different data items are held in different tables, you can perform one-off enquiries that entail combining data from different tables; thus, to find out whether a certain engineer paid any maintenance call to a house in a certain district at any time in the past year, you would join the customer table to the maintenance table by. . .' Note: this kind of feature is (or should be) only for relatively unusual, complex accesses; if any specific multi-table accesses are needed frequently, then the people who designed the system ought to have provided specific features with the delivered system.
- Gradation 4. Users build up personal or departmental **libraries** of useful, one-off access instructions that can be reused. Having succeeded once in setting up the correct instructions to find out whether a certain engineer. . . etc, they store them with some meaningful name (eg ENGMAINTCUS). Then, to make the same access on another occasion the system can be asked to execute ENGMAINTCUS. Moreover, for an access that is similar but not identical, it is easier to make small changes to the existing instructions than to work things out from scratch.
- Gradation 5. As well as specifying the information they want extracted, users **design and modify the formats** of the screens and printed reports on which the information will appear. Thus, either the handbook for this specific system or the DBMS supplier's manual will say: 'In order to tell the system which fields you want to appear and where and in what format, proceed as follows . . . etc.'
- Gradation 6. Users go beyond just displaying information already in the database or designing formats for screens and reports, and start **developing software for extra runs**, one-off or regular — albeit not adding to or amending the database itself. Examples are: producing extra reports selected, sorted and sub-totalled in new ways; or extracting certain data from the main database and loading it into a spreadsheet.
- Gradation 7. Users go as far as doing things that will (or may) **affect the operational database** of the system. This may range from apparently trivial things such as altering the validation criteria of a certain field to allow an extra code-value to be accepted, through to creating new tables and wiping out old ones.

Gradations 6 and 7 form the overlap-area where access features turn into system development. This is really a convenient break along a spectrum of gradations rather than a sharp difference of principle. Understanding these gradations can be useful in combatting the confusions that often arise from vague language in discussions of end-user computing.

Distinguishing between Interface Styles: Language and Facility

As the opening examples show, the same command (eg extract all the records meeting certain criteria) can be given through different styles of interface. Here is a four-way distinction between styles of interface relevant to database access by a user within an operational system.[1] The first two are vastly more important than the third and fourth:

- **Classic language.** You formulate commands on a blank screen, using the conventions of a computer language; as if trying to compose grammatical French sentences on a blank sheet of paper. Ease or difficulty depends on how complicated the language is and how much fluency you have acquired.
- **Access facility.** The system finds out the commands you wish to formulate from the data you key in on well-structured forms on screens, or from the options you choose on menus, or from the answers you make to choice-posing questions.
- **Special restricted language.** In some applications, there are high quantities of rather uniform transactions to be dealt with in an absolute minimum of key-strokes. Therefore the designers of such an application sometimes create in effect a special language of great concision; eg key alt+F7 for some particular type of transaction, ctrl+alt+F7 for some subtle variety of the transaction etc
- **Natural language.** This is not that common, currently at least. You formulate commands on a blank screen, but in English, rather than the conventions of a computer language — except that it isn't really English, because you can only use certain words and grammatical constructions. Thus, from a logical point of view, it is just another computer language, albeit relatively easy to get right, somewhat limited in commands and verbose.

There is a loose correlation between style of interface and gradations of access criteria. Though not shown in the opening example, it would still be feasible to join data from two tables by using a QBF interface or some related instruction-less style. But it does start to become rather awkward: two table-forms have to be fitted onto the screen; there must be conventions for filling them in to show exactly what is required; etc. The general point is that, as enquiries get more complex, the approach of keying instructions in a language onto a blank screen becomes more and more appropriate, tedious though it still may be.

Distinctions between the Interface Styles within Access Facilities

With a classic computer language you formulate commands on a blank screen; with access facilities there are far more varieties of interface style. Here are the main distinctions:

• **Query-by-forms (QBF).** As shown in the opening example, you key in values for blank fields on a screen layout designed like a paper form. For enquiries based on selection criteria, the form usually has a design similar to that of the database table itself. For new input or other database updates the design may be less tabular, to give more scope for helpful messages such as: 'Enter 'V' here for a VIP customer; otherwise, the system will automatically store 'N' for normal'.[2] Some, not all, forms-based interfaces allow update in ways other than just entering a new value (eg by entering *1.2 to multiply the currently stored value by 1.2).

• **Query-by-example (QBE).** This variety of QBF is intended to permit relatively complex accesses. Here is how it might be used for the access specified by the last of the SQL examples. The system displays empty forms for *several* tables from the database, eg *Customer* and *Maintenance*. You key in certain field values as search criteria, as with QBF; thus 'Brandt' in the *engineer* field, '19' in the *district* field and so on. But you also key in imaginary example values to other columns, underlining to show they are *examples*, not constants. Thus you might put the same example value <u>11111111</u> in the columns headed *account-no* of both tables. The facility understands this to mean that you want it to match the records of the two tables on *account-no* and select on the criteria 'Brandt', '19' etc.

Many people find this style of interface more pleasant than that of a classic language; it certainly saves having to remember the specific words and format for instructions. Even so, you still need the ability and patience to grasp some sort of logic, formulate requests precisely and think through the reasons for any surprising results that may come up.

• **Question-and-answer interface.** On a blank screen the system poses a question — either multiple-choice or one where the answer is severely constricted; eg which field (out of the ten in this record) do you want to search on? Each answer is followed by another question, depending on the previous answer. The use of this kind of interface is relatively limited.

• **Graphical interface.** Sometimes this term is used broadly for any interface that is not classic language or question-and-answer on a blank screen. It is best to use the term narrowly for the *diagrammatic* (rather than just form-like) kind of interface; eg to show that your access criteria depend on joining two tables you might use a mouse to draw arrowed lines between boxes representing the *Customer* and the *Maintenance* tables.
• **Menu-based interface.** The system offers a set of choices on a menu. These in turn lead to further options for choice on a lower-level menu and so on. Most systems need some degree of menuing, but menus are rarely a complete form of interface. Nevertheless, in designing a system there is usually some choice in setting the weight of menu use relative to other styles of facility and classic language.

Aspects of Presentation

A really careful analysis of presentation would begin by splitting the topic in two between the selective view (an important *logical* concept) and representation resources (how information is presented *physically*); after that, a number of different representation resources could then be separated out. That is why the following list of aspects of presentation contains one long point about views, followed by four brief points:
• The **selective view** (aka user view, external schema, virtual schema), at its most simple, is an edited subset of a table that filters out irrelevant fields. People working in a certain department may need to access data about customers, but the field *status-code* may be of no conceivable relevance to their work. The database administrator defines a 'view' so that, when these people access records from the *Customer* table, *status-code* simply doesn't appear.

Views can be much more sophisticated than this. Suppose you frequently need to access the database in a way that extracts 20 fields from four different tables, that contain in total (say) 40 fields. Coded in SQL this might take ten lines or more. The database administrator defines for you a view consisting of just the 20 fields; after that, it will be far less trouble to access the database by citing the name of the view than by keying in many lines of instructions each time.

Views may seem to be among those things that are obviously-nice-to-have, but there are snags to watch out for. If one department's view excludes *status-code* and if *status-code* is a mandatory field, it follows that the system must have safeguards to ensure that nobody in that department ever adds a new *Customer* record to the database — since nobody there is ever capable of

SUMMARY OF WARRANTS

Example of Query-by-forms, an Access Facility: Input, standard access, one-off multi-criteria access to customer data

Example of SQL, a Language: Accessing customer table and joining customer table to maintenance table

Aspects of Database Access: Access criteria; User initiative; Interface style; Data presentation

Gradations of Access Criteria: Single-record via Processed-set-of-records-from -single-table through to Processed-set-of-records-from-multiple-tables

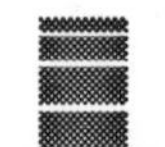

Gradations of User Initiative: Delivered-system-only via Sophisticated-general-purpose-one-off-access through to Software-affecting-database

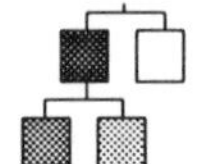

Distinctions between Classic Language and Other Interface Styles: Classic language; Access facility; Special restricted language; Natural language

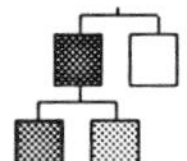

Distinctions between the Interface Styles of Access Facilities: Forms-based interface (QBF); Query-by-example (QBE); Question-and-answer interface; Graphical interface; Menu-based interface

Aspects of Presentation: Views; Typographic presentation; Windowing; Presentational graphics; Business graphics

---

inputting *status-code*. Again, if you work with a view that includes 20 out of the 40 fields of four tables, then you are working with a subset of the database's conceptual schema. The real conceptual schema has doubtless been devised with some care to be a coherent logical structure following the main tenets of relational design. But is it safe to work with the 20-field subset? You might draw false conclusions or make false updates that would never occur to you if you could see the whole picture.[3]

• **Typographic presentation**. In the extreme limited case, the numbers and letters from the database, as well as those of the legends and messages, will all appear on the screen in the same size, same typeface, same colour, same spacing. A richer system might allow different sizes, typefaces and colours; then, some lines of data could be shown more closely spaced than others, some text-rich lines could be justified and hyphenated and arranged in two or more (not necessarily equal-width) columns on the screen.

- **Windowing**. It can be a useful resource to present data in separate screen windows; eg data from the *Customer* table might be viewed and scrolled in one window without affecting *Maintenance* data in another window.
- **Presentational graphics**. Additional resources include: notebook- or index-card- or other styles of graphic containers for data-items and (more advanced) clarifying the relations between data items through diagrams that have boxes and arrows.
- **Business graphics.** Another possibility is allowing raw data extracted from the database to be shown also in the form of bar-charts or pie-charts.

POSSIBLE DECISION-MAKING

Plainly, it should be easy rather than awkward to formulate search requests and information on screen should be clear rather than muddled. That is easy to agree, but among issues calling for tricky decisions, one dominates others: How much freedom and responsibility do you give to the user?

The two opening examples depict different styles of interface, but in showing operations of differing complexity, they reveal another point: some of the access features contained in an operational system are more specific than others. The users' handbook may very well spell out: 'in order to see the details of a customer account, key in the following . . .', but it can scarcely be so specific for searches based on (say) the fields *type-status-district* and every other conceivable combination of fields too. Instead, the handbook will probably say: 'The system offers a generalised search feature; you can search on *any* combination of data fields by doing the following. . .' This leads to a tradeoff:

- A user provided with a generalised access feature has a more flexible, **more powerful instrument** to exploit the database. Moreover, there is a growth path, since, with practice and experience, it becomes feasible to make steadily more ingenious use of the feature.
- On the other hand, more generalised features tend to call for **more sophisticated users**, possessing the capacity to see how an actual, specific request for information can best be poured into the mould of

the generalised feature — and even for them, more upfront investment is needed to become fluent in using the features.

And there is another tradeoff:

- Using a generalised feature to carry out a certain task may require more **mental effort** and more key-strokes than a system feature set up for that very task.
- On the other hand, the more detailed the application-specific features that are built in, the greater the **investment** in system development. By contrast, general-purpose access features are relatively cheap because they are not normally developed in house. They come as part of the DBMS or are bought-in from some other source.

Given this analysis, the Forest Oak steering committee decides that, although everybody will be using the same database, different people in different departments will be provided with different access features — but in a dynamic kind of way.

- Front-line staff dealing face-to-face with (perhaps) angry customers will possess a repertoire of carefully designed QBF access facilities supporting all the most commonly met requirements.
- Occasionally they will require information not easily accessed with these facilities, or it may be that unnoticed subtleties in the case cause the information extracted to seem very odd; perhaps the angry customer has kept quiet about some complicating details. These cases will be referred to a small back-office team of people skilled in SQL and other access methods.
- The back-office people are expected to notice if many of the awkward cases they deal with exhibit a similar pattern. If so, they are to develop an appropriate standard access feature that can be added to the front-line repertoire.

This is a neat example of a case where the characteristics and constraints of the technology play an important role in designing the organisation structure and job-content of non-technical people.

CONNECTIONS

9. Client-server Architecture	SQL as intermediary in a client-server setup
15. Development Tools and Languages	The development end of the access-development continuum, including the role of SQL
16. Mix, Match, Amend	SQL the link between separate system compartments
27. Rules-with-Mainstream Systems	SQL as a resource in hybrid systems

6. Database Integrity

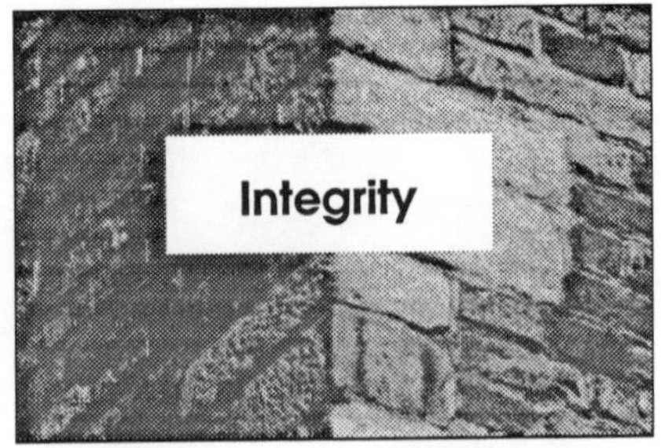

BEARINGS

Integrity is slightly nearer the demand pole of the demand-supply axis than the three topics within CRS: concurrency control, recovery and security.

Like CRS, integrity is an infrastructure-like thing, perhaps calling for supply facilities of great intricacy, ingenuity and cost, but — if it never fails — largely hidden from most users of the system. However, integrity should lead to rather more discussion in demand terms than the CRS topics: Do you need an automatic integrity safeguard so that an order can't be added to the database for a product that doesn't exist in the *Product* table? Should you prevent a product ever having a standard price of zero, or are there some products where that might be allowed, or even necessary?

Such questions can only be resolved by discussing integrity controls together with the conceptual schema and taking account of wider business considerations.

POSSIBLE CONTEXT

Buloke is a distributor of commodities such as olive oil, rape seed, soya beans and so on. A small group of computer-literate senior managers and directors forms the committee that oversees IT strategy.

Plainly, there is little sense engaging in detailed technical work on the supply side of a company's systems until decisions have been taken on the general shape of the demands to be met. But does this mean that no account whatsoever should be taken of supply matters until the last detail of the demand has been engraved in stone? Surely not. Supply and demand should interact to some degree, and integrity control is one place where this should happen. Some decisions about integrity may be too far-reaching to be regarded as purely matters of technical competence..

But this is all terribly abstract. If Buloke's computer-literate managers are to have any useful involvement in issues of integrity control, they need to be briefed, so that they see the contours of the beach rather than all the pebbles.

WARRANTS

This briefing is largely concerned with analysing two things: the different kinds of integrity controls that may be wanted and the different ways of achieving them. Of course, they interact.

Foreign Key: Example of an Integrity Issue

The diagram gives a representative example of one of the most prominent problems of database integrity. The database of a distribution company holds a *Customer* table (primary key *customer-number*), and each record includes the field *customer-rep* — the customer's main contact at the distribution company for discussing contracts, complaints and other aspects of business. This person may be a depot manager or regional sales manager or hold some other position. There is a *Customer-rep* table (primary key *customer-rep*), that, among other things, holds data about the person's performance in developing business with satisfied customers.

In this situation, the *customer-rep* field in each record of the *Customer* table is said to be a **foreign key**. It is not the key of the *Customer* record itself, but it is, or ought to be, the primary key of some record in another table, *Customer-rep*.

The data about customer-reps contained in the two tables must keep in step. It seems undesirable for a certain customer-rep to be mentioned in a record of the *Customer* table, but not in any record of the *Customer-rep* table. If this inconsistency did arise, the database would be said to have lost **referential integrity**, and trouble might ensue. Any operation that combined the content of the two tables might yield strange results. More generally, people might begin to doubt the reliability of the whole database system, and mistrust other information that in fact had perfect integrity.

Distinctions between Types of Integrity Defect

The opening example gives a flavour of integrity matters, but it only represents one out of many types of integrity issue. This is a topic

Referential Integrity

Data from the Customer table of the database

Customer-Number	Name	Street	Town	Customer-Rep
1358479	Vink	Nachtstraat 34	Baarn	126
1358481	Ahrend	Bossingel 18	Hoorn	119
1358487	Boer	Meent 142	Olst	241
1358488	Wiegel	Dorpsstraat 579a	Emmen	126

Data from the Customer-Rep table of the database

Customer-Rep	Name	Grade	Budget-%
119	Visser	1D	89
121	Pronk	2A	72
126	Jansen	1D	69
127	Mol	1E	85

Loss of Referential Integrity can occur:
if the Customer-Rep field for Vink is changed to 120
(and there is no such record in the Customer-Rep table)
or if Customer-Rep record 119 is deleted,
(and the Customer-Rep field for Ahrend remains unaltered)

that encourages distinction-drawing and classification. Here, devised for this briefing, is a four-way breakdown of integrity defects that a database may suffer from:

- **Basic relational integrity:** defects that break fundamental rules of relational form. You could detect these by examining the current version of the database, even if you knew nothing of the application. Loss of referential integrity is one. The other main one is sometimes called loss of entity integrity: eg two records in the same table with the same primary key. These defects are analogous to those you might find in a Hungarian book, even if you didn't speak Hungarian, provided only that you were aware of the usual conventions of a book: pages should not be printed twice, the page-numbers referred to in the index must exist etc.

• **Business integrity:** defects that you could detect by examining the current version of the database, and applying knowledge of how its data is used in the particular application — analogous to printing errors in a Hungarian book only detectable if you did know the language. Examples: the field in the *Orders* table showing the product quantity ordered is wrong because it contains letters; or, though numeric, it is wrong because it is higher than some standard limit; or it is both numeric and less than the normal limit, but still wrong because other fields show that for this type of customer with this type of contract, other stringent conditions apply.

(Controls and defects within this category are often categorised much further: controls at the level of the individual field; consistency between two or more fields in the same record; consistency between two or more records in the same table; consistency between records in different tables; etc. But such analysis is not particularly relevant here.)

• **Dynamic integrity:** defects that, like business integrity defects, are dependent on the particular application, but can't be detected by examining the current version of the database — only by comparing two versions of the database. Suppose the current version of the database contains one and only one customer account, 1358492, which seems valid. Last month's version also contains one and only one account 1358492, but its field *account-type* is 'export' and in the current record it is 'home'. However, alteration of the field *account-type* isn't allowed in this system (perhaps because it would make the quarterly statistics prepared for the customs authorities too complicated). Therefore this rule must have been broken or something else must have gone wrong.

• **Other:** errors not obviously covered by the above. Some may be undetectable by any systematic procedures, eg a customer's name is stored as Brown when it should be Browne. But others can be covered. If, through some mishap, a field stores a valid but wrong numeric value, that error may still be discovered if control totals are kept too, and business integrity rules check for consistency between control total records and individual transaction records.

Gradations of Approaches to Integrity

The opening referential integrity example, and most of the others given too, could be tackled by a variety of generic approaches:

- Gradation 0: **Do nothing**. You accept the possible loss of integrity. Not to be done lightly, of course. But suppose the whole customer-rep concept is to be abolished as part of a reorganisation. This can't all be done overnight, and during the transition period the loss of integrity may be tolerable, because it could lead to no serious problems. This is a relationally incorrect approach and some authorities are quite insistent that it should never, ever be permitted. This prohibition has less force than at first appears. It is a fair enough principle that, if, as part of your relational design, you explicitly define *customer-rep* as a foreign key in the *Customer* table, then you should have controls to maintain referential integrity. But you can, if you like, change your design, so that *customer-rep* is no longer defined as a foreign key, and perhaps (though this is not essential) change its name to (say) *customer-contact*.
- Gradation 1: **Application program**. You ensure that any application programs handling updates to either the *Customer* or *Customer-rep* tables carry out the checks needed to avoid loss of integrity. The trouble is that many different programs may be concerned and their integrity controls must be absolutely identical, otherwise niggling inconsistencies will arise. If the integrity checks have to be altered later, then all the programs will need to be amended; suppose one is forgotten, because it hasn't been used for the last three years; but two years after that somebody does use it . . . Apart from the fact that there may be, so to speak, many gates to guard, there is another drawback. If users of the system can set up new ways of accessing the database through QBF or SQL, it may be difficult or impossible to guard those particular gates at all. Clearly, the approach of enforcing integrity within the logic of each individual program has considerable disadvantages.
- Gradation 2: **Stored procedure.** You have the integrity checks programmed once in a piece of software, a stored procedure, that is kept with the database, rather than in any application program. Application programs invoke that stored procedure for integrity control, rather than use program code of their own. Thus, if any change to the details of integrity controls is ever required, it need be done only once within one piece of software. This approach is only feasible if the DBMS used does provide a stored procedure facility. Incidentally, a stored procedure need not only be used for integrity control; it can be used for any type of processing.

- Gradation 3: **Trigger.** As Gradation 2, but the integrity controls are programmed as a special kind of stored procedure, a trigger. The DBMS itself ensures that this trigger always comes into action when updates are done, without any action on the part of the program or person making the update.
- Gradation 4: **Declarative integrity.** Within the conceptual schema, you declare *Customer-rep* as primary key of the *Customer-rep* table and foreign key in the *Customer* table. Then the DBMS software itself guarantees that integrity. This approach has much the same effect as Gradation 3. The advantage is that you don't have to write the checking software yourself, as you do with a trigger; you just declare the nature of the integrity control and the DBMS works behind the scenes to carry out the necessary checks. This is the approach most favoured by relational theorists.

Distinctions between Declarative Integrity Controls

From this it may seem that declarative integrity is the best approach to enforcing integrity, and any deviations from it will stem from incompetence or use of outdated technology. But things are not so simple; to see why, break down the types of integrity from a different angle:

- **Entity integrity** (part of basic relational integrity). It is relatively easy for a DBMS to provide a general-purpose, declarative integrity facility to check that any new or updated record has a unique, non-null key. The requirement is easy to define and the action to be taken on a violation is simple.
- **Referential integrity** (part of basic relational integrity). The requirement that foreign keys don't become inconsistent with the primary keys of other tables is also a generic one, for which it is fairly easy to define standard DBMS facilities. However, there are some complications. If somebody wants to delete the *Customer-rep* record with key 119, and thus leave the *Customer* record of Ahrend without a valid *customer-rep* field, there are at least three possible ways of maintaining integrity: refuse the deletion, or delete both the *Customer-rep* record and the *Customer* record of Ahrend, or delete the *Customer-rep* record and set the *customer-rep* field in the *Customer* record to a null value. Thus, it isn't enough to declare the fields for which referential integrity is needed; you must also declare which action is required on violation.
- **Domain integrity** (part of business integrity). This is the technical term for integrity at the level of the individual field. It seems straightforward for a DBMS to enforce a declaration that a certain field must be of a certain type (eg numeric), within a certain range

SUMMARY OF WARRANTS

Example of Integrity Issue: Foreign key — referential integrity, ie consistency between tables

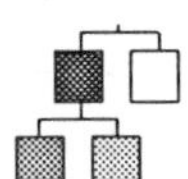

Distinctions: Types of Integrity Defect: Basic relational integrity; Business integrity; Dynamic integrity; Other errors

Gradations: Approaches to Integrity: Do nothing; Application program; Stored procedure; Trigger; Declarative integrity

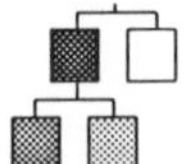

Distinctions: Declarative Integrity Controls: Entity integrity; Referential integrity; Domain integrity; Business rules

---

(eg $1-100,000). This can be a generic facility. But many such controls really need to be more complex, eg numeric and in the range $1-100,000, unless *customer-number* starts with a 9, in which case . . . This soon drifts into complicated, application-specific rule-making, that is difficult to handle in a generalised DBMS facility. In any case, *declaring* such complicated constraints is hardly any easier than *coding* them as a trigger.

- **Everything else (aka business rules).** Suppose two *Delivery* records are each valid in themselves, but, taken together, can't be valid, because they show that the lorry was at two places 100km apart at the same time. Such controls don't lend themselves so well to a generic declarative integrity feature, because they are too application-specific. They may be better handled as stored procedures or triggers.

The above notes help explain the current situation. Most DBMSs for minicomputer and mainframe provide declarative integrity features for referential integrity and entity integrity, and this is now the natural way of handling these things in newly developed systems. But for more application-specific integrity controls, stored procedures and triggers are far more common than declarative integrity.

POSSIBLE DECISION-MAKING

The word 'integrity' suggests a commodity that you can't possibly get too much of. From the content of the briefing it may seem that the policy of any sensible company should rest on two simple principles. One is to build in as many integrity controls as you possibly can. The other is to do so by the declarative integrity approach as far as possible, failing that by triggers, failing that by stored procedures, and only in the last resort, through application programs.

These principles, if valid, are straightforward enough to avoid the need for awkward judgements about best-buys, tradeoffs, influence of supply on demand and the like. In fact, they seem to rule out the need for any further *decisions* of consequence about integrity; all that remains is to follow the principles in detail. But in practice, the issues are usually more complicated. Take Buloke, for example:

'The system has an integrity rule that no record may be added to the *Weighbridge-calibration* table, unless there is a corresponding record for the same depot and same quarter in the *Depot-health* table, and vice versa. Since these tables are the responsibility of different departments, the constraint makes updates more cumbersome than they would otherwise be. The rule is wise in that inconsistencies between these tables could lead to strange results if data from the two tables were ever combined. But the rule is stupid because nobody in a thousand years would ever want to combine these tables; the idea of producing statistics to correlate the health of depot staff with the way their weighbridges are calibrated is just absurd.'

'We already have a substantial database, whose data was and still is captured in the bad old way, ie with integrity controls in the application programs. At the time of conversion to make a completely new database system, we ought to find and correct any inconsistencies. The natural approach is to be extremely rigorous indeed. But suppose (say) 70% of the records are (or seem as if they may be) wrong or inconsistent in some way, however tiny. The task of sorting all that out would be just too great. Now here is an ugly pragmatic solution. Divide all the possible integrity defects into two classes: unacceptable (eg two records with the same key) and acceptable (eg order placed for an absurdly high quantity). Eliminate all the unacceptable defects at conversion time, and deal with the others at leisure afterwards. If we do adopt this policy, the next issue is which integrity defects to put in each category.'

'We use one of the best-known DBMSs in the industry, but it doesn't support triggers or stored procedures, and its declarative integrity features are limited to referential integrity and not much more. Therefore, most integrity control is done in application programs. Of course, the supplier is always promising new features, without being specific about time-scales. What should we do with systems and databases currently under development? We could carry on as before. *Or* we could make assumptions about the features the DBMS will provide in (say) three years time, and design our systems on that basis. *Or* find some way of our own to organise application software, so that the logic of integrity control is reasonably centralised and standardised. *Or* switch to whichever rival DBMS has the most advanced integrity control features.'

'We need to allow managers in the departments to access and combine data for management information. There seem to be three broad approaches to choose between: *either* allow them to access the main database, having assured ourselves that cast-iron integrity controls are in place; *or* give them facilities to use a separate version of the database, with strong integrity controls, thus making it less easy to use than it otherwise might be; *or* give them a separate version of the database, but sacrifice most integrity controls to ease of use, on the grounds that this database will be replaced by a new version of the main database at regular intervals anyway.'

How should Buloke tackle this kind of problem? Probably the most important decisions to take are decisions about the organisational arrangements needed to find best-buy solutions on integrity matters. That may mean getting three types of people to work together: people steeped in relational theory (who can say what is desirable in principle); people expert in the features and limitations of the specific DBMS to be used (who can say what is technically feasible); and people who know the Buloke business thoroughly (who can judge what is sensible).

CONNECTIONS

4. Conceptual Schemas	More about relational theory
7. Concurrency, Recovery, Security	The other three infrastructure-like topics
14. Data Dictionary Control	More about the idea of holding integrity rules centrally
25. Geographic Information Systems	Integrity control gets more challenging with complex hybrid systems

7. Concurrency, Recovery, Security

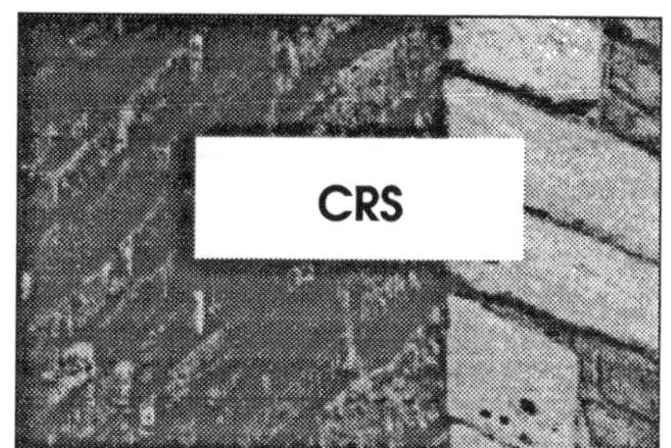

BEARINGS

In most of the other briefings matters of demand predominate. But it is important to remember that many attractive demand features exact a cost in the complications of supply-side matters, such as concurrency control, recovery and security. This briefing gives an impression of how these factors can affect the supply-demand calculus.

POSSIBLE CONTEXT

Corkwood Bank is large and profitable. It is taking a fresh, top-down look at all aspects of its use of IT.

This kind of study will begin with discussions of some general, non-technical business issues, develop them by expressing demands in ever greater detail and only turn attention to purely supply matters when the shape of the demands to be met is fairly clear. But this cautious formulation conceals a rather acute difficulty:

- It would plainly be irresponsible to devote effort to most supply matters before deciding fundamental demand matters.
- But this surely can't mean that every detail of a completely non-technical system definition must be firmed up and definitively signed off before any technical decisions whatsoever are taken. This would remove any possibility of making tradeoffs between demand benefits and supply costs.
- So, in order to take a useful part in debates, non-technical decision-makers at Corkwood need *some* awareness of the way demand and supply factors can interact. But in a computer science text about concurrency control, it is very difficult to see the bulb-fields for all the individual tulips.

What they need is a briefing about database supply matters in general terms, specifically intended to show how supply matters can affect demand considerations.

WARRANTS

These are immense topics consuming hundreds of pages in the textbooks. What should one briefing contain? Mainly two *kinds of* material:

- **Examples**, that give an impression (as opposed to a precise definition) of the sort of problems, challenges and technical choices that typically arise;
- **Distinctions**, breaking down each topic one level further, to show what different matters are covered and how they relate to each other.

Example of Concurrency Problem and Solution

The database is often said to be a shared pool of information. Problems arise when several people want to take the same information out of the pool at the same time. Here is one version of the classic concurrency problem:

- The *Customer* table in the database contains a field, *account-balance*, with, for one particular account, a value of (say) 100.
- Users A and B at different terminals access the *account-balance* field for this same account at almost the same time; each sees a value of 100 on the screen.
- A updates *account-balance* by adding 50. The value of 150 for *account-balance* is then stored in the database. While this is happening B still sees 100 on the screen.
- Two seconds after A, B updates *account-balance* by adding 70 to the 100 on the screen, giving 170. This value of 170 is then stored in the database, replacing the previous value of 150.
- It depends on the application, but probably 170 is not correct. Perhaps it should be 220 or perhaps there is a restriction on applying two updates on the same day or perhaps there are other considerations. Whatever the case, an unacceptable lack of control has crept in.

To combat these problems, ie to control concurrency, DBMS products provide locking mechanisms. A could lock *account-balance*, read it, amend it, write the amended value back to the database and then unlock it. There can be varieties of locks; depending on the lock chosen, B might be prevented from looking at *account-balance* at all until it is unlocked, or allowed to look but not update.

There are other variations. The lock may be applied to different extents of the database — record, group of associated records, whole table etc — depending on the ramifications of the possible changes to the information. If a certain kind of lock is already in force for one user, complicated rules may determine whether another user may apply additional or overlapping locks.

Optimistic and Pessimistic Approaches to Locking

Locking buys control at a price: it may hold up the work of those who are temporarily locked out. This becomes a real problem in cases where different parts of the database need to be kept consistent: eg if a transaction is transferring money from one account to another, then the information about *both* accounts may need to be locked. Other, more complicated cases can arise, where various related items of data may all need to be locked. Deadlock can arise: perhaps you can't finish the transaction to update X, until Y has been accessed; but Y is locked, and the person who locked it is waiting to access X, which you have locked . . .

There can be a tradeoff between so-called pessimistic and optimistic locking approaches (these are just vague labels, without any connotation that one is rasher than another):

- With an extreme **pessimistic** approach the logic is something like: 'If you want to access information X, X will be locked automatically (even if it is unclear whether X will be updated) and so will all other parts of the database that might ever be affected by any conceivable change to X, however unlikely. Locks will even be applied to any other parts of the database that might be accessed within any transaction, that might conceivably cause a deadlock to arise. Thus, if X is then updated, this can be done without danger.'
- With an extreme **optimistic** approach: 'If your terminal or PC wants to access information X, X will not be locked, but the system will note that an access was made at a certain time. Should the terminal or PC then send in an update of X, the system will consult its notes to see whether anybody else has updated X *in the meantime*. If so, it follows that the update is unsafe; the system will refuse it and ask you to start again with the current version of X. Similarly, the system will not try to prevent deadlock occurring; but if it happens it will automatically unravel it.'

These are extremes; many in-between possibilities exist. The best tradeoff for the situation will depend on factors such as the volumes of transactions relative to the size of the database, how many different parts of the database one transaction affects, and how inter-related are the different parts of the database. If the approach is too pessimistic, users may be kept waiting at their terminals too often because the data needed to process their transaction is currently locked, even though it probably need not be; if too optimistic, the system will have to refuse or unravel updates too frequently.

Computer science books go into these things in detail. One tradeoff influence often missed out is the user interface. With a modern graphic interface, the system may send out large numbers of database records to be displayed on screen as a list. Clicking with the mouse on one item in such a list is easier than keying in a whole account number, as with an old-fashioned interface. But the graphic-list approach means that the great majority of records sent out from database are for display only, not update. Therefore, *other things being equal*, this factor argues for a relatively optimistic concurrency approach.[1]

Examples of Recovery Techniques

Any grown-up database system will include facilities to recreate the database if it should become corrupt or damaged, through hardware failure, human negligence or malice. Such facilities are provided by the DBMS, and can spring into action automatically to recover the database speedily and accurately.

There are many different recovery options. The problem is to make the best choice out of those offered by the DBMS. The best recovery approach for any one database system might be some combination of any of the following:

- the most obvious: **complete backup** copies of the database taken regularly, together with a **log-file** of all incoming transactions (with sequence numbers or times or both) since a certain backup copy was made;
- or more cleverly: frequent **partial backups** of certain portions of the database, together with a log-file;
- or, more subtly still: holding a log-file together with some choice from **before-images** (ie storing each database record as it was before update) and **after-images** and periodic **check-point** records, containing the identities of transactions that are in progress at a certain moment;
- or, getting away from backups and log-files, though perhaps extravagantly: having **mirror versions** of the whole database (on different disks or even different computers) kept up to date at all times;
- and perhaps as well: providing **temporary facilities** even while the recovery process is going on; eg allowing new updates to go into the system, and new enquiries to be made against an earlier version

of the database (tricky stuff: as soon as the recovery has been done, the system has to go back and see if the updates input during the period of temporary facilities were valid or not — and while that is happening, it might just happen that a new disaster occurs causing a new recovery process to start . . .)

This is just an impressionistic view of the possibilities (to give one simplification, you might mirror part of the database rather than all of it). Choice from such a range isn't easy; it entails visualising awkward combinations of circumstances and assessing how certain solutions cope with some of the problems but not others. Suppose one disk-drive containing the whole database and the log and the before-images is out of action completely; combat that problem perhaps by keeping log and before-images on separate drives from the database. But suppose two logs, each logging alternate transactions, were stored on different drives; would recovery be easier or more difficult?

In crude terms, the technical designer faces a tradeoff, roughly as follows:

- If you are prepared to accept a **huge overhead**, so that the system spends most of its time keeping logs, before-images, mirror versions etc, and only a small part doing real work — then you can have an automatic recovery system to recover from almost any imaginable disaster **very quickly**.
- But if you want to reduce overhead to the absolute minimum — then the system may take a long time to recover, even from rather simple breakdowns.
- Therefore the 'best buy' is the approach that pays with a moderate amount of overhead for a recovery system that, for most likely breakdowns, recovers in a reasonable time.

Notice that the *ability* to recover automatically and reliably is normally not a negotiable demand. The real issue is: how slickly and at what overhead?

Examples of On-line Transaction Processing

The matter of recovery is at the heart of one of the most high-powered types of system, on-line transaction processing. The term transaction can have several meanings:

- **Simple transaction:** updating data in a certain record of a certain table or else adding one new record to a certain table. When a customer withdraws some cash from an ATM, the balance in the *Account* record is updated. There are no other repercussions (at least, assume so, for the sake of this argument).
- **Logical transaction:** updating several different parts of the

Recovery in On-line Transaction Processing

Representative Transaction:
Transfer 300,000 from account 1086431 to account 4653298
ie update record 1086431 and also record 4653298 (more or less) simultaneously

Hundreds of similar transactions are in progress when the system crashes

	Account Record	Update to Balance
at time of crash the balance field of these account records had just been updated in the database	1856382	-50,000
	3926173	-150,000
	2555417	+50,000
	1086431	**-300,000**
	2266341	+200,000
at time of crash these account records were not yet updated in the database	2995181	-40,000
	4653298	**+300,000**
	4446718	-200,000
	7113642	+40,000
	2227762	-150,000

The system must automatically roll back the update to 1086431, because it knows that an associated update (to 4653298) was thwarted by the crash; and it will perform the same service for perhaps dozens of other updates from around the time of the crash (but without rolling back any update unless really necessary)

database. Suppose a customer uses a high-speed service to transfer money straight from one account into another, eg at the time of transferring ownership of a house. From a technical point of view, there are two updates of the database, but they belong together as one logical transaction (aka business transaction)

Transactions of the second sort make recovery far more complex. As the illustration suggests, technical failure could occur at a moment after one update and before another, and the DBMS needs to know which updates belong together, so that, if necessary, one or more can be rolled back.

OLTP (on-line transaction processing) is a term applied to a system that can process massive volumes of multi-update logical transactions and then, no matter what kind of fault occurs, recover fully automatically, sorting out all the transactions, no matter how intricate. The term 'fault-tolerant' is also used.

Gradations of Transaction Processing and Other Updates

There are actually more than just two gradations of transaction processing. It may not be worth paying the considerable price of additional complexity resulting from sophisticated OLTP. If you suspect that a multi-update transaction *may possibly* have been spoiled by a technical interruption and not fully resolved by recovery procedures, you can always examine the state of the database records afterwards and, if inconsistent, put them right. Whether this is sensible or not depends largely on the volumes of transactions pouring in, and also on factors such as possible adverse consequences from the database containing false information during a brief clearing-up period; with a banking system, this is probably unacceptable, but with (say) a bulk commodities depot or a chain of fast-food restaurants, maybe not.

Here in brief are the main gradations of transaction processing:

- **Simple transaction:** update in only one part of the database.
- **Simple but integrated transaction:** update in only one part of the database immediately, but later effect on other parts too; eg at the end of the day, data on all new customer accounts is used as input to the customer statistics part of the database.
- **Complex transaction:** update multiple parts of the database straight away, though without fully automatic recovery of logical transactions if disturbed.
- **True OLTP:** automatic recovery if logical transactions are disturbed.

These are still gradations rather than firm distinctions. The complexity of transaction processing is defined above in terms of its updating, but the elaboration of the validation procedures (eg checking a new piece of input for consistency against data in other parts of the database) is a factor too.

Aspects of Security

There are four main aspects of security — authorisation (the most important), password, audit trail and encryption.

Authorisation is concerned with allowing certain people to access certain information and not other information. This has three main levels, any of which can get quite complex:

- allowing a person (or class of person) to see certain items of **data** and not others; eg only certain tables or certain records within a table or certain fields within each record of a table;

- allowing a person (or class of person) to see certain data but carry out only a restricted range of **operations**, eg amending a field but not adding a record, or adding a record but not deleting etc.
- allowing a person (or class of person) to grant further **authorisations** to others; in the straightforward case, one database administrator (DBA) is responsible for setting up and withdrawing all authorisations, but it may be desirable for the DBA to delegate some authorisation rights to others as well (this can get as complicated as medieval feudalism: suppose some of the delegated authorisation rights are withdrawn again later; what about the authorisations to other parties already granted under the now-withdrawn authorisation rights?).

Authorisation really depends on also having controls for checking **passwords**. However, some systems have password without authorisation controls.

An **audit trail** facility maintains a log file of transactions affecting the database, specially designed to enable an auditor to check that things have in fact gone correctly or, if there is cause for suspicion, to find out exactly what has happened in order to track down embezzlement.

Encryption entails storing information in a coded form; a trivially simple approach would be to subtract (say) 789 from every numeric field, but naturally the encryption algorithms used in fact can be far more intricate.

Encryption only has any point if the encryption algorithm itself is secure (or at least more secure than the data itself). In telecoms, encryption can be sensible, because anyone who intercepts data may well not possess the algorithm. But encrypting the data actually stored in the database is more questionable. The encryption algorithm must perforce be contained in the software of the system, including very likely the software used by PCs and other remote devices. Therefore it may well be just as easy to steal as the database itself, and, if so, encryption is pointless.

Of course, special schemes can be devised; eg the encryption algorithm depends on input of some special value known only to a few and never written down. But on the whole, database (as opposed to telecoms) encryption is uncommon — except in extreme cases such as military applications, or perhaps some business applications where it makes sense to set up special safeguards for some tiny subset of the whole database.

SUMMARY OF WARRANTS

Example of Concurrency Problem: Updating a bank account with several transactions at the same time

Comparison of Optimistic and Pessimistic Locking: Tradeoff factors: Locking overhead — minimal or extensive; Frustrating lockouts — frequent or rare; Backing out transactions — frequent or never

Examples of Recovery Techniques: Backups, transactions logs, partial backups, before-images, after-images, check-point records, mirrored databases, temporary facilities

Examples of Transaction Processing: Simple, one-update transaction; Genuine OLTP with automatic integrity

Gradations of Transaction Processing: Simple-transaction through simple-but-integrated-transaction through complex-transaction through true-OLTP

Aspects of Security: Authorisation; Password; Audit trail; Encryption

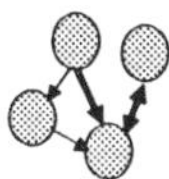

Chart of DBMS Product and Supply Features: Theoretical techniques; DBMS-specific techniques; Particular requirements; Efficiency; Reliability; Tuning

Charting the DBMS Product relative to Supply Features

The computer science books describe various approaches to concurrency control, recovery and security. Any individual DBMS product will offer a selection of facilities based on certain of these approaches, another DBMS a different range. The technical designer using a given DBMS still has to judge which of its proffered facilities to make use of and how.

Different theoretical approaches suit different real-life cases. It is conceivable that, for a certain application system, DBMS A, if used with skill, may be superior to DBMS B — a rival product with a comparable reputation, that happens to offer different approaches to CRS. This is something not really true of (say) rival spreadsheet products.

It is entirely possible that DBMS C may turn out to have

superior CRS features to DBMS D under all circumstances — if (say) DBMS was designed by a small group of very bright people, while D was developed within some stultifying, bureaucratic corporation.

The DBMS software product has to balance two considerations: given the infrastructure character of CRS functions, the reliability of the software must be rock-solid; on the other hand, ingenious, subtle design can bring great dividends in efficiency. These two things pull in opposite directions, since cleverly written software can be more bug-prone than methodical, unimaginative software. A DBMS may go through many years of teething troubles before it possesses both robustness and efficiency.

There is another twist: the programmers of a certain DBMS don't just aim to develop efficient, robust software for CRS functions. Their real task is to build in CRS options so that, *with competent tuning* (ie choice between options by an expert, carefully weighing the factors of the specific application), the DBMS product can be made to perform well in a variety of applications. Therefore choosing the most appropriate DBMS achieves little unless you also have people competent to make best use of the options it offers.

POSSIBLE DECISION-MAKING

It may seem tempting to complete the conceptual schema, hand it over and leave technical matters to the specialists. Only they have the time and temperament to master all the details of concurrency control, recovery and security. The trouble is that questions arise such as whether speedy system recovery (with the associated overheads) should take precedence over (say) fast terminal response time during normal operations. Surely some non-technical decision-makers ought to be involved here.

Moreover, it may not really be sufficient for the non-technical people to define some simple priorities on these matters as a diktat to be implemented by the technologists. Sensible decisions are more likely to ensue if the options and tradeoffs of supply are articulated by the experts first, but then discussed, with interaction and feedback, by those more concerned with demand.

Even well briefed with knowledge about these supply matters, Corkwood's non-technical decision-makers are unlikely to suggest imaginative new approaches to recovery or concurrency control in an active way. But they may still play a very useful role; eg:

'We originally expressed the demand that the system should be able to handle two cash withdrawals through different ATMs *for the same account at the same time*. Why? Because a husband and wife with a joint account might conceivably want cash from different machines at exactly the same time. Now a perfect system to handle this is presumably quite complex in the areas of concurrency control and recovery and security so on, and thus expensive. Suppose we watered down that demand. Would we be looking at big savings or negligible savings?'

'You have built in numerous controls to ensure that only certain people are authorised to do certain things with the database. I know you agreed them with some of the other managers, but I suspect you got carried away with the richness of security features offered by the DBMS. Must they really be so complicated?'

'The system design is based on the demand that, on the basis of probability estimates of possible disasters, the main on-line facilities should never be out of action for more than two hours, except for once in every five years. All the database recovery features are designed on that basis. Now we hear that one of our competitors has a target of not more than *one hour* except for once in every five years. How easily could the design be changed to match that?'

CONNECTIONS

9. Client-server Architecture	Role of supply-side matters in client-server and other architectures
10. Special Architectures	Role of supply-side matters in distributed database and other architectures

8. Internal Schema Design

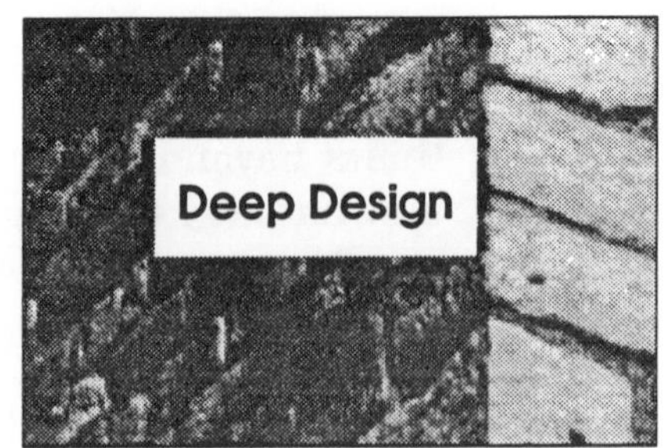

BEARINGS

Briefing 4 defines the conceptual schema as, roughly speaking, the design of the database with the technical bits left out. The internal schema is the one that includes the technical bits, or, better, it is the deep design of the database.[1]

Unless you are a professional database designer, you won't normally be asked to compare the merits of (say) dynamic, extendible and linear hashing. But awareness of the *kind of* supply-side challenges and options that may exist is of value to many more people than database specialists. It provides an essential foundation for sensing how elaborations on the demand side can lead to supply-side complications.

Moreover, even here in the most supply-oriented briefing of all, deep design turns out to be no neat, self-contained topic. During the process of weighing technical options there may well be a vital loopback to reappraisal of the thoroughly demand-side conceptual schema.

POSSIBLE CONTEXT

PTR (originally Pink Tea Rooms) is a chain of fast-food restaurants. Its computer-literate general managers take a keen interest, in fact a decisive interest, in the development of new database systems. Naturally most of their involvement is on the demand side: working with information analysts to develop the conceptual schema, deciding about the kind of access facilities required and so on.

As attention shifts to the deep design process that will define the internal schema, an interesting problem arises:

- Deep design can get immensely technical.
- Plainly the computer-literate general managers need to ensure

that the technology people charged with deep design are knowledgeable and competent.

• But beyond that, should they have any involvement at all? If so, in what kind of things?

They can't even think about these questions, let alone decide them, unless they obtain some appreciation of the essential nature of deep design work.

WARRANTS

On this topic a certain tool for critical thinking comes in useful: distinguish *product* (eg a pile of documents or an installed database) from *process* (the meetings, discussion-papers, emotions and arguments that produced the product). Textbooks concentrate on the internal schema as product; this briefing says just as much about the process of making it.

Deep Design: Chart of the Process

Is the work of deep design essentially that of adding an additional level of detail to a logical design, so that the database can function technically? Is it like taking a design for (say) a mural painting already completely drawn in outline and going on to decide the colours each part should have? This is a fruitful, but not exact, analogy:

• First, a **clear parallel**. The conceptual schema shows clearly that the records of all branches of the business in a certain town could be extracted from the database, but there is nothing about *how* this might be accomplished. The internal schema, once completed, may show that the database maintains a special index on the field *town*, making access of records of all branches in a town very efficient. Or it may show that, though indexes are held for some important fields, *town* is not one of them; the database can still extract all records for a certain town, but, without the aid of indexes, perhaps more slowly. Or maybe some technical device other than indexes has been employed instead. Thus, deciding which of the fields contained in the conceptual schema should be given indexes and which not is very similar to *adding* colour to a monochrome design, without redrawing any of its lines.

• Now here is a **development** of the analogy. Before making technical choices, the technical designer has to collect some factual detail — in particular, how many records are likely to be in each table. The conceptual schema doesn't normally record whether the business has 10 branches or 10,000. Also, some account is needed of which pieces of data will be used to support which processing or to produce which reports.

Within these working notes, the database designer has to take account of a variety of factors that may conflict. A design that will give excellent response time at the terminal may not have optimal transaction throughput (the quantity of transactions processed per hour) or may have excessive space utilisation (amount of storage required on disk). The design optimised to handle enquiries may be inferior in speed of adding and deleting records. Integrity and CRS factors enter this calculus too; requirements for rigorous security or exacting recovery performance will impose overheads. Thus, as with a mural, it isn't just a matter of choosing the best colour for each part of the design by itself; the challenge is to find the best *combination* of colours for all the parts of the design taken together.

● Here is a **deviation** from the analogy. In principle, many possible tradeoffs exist, but the DBMS software itself will generate a set of *default* design choices automatically. At a simple level, it might suggest that the primary key field of every table be indexed, but other more intricate assumptions are possible too. With a mural, automatic default colours would probably be worthless, but with a database, it is usually sensible to let most defaults stand and concentrate on the options for the most critical parts of the system.

● Here is another **complication**. Many of the deep design choices are not final in the way the colours of a mural would be. You can work out a plausible deep design on paper and set up the database; then study system performance during a trial period and tune the design (eg by adding or dropping indexes); six months after going live, tune again; after that, return to assess and tune system performance at regular intervals . . .

Examples of Deep Design Options

The deep designer deciding how best to colour in the design technically has many options. The task is to find the supply choices that best meet the demands (response time etc). Here are examples of some of the less arcane options:

● **Sequence.** One cardinal feature of a relational conceptual schema is that it says nothing about the sequence of records in any table. But the deep designer may decide that the records of should be stored in sequence of value of one field or a combination of fields. (This is called clustering, but there are other forms of clustering too.) Suppose there were frequent accesses to the *Supplier* table such as: 'all suppliers whose postcode lies between value x and value y'. Holding the records in sequence of postcode could make that access very efficient. Of course, there can only be one sequence; other fields, used in more common or more complicated accesses might have stronger claims still.

- **Data placement.** One piece of added detail is the physical location of the pieces of a large database on the disks — something entirely irrelevant to the logical design. If two small tables were often joined together in the intended application, it might be good for performance to ensure that they were stored close together on the same disk. But then again, the calculus based on hardware technology, DBMS, operating system and data volumes, might show that it was more efficient to locate two commonly-joined tables on different disks.
- **Multiple indexed fields.** The DBMS can maintain an index table giving for each value of a certain field (eg *postcode*) the address on disk of every record with the corresponding value. This can be done for several fields; eg the *Supplier* table could have one index for use in accessing records when *supplier-number* is the key, another for accessing by *postcode* and another (perhaps for management information enquiries) by the combination of fields *product-category* and *supplier-type*. But, the more such indexes there are, the more overhead is incurred whenever the database is updated, since all the indexes must be updated too. Tradeoffs arise between swift access and sluggish update.
- **Levels of index and B-tree.** The design for a high-volume database might have several *levels* of index. A slim top-level index might record that all records whose *postcode* fell within a certain range of values were on a certain track of the disk, those within another range on a different track etc. Then every track would have its own lower-level index. Such a scheme must be robust in the face of change; new records added to the database may have to be held in overflow areas away from their natural track and extra indexes are needed to point to them or even to overflow-overflow areas. The so-called B-tree technique is a mathematically-based way of designing index-structures in such a way as to minimise overflow problems.
- **Hashing**. Since the indexes for a large database are stored on disk, it may take several time-consuming disk accesses to work through the levels of indexes to find a desired record. The hashing technique translate a key's actual value straight into an actual address on disk, without any indexing. Thus (say) *product-number* 1548056 becomes 'disk track 42, sector 3, record 2' How? The seven digits of the account number are processed by an algorithm: eg they are multiplied together, the result is divided by 737, the square root of the remainder . . . etc. This approach increases speed by avoiding disk

accesses to retrieve indexes — in principle, but it raises other delicate problems. Here the challenge isn't just whether or not to use hashing, but, if so, what algorithm to use to fit best the patterns of data in the database.

These examples give only a taste of deep design. Many more esoteric possibilities exist: 'compressed heap', 'compressed B-tree', 'compressed B-tree with unique keys' and so on. Still, deep design is not as onerous as it might appear from some textbooks. Often the designer of a specific database doesn't have to evaluate all theoretical options, only those offered by a chosen DBMS, a much more limited range; one DBMS may offer (say) elaborate indexing possibilities but no hashing, another the reverse.

Denormalisation Examples

There is another resource of great importance for the deep design process — denormalisation. Suppose the deep designer makes the following case: this conceptual schema results in an extravagant system that will consume considerable hardware resources, no matter how cleverly the deep design options are chosen; but if the conceptual schema itself is altered, then a leaner, more efficient system will be feasible.

Usually this kind of judgement is associated with denormalisation. The conceptual schema in third normal form has (say) 45 tables; if a few critical tables were merged so that there were only 41 tables, deep design could provide better performance. The drawback, which different people may assess very differently, is that the conceptual schema is no longer entirely in third normal form. To help focus on this matter here are some examples where denormalisation is plausible:

• **Merging one-to-ones.** Suppose the conceptual schema has a table *Branch-type*, containing *location-code* (down-town, suburb, village etc), *status-code* (all products and services, restricted range) etc. There is another table, *Branch-building*, with data about the branch as a property: *floor-area*, *book-value* of the property, *last-valuation-date* etc. It is natural and logical to think of these as two distinct tables containing different sorts of information. But suppose that whenever any *Branch-type* record was accessed, the system usually needed to access the corresponding *Branch-building* record too, and vice versa. Then there would be a case for putting all that branch data in one table, *Branch*. This might produce a more efficient system at the price of a slightly less natural database structure.

But another issue could be relevant to the tradeoff: Who is

responsible for maintaining this data? It is generally best to keep responsibilities as simple as possible. If one head office department is responsible for all the branch-type data, and another department for branch-building data, then that would favour the notion of keeping two separate tables.

- **Two tables instead of three.** In practice a more complex version of the previous point often arises. The most exacting transactions to optimise are often those that access data from *three* different tables. Redesigning the database so that the content of the three tables is held in just *two* rather-more-complicated tables may seem attractive. But then building in safeguards so that, whatever updates are made, no inconsistencies can arise between or within tables may be a considerable problem.

  Here, as with most denormalisation possibilities, quantification has to enter the debate. Suppose the correct design in third normal form includes three tables: *Supplier* and *Supplier-product* and *Supplier-schedule.* If 295 out of 300 suppliers deliver only one product according to quite a simple schedule, then reorganising the three tables as two could be very attractive — provided that the data for the five multi-product suppliers doesn't become unduly distorted. On the other hand, if there are 50 suppliers and nearly all of them deliver many products, whose deliveries are scheduled in complex ways, and if all their data is often combined in quite intricate ways, then . . .

- **Derived data.** Suppose the system allows access to a certain total figure, eg total of deliveries to branch from depot of a certain fast-moving product since start of business today. The logical, clean way to do this (theoreticians agree) is to store the data of each delivery in the database, but not any total (except maybe for auditing or recovery purposes, but that is a different topic altogether), and calculate the total afresh whenever the access is made. This is based on the principle that it is best to store data in an atomic way and avoid storing pieces of data that are completely derived from other pieces of data. But if there are many thousands of transactions to be added up, this clean approach may strain system resources. To overcome this, you might consider being slightly less neat and storing the derived total in the database as well. The downside is that the system will then have to bear the burden of updating this total every time a new transaction comes in. And recovery procedures will be more tricky too; the system might conceivably crash *after* a transaction has been received, but *before* the running total has been updated.

These examples are fairly representative of the kinds of tradeoff factors that may come up in decisions about denormalisation.

Denormalisation Complicates the Process

The Classic Approach

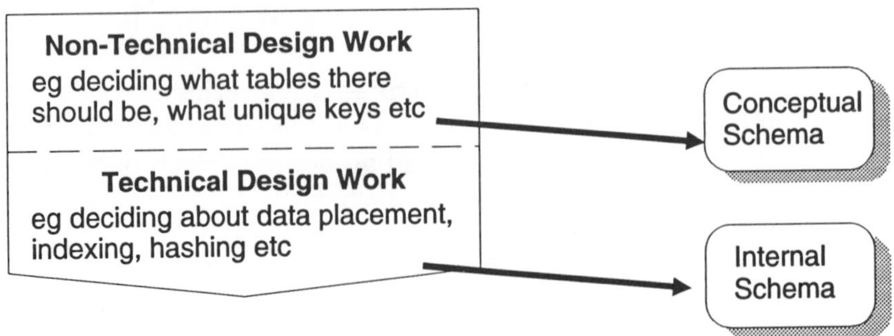

But suppose the Technical Design work raises the possibility of denormalising the Conceptual Schema

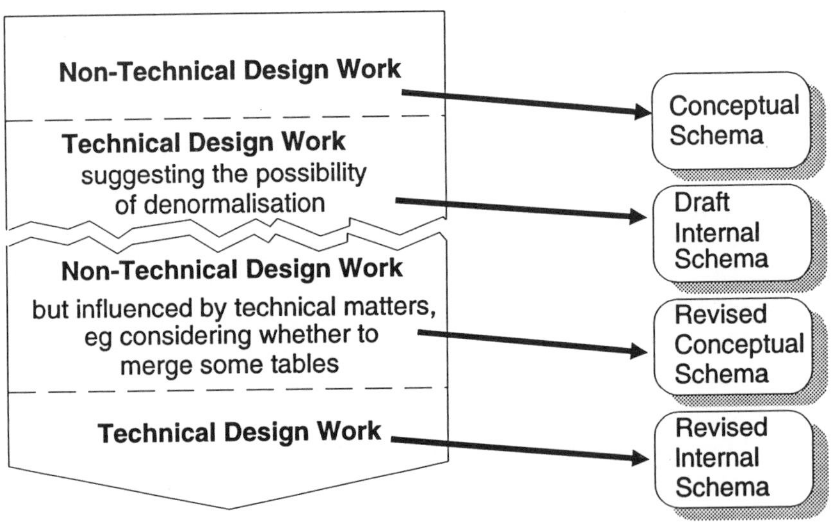

Revising the Conceptual Schema: Chart of the Process Implications

Now to return to the mural analogy of the deep design process. Denormalisation makes the analogy utterly false. Much of deep design certainly entails colouring in a fixed, pre-existing conceptual schema, but denormalisation doesn't colour in. Rather, it changes the shapes contained in the starting design in order to make them easier to colour.

Denormalisation, though the most common, is not the only way that the conceptual schema may be revised during deep design. There are a couple of other possibilities:

- The conceptual schema at the outset might be in third normal form (3NF) and generally agreed to be the most natural design available. But consideration of data volumes and other factors of deep design could lead to the idea of reorganising part of the conceptual schema to make a schema that, though slightly less natural, still met the criteria of 3NF, and made a more efficient operational system.
- The deep design process might even lead to ideas for altering the conceptual schema in a way that met higher relational criteria. The conceptual schema at the outset might be in third normal form (3NF), but reorganising it to handle the data volumes of the case as efficiently as possible might produce a design in some higher normal form, eg BCNF. It is true that higher normal forms usually lead to more tables and thus to a heavier load on hardware resources; but they can also lead to simpler tables with fewer records. Thus, there *can* be particular quantities and patterns of data that are more efficiently handled in (say) BCNF than the usual 3NF.

Nobody but the most technical people need usually enter debates about levels of indexing or hashing. But with revision of the conceptual schema (usually by denormalisation) the situation is quite different. Since the conceptual schema was probably designed by other people — say, systems analysts in collaboration with company managers — feedback from the subsequent deep design stage of the process may have important organisational ramifications, that don't arise with hashing and the like.

Many books and articles on deep design mislead by lumping choices about indexes, hashing and so on together with decisions on denormalisation, as if these were all useful resources belonging together in the technical designer's specialised repertoire.

This obscures a vital point. Some design decisions (eg about indexes) just add technical content in its natural place in the design process, but others (eg about denormalisation) complicate the whole process, as the diagram shows, by going back to discuss alterations to what had previously been thought firmly established.

POSSIBLE DECISION-MAKING

Plainly the technical expert must do most of the work on data placement, B-trees, hashing and so on. But, as the account just given suggests, the database internal schema may very well be the result of tradeoffs between technical and non-technical factors. If the

SUMMARY OF WARRANTS

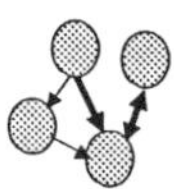

Chart of Deep Design Process: Adding technical content to given design; Tradeoffs; Defaults; Tuning

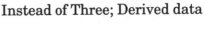

Examples of Denormalisation: Merging One-to-Ones; Two Tables Instead of Three; Derived data

Examples of Deep Design Options: Sequence; Data placement; Multiple indexed fields; Levels of indexes and B-trees; Hashing

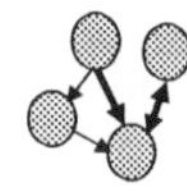

Revising Conceptual Schema: Chart of Process Implications: Denormalisation and other schema revisions; Denormalisation etc and other deep design techniques; Colouring in and changing shapes; Conceptual schema and internal schema

design choices that lead to optimum performance for one part of the system requirements result in poor performance in some other area, then compromises will have to be made. They can only be made rationally if demand-side interests are fed into the calculus too.

PTR's computer-literate general managers won't interfere with deep design to the extent of arguing about whether one hashing algorithm is more suitable than another or criticising the way different parts of the database are located on different disks. But their guidance may still be valuable; eg:

'You want to denormalise parts of the conceptual schema to make operation more efficient. We are not against that idea on principle, but the denormalisation should be kept to a minimum and well controlled. Decisions on this will be taken by a small group with equal numbers of information analysts and technical specialists.'

'If your deep design only manages to meet some of the most exacting access requirements by inventive use of clustering sequence, that could have unfavourable implications for other accesses that are as yet undefined. Somebody more demand-oriented should be involved to bear in mind longer-term developments.'

'You say that the deep design for the database has been contrived to optimise the speed of processing the *average* transaction. But is that a sensible aim? Perhaps a better aim would be a deep design tuned to give *priority* to certain transactions, even at the expense of average performance, or one tuned to optimise processing of the *95% of standard* transactions at the expense of the others — or any number of other possibilities. Supply and demand are surely interlinked here.'

As these pseudo-quotes suggest, the important management decisions about deep design are not decisions such as 'Yes, hashing is the technique to use' or 'No, don't use a B-tree there'. They are decisions about how the design process should be organised — who should be involved, what factors should be brought in, where feedback should be encouraged and so on — to ensure that the supply-side decisions of deep design fit well with demand-side choices.

CONNECTIONS

4. Conceptual Schemas	The conceptual schema — input to the deep design process
12. Data Modelling Method and Process	More about the process of modelling and designing
16. Mix, Match, Amend	Why denormalisation means going back to the conceptual schema
19. Classic Text Systems	Deep design options with text database
24. Document Image Systems	Deep design for systems that hold bit-mapped images

9. Client-server Architecture

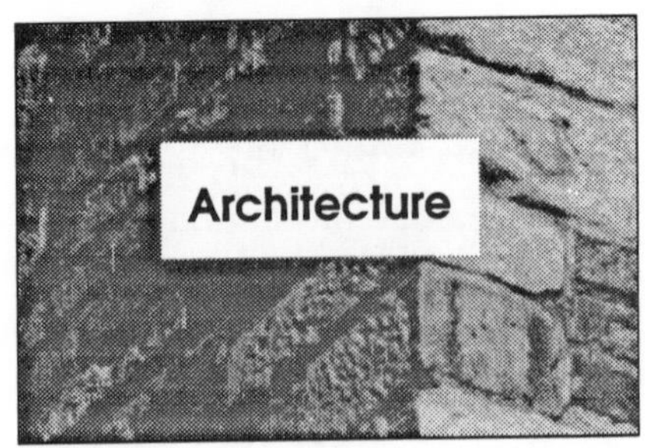

BEARINGS

The architecture of a system is the way its components fit together. Design of the system's architecture is macro-design, in comparison with the micro-level deep design, discussed in the previous briefing. For this reason, its interactions between supply and demand are more prominent in management decision-making.

This briefing covers three generic types of architecture — host, file-server and client-server. As it shows, there is far more knowledge worth knowing about client-server architecture than about the others.

POSSIBLE CONTEXT

Sassafras Magazines publishes 50 magazines about medical equipment, agricultural machinery and various other areas of technology. The Commercial department takes orders from companies and individuals to advertise in the magazines and looks after the associated accountancy, credit control and debt collection. The department needs a database system to support these tasks. During most of each working day, 10-15 people will be accessing and updating information in the database.

The quality, scope and other features of any arrangements for sharing the database are strongly related to the architecture of the whole system. At first glance it may appear that the decision-making logic (though not necessarily the technical design itself) should be rather simple:

- first, decide what data needs to be shared, and by whom; ie define the demands of the system;
- then work out the most appropriate architecture to **supply** these demands.

But this is inadequate for well-warranted decisions. Absolute, inflexible demands rarely exist in isolation, and sensible, realistic demands are generally guided by some instinct for the different supply possibilities. The important thing is to be aware, at least in outline, of the pros and cons of different architectures and grasp how they permit certain database system facilities and limit others.

WARRANTS

Meeting the demands for kind of data, structure and access means finding an architecture to deal as efficiently as possible with supply matters such as integrity control, concurrency control, recovery, security and deep design.

There are various generic styles of architecture for a database system. Much the most talked about in recent years is client-server, whose promise is to harness the vitality of the PC within large-scale database systems. But to appreciate the issues within client-server you need to relate them to the less glamorous host and file-server architectures.

Comparison of Host Architecture with Other Possibilities

In a simple host system a department has a minicomputer, controlling terminals scattered around the office. The database is managed by a relational DBMS at the minicomputer and all processing takes place there.[1]

This architecture has some strong and some vulnerable points:

- **Integrity, CRS and deep design.** The DBMS and operating system software products have to fit together hand in glove to meet the aims of efficiency and robustness, but over the years this has been achieved and the technology is now mature. This is the area of strength for the host architecture.
- **User interface.** In the PC world, the trend is towards ever more sophisticated interfaces: graphics, different letter sizes, different colours, different shape windows, pointing through a mouse, etc. A mini-computer typically displays monochrome 24x80 character screens on its terminals; getting it to support interfaces an order of magnitude more sophisticated on all its terminals at a reasonable cost is often out of the question. Thus, the host approach tends to condemn users of the database system to an interface from the dark ages. This (many people think) is a really big weakness.
- **Architecture cost-effectiveness.** The host architecture misses out on the tremendous price-performance ratios of the effervescent

PC market. The approach of massing all the processing in one expensive minicomputer and treating the devices on the users' desks as mere slaves seems to make the host architecture vulnerable — a big target for improvement.

• **Software development.** Testing out new software under development entails either using a host configuration that is also running the live system (perhaps risky), or using a whole configuration dedicated to software development (expensive). Also, the software development features available here are less varied and innovative than those for use on the PC. Thus, the host approach is also vulnerable on this front.

Chart connecting Elements of File-server Architecture

File-server architecture is a much cruder approach, but it does make use of the power of the PC. There is no minicomputer — instead **PCs** are linked together in a **LAN** (local area network). The database is stored at one PC, the **server**.

With this setup, each PC can be used by itself, whether for database or non-database work, such as word processing, spreadsheet etc. But when necessary, a PC can also request a file (say a word processing document) stored at another PC, receive it, amend it and return it.

The software of the **network operating system** (say, Novell Netware) arranges all this, and looks after CRS functions; eg it handles recovery in the event of breakdown and, if two PCs want the same file, it provides concurrency control. This network operating system knows nothing about word processing, database or any other application. It is simply concerned with arranging access to files — for any application.

Suppose there are 10 PCs in the department at which database-related work is done. Each has a separate copy of a **DBMS** software package (say, Paradox or dBase IV), but the database they share is stored at the server. The network operating system will arrange access to the data from the database and pass updated data back.

However, the network operating system will only deal in whole files. The database at the server is made up of a number of files, but probably not all that many. If you want information about adverts in *Plough Illustrated*, there may well be no such file — only a file for adverts in all 50 magazines. The network operating system can only pass you that whole file across the network.

Comparison of File-server Architecture with Other Possibilities

This architecture is a kind of theoretically flawed compromise — though it may still be the most pragmatic choice in an individual case:

- **Integrity, CRS and deep design.** The system relies on the facilities of the network operating system for concurrency control, recovery and other supply-side capabilities.

  But a network operating system isn't designed to support database systems *per se*. It provides generic facilities for one PC to access files from the disk of a server PC; these are designed just as much for the data of a spreadsheet or the electronic-mail messages of a person's mailbox as for information from a database.

  One practical problem is the granularity of the concurrency control. The network operating system allows one PC to access and amend a whole file from the server, and can prevent any changes to any part of the file by a second PC. But a network operating system doesn't provide locks on parts of files, such as: 'This file contains advert records of 50 magazines; lock any changes to *Plough Illustrated* data, but allow changes to data of any of the other 49.' Still less: 'Lock the data of *Plough Illustrated*, September 1994 issue.' This, of course, can be very unsatisfactory: the person working on *Plough Illustrated* may prevent any work being done on *Bobsleigh News* for no good reason at all.'[2]
- **User interface.** The power of the PC does allow a more sophisticated interface: graphics, mouse etc. Note also that the scope for improved interface isn't limited to attractive graphics: it is now more feasible to employ techniques such as textual help screens, lists of valid values for input fields with explanations, display-only of possibly relevant data (eg customer's credit history) in separate windows etc.
- **Architecture cost-effectiveness.** File-server does avoid leaving the processing resources of the PC unused. On the other hand, it introduces a source of inefficiency: if a certain PC needs to access information in a certain file, then it requests that file from the server. The whole file (perhaps thousands of records) is transmitted across the network and the software at the PC selects the part required and perhaps updates it. After the update, the whole file is transmitted back across the network, and the server then replaces the whole of the old file with the whole of the new. This puts an undesirable load on the network, on the PC and on the server.

Comparing File-server and Client-server

File-server Architecture

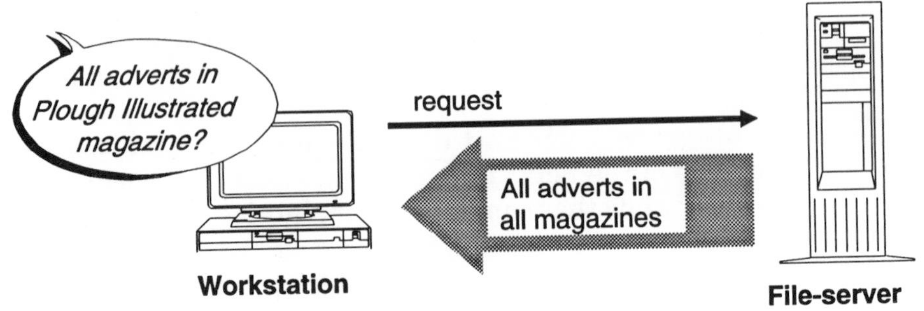

The workstation receives the whole file and selects the adverts it needs

Client-server Architecture

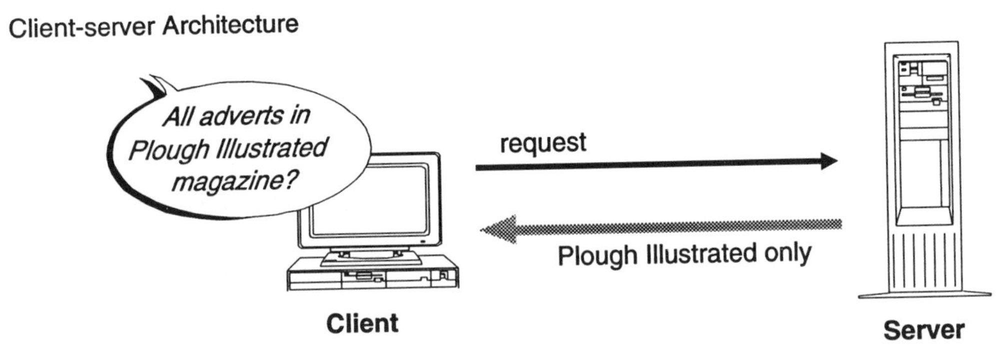

Client and Server work together to optimise use of resources

- **Software development.** File-server takes advantage of the PC as a machine for developing software — a considerable benefit.

Chart connecting Elements of Client-server Architecture

Clearly an architecture with all the good and none of the bad points of the other two architectures would be ideal. The client-server concept is illustrated in the two diagrams:

- Keep the main database at the **server PC**, with a powerful DBMS to provide efficient, reliable supply functions;
- but keep much of the application software running on each of the **client PCs.**
- Let the application program work by itself on the client until the

Client-server Architecture

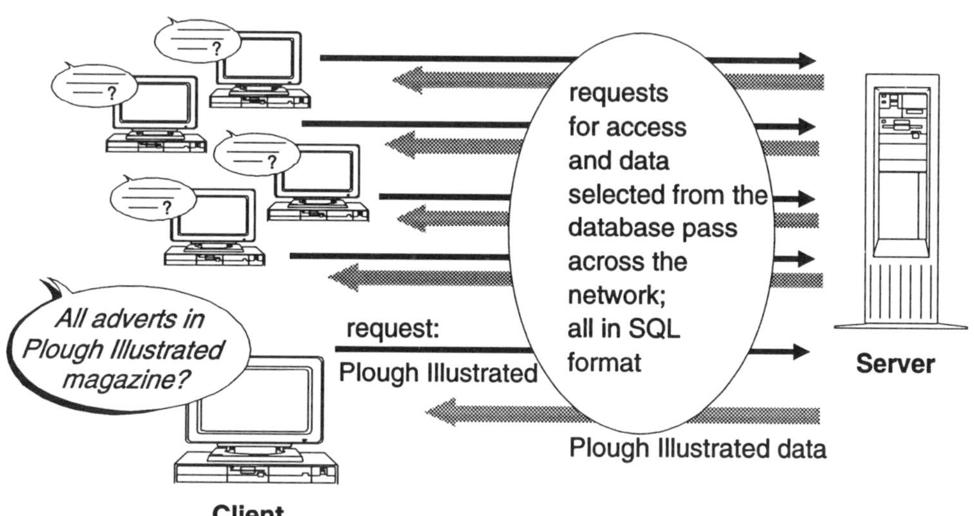

Client runs application programs with the power to provide sophisticated interface features

Server runs DBMS software, clever enough to select requested data from database - for numerous clients, providing powerful integrity, CRS and deep design features

time comes to retrieve data from the database or to send it over there. At that point the client can send a message across the **network** to the server.

- Have the **server DBMS** both subtle enough to extract and update just that information required by the client (rather than deal in whole files) and powerful enough to provide sophisticated integrity, CRS and deep design features.
- Use **SQL** as the lingua franca of this arrangement. Have clients define their access requirements in SQL and send them across the network to the server, which receives SQL statements and executes the database accesses they demand.
- As an important refinement of the concept, allow programmers and users to work with **client software**, offering a less taxing interface than SQL, and *translating* the accesses required into the necessary SQL messages behind the scenes.

The definition of client-server is somewhat blurred at the edges, as the definitions of fashionable terms usually are. The central concept is the sharp distinction between one piece of software at the client and another piece at the server, with an industry-standard language, SQL, to mediate between them.

Architectures based on a so-called multi-user version of a PC DBMS (Paradox, dBase IV etc) also provide a database on a server accessed by PCs across a LAN, and also provide concurrency control with the granularity of records rather than files, but they are not usually called client-server, because they don't break neatly into client and server components.

Examples of Client-server Architecture

To see how the components of client-server architecture work together, take two representative example applications:

- **Transaction.** To add one new order for magazine adverts, perhaps three successive input screens with multiple windows and clever graphical layouts might be used. The sequence of screens and fields to be filled in might depend on the input itself; there might be complex logic to check that the information input was consistent; various pricing calculations could be needed; all the time various help screens could be available. The client PC could handle all this up to the point of having a complete new record for adding to the database; it would pass this across the network to the server; the server would just add it to the database.
- **Decision support.** Somebody at a certain PC wants to see all customers owing more than $15,000, with more than three future adverts outstanding in at least two magazines, and . . . and . . The client PC accepts this request from the user and sends it over to the server. The server does the demanding work of searching many thousands of database records for the few which meet all the conditions; it sends them back to the client, which displays them.

Note that in this setup there is no necessity for DBMS software to run on the client PC, provided that its application software sends messages across the network in SQL recognised by the server DBMS, and provided it can decode the messages it receives back.

Comparison of Client-server Architecture with Other Possibilities

The client-server approach seems to meet the major architecture issues very well:

- **Integrity, CRS and deep design.** In principle, the required facilities can be provided just as well by a DBMS running on a powerful server PC as by the DBMS on the minicomputer in the host architecture. As in the host approach, concurrency control, recovery and such facilities are provided by a collaboration between the DBMS — general-purpose, ie not application-specific — and operating system (of network or server PC or both) — more general-purpose still, not even specific to database systems.

- **User interface.** Great possibilities, as for file-server.
- **Architecture cost-effectiveness.** Client-server avoids leaving the processing resources of a PC unused and also avoids the inefficiency of transmitting entire files over the network.
- **Software development**. As for file-server. The bulk of application software developed by an organisation will be for the client, not server. There is a healthy market in products assisting software development.

Examples of Client-server Supply-side Issues

Client-server seems such a natural and attractive approach that a problem of comprehension can arise: What is so difficult about it? Unless you have some sense of the challenges faced by developers of client-server software products, and of the technical alternatives that a system designer has to weigh, you are ill equipped to appreciate what client-server really entails.

Here are a couple of examples of the complications that client-server throws up in the areas of CRS and deep design:

- **Concurrency control.** Any system has to deal with the problem that somebody may extract a record from the database, see it on the screen, but before updating it, go off to a meeting. It seems undesirable to lock that record so that nobody else can access it, perhaps for hours.

One solution is 'optimistic' concurrency control: allow several people to access at the same time, but with safeguards to prevent confusion from overlapping updates of the same data. A sophisticated version of this approach is to accept an update from one user and, if any other users are currently accessing the same record, update the data shown on their screens. It is tricky but feasible to make the DBMS do this in a foolproof way in a host architecture; at least all the logic is contained within one computer. With client-server such features are more difficult to build in: the logic of this concurrency control is contained in the server computer but it can't display updated data itself, only send it off in messages to the client, which may use it in ways the server knows nothing about.

- **SQL optimisation.** Suppose the server receives an SQL instruction from the client, saying in effect: extract details of all adverts published in the year 1994 in a leisure (as opposed to professional) journal for which payment was not made within 60 days. The server might satisfy this request by first extracting details of all 1994 leisure adverts and then going to the accounts part of the database to see which of them were not paid within 60 days. But an alternative way would be to extract all the not-within-60-days advert data first, and then see which met the 1994-leisure criteria. In logic, both ways will produce the same result, but the speed of producing that result may vary. Suppose 99.9% of all adverts were paid in less than 60 days; then the second approach is likely to be most efficient. But if hardly any bills are paid that quickly, then the first approach is probably better.

One of the cardinal features of SQL is that it defines the desired ends but not the means. But, as this example shows, it is tempting to find ways of optimising SQL accesses. One crude approach is based on the fact that complex search criteria can be expressed in different ways with equivalent effect. If the software company supplying the server DBMS publishes details of the sequence in which that DBMS processes the constituents of SQL statements, the programmer of client SQL software can take this into account when formulating the request.

With a more sophisticated approach the software of the DBMS server itself makes intelligent decisions about the most sensible sequence of accesses to follow. A relatively simple piece of reasoning might be: the *Adverts* table possesses indexes on the fields *magazine* and *date*, but the *Payments* table has no indexed field called days-since-invoice; therefore, other things being equal, it seems best to start by finding the *Adverts* records that meet the 1994-leisure criteria.

Much more sophisticated logic is possible. Some advanced server DBMSs maintain statistics about the distribution of *field values* in tables (eg 5% of records in the *Adverts* table are for magazine A, 11% for magazine B, and so on). This information can be used by the DBMS to optimise the accesses arising from any given SQL request. Naturally the overhead of maintaining and processing all the extra data about the distribution of values is a factor too; in a poorly tuned system it might even outweigh any savings through optimisation.[3]

Examples of Client-server Variations

Client-server isn't one specific approach to be either adopted or not; rather, it is a classic scheme on which numerous variations are possible.

Suppose the essential idea is that all processing attached to a new order should be done at the client PC; then the data will be sent to the server which adds it to the database. But for each new order a price has to be calculated, based on some discount tables, stored in the database. It seems rather odd for each client to extract this same information about discount rates from the server repeatedly for every order throughout the day. The natural alternative is to store these discount rates in a very small database at each PC.

The system can be kept under control by the following procedure. The master tables of discount rates are stored at the server; there they may be modified, but any changes only take effect the next day. Every morning, the current discount rate tables are sent out from the server to all the clients: a daily snapshot. Each client PC has a copy on its disk in a small database; the information is accessed during order processing but never amended. But the system's architecture has become more complex; the entire database is no longer held and controlled at the server. This can even be called a case of distributed database, albeit in an extremely weak sense.

Here is a different example of the concept. Each client PC holds a copy of a database containing several million characters of statistical information about the readership of different magazines. This makes it possible to generate (say) a pie chart in colour of the breakdown of the readership of a medical journal by reader specialism, while discussing advertising rates on the phone with a pharmaceutical company. A new copy of this statistical data is sent out to the clients once a month.

These two variants raise no great problems of supply, but as more volatile data is distributed, the problems get more formidable. It might seem attractive to download once a day a snapshot of the complete customer file to a database at each client PC, so that customer information is immediately available at the client when processing a new order. But then how would changes to customer details be handled? Suppose one morning a certain customer's credit rating is changed; do the workers at the PCs need to know immediately so that their daily snapshot information is overridden? This can be done, but at the price of complications.

Chart of Client-server Variations

The ideas conveyed by the examples can be summarised in a more generalised form. Divide the work of a client-server system three ways:

- **Presentation and interface:** the work of taking raw data and displaying it on screen in an attractive, typically graphical, way.
- **Business logic:** eg the processing to test whether an attempted update is valid — numeric, within valid ranges etc.
- **Data management:** the processing to retrieve raw data of (say)

SUMMARY OF WARRANTS

Comparison of Host Architecture and Other Possibilities: Integrity, CRS and deep design; User interface; Architecture cost-effectiveness; Software development

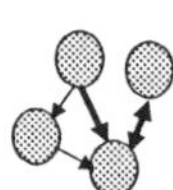

Chart connecting Elements of File-server Architecture: PCs; LAN; Server; Database; Network operating system; DBMS; Files

Comparison of File-server Architecture and Other Possibilities: Integrity, CRS and deep design; User interface; Architecture cost-effectiveness; Software development

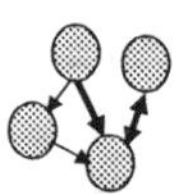

Chart connecting Elements of Client-server Architecture: Server PC; Client PC; Network; Server DBMS; SQL; Client software

Examples of Client-server Architecture: Transaction; Decision support

Comparison: Client-server Architecture and Other Possibilities: Integrity, CRS and deep design; User interface; Architecture cost-effectiveness; Software development

Examples of Client-server Supply Issues: Concurrency control; SQL optimisation

Examples of Client-server Variations: Discount tables at client; Summary statistics at client.

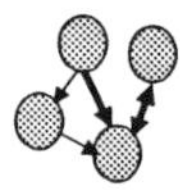

Chart: Elements of Client-server Variations: Presentation and interface; Business logic; Data management

an existing customer or to update the database with a newly amended record.

Though used by a number of authorities, this breakdown isn't always too easy to apply; it is best to treat business logic as all the work that isn't either of the other two.

With a host architecture all three occur at the mainframe; the essence of client-server is that the body of work represented by the three be split between client and server. But it may be split in any of a variety of ways. You may place all the presentation and interface and part of the business logic at the client, with the rest of business logic and all data management at the server. But then again you may place only part of the presentation and interface at the client and everything else at the server. Not all theoretical variants will be practically sensible in a particular case, but it may well be that more than one is.

Thus, this chart of the three work components is a good tool for uncovering options to decide between.[4]

POSSIBLE DECISION-MAKING

From this briefing there seems to be a prima facie case for choosing the client-server option at Sassafras Magazines. It is the up-to-date approach that, in principle at least, has numerous advantages.

The natural first step is to check whether these theoretical advantages do apply in the specific case. Yes, Sassafras does stand to benefit from such things as better user interface, easier software development and so on. No, there is no obvious reason why its applications should be less suitable than those of thousands of other companies.

Are there any major risks or disadvantages to balance against these advantages? Not really, given reasonable technical and managerial competence.

But these are merely preliminaries, showing that the important question is not 'Shall we use client-server?' but 'How should we best use client-server in our particular case?'

As in other areas of technology, here a variety of concepts and possibilities huddle together under the shelter of one term. Client-server offers several distinct advantages in principle, but not all possible uses of the concept achieve all these advantages to the same extent:

- If efficiency factors such as optimum use of the network and speed in accessing an enormous database by complex selection criteria were top priority, then a client-server system might not have any very special user interface.
- But if the main reason for using client-server was the scope it offered to present an attractive, exceptionally easy to use interface, this area might well be elaborated, if necessary even at the expense of configuration cost-effectiveness.

The next step at Sassafras is to weigh up the relative importance of such factors as integrity, CRS, deep design, user interface, architecture cost-effectiveness and software development. That will bring further progress towards recognising demand and supply options . . .

CONNECTIONS

5. Accessing the Database	Access options, including the role of SQL
7. Concurrency, Recovery, Security	Underlying CRS factors in client-server architecture
10. Special Architectures	Distributed database as a more advanced gradation of architecture
16. Mix, Match, Amend	Client-server and SQL facilitating a flexible architecture
17. Mainstream Software Products	Software products for various client-server roles

10. Special Architectures

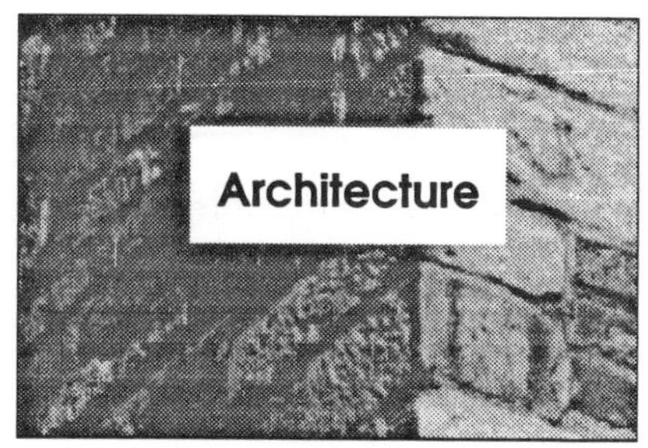

BEARINGS

This briefing discusses three varieties of architecture that are more esoteric than host, file-server or client-server, but still worth knowing about:

- **Distributed database.** Storage of the database is split over two or more computers, normally in different locations — thus raising the problem of keeping the different parts of the database in step with each other.[1]
- **Database machine.** Special combinations and variations of processors and storage media are arranged to optimise database storage and access.
- **Data warehouse.** One database is kept for normal operational use in processing transactions and the like, and a separate but loosely related database is a warehouse (aka refinery) of history data for analysis in decision support (aka executive information) systems.

POSSIBLE CONTEXT

Turpentine Tours is a travel agent and tour operator with a network of branches. A new generation of systems is under consideration. One party among the senior managers of the company has become convinced that distributed database technology is essential. The argument runs as follows:

- We have already done some outline data modelling for the new family of systems. It defines in non-technical terms who will need what data in what location.
- Much transaction information (eg about a simple flight booking) is of interest to the local branch and to nobody else. It would be bizarre to store that information hundreds of miles away from the branch in some central database.
- You might say then that each branch should have its own self-con-

tained database. But that would be a very clumsy arrangement for certain other bookings. As a company we may have a deal with some hotel on a Greek island, enabling us to offer up to some maximum number of low-price bookings to our customers. Clearly a centralised database is needed to control those bookings.

- Also Turpentine may have several branches in the same large city that may need to share data with each other, eg so that a customer can use both the branch closest to home and that closest to work and still be treated by the computer system as one customer.
- Therefore Turpentine needs to use technology that permits a database to be split up in quite complex ways, with different pieces at different locations around the country, while allowing somebody at any location to work on whatever data is needed, wherever it may be.
- Therefore Turpentine needs a **distributed database** architecture.

But an opposing faction within Turpentine develops a more cautious line of reasoning:

- If it is true that a large part of the whole database is of purely local interest and other parts must be managed centrally, that is a prima facie, though not conclusive, argument for distributed database *in some vague sense.*
- But distributed database is not one unambiguous concept. The term covers many possibilities, some more intricate and adventurous than others.
- Moreover, though the possible options may, in a sense, be purely technical options, we suspect that the implications may be sufficiently great for non-technical people to be involved in decisions about them, at least to some degree.
- Therefore in order to make sound decisions about distributed database in our particular case the vital general knowledge we need is a briefing on distributed database options.[2]

WARRANTS

The briefing has four warrant sections on the distributed database topic, three on database machine and three on data warehouse.

Initial Gradations of Distributed Database

Why not split up a database over a number of different locations in the organisation? That innocent question can mask a great variety of alternative arrangements, with technical challenges ranging from straightforward to trailblazing.

First, what does it really mean to assert of a system that its *one database* is broken into several parts — as opposed to saying that it uses *several databases* that fit together neatly? The best preliminary answer is an account of three very rough gradations of cases where the database is certainly not all stored in one location:

- **Gradation 0.** This is something some may call a distributed database architecture — but erroneously. An organisation with 20 branch offices might have 20 small databases, similar in format, with each office running an entirely self-contained system. This architecture might well be more cost-effective than having all terminals in all offices on-line to one central computer with one huge database, but it doesn't really count as running a single database distributed over 20 sites. After all, one office's database might disappear and the other offices might never notice. It is more useful to regard this as a system with 20 similar but separate databases — not a case of distributed database.
- **Gradation 1.** In this, data stored at each of 20 offices is both accessible and updatable by people at the other 19 locations. Here it is more reasonable to think of the whole body of data as making up one single database. But suppose that accessing data at another location is something of an exception, and entails a more involved procedure than accessing the local data. If so, this is the **basic case** of distributed database.
- **Gradation 2.** This introduces the fundamental concept of **location transparency.** Here accessing data elsewhere entails just the same procedures as accessing local data. The user doesn't need to know where the data is stored — here or somewhere else, and if so where. The system itself, so to speak, knows where to find any data requested. In discussion of this topic, the user to whom location is transparent is always taken to include the application programmer, as well as the person using the operational system. Of course, location can't be transparent to everyone; the people masterminding the whole setup (database administrators and the like) are very much concerned with knowing where everything is.

Gradation 1 of distributed database is generally regarded as rather a poor thing. It is generally assumed that the location transparency of Gradation 2 is a necessary feature of a distributed database system. The main issues come in further complications of the Gradation 2 case.

Aspects of Data Distribution

Splitting a database makes things more complicated. It only has a point if there are, on balance, advantages to be gained in such areas as deep-design efficiency, recovery, security and so on. To go further into the subject it is best to identify a number of aspects of distributed database that may affect a Gradation 2 (location transparency) system. They are also illustrated in the diagram.

- **Fragmentation.** If the whole database is split over several locations in a natural way (eg each customer's data stored at the local branch office, all supplier data at head office etc), this is horizontal fragmentation. Vertical fragmentation occurs when certain fields from (say) each *Customer* record are held in one place and other fields (belonging logically to the same record) in another place. This tends to pose more integrity problems than horizontal fragmentation.
- **Replication**. Another concept is to hold copies of certain fragments of the database (or all of it) in several different places. Usually one copy of the data has a primary status: any update is always done on that copy and changes are passed to any other copies afterwards. The DBMS has to look after the problems of integrity and CRS that can arise; eg copies of the data getting out of step through hardware failures in certain parts of the network.
- **Distributed updating**. If one transaction can cause update of data *at several locations*, this raises considerable integrity and CRS complications. If data is replicated, then an update to one copy unavoidably entails update of another copy in another location. If data is fragmented but not replicated, it may or may not be the case that one transaction causes distributed updates. Many genuine distributed database systems, particularly those based on horizontal fragmentation, are designed to avoid it. With vertical fragmentation, however, distributed updating is more likely to be needed.

Advanced Aspects of Distributed Database

Distributed database has many more complicated aspects. Here are some of the main ones:

- **Transaction recovery.** The term logical transaction applies to the case of several related updates to the database, where either all or (in case of hardware failure) none must be carried out. This is tricky enough with a single-site host architecture, but things become even more complicated if the updates and the technical failures can affect several different parts of the database at different sites; ie if

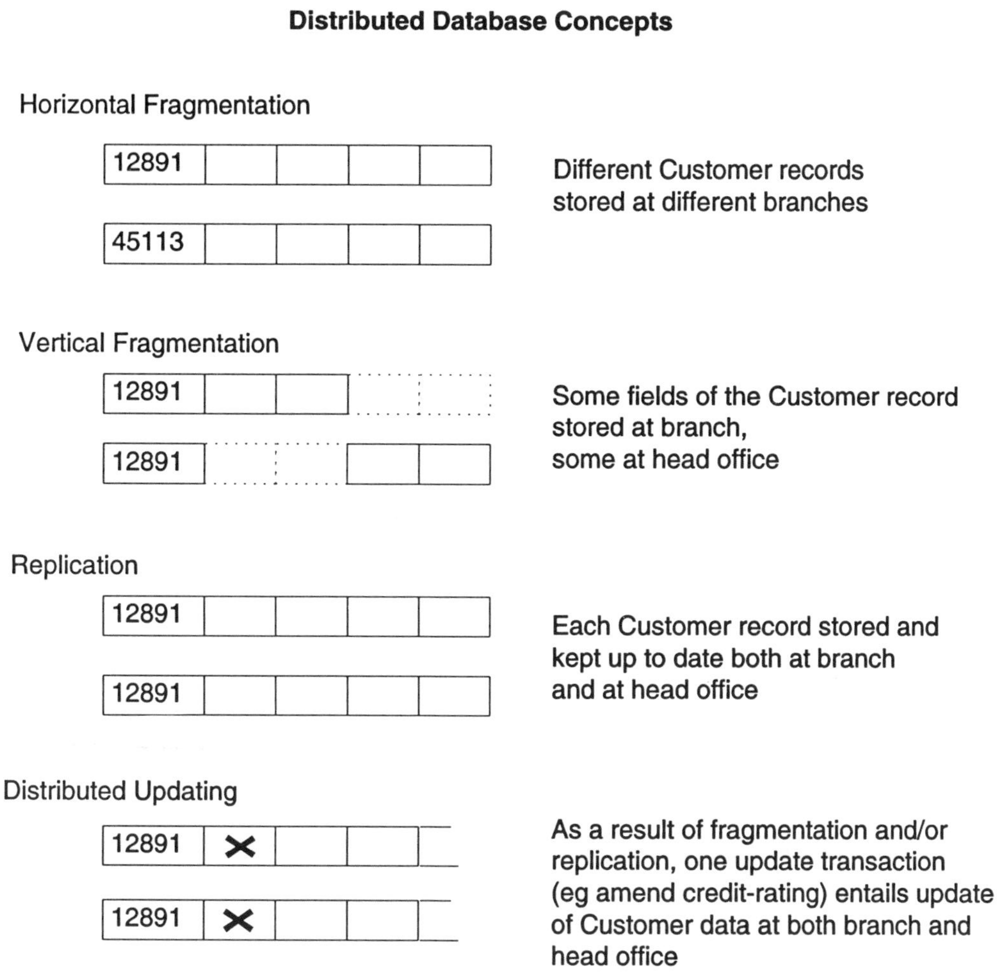

Distributed Database Concepts

Horizontal Fragmentation

12891				
45113				

Different Customer records stored at different branches

Vertical Fragmentation

12891				
12891				

Some fields of the Customer record stored at branch, some at head office

Replication

12891				
12891				

Each Customer record stored and kept up to date both at branch and at head office

Distributed Updating

12891	×			
12891	×			

As a result of fragmentation and/or replication, one update transaction (eg amend credit-rating) entails update of Customer data at both branch and head office

the logical transaction theme is combined with distributed updating. During the period of any partial failure, the system will have to store in some part of the network messages about updates outstanding, and perhaps any updates already made that ought to be unrolled. It will have to deal with them smoothly as soon as things come back to normal, without violating any of the integrity constraints.

- **Transaction concurrency control.** With a one-site database the DBMS software can control logical transactions to avoid undesirable updates of the same data by different people at the same time. With distributed database, this task is more exacting, because several different pieces of DBMS software in different locations have to control access to physically different portions of the database. The mere names of the techniques used give a flavour of the complications: centralised two-phase locking, primary copy two-phase locking, circulating control token, majority consensus, conservative timestamp ordering scheme . . .

- **Optimum routing.** To extract data from the database, the DBMS needs to know where to find it and how to route it to its destination. An advanced DBMS may *optimise* this routing, by taking account of the amount of data to be sent from different locations, the possible paths through the network and the capacity of different elements of the whole configuration.
- **Emergency routing.** If certain elements of the whole configuration (eg particular computers or telecoms lines) are temporarily inaccessible through technical failure, an advanced distributed database system may switch automatically to using alternative routes for exchanging data in the meantime.
- **DBMS transparency.** Suppose the databases at different sites are managed by different DBMS products: at one location by Ingres (say), at another by Informix. In these circumstances it is quite a challenge to provide all the features above, just as if everything was all-Ingres or all-Informix. It may in fact be hopeless: two DBMSs could have such different concurrency control features that creating one uniform concurrency control function for the whole system was impossible.

Example of a Distributed Database Challenge

Examples are often useful to give an impression of the difficulties inherent in something that, otherwise described, may appear misleadingly simple. That danger is probably slight in this case, but still, here is a representative example of the challenges.

A DBMS equipped for a sophisticated distributed database needs a **global dictionary** facility to record what data is located where; this is quite distinct from the usual data dictionary consulted by users, which should have location transparency. Moreover the global dictionary will store data about the configuration of the network and all manner of quantitative data and algorithms relevant to the optimisation of routing.

Thus on a certain computer, somewhere in the network, a global dictionary is stored and continually accessed by special software that routes data around the network. But if this part of the system were ever out of action the whole system would be paralysed. That risk, however remote, may well be unacceptable. A recovery facility needs to be built in; eg have a duplicate of the global dictionary data and software on another computer 500km away, that can take over automatically if necessary.

This may seem not too difficult, even though expensive. But what about all the quantitative data and algorithms stored in the global dictionary for use in the optimisation of routing? The reserve global dictionary can't simply carry on using a duplicate of this information, because it is certainly wrong (ie since one of the main points in the network is out of action, many of the normal routing possibilities are not available).

Therefore the recovery facility must switch over from one global dictionary to the other, but also amend the content of the global dictionary with new routing data — and these amendments can't be defined easily in advance, since they depend on what precisely has gone wrong elsewhere in the network. It is a tall order to develop generic DBMS software for such tasks, that will be sophisticated, utterly reliable, but not absurdly extravagant in resources.

Initial Distinction between Database Machine Approaches

This is another area where it is often difficult to see the hedge for the twigs and foliage. As a modest start, distinguish two ideas for making a system based on the *host architecture* more efficient:

- **Division of labour.** With the classic host architecture, there is one large host computer at the hub. A more subtle variant is possible: all database work (eg extracting data, updating data etc) is kept in certain parts of the host configuration, separate from other work (eg handling calculations, some validation checks, message formatting etc), done in other parts. Of course, this isn't merely a matter of hardware configuration; appropriate software (eg a special version of the DBMS) is needed to co-ordinate things.
- **Special hardware.** Most computers sold to business are general-purpose machines, capable of receiving bookings through a terminal, producing sales analysis statistics and a hundred other types of work. Rather than use ordinary computers, maybe powerful but general-purpose, it could be more efficient to use hardware specifically designed for database work, as opposed to other types of processing. Again, to take proper advantage and keep things in order, clever software is needed.

These are distinct but overlapping possibilities; you could adopt the first idea, without the second. However, the reverse isn't true; the second practically implies the first.

A host architecture, that uses the division of labour idea gives a **backend machine** a role analogous to that of the server in a client-server setup. The backend or database machine concentrates on the reading and writing of data from the database while a frontend computer does everything else. Special software ensures that the two computers keep in step. In an advanced form of this approach the backend machine uses a stripped-down version of an operating system.

The analysis so far applies to host architecture. The whole point of client-server architecture is to divide labour between the database server and its clients. The server is by definition a database machine. But the second idea, using special hardware for the server configuration, may well be relevant. This raises many issues and options.

Aspects of Parallel Processing

Whatever special hardware you configure, its justification is increased efficiency — and that will come mainly from causing certain operations to occur in parallel. Here are four main aspects of the complicated field of **parallel processing**:

- **Processing aims**. The aim that is usually called **parallel transaction** is to handle a number of distinct transactions from different terminals, simultaneously in different parts of the host or server configuration.

  The term **parallel query**, by contrast, applies to the case where work on *one particular* transaction is shared between different parts of the configuration that can work simultaneously. Suppose one access request entailed extracting all records meeting certain criteria from a database table of several million records; this work might be split between (say) four parts of the configuration, each searching a quarter of the table. Or the request might call for extracting certain records from two tables, joining them together and sorting the results. Tasks might be allocated so that one part of the configuration was scanning table A and another table B, while another was joining together records already extracted from tables A and B, and a fourth was sorting the results.

  These processing aims can be seen as the demand that the other three aspects are meant to supply.
- **Special hardware.** What are these parts of the configuration that may work in parallel? There are three main possibilities: separate processors that can work in parallel but are tightly coupled, ie they share the same memory and disks; loosely coupled processors that own at least some dedicated memory and disks; and special disk sub-systems capable of looking up keys in indexes stored on disk, in parallel with whatever the rest of the configuration is doing. Combinations of these possibilities are feasible.

- **Database partitioning.** The database may be stored on one disk or disks in a straightforward way, or it may be deliberately split over several disks to facilitate parallel processing; eg a table of several million records might be split over four disks in a predictable way, according to the value of the primary key. This is rather like having a distributed database whose horizontal fragments happen to be physically next to each other.
- **DBMS Copies.** The DBMS software controlling parallel processing may be essentially one piece of software, albeit a complex one, or several copies of the software may run on different processors in a somewhat autonomous way. The latter option brings many of the complications typical of distributed database systems.

A good way to clarify any technical proposal you encounter is to see where it stands on the options given above for these four aspects. Though some combinations of options may be pointless, many are credible. A relatively straightforward approach might take the following four choices: parallel transaction; tightly coupled processors; undivided database; one DBMS copy. A more advanced one: parallel query; tightly coupled processors; partitioned database; one DBMS. A fairly ambitious design: parallel transaction; loosely coupled processors, undivided database; several DBMS copies.

There are generally two main determinants of complexity: the delicacy of co-ordinating and optimising work under normal circumstances, and the difficulties of providing integrity and CRS arrangements that will be robust under any circumstances. These are largely challenges for the DBMS supplier. Understandably, the more complex the architectural options desired, the fewer the DBMS products available to support them.[3]

Comparison of Database Machine with Conventional Approaches

As the previous analysis shows, the term database machine covers a great range of complex possibilities. In a very general way its pros and cons can be set against those of a more straightforward approach.

First, most database systems of any size provide facilities for integrity control, recovery, concurrency control and so on. These things become more complicated if two or more computers or parts of computers have to be co-ordinated. So a considerable software overhead may be required if a database machine architecture is to provide decent integrity and CRS facilities.

Another crude objection to an intricate architecture with sophisticated optimisation techniques is that, after accounting for all software and technical support costs, it may be no cheaper than having an expensive but powerful and straightforward configuration.

A special database-machine architecture only becomes really competitive when the work profile permits extensive parallel processing. The co-ordination of parallel operations on the database usually brings a substantial overhead, and for moderate data volumes this overhead may cancel out the theoretical savings brought by parallelism. In short, the approach works best when volumes are massive and work is easily broken into fairly independent parallel tasks.

It follows from this that much typical database work — eg simple searches on average-sized databases — will gain little benefit from the complications of these special architectures.

Distinctions between Three Roles for Data

To see the point of the **data warehouse** architecture, make a rough and ready distinction between three roles for data:

- **Static data** is data such as a customer's name and address or the current timetable and prices of an airline.
- **Dynamic data** is data such as the details of one particular booking made by a customer, outstanding items on a customer's account, or places still open on a certain package tour.
- **History data** is static and dynamic data retained from the past, either individually or summarised in totals and sub-totals. Last year's accounting transactions may still be needed if current-year-to-date figures have to be compared with those of a previous year. A history of changes to a customer's address may have to be kept, in order to generate statistics such as sales analysed by customer location in each of the last five years.

The use of history data in any system is usually quite distinctive: no on-line update, only enquiry; relatively many ad hoc (as opposed to predefined, regular) enquiries; certain enquiries that are extremely complex (eg what-if analyses based on extrapolation of trends); intricate sorting out of data over time — eg changes in supplier status within an analysis of business by supplier type; perhaps, specially easy interface for commands (eg touch-screen or mouse) and for presentation (eg data shown as pie- or bar-charts); and, most striking of all, irregular usage — some days none at all, occasionally intensive.

This analysis leads straight to the idea of having two systems: the main operational system with its own database, with up to date static and dynamic data, and a separate DSS (decision support system) with a database of history data, perhaps called a **data warehouse** or **information refinery**.

Gradations of Data Warehouse Architecture

There seem to be at least six options of ascending complexity for data warehouse architecture:

- Gradation 0: **Same database.** One database serves both DSS and operational processing requirements.
- Gradation 1: **Separate databases, same schema, same DBMS.** Operational and DSS databases are separate. They have the same conceptual schema and DBMS. The DSS database is either a literal copy or simple subset of the operational one (eg a snapshot or edited snapshot, taken at the end of each day or week).
- Gradation 2: **Separate databases, consistent schemas.** Operational and DSS databases are separate. They use the same DBMS. Their conceptual schemas are not identical (eg the DSS schema contains many summary totals not in the operational), but they map onto each other neatly. Once a day (or week), certain data is shuffled out of the operational database to be loaded into the database of the DSS. Since no data comes into the database of the DSS from any other source, the two databases should remain consistent with each other.
- Gradation 3: **Separate databases, consistent schemas, extra data.** As above — operational and DSS databases separate, same DBMS, consistent schemas, DSS database fed by operational — but the DSS database also receives much data that doesn't pass through the operational system; eg monthly statistics about the economy in general and particularly about the industry in general.
- Gradation 4: **Separate databases, separate schemas.** As above with operational and DSS databases separate and same DBMS — but schemas not consistent. The DSS might use a completely different way of analysing types of business, customer and supplier. Why? Because statistics pouring in each month from outside sources (eg government, foreign subsidiaries etc) have different ways of analysing types of product, customer, supplier etc.
- Gradation 5: **Separate databases, separate schemas, separate DBMSs.** As the previous possibility, except that different DBMSs are used.

Aspects of the Data Warehouse

Particularly with the higher gradations, design issues have some interesting aspects:

- **Atomic data.** One extreme approach is to maintain a vast archive of past transactions in atomic, ie not summarised, form. The reasoning here is that, although summarised figures *appear* on screen in response to an enquiry, it isn't acceptable to *store* only summarised figures in the database. Any kind of summary inevitably makes assumptions about what *basis* for summary is likely to be useful and thus narrows the options for ad hoc requirements. For instance: 'I want the figures for Mediterranean package tour bookings made in each week from January to March 1994, but our so-called data warehouse consolidates bookings *of all types* by branch on a weekly basis. It does analyse bookings keenly enough to identify Mediterranean package tours, but then only on a monthly basis.' On the other hand, some degree of summarising is practically inevitable; otherwise the system may have to total up millions of atomic data items even to handle simple enquiries.
- **Temporal data.** Dynamic data by its very nature is transitory, but static data isn't literally static in the sense of completely immutable. Changes to static data raise problems. The current value of *supplier-status-code* may show that tour-operator A is in strategic alliance with your company; but for proper analysis, the system needs to record that during a certain period in the past, this code had a different value, meaning that the supplier was a bitter rival, one you only took bookings for if the customer really insisted. It may not seem hard to design a database that stores not just the current value of a field, but also past values and dates of change; the challenging task is to make the design both correct and efficient in its use of hardware resources.
- **Business model.** If the data warehouse has a different and inconsistent schema from the operational database, why not make it *completely* different? You could make a model of the business, based on say critical success factors or value chain analysis or something of the sort — quite independent in structure from the operational systems and database. Then data from the operational systems could be fed in and processed as necessary to produce appropriate summarised information in the structure of the business model.
- **Several warehouses and databases.** Once the warehouse is separate and different from the operational database, why not go further and allow the DSS workstation to access *several* warehouse databases, with different structure and content — eg a warehouse of sales data and another one of general economic data? A variation is to access several operational databases, not necessarily warehouses.
- **Hybrid database.** For more support to management, other types

SUMMARY OF WARRANTS

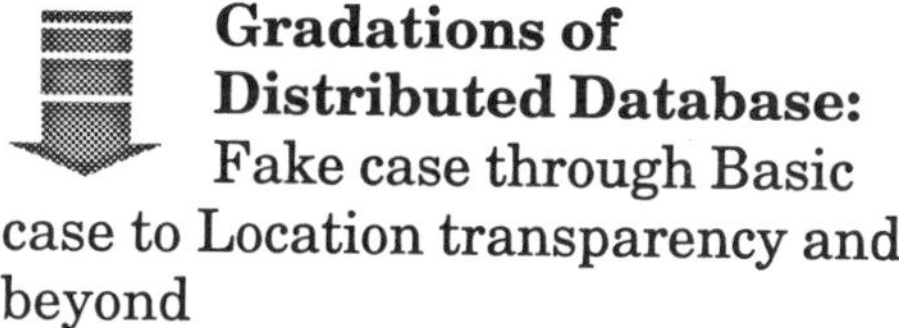

Gradations of Distributed Database: Fake case through Basic case to Location transparency and beyond

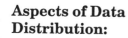

Aspects of Data Distribution: Fragmentation, horizontal and vertical; Distributed updating; Replication

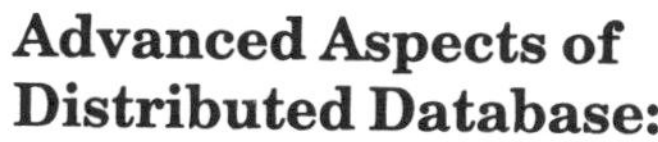

Advanced Aspects of Distributed Database: Transaction recovery; Transaction concurrency control; Optimum routing; Emergency routing; DBMS transparency

Example of a Distributed Database Challenge: Global dictionary and recovery

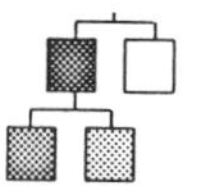

Distinctions between Database Machine Approaches: Division of labour; Special hardware

Aspects of Parallel Processing: Processing aims; Special hardware; Database partitioning; DBMS copies

Comparison of Database Machine and Conventional Approaches: Complex Integrity and CRS; Ingenious or simple but strong architecture; Natural breakdown into parallel tasks

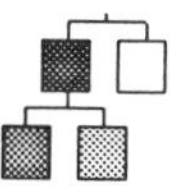

Distinctions between Data Roles: Static data; Dynamic data; History data

Gradations of Data Warehouse Architecture: From Separate databases, same schema and same DBMS, through to Separate databases, separate schemas, separate DBMSs

Aspects of Data Warehouse: Atomic data; Temporal data; Business model; Several warehouses and databases; Hybrid database

of data may be stored along with mainstream fields and records. Voice and bit-mapped image data may seem a little gimmicky, but text is a strong possibility; eg the figures for certain sales-periods could have excuses attached: 'Bookings for Algeria are down this month — perhaps because of the TV serial *La Peste* . . .' etc.

POSSIBLE DECISION-MAKING

These warrants show that, as one party at Turpentine Tours suspected, distributed database technology can be complicated, delicate and risky. Therefore, it may reasonably be thought, senior managers ought to have some control — or at the very least some awareness — of the risks run on their behalf. But, it seems, Turpentine Tours managers will have difficulty understanding these risks unless they spend all their time studying database technology.

There is a better way forward. In any risky, advanced technology the challenge is surely to find the least complex gradation of the technology that supplies the demands. Even though they won't investigate every detail, the Turpentine managers can at least ensure that their technical people do see this as a 'least complex gradation' problem. Then the approach finally chosen can be justified by comparison with other options of slightly less and slightly greater complexity.

This may not be so simple: tradeoffs probably have to be exposed and dealt with iteratively. If the only way of meeting certain demands in a reliable, competent way is through a high-powered, state-of-the-art version of distributed database, it would be rational at least to double-check whether the demands are truly immutable.

The senior managers of Turpentine Tours set up a study, to be dominated by technology experts, but with these bluff, no-nonsense terms of reference:

- There are many gradations of distributed database and since they are successively more complex, risky and potentially troublesome, we should choose the lowest gradation we can (as any sensible company should).
- Please sketch out the main gradations of distributed database (perhaps two or three) that are relevant to our situation. Define these options as simply and non-technically as possible.
- From our current knowledge, it seems that a system where no individual transaction ever needs to update data at more than one location would be one of the relevant lower gradations. Distributed updating would come much higher up. But all this is the kind of thing we want you to spell out for us.
- Our intention is to choose one of the options you define, following the principle that it must be justified as the best buy, by comparison with the nearest upper and lower gradations.

CONNECTIONS

6. Database Integrity	A big factor in distributed database architecture
7. Concurrency, Recovery, Security	Underlying factors in distributed database architecture
9. Client-server Architecture	Client-server and other architectures

11. Untangling Models, Tools and Control

BEARINGS

In the chart of database technology that helps organise this book, the first seven elements — kind of data through to architecture — describe the state of a given system at a given moment.

The other three elements — data modelling, software development and database system control — are concerned with a different angle: activities and processes in the development and life of a system, rather than its state at a given moment.

In this general area, some topics that seem distinct at first sight turn out to be confusingly interwoven. This briefing begins the task of sorting things out and thus provides an outline view of the content of Briefings 12, 13, 14, 15 and 16.

WARRANTS

To ask 'Shall we use an upper-CASE tool, a repository or an I-CASE system?' is to succumb to a confusion of category, as in 'Which is most dangerous — a lion, a tiger or a peril?' This briefing contains some charts to help combat that kind of confusion.

Chart connecting CASE and Associated Concepts

Intellectual methods exist in this field as suggested conventions and techniques for making models of data, processes, systems and so on. Logically, they are entirely distinct from any software products: you could carve an ER (entity-relationship) data model in a piece of sandalwood. But in practice, modelling is too laborious to do in any detail unless there is software to automate the production of diagrams and the like.

Software can do more than draw model diagrams. The broad class of **software** products needs charting out:

• **CASE** (computer-aided software engineering) is an elastic term that may describe any software product that helps in the activities of developing systems and databases.

• Some activities occur earlier in system development than others; eg data modelling comes before design of report layouts. Software tools for the earlier activities (roughly, the system design work, where intellectual methods are prominent) are called **upper-CASE**, and those for activities further downstream (roughly, software development work) **lower-CASE**.

It is possible to use a variety of CASE software to develop a system: one upper-CASE tool for data modelling, a different one for process modelling, a lower-CASE software product for making reports and another for the programs to handle input transactions. But successive development activities are related (the data items defined in the data model will crop up in the process model too) and need to fit together. Therefore many CASE software products support several development activities. The following are the three important classes of CASE software product and CASE system:

• The CASE software that supports and co-ordinates several lower-CASE activities. Since the term lower-CASE sounds vaguely inferior, many products are given a more glamorous name; eg **4GL** (standing for the meaningless phrase fourth-generation language).

• The **upper-CASE** software tool that supports a major activity (eg drawing the diagrams of an ER model), and to some degree other adjacent activities as well, eg automatically translating the ER model into instructions that can be used to set up the database. Analyst's workbench is a roughly equivalent term, but is best avoided as too vague.

• The **I-CASE** (integrated CASE) system. This supports the chain of development activities by keeping consistent the products of different activities and avoiding duplication of effort. There is scope for mild confusion: I-CASE sometimes refers to a complete set of co-ordinated upper-CASE and 4GL tools, but in other usages it refers only to the software that does the co-ordinating, excluding the individual tools.

Chart connecting Data Dictionary to CASE and Repository

Now the **data dictionary** has to be added into this charting of concepts. The natural way for any CASE system to achieve consistency between different tools and activities is to hold information describing the database tables, records and fields. This may well contain much more than the conceptual schema; eg the range of permissible values for many fields and some verbal explanation of their use. Both a 4GL and an I-CASE system store a data dictionary separate from any instances of diagrams or software coding. An upper-CASE system as defined above may or may not, depending on whether it is narrowly focused or supports several adjacent activities.

But the importance of the data dictionary isn't confined to CASE. Whatever the policy on CASE, most installations maintain a data dictionary for the *operational* database, at least as a source of reference. When any kind of change to data definitions is discussed or when any perplexing data is found in the database, the data dictionary is invaluable in thinking through all the complications. Seen from a purely operational point of view (ie ignoring CASE) there are two broad types of data dictionary:

- **Reference**: eg tells you that a certain field must always have a value within a certain range.
- **Active**: eg tells you that a field must have a value within a certain range, and actively prevents any update with a wrong value.

The main item missing from this charting of concepts is the **repository** — perhaps second only to 'object-oriented' as a plastic, status-symbol term. Repository is to data dictionary as mansion is to house. One system may store such a variety of information, documenting database and system in such elaborate ways, that repository is indisputably the right term; another may be so plainly limited to the basic description of database content that any more elevated term than data dictionary would be misleading. But drawing the line across the continuum is really a matter of taste. Marketing brochures tend to adopt repository because it is prestigious and fashionable. This book uses whichever seems most natural in context.[1]

To make real progress in demystifying repository, it is of first importance to disentangle two separate purposes:

- You can have facilities to store descriptive data (models, data definitions, even business plans etc) in order to further the activities of **developing** new systems.
- You can define rules about a system (particularly but not only validation criteria) in a rigorous, highly structured form to be stored in part of the database, for automatic, active use by the **operational** system.

Evidently, an ideal, all-embracing repository could handle these two different things in an entirely integrated way — but that doesn't mean that any less ambitious approach is worthless. It could be quite rational to concentrate on one purpose more than the other, or to have a development repository and an operational one, only crudely

SUMMARY OF WARRANTS

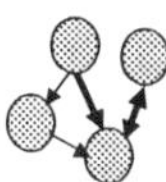
Chart connecting CASE and Associated Concepts: Intellectual methods; Software products; CASE; Upper-CASE; Lower-CASE; I-CASE; 4GL; Analyst's workbench

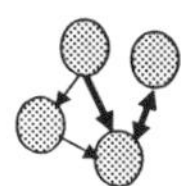
Chart connecting Data Dictionary to CASE and Repository: I-CASE; Data dictionary; Active data dictionary; Repository; Development; Operations; Types of Customers

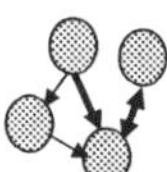
Chart connecting Concepts to Elements: Data modelling; Software development; Database system control; Upper-CASE; I-CASE; Lower-CASE; 4GL; Data dictionary; Repository

linked together. Some software products are more suitable for one purpose than the other. Many magazine articles about repository discuss one as if the other didn't exist, while others are so vague that the different purposes are not clearly distinguished.

One way of deepening this analysis by purpose is to think of a full-scale repository offering services to several different types of customers:

- **Development people**, who use it for reference while developing systems;
- **Upper-CASE** software tools, that use it during development, eg to make and store ER diagrams;
- **Lower-CASE** software tools, that use it during development, eg to generate software for input of transactions;
- **Control people**, who use it for reference while controlling operational systems;
- **Operational software**, that uses it to control actual data updates in operational systems.

Chart connecting Concepts to Elements

The above charting is offered as the least misleading way of sorting out the most frequently met terms and concepts in this part of the database world. But how do they relate to the three elements of data modelling, software development and database system control? Here is a final chart:

- **Data modelling** is concerned with intellectual methods (ie modelling conventions) and with upper-CASE tools — which may be self-contained or may be co-ordinated in an I-CASE system.

- **Software development** is concerned with lower-CASE software, that may or may not be contained within an I-CASE system, and may or may not be labelled as a 4GL.
- **Database system control** embraces quite a range of associated activities: maintaining documentation about the database to help people model and develop systems; checking that the system as defined actually works (ie people do in fact update the system with transactions as they are supposed to); maintaining documentation about the database so that people can understand what is going on and can also make incremental changes to database or system safely. These may seem disparate activities, but they are linked together in their dependency on a data dictionary or repository.

CONNECTIONS

12. Data Modelling Method and Process	The intellectual methods side of data modelling
13. Data Modelling Tools	Upper-CASE tools for data modelling; their place within I-CASE; role of repository in system development
14. Data Dictionary Control	Data dictionary or repository in operation, ie those matters falling under the element of the chart called control, and excluding I-CASE matters
15. Development Tools and Languages	Lower-CASE products and all kinds of languages and tools
16. Mix, Match, Amend	A database system's flexibility for development and change over time (a topic falling under both the control and architecture elements)

12. Data Modelling Method and Process

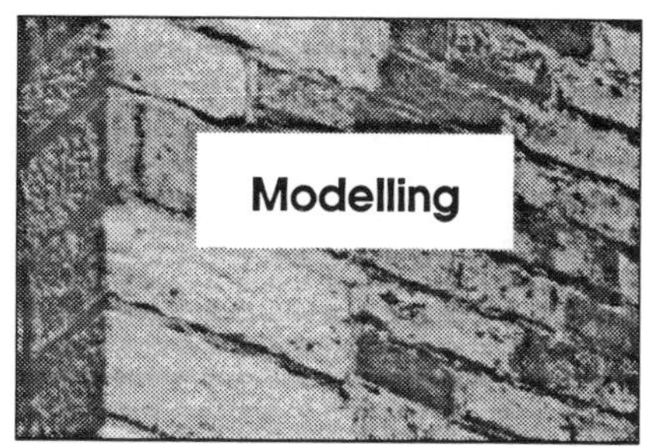

BEARINGS

The conceptual schema (Briefing 4) is a rigorously organised description of the content and structure of a database. But it isn't usually the starting point for design of a new database. More often, people begin with an ER (entity-relationship) model, and convert it later into a relational conceptual schema.

Whether you do that or adopt some variation of the approach, the important point is that options arise and decisions are called for concerning the whole *process* of modelling that leads up to a conceptual schema. These are more fundamental than any that arise within the detail of the modelling.

A good start is to arrange issues in two clusters: first, the modelling process in logical terms, eg content of ER model, breadth of its terms of reference, rigour of analysis, depth of detail, transition to relational schema; second, the practical details of modelling-support arrangements, ie how CASE software eases the task of drawing, revising and verifying the model.

This briefing concentrates on the modelling process in logical terms. Automated support for modelling is covered in Briefing 13.

POSSIBLE CONTEXT

The LP Library (of Lilli-Pilli, another hypothetical case named after an Australian tree) hires out recorded music on CDs and vinyl records. The director of the library has a large budget for new computer systems and is sympathetic to the idea of developing data models as the springboard for database systems. In fact, several people have urged this as the obvious thing to do. But there is an awkward quandary:

• The director might set up a team of experts on data modelling, provide whatever co-operation they required and receive a bulky document after six months or a year. But this seems too passive; it gives away too much responsibility. Surely the director and his colleagues ought to play some active role in determining the shape and scope of the data model.

• An alternative might be to appoint one of the most senior people in the organisation to find out a great deal about the subject of data modelling and manage the modelling process personally. But this seems such a large task that it is like switching to a different career.

The director and senior colleagues want to participate in decisions that shape the modelling exercise, but without dominating it and without getting heavily involved in the detail. Therefore they need, at a minimum, an understanding of what the critical decisions associated with data modelling are likely to be.

Probably the most important decision is choosing good people to do the work, but that depends largely on judgement rather than on any knowledge that can be acquired readily from a book.

But apart from this, there do seem to be areas for decision where summarised knowledge of the subject may help. Since data modelling may be done in several different ways, one decision is the choice of one way rather than another. Then there is the issue of scope. You could make a comprehensive model in great detail of the whole organisation; that may indeed turn out to be necessary, but surely it isn't self-evidently the only possible course. Some decision is required. Perhaps, on this point, the judgement of the director of the library, if well-informed, could be as valuable as that of a modelling expert.

WARRANTS

This briefing isn't concerned with explaining *how* to model — not directly. Two different kinds of knowledge are useful on this subject: factual (eg 'this modelling method can represent the following kinds of things . . .') and impressionistic (eg 'to get a feeling for how tricky it is to model certain things, take this example . . .').

ER Modelling: Simplified Example

The conceptual schema concentrates on logical structure rather than technical detail, but it is still quite a rigorous, even forbidding, document. There is a strong case for producing a different kind of data model at an earlier stage to provide a more convenient basis for discussion.

Some variety of entity-relationship (ER) modelling is the usual

Typical Entity-Relationship Modelling
LP Library of Recorded Music

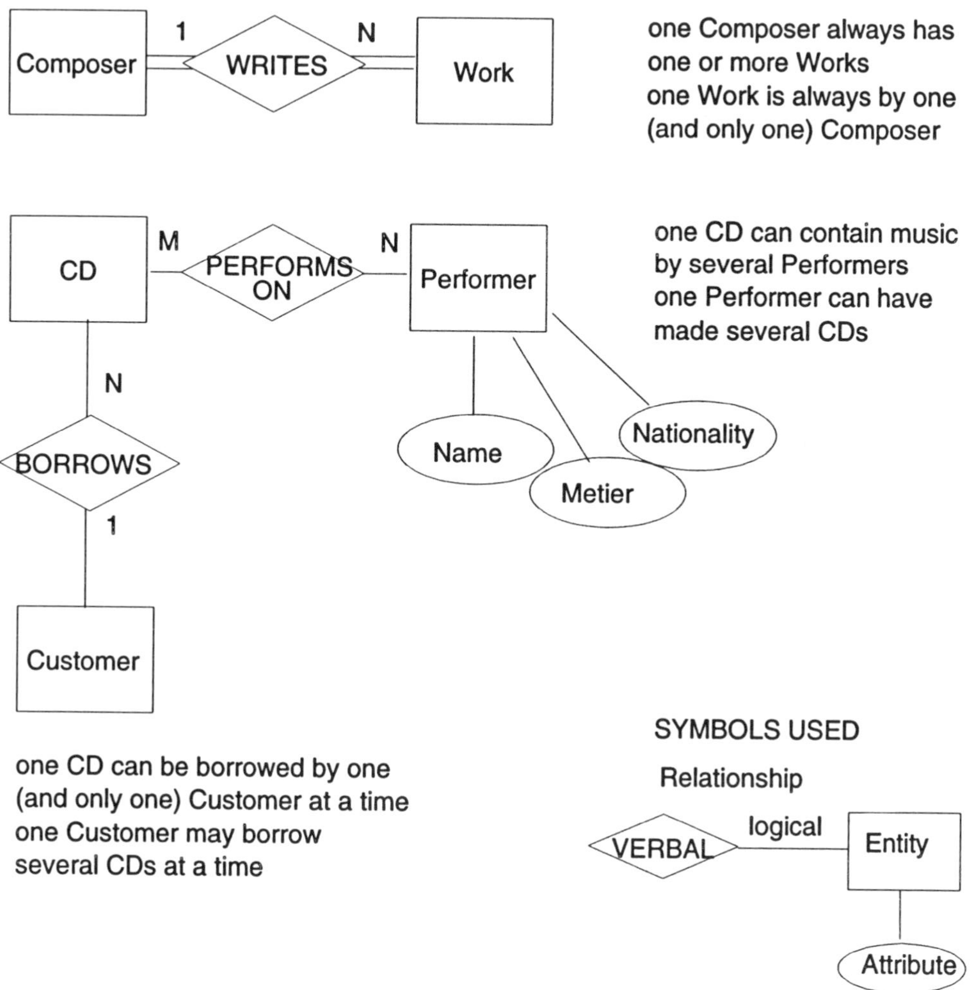

This simple model omits many complexities.
For example:

- suppose the library possesses several copies of a certain CD
- suppose the same performance appears on both CD and LP
- what is the relationship between Work and CD?
  (remember some Works take less, some more than one CD)

choice. An ER model identifies the *entities* relevant to an organisation and the *relationships* between entities and thirdly (although it isn't apparent from the name) the *attributes* of the entities.

As the first diagram shows[1], for a library lending out CDs, *Customer* and *CD* are obvious entities. Provided the scope of the modelling covers the music contained on the library's disks, then *Composer* and *Work* and *Performer* are entities too.

Attributes are data-items associated with an entity, one of them identifying it uniquely. Among the attributes of *Performer* may be *name*, *nationality* or *metier* (pianist, harpist etc).

The difficult part is defining the relationships between entities. The entities *Composer* and *Work* have a **one-to-many** relationship; there can be many different works by one composer, but a work is generally by one and only one composer. The relationship between the two entities *CD* and *Customer* is also **one-to-many**. But the entities *CD* and *Performer* have a **many-to-many** relationship: one performer can have made one CD or several, and any CD may contain performances by one performer or by several.

Any database system based on this model will very likely enable certain enquiries: given the name of a performer, the system can tell you the performer's metier and nationality; for any customer, the system knows which CDs are currently borrowed; for any CD, which customer is currently borrowing it; and so on. Still, the model is only concerned with describing information relevant to the organisation as logically and clearly as possible. It says nothing about database technology and contains no indication whether the system will need two seconds, two hours or two days to tell you which CDs a customer is currently borrowing.

ER Modelling: Problems with Entities

Here is a brief taste of some practical challenges that confront the data modeller in arriving at the entities for a model:

• **Synonyms**: two or more terms referring to the same thing, eg customer and client and account;

• **Homonyms**: one term used in different parts of the organisation in different ways, eg product;

• **Unmentionables**: an entity existing in the real world, but not hitherto identified as such, eg household, the group of related customers all living at the same address;

• **False entities**: terms too vague to apply to any clear entity, eg turnover or inventory.

It can be a tough task for the data modeller to recognise imprecisions of this kind in discussions with managers and clerks and

Detailed Distinctions in Data Modelling

Modelling conventions can describe the logical relationships between composers and their works for a library of recorded music.

Four Possible Descriptions

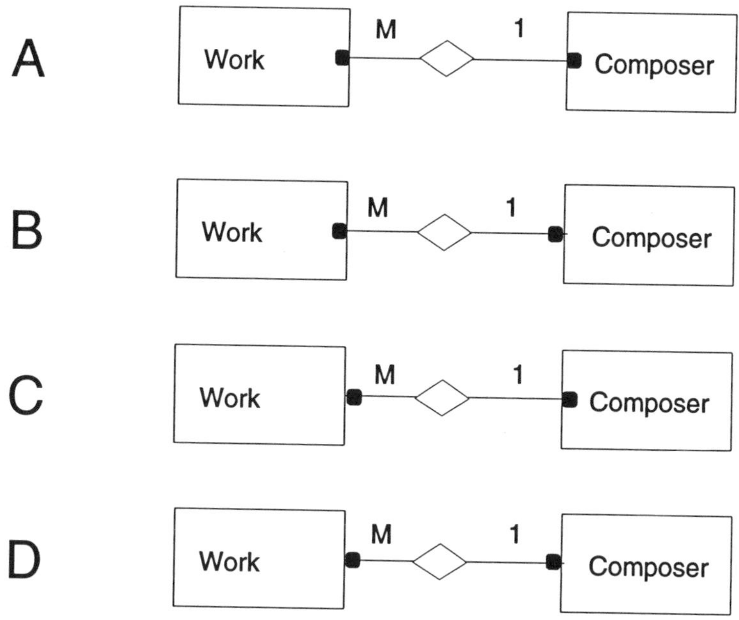

Explanation

To begin with, ignore the heavy dots. All four of the above tell you that any musical work is written by ONE composer (rather than several), but on the other hand, any composer may well write SEVERAL works.

The placing of dots inside or outside boxes conveys additional information:

In A and B, the dot by Work tells you that a work MUST be written by one composer (a zero-composer work is impossible)

In C and D, the dot by Work tells you that a work MAY be written by one composer (a zero-composer work is possible)

In A and C, the dot by Composer tells you that all composers write at least one work and maybe more

In B and D, the dot tells you that there can be composers who have written no works at all

Which is the correct (or most useful) model of reality - A, B, C or D?

directors, to spell out the nuances to them, explain why they matter, and get things properly thrashed out. But it has to be done, if a decent ER model is to be produced. A system based on an ER model that is blighted by homonyms and false entities is practically doomed from the start.

ER Modelling: Problems with Relationships

The relationships documented in an ER model generally have to be a degree more complicated than in the outline above. There are two distinct concepts, abstract but readily illustrated:

- **Cardinality**: *Customer-CD* is one-to-many; so is *Composer-Work*. The other cardinality possibilities are one-to-one and many-to-many.
- **Optionality**: *Composer-Work* is a *mandatory* one-to-many relationship; since composerless works or workless composers don't normally exist. But *Customer-CD* is *optional*; since there are at any time some CDs not being borrowed and some customers not borrowing CDs.

As the second diagram suggests,[2] if the cardinality of relationship between two entities is one-to-many, there are four different optionality possibilities, and precise modelling conventions need to distinguish them clearly.

This gives an impression of the practical challenge of modelling. Ideally, the modelling analyst talks to responsible people in the organisation, draws such diagrams and comes back to have them checked. But this process only has a point if the representatives of the organisation do in fact make comments such as: 'You put a dot outside the line here in this box, indicating, according to the modelling conventions, that every *Work may have* one *Composer*. That is wrong. You should have that dot inside the line.'

This example illustrates another point. However great the analyst's facility with modelling conventions, the subject matter itself may call for quite subtle debate, combining logic with practicality:

- Is it really true that every work has a composer? That depends on how you want to deal with anonymous works. You could pretend there was a pseudo-composer called 'Anonymous'.
- But should this 'Anonymous' be considered as the composer of both Gregorian chant and *Greensleeves*? Perhaps the model should subdivide 'Anonymous' into several anonymous pseudo-composers for different styles and periods? If so, what are their attributes — *birth-date, nationality* etc?
- It seems unassailable logic that a composer must have written at

least one work — otherwise a composer wouldn't be a composer. But might not workless composers occur in practice? Suppose there is just one CD of music by a certain composer; that CD is then lost and not replaced. Does that produce a workless composer? Or should you say that the composer ceases to exist when the CD is lost? If so, what about the period when the CD is in the state of 'lost but being searched for'?

- And is it really true that all works have only composer? What about a work written by one and orchestrated by another? Should you treat Mussorgsky-Ravel and Bach-Elgar as artificial, separate composers? If so, what are their attributes — *birthdate, nationality* etc?

And that is not the worst of it. When three or more entities are closely related, even an experienced data modeller can easily draw a model diagram whose dots and lines make unwarranted, perhaps false, assumptions or fail to cope with subtleties like those just mentioned.

ER Modelling: Example of Problems of Principle

The modelling problems above are at a micro-level by comparison with certain macro-problems affecting the whole terms of reference of the modelling exercise. One book about database[3] presents an example of ER modelling that includes the following:

- There are two entities *Client* (with various attributes) and *Payment* (whose attributes include *client-number, date-paid* and *payment-value*).
- Each *Client* is uniquely identified by *client-number*. Each *Payment* is uniquely identified by the combination of attributes *client-number* and *date-paid*.
- Over the years a client will make several subscription payments; therefore the relationship *Client-Payment* is one-to-many.

This makes a valid piece of ER modelling, but 'valid' doesn't necessarily mean 'true' or 'sensible' or 'useful'. Here is an alternative piece of modelling:

- There are two entities *Client* (with various attributes) and *Payment* (whose attributes include *client-number, date-paid, payment-value* and also *payment-number*).
- *Client* is uniquely identified by *client-number*. Each *Payment* is identified by *payment-number*, a unique sequence number allocated by the accounts department (rather than by the combination of *client-number* and *date-paid*).
- As before, *Client-Payment* is a one-to-many relationship.

The second is just as valid a piece of ER modelling as the first one; but plainly both can't be correct as a description of one specific organisation. How can you decide between the two? Only by raising the question of the terms of reference of the modelling activity. If the library already exists and the aim is to make an accurate description of its current situation, then only one of the two possibilities above (or perhaps some third one) can be true and any others will be false.

But describing the present situation is rarely the sole purpose of the modelling. Usually this work is meant to help in deciding about and designing *new and better* systems. Suppose, for the sake of argument, that the library already does things in the way suggested by the first piece of modelling, but a management consultant argues that new procedures based on the payment-number concept seem superior. This is plausible; the present system can't cope if two payments made by a client have the same *date-paid*; also, the meaning of *date-paid* can cause confusion (the cheque might be dated the 23rd, mailed on the 24th, received on the 25th, paid into the bank on the 26th and credited to the account on the 27th); also, a unique, sequential payment-number could make reconciliation of bank-accounts easier.

These arguments seem powerful, but somebody else might find even weightier ones in favour of some different procedure altogether. Suppose other parts of the system offer options too — perhaps more important than procedures in the accounts department. If so, many variant-models may have to be drawn and discussed. As this suggests, ER modelling often poses a serious dilemma:

- If done in any detail, ER modelling is suitable for describing only **one version of affairs** — either the present situation or some proposal for a different system. It soon becomes too awkward to record options for possible new systems in the form of detailed ER models.
- But one of the most common aims justifying the considerable effort of an ER modelling exercise is to **design better systems**. How can you design better systems unless you brainstorm through radical, imaginative, overlapping, contradictory ideas?

This dilemma is most serious in the parts of a model describing things that you have the power to change, eg the way the accounts department works. Other things, eg the content of CDs, come closer to being objective fact; even then, different versions of a model with different selection of detail are often possible. Many books that discuss ER modelling in detail say nothing at all about this dilemma. And yet there is little point knowing the theory, if the whole modelling activity is based on hazy, question-begging terms of reference.

ER Modelling: Examples of Problems with Relational Conversion

The macro-level problems of principle above can arise all through the ER modelling exercise, but particularly at the beginning. The other macro-level problem occurs, logically at least, at the end. When the ER model is complete, how does it become a conceptual schema in relational form?

At first glance it may seem that an ER model and a relational schema are equivalent: each entity in the ER model corresponds to a relational table and its attributes correspond to the fields in the table; relationships between entities are conveyed by the unique keys of the relational tables. But this is deceptive. Many ER models can't be converted into relational format in a straightforward judgement-free way. Here are some examples of problems that arise:

- **Repeated attributes.** With many forms of ER modelling some convention (eg enclose the name of attribute in a double circle) shows that there can be *several* of this attribute attached to one entity; eg perhaps an unlimited number of *award* attributes (silver disk, grand prix de Paris etc) can be attached to a CD entity. A relational schema doesn't permit this within a table; probably an extra *Awards* table will have to hold the data.
- **Transaction relationships.** It is easy to show on an ER model that two entities can be related in a transaction-like way; eg a customer is related to a CD by borrowing it. A relational schema can show this in alternative ways: either have a field within the *CD* table to contain the *customer-number* of the person currently borrowing it, or set up an extra table called *Loan* with records containing pairs of fields, *CD-number* and *customer-number*. A choice has to be made.
- **Many-to-many relationships**. An ER model can easily show a many-to-many relationship between two entities; eg one *CD* can contain music by several *Performers*, while one *Performer* may have recorded several *CDs*. But if there is one relational table for *CD* and another for *Performer*, it is impossible to represent this relationship within the conventions. Extra tables have to be devised.
- **Primary key.** Every entity in the ER model should be a distinct thing that is uniquely identifiable. It is easy enough to see that a *CD* entity in the ER model should correspond to a *CD* table in the relational schema. But there is more than one way of identifying a CD uniquely: either the record company's number for the CD or the library's own internally allocated number could do the job. Satisfied that this entity *can* be identified uniquely, you might not worry during ER modelling about precisely how. But the conventions of the

relational schema demand that one out of those two numbers be nominated specifically as the table's primary key, while the other is given a much lower status. According to relational theory you should make the choice that seems simplest, but simplicity can be a problematical criterion. In any event, judgement is required.[5]

The above is not an *analysis* of the problems of ER-relational conversion; it is a selection of examples that give an *impression* of the kind of judgements that may be needed. Quantitative factors often play a part. How many CDs have *award* attributes — one in a hundred or one in ten thousand? Is the library run as a business attempting to maximise the volume of borrowing or, at the other extreme, is it a reference library where borrowing is possible but rare? And so on.

ER and Relational Modelling: Gradations of Process

If the above examples provide a fair impression of the nature of modelling work, the question arises: How should you divide a substantial modelling process into orderly steps? One representative standard approach has 26 steps all the way through to a database's deep design: in step two, identify major entities; in step three, determine relationships between entities . . . in step seven, identify, decompose and add nonkey attributes; in step eight, validate through normalisation . . . and so on.[6]

The difficulty in appraising any such approach — whether proposed as a standard or devised for a particular case — is that of seeing the shape of the storm for all the hail and sleet. How can you compare one person's 26-step approach with some other 19-step approach? And if you can't, how can it be rational to opt for one approach rather than another?

To demystify any multi-step modelling approach, cut through the detail to examine its stance on the issue of converting ER model to relational conceptual schema. The possible solutions can be seen as gradations:

- Gradation 1: **Rich-ER.** Produce an ER model that is logically rigorous and subtle (eg thrashing out matters such as pseudo-composers and workless composers, perhaps using extra conventions to represent certain nuances) — in the full knowledge that some of the subtlety can't be easily translated into relational form. Rely on particularly bright people and/or a battery of guidelines (as opposed to fixed rules) to cope with the transition from a rich ER model to relational schema.
- Gradation 2: **Classic-ER.** Draw classic ER diagrams on the lines described in many books, but without probing some of the more

SUMMARY OF WARRANTS

Simple Example of ER Modelling: Entities, attributes and types of relationships

Examples of Problems with Entities: Synonyms, homonyms, unmentionables and false entities

Examples of Problems with Relationships: Optional and mandatory; Logic of pseudo-composers and workless composers

Examples of Problems of Principle: Correct modelling, modelling existing systems, modelling options

Examples of Problems with Relational Conversion: Repeated attributes; Transaction relationships; Many-to-many relationships; Primary key

Gradations of Process: Rich-ER via Restricted-ER through to Non-ER

---

esoteric questions of logic. When the ER model is ready, convert it to relational form, making the kind of judgements sketched out in the examples above.

- Gradation 3: **Restricted-ER.** Draw ER diagrams, but (at any rate where it is easy to do) eschew features that may give trouble at the ER-relational transition. When the ER model is ready, convert it to relational form, a task needing fewer judgements than with the previous gradations.
- Gradation 4: **Pseudo-ER.** Draw ER diagrams, but within certain constraints intended to eliminate altogether the need for judgements at the ER-relational transition. In other words, model according to relational conventions, but using ER notation.
- Gradation 5. **Non-ER.** Don't draw ER diagrams at all. Model according to relational conventions explicitly from the start.

From the documentation of some multi-step processes it may be unclear which of these five is being recommended. If so, that is a sign that the method, however detailed, is flawed by failure even to recognise the essence of the problem it tackles.

POSSIBLE DECISION-MAKING

Many books and articles about modelling concentrate on describing the nuances that a finished model will have, with only occasional hints about the problems of arriving at it. This is to concentrate too much on model-as-product at the expense of modelling-as-process. There are two distinct areas for decisions:[7]

- What kind of model do you want as your **product**? How deep (ie what type of things shown, and how subtly) and how broad (covering what areas of the organisation, with what terms of reference)?
- How will you organise the **process** of achieving this, bearing in mind the need to invest people's time sensibly, and all other situation-specific constraints?

Decisions on the two issues need to be coherent. It is no use deciding exactly the kind of model that will be ideal, if there is no practical chance of organising a team of people, with the right mix of skills and knowledge, to spend enough time in the right sequence, exposing and checking out all the subtleties.

The data modeller generally depends on input from people throughout the organisation, whose normal work does not require the meticulous attitudes essential to data modelling. Moreover, data models are often not only subtle but voluminous, extending into hundreds of pages covered with shapes and lines and arrows, all expressing fine distinctions. Such models can easily become, as they say, unreadable at any speed. Many people may be well enough motivated to check out a few vital relationships thoroughly, but not rigorously to scrutinise dozens of pages of diagrams.

How much detailed modelling is truly necessary depends on the case, but it is certainly attractive to organise this work as elegantly and economically as possible. Thus, there are tradeoffs to be struck between product desirability and process practicality:

- The richer the modelling techniques employed, the **deeper** the analysis contained in the model, and the better it will capture nuances of data structures, that could make all the difference between a humdrum and an excellent database system. But, on the other hand, the richer the intended model, the more work required to make it, and the greater the risk that some of the people involved fail to find enough time away from their normal work to grasp the full implications of some of its more subtle analysis.
- The **wider** the model's scope, the better it enables data from different departments and functions to be brought together coherently in a database. But, on the other hand, the wider the intended model, the more work required to make it and check out all its detail.

Once the problem is viewed as a matter of tradeoffs, any number of pragmatic solutions suggest themselves for the LP Library:

- Use a simple form of ER modelling throughout the organisation, avoiding any temptations to go into subtleties such as workless composers. Having produced a complete, reasonably correct but coarse model, go round a second time looking for places in the model that need to be refined, because their detail could be critical.

- *Or* concentrate first on making a fairly complete and reliable model of just one part of the organisation. That done, assuming that skill and enthusiasm for modelling has been built up, expand to the rest of the organisation.
- *Or* begin by making an outline model of the whole organisation, with insufficient detail to be the basis for a conceptual schema. Use that outline to decide which are the really critical areas for probing, thoughtful modelling.

These are just three generic conceivable decisions about the approach to modelling within an organisation. Plenty of others are possible. How do you decide what is appropriate to the specific case?

There is no substitute for taking a view on the relative importance of different factors in the situation. For example, the director of the LP Library should be able to see *before detailed modelling begins* that any data model of the whole organisation would certainly contain detail on two fairly (though not completely) distinct areas. There is *customer* information (eg about customers paying annual subscriptions, borrowing CDs, reserving them etc) and *music* information (eg about composers and their works contained on CDs made by performers etc.)

Are these two areas equally important? If the administration of the library is currently in bad shape, perhaps it would make sense to concentrate on getting only the customer information properly modelled. But maybe this isn't so; perhaps a central objective is to offer a clever new service that helps people choose music; if so, that will call for quite careful modelling on the music side. In any event, two points are inescapable:

- Setting up a data modelling activity shouldn't merely be a matter of choosing competent people to carry out some self-evidently necessary task (ie it isn't like appointing an auditor or a plumber). A decision is required on the scope and nature of the task itself, and there are usually several distinct options to decide between.
- Good decisions between options for the data modelling task need to rest on some view of the whole situation, and some choice between general objectives, possibilities and priorities.

CONNECTIONS

13. Data Modelling Tools	Using upper-CASE software tools to facilitate the work of data modelling
14. Data Dictionary Control	Repository and other techniques for maintaining a data model and its database
29. Object-oriented Topics	As you make your ER model richer and more sophisticated you may arrive eventually at EER (aka object-oriented) modelling
31. Untangling Database and Wider Issues	Relation of data modelling to wider issues of information management

13. Data Modelling Tools

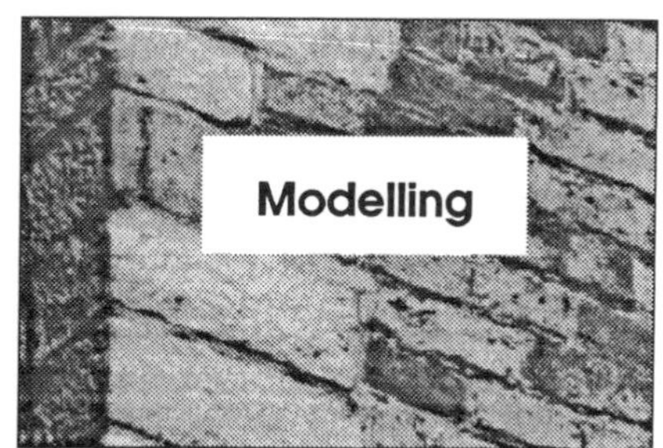

BEARINGS

Briefing 12 concentrates on the nature of the data model.

This briefing is about the options of automated support for modelling and related decisions about their use in the modelling process.

As the other briefing emphasises, building the data model requires considerable work. Just as the labour of writing books can be alleviated by word processing technology, so part of the labour of modelling can be considerably reduced by upper-CASE software tools.

Tools can help in drawing and updating diagrams with the appropriate lines, arrows and shapes of the modelling conventions, but, more important, they can perform checks that keep different parts of the model consistent, and enable work done in one part of the project to be accessed and used elsewhere. Discussion of these more powerful features leads naturally to issues associated with the I-CASE system and the repository.

POSSIBLE CONTEXT

Ironbark Insurance is a small company but it underwrites all the main classes of insurance. Its managers decide to replace all their administrative systems, to take better advantage of the opportunities of modern IT.

It seems a natural decision to set up a data modelling exercise, and just as natural to invest in upper-CASE tools. Straight away, two main issues arise:

- what kind of upper-CASE **software product**;
- how to fit the data modelling activities based on upper-CASE tools into the wider **process** of developing systems, using other CASE tools, linked together in an I-CASE system.

The first step towards decisions in the first area is to get a good view of the main types of software tool that exist, the features they offer and the factors that expose the scope and nature of any particular product. Tackling the second area calls for a similar exercise. It is important to know what are the main general problems to be solved in organising work with these tools and what are the main different options for approaching these problems.

WARRANTS

The potential advantages of automated tools for data modelling are obvious. The following warrant sections show that, as soon as tools go beyond the basic task of drawing diagrams, some considerable challenges arise.

Single-level Aspects

It is best to start with some aspects of upper-CASE data modelling *per se*, leaving aside for the moment those associated with the co-ordination of data modelling with other activities in an I-CASE system:

- **Graphics sophistication.** Any decent system includes features for screen graphics to cope with the inevitable diagrams. But there are many degrees of graphics sophistication. How big is the screen? Is colour used? How many windows can there be, what kind and how flexible are they to use? Can you drill down through models, exposing detail at different hierarchical levels in a graphical format that maintains a sense of context? How flexible and powerful is the user interface? If you want to amend a design in some way that causes you to reconsider and perhaps amend several different portions of the system, how easy is it to bring up those different parts of the system on the same screen in different windows?
- **Typographic sophistication.** With any system in any field attractive print output is better than ugly, but the issue can be particularly important here in making sense of voluminous documentation. For instance, detailed text describing data items could be in double-column format, with vital text about relationships in a larger size, single-column on the same page. You may want import and export of text between upper-CASE tool and word processing software (perhaps even desktop publishing software) without (and this is the exacting requirement) loss of formatting, such as italics, font sizes, bullet points, paragraph indents etc.
- **Database access.** An upper-CASE tool may also provide access

to its data in the way that any other database (eg one of sales statistics) does. Suppose you are wondering whether to store an insured person's first name as a separate field from surname, or to have them both together as one field. You may want to call up on the screen a list of all the places in the system where this information is used, in order to judge whether this is a good idea. Can you do this as if accessing a mainstream database, by using SQL to frame multiple search criteria on relational structures?

- **Extent of data modelling features.** Taking ER modelling as a given, what adjacent activities are covered? Several associated but slightly different things may be. One is to convert an ER model automatically (or as far as possible) into a relational model in third normal form. Another is to check a model defined in relational tables to point out things that seem inconsistent with third normal form. Another is to take a model defined in relational tables (irrespective of the quality of their normalisation) and generate appropriate SQL code to set up the internal schema of the database — largely a formatting task. Another possibility is to generate a data dictionary from the ER model, leaving gaps for the extra descriptive information about database content to be added. From this data dictionary, a system may also go on to generate draft formats of the necessary screens for transaction input.

  Reverse engineering is another important possibility; some tools can work back from a definition of relational tables to generate a corresponding ER model. This is particularly relevant if you are moving from an existing database system to a new one.

- **Data dictionary.** Upper-CASE software *can* support data modelling by essentially storing the diagrams *or* it can hold a data dictionary and use that to generate the diagrams and any other output too. The data dictionary approach has a couple of advantages. First, it is neater and more flexible and thus makes it easier for data modelling to extend into adjacent activities such as checking for third normal form. Second, it allows different departments in an organisation to continue to call things by different names; eg one person's *insured-risk-code* is another's *statistical-analysis-code* and another's *type-of-business-code*. A data dictionary can allow the different names to be used in different charts and sort out the correspondences behind the scenes.

I-CASE Aspects

Most of the following aspects apply to upper-CASE systems, but they become far more prominent in an I-CASE system, where (as sug-

The Repository's Role in Development

The Products of Development Activities go into the Repository
The Repository supports the Development Activities

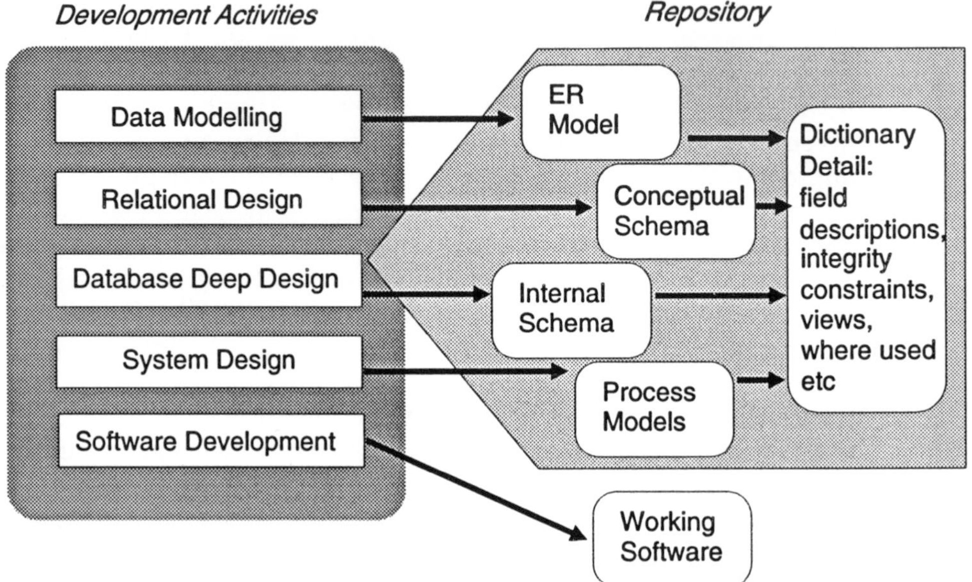

Thus the Repository supports an integrated development process.
It allows the product of one activity to be the starting-point for another.
It controls the consistency of models and designs produced.

---

gested in the diagram) the data model is contained in a repository that co-ordinates the other development activities:

- **Documentation deluge.** Detailed models tend to generate many pages of printout. When several related levels of models are printed out the volumes can be immense, and when revised versions of several levels are printed the body of pages can be overwhelming. The documentation deluge can be quite a big issue; sometimes the thick listing generated by a system can be so inconvenient to use that it just never is used and is therefore worthless. Thus one test of the quality of an I-CASE system is how elegantly its printed output presents essential design information.
- **Consistency control.** If you add some new detail to the system design in a certain phase of system development (eg the fields to be contained in a report), an I-CASE system will normally check that

the new detail is consistent with what is found elsewhere (eg the list of fields contained in the database). That is the easy part.

The real test comes with backtracking. Suppose that in the middle of (say) phase 4 of system development, it becomes clear that some part of the design firmed up in phase 1 will have to be altered. Since the work in each phase proceeds from the product of the previous one, very likely some models and designs generated in phases 2, 3 and 4 will have to be changed too. How much of this does the system do automatically? Does it signal some inconsistencies without resolving them? These questions may be answered in different ways for different types of change.

Manifestly, consistency control is a big theme; here are some more critical questions. Some documents are permanent documentation, but others are merely transitory working-papers; is that distinction made in handling consistency control? Does the system do all its consistency checking in special massive processing runs from time to time or is input checked for consistency immediately it enters the system? If the latter, can you switch off the rigid checks and consequential alterations while you doodle, trying out new ideas for system design? Can you have two separate versions of your models — one operational, one under development? Or several under development, since several development projects are in progress? What happens when one of these projects goes live?

- **Multi-user facilities.** Most new computer systems are developed by teams of people working together on a project in an office — inevitably with some degree of overlapping responsibilities. Suppose one person wants to modify a piece of the system that somebody else is currently working on; are there concurrency control facilities? Suppose the piece of system modified was designed by somebody else yesterday; are there any control or notification features? Suppose the modification will have far-reaching implications for some distant part of the system that is somebody else's responsibility; are there any safeguards against a tug-of-war developing?
- **Portability**. Can you start sketching out a data model on a cheap PC and move on easily to a high-powered workstation when the graphics and consistency checking requirements get heavier? Can you move on from the workstation to the mini/mainframe operational environment?
- **People and culture.** Other factors need to be fed into any calculus of the best-buy way of developing systems: the characteristics of the people in the organisation and the way their responsibilities are — or could be — defined. You might decide that some strongly defined, highly-integrated I-CASE approach was, though in some abstract sense ideal, inferior to some slacker, less ambitious approach — *for*

the organisation in question. Perhaps the pervasive culture of this particular insurance company favours personal initiative at the expense of strongly co-ordinated planning, more than most. That is a crude example of a point with quite extensive ramifications.

Advanced I-CASE Aspects

The following issues are for more advanced systems. Many of these items, particularly those towards the end of the list, are barely touched by I-CASE systems at present.[1]

- **Explanation.** Tight consistency checking is all very well, but when a system detects an inconsistency or incompleteness that prevents you moving on, it ought to explain what the trouble is. Designing software that explains complex errors in a way that is neither too cryptic nor too tedious is surprisingly difficult.
- **Program code generation.** Some systems provide automatic translation of the verbal and diagrammatic design of the system into program code. This code may only be good enough for use as a rough draft of the real program, but the facility can still be a rather powerful one.
- **Operational documentation.** What about the documentation needed to go with the delivered operational system, such as the handbook for users? In principle that might be generated semi-automatically too. The same applies to the 'help' screens that have to be included in the operational system.
- **Repository scope.** How extensive is the content of the repository at the heart of the I-CASE system? As well as storing models and system designs does it store other kinds of information? Minutes of meetings; lists of action points and discussion points; project critical paths and weekly activity reports; presentation slides and transparencies; discussion papers on technical design considerations; bibliographic references and abstracts of documents whose actual content can't be stored in a database (eg letters received from outside parties; relevant magazine articles; suppliers' technical brochures)? Can things of this sort be cross-referenced to some degree with hard documentation such as data models, internal schemas etc?
- **Technical design.** Few systems offer much automated help in areas such as deep design and CRS; eg deciding whether to use hashing or indexing on a table, working out the most appropriate recovery procedures, designing security schemes. This is a field where advanced systems may well expand in the future.
- **CAD-like calculations.** I-CASE systems might be regarded as CAD (computer-aided-design) applied to the development of com-

puter systems, as opposed to (say) cars or nuclear reactors. For purists true CAD must include calculations as well as graphics; ie not just designs for a racing-car, but calculations of its top speed when going round corners. By analogy, real CAD for computer system development, if it existed, would embrace calculations such as the response time expected from a certain technical design under certain usage conditions.

- **Artificial intelligence techniques.** Some products' suppliers boast of using artificial intelligence techniques, but usually this is misleading. They mean that, in order to carry out all the cross-checking inherent in controlling consistency of system design, their software uses a language like Prolog, which is also used to handle the logic in artificial intelligence applications. There are more exciting opportunities than this for artificial intelligence technology in the I-CASE system. Expert systems might be used to identify issues and information that are likely to be relevant to system analysis and design; or identify areas that are not actually contradictory, but are unusual enough to be double-checked; or, if a certain change potentially affects many parts of the system, decide which of the implications are likely to be of great relevance and which trivial.
- **Fundamental decisions.** Some systems support high-level business modelling, but hardly any assist fundamental decisions of information management. For instance: Should we develop a full-scale database system taking three years or be more modest and adopt a two-year programme of development? Is a company-wide database appropriate for this organisation or should each main division have its own database? Should this project be organised as a regular development or as a pure experiment? This is not a severe criticism because the really important issues are usually situation-specific and difficult to encompass in any standard approach. Still, it is important to remember that usually an I-CASE system only starts after some of the really important things have already been decided — or tacitly assumed.

Gradations of Standard Method

The analysis so far has ignored one issue that cuts across many others — the issue of **standard method**. Different tools are bound up with different standard methods to various degrees.

Within the class of **upper-CASE** data modelling tools these gradations:

- **Gradation 1.** The tool supports data modelling usi ticular set of conventions already well-established in t
- **Gradation 2.** The tool supports data modelling ir

range of the established conventions; eg there is a choice between the Chen, Bachman and Elmasri-Navathe conventions.

- **Gradation 3.** The tool is general-purpose; it supports whatever conventions for data modelling you like, including any you may invent yourself. Generally the tool is delivered with one or more of the established conventions already set up.

Analogous gradations exist on a larger scale in setting up an **I-CASE** system:

- **Gradation 1.** The I-CASE system supports standard methodology in two senses. First, its different components each follow an established convention (eg the ER modelling part uses Chen conventions; process modelling uses SA data flow diagrams; for program logic Warnier-Orr diagrams are used etc). Second, the way these components fit together is standard in a different sense: a standard structure intended to be suitable for all or most development projects.
- **Gradation 2.** As 1, except that within certain stages the conventions supported by the software tools are not exactly industry-standard. They may be a dialect of an established convention or perhaps something completely different devised by the makers of the I-CASE software. But still, the project structure as a whole is intended to be standard, in the sense of suitable for all or most development projects.
- **Gradation 3.** Again, every project follows a standard stage-by-stage structure. But there can be variation in the content of each stage; for each (or at least some) there is a choice available between several different conventions.
- **Gradation 4.** As 3, but the people managing a project are also expected to choose the most appropriate stage-by-stage structure; they need not follow the standard. This still counts as I-CASE (just), because software tools may help carry forward work from one stage to another.

Comparison of Standard Method Approaches

Different software products are appropriate for different gradations. The choices of gradation and tool generally rest on evaluation of tradeoffs. Quite a few factors can come in:

- **Consistency and Integration.** Very often, the salesman for a certain tool will explain that this product, as well as being highly integrated, provides flexibility to deviate from the prescribed norms or perhaps offers the choice between several conventions. But that may not mean very much.

Suppose your multi-stage approach to developing systems

produces six main types of document, type-A to type-F. Maybe, a piece of data mentioned in document B11 ought also to be in document D34. That can be checked quite rigorously if the tool is specifically built to check all relevant links between any of these six types of document. It is more exacting to set up such checking with a general-purpose tool. Similarly, smooth, labour-saving integration of work done in different activities is impaired.

In principle, the more the I-CASE is based on some detailed, standard, rigid methodology, the more easily it can achieve powerful consistency and integration features. Of course, that which is in principle feasible is not always realised successfully in practice.

- **Fit with requirements.** With any standard approach the question arises: Does it fit the particular situation? This is not a purely theoretical consideration: your case may genuinely need some intricate form of data modelling that is not adequately covered by the standard approaches of any I-CASE product.
- **Hybrid data.** A strong case of the previous point arises if you need to store map data or text data along with the mainstream data. Since I-CASE systems are mainstream-oriented it may be impossible to use one, apply its standard approach *and* achieve adequate consistency and integration.
- **Other upper-CASE tools.** Perhaps there is one particular upper-CASE software tool handling just one type of modelling that you want to fit into the I-CASE structure. The more tightly a standard methodology binds the phases of the development process, the more awkward that will be.
- **Green-field basis.** Many standard methodologies are for developing complete new databases and systems from nothing. If you have to build a new database by taking what already exists, scrapping some parts, altering others and building on new ones, then a standard approach is likely to be somewhat less useful.
- **Human factor disadvantages.** Presenting people with one huge set of standard methods to follow is often poor psychology. Bright people may feel demotivated at having methods imposed on them and quickly discover areas where the standards are too pedantic or not sophisticated enough. Some other people may follow the methods religiously, but without real understanding and produce uninspired, mediocre work.
- **Human factor advantages.** But in some cases you may judge that the people concerned badly need the discipline of following some standards. Moreover, if presented as current best practice, the methods may enjoy considerable prestige and be used with enthusiasm.

SUMMARY OF WARRANTS

Aspects of Single-level Systems: Graphics sophistication; Typographic sophistication; Database access; Extent of data modelling; Data dictionary

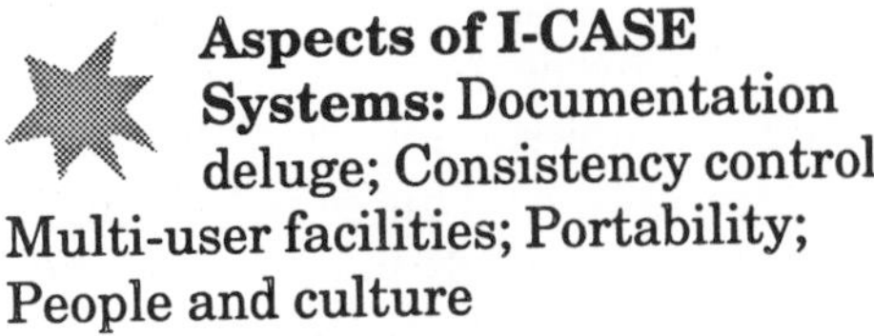

Aspects of I-CASE Systems: Documentation deluge; Consistency control; Multi-user facilities; Portability; People and culture

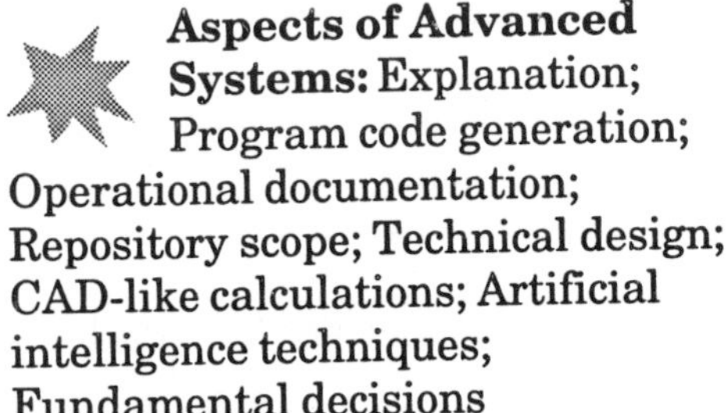

Aspects of Advanced Systems: Explanation; Program code generation; Operational documentation; Repository scope; Technical design; CAD-like calculations; Artificial intelligence techniques; Fundamental decisions

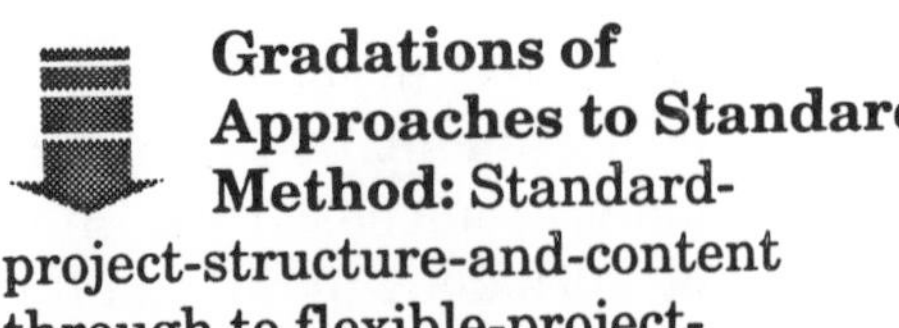

Gradations of Approaches to Standard Method: Standard-project-structure-and-content through to flexible-project-structure-and-content

Comparison of Approaches to Standard Method: Consistency and integration; Fit with requirements; Hybrid data; Other upper-CASE tools; Green-field basis; Human factor disadvantages; Human factor advantages

POSSIBLE DECISION-MAKING

Faced with so many issues to consider Ironbark's computer-literate managers home in on three major choices to be made:

- What **modelling method** (an intellectual construct)?
- What **technology** (one or more software products)?
- What **organisation** (of the work of people using these things to design new computer systems and databases)?

They examine the features of a number of different software products — not to evaluate them directly, rather to get a better instinct for the way the possibilities on these issues interact and work out.

The consensus is that the questions are too complex to permit clear decisions on all these matters straight away. This leads to a policy of a rather indirect character:

- 'We will choose an upper-CASE software product for data modelling, without caring about which dialect of ER modelling it uses. We will try it out on a couple of lesser projects to gain experience.'

- 'In parallel, we will experiment with an I-CASE tool to co-ordinate the stages of work on one complete project.'
- 'Once we have garnered all that experience and drawn some conclusions from it, we will be in a position to take the really important decisions.'
- 'We can't say now what will happen at that point, but we already have a suspicion of what our approach to decision-making will be. First, based on the experience, decide what the most appropriate way of organising system development projects is for our particular insurance company; eg what pattern of stages, what pattern of responsibilities between MIS people and users, how highly integrated and standardised to be, and so on. After that, and only then, decide which CASE tools best suit that way of organisation.'

CONNECTIONS

12. Data Modelling Method and Process	Different modelling methods and conventions that may be automated by upper-CASE and I-CASE software tools
14. Data Dictionary Control	Repository and other techniques for maintaining a data model and its database
17. Mainstream Software Products	Categories of software product, including upper-CASE and I-CASE software tools

14. Data Dictionary Control

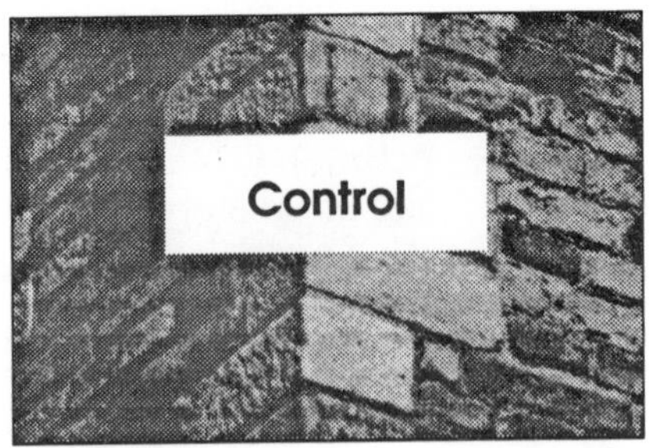

BEARINGS

Suppose you employ upper-CASE tools to build an impeccable data model and make it the basis for a skilfully designed database. The database system goes live. What next? A number of important issues are associated with the control of the operational database.

The unifying theme is the role of the data dictionary (aka repository) — a complicated subject with ramifications in several areas: control (discussed here), modelling (Briefing 13) and software development (Briefing 15).

POSSIBLE CONTEXT

The Acacia Authority is an independent agency recently set up to handle many functions previously performed by ministries of central government, local government and other agencies. All its activities are broadly concerned with environmental matters and above all with combatting pollution. The authority monitors the application of environmental controls, issues various licences, carries out inspections, organises various planning and consultative bodies and so on.

There is both a crying need and a great opportunity for a well co-ordinated new family of database systems. One decision-making problem has to be considered at an early stage:

- Since the information required in Acacia's database or databases is so varied and yet interrelated, it will be hard to keep all this data in step, once systems become operational.
- This is partly a question of having controls to ensure that when new data is keyed into the database system, it doesn't contradict other data already there or leave information inconsistent or defective in some other way. Perhaps more demanding is the problem of ensuring that when new systems are developed and new segments of the database added, everything will remain consistent.

• Managers at Acacia are aware that the well-established concept of the data dictionary helps with these problems. But they also know of more advanced concepts that are often claimed to be far more powerful. The trigger is a better way to ensure that only consistent new data is accepted. The repository is meant to store and control a complete model of the database systems in such a way that extensions can be added over time organically, without confusion or inconsistency.
• It may seem that these and related concepts, though doubtless important to general efficiency, don't really have far-reaching implications. But some Acacia managers are not so sure. Perhaps commitment to a repository could be a major decision with many implications. But, if so, how exactly?

The challenge is to avoid the trap of missing the plantation for the palms and to extract the implications for decision-making of the repository and related techniques.

WARRANTS

As this briefing shows, the originally mundane, record-keeping role of the data dictionary (from now on usually DD) has gradually been expanded into the more ambitious concept of the repository that plays the role of unifying the models and documentation associated with a database system.

Chart of Data Dictionary Content

It is clearly a useful idea to have the computer store information about the database as a whole: What different tables exist? What are the data fields and their formats in each table? What are the keys of each table and, hence, how are the different tables related to make up the whole database? What are the contents of each user view (aka external schema)? This introduces the concept of meta-data:

• **Data.** The database proper has (say) a *Protected-buildings* table. In one of its records is stored the value 'St Martin's Church' for the field building-name and the value '5.5.94' for the field *last-inspection-date.* It contains equivalent data about all the other protected buildings too. This is real data describing things in the world.

• **Meta-data.** The DD contains the information that one of the tables of the database is the *Protected-buildings* table, that the record for each building has a unique *building-number* as its key, that one field is *last-inspection-date*, in date format; another field is *building-*

name, a text of up to 50 characters, etc. This is not data about any particular buildings or about anything out in the world; it is data about the database, which in turn contains data about actual buildings.

The meta-data held in a DD need not just be about the database in a narrow sense: it could be about the database system. As well as saying that *last-inspection-date* is a date within a *Protected-buildings* record, it might contain the following additional types of meta-data:

- **Complex validation criteria.** 'When this date is updated by a normal update transaction, the new date must always be later than the old, and always in the current or previous year. Further, this date must always be earlier than the date stored in another field, *next-inspection-date*, except that . . . etc'
- **Explanations.** 'Every protected building is inspected regularly; the inspection cycle depends on the type of building. . . The field *last-inspection-date* is one of those updated when the data from the inspector's report is keyed in. It can happen that the inspection is not completed, because the inspector decides half-way through that a special expert is required. In this case, the field *last-inspection-date* is updated, but also . . . etc.' As this suggests, complex validation criteria and explanations are not really separate things; they tend to run into each other.
- **Cross-references.** 'The field *last-inspection-date* appears on the following standard screens, IN5, IN6, IN13 . . . etc and printouts IN41, IN42 and external schemas INA, INB, INF'.

A computerised DD holding such meta-data seems a useful thing. But what deeper issues arise?

Gradations of Integrated Data Dictionary

Plainly it would be possible to use a word processor to record the database's meta-data, but many DBMSs offer a special DD facility. This is in fact a classic general-purpose DBMS facility, since DD facilities for storing meta-data are much the same, whether the systems are for a government agency, rubber plantation or mortgage broker.

A DD facility that merely provides convenient formats for keying data in, displaying it on screen and printing it out can't be said to be integrated. If anything is changed in the database or system (eg the format of a field or content of a report), somebody has to remember to update the DD to keep it consistent. By contrast, an integrated DD accepts an amendment of (say) a field format and automatically keeps the other parts of the meta-data consistent.

However, there are gradations for a DD between fully integrated and not at all:

- Gradation 1. **Separate DD.** The DD merely acts as a kind of special-purpose word processor.
- Gradation 2. **Classic integrated DD.** Any amendment of the conceptual schema (tables, fields, field lengths and formats) can be made once and it will be applied by the DBMS to both the actual database and the DD; therefore the consistency of these two things is guaranteed. However, validation rules (except for simple things like 'must be numeric') are not integrated; they are coded in the application software and written down separately in English in the DD (or maybe left out of it).
- Gradation 3. **Active integrated DD.** As Gradation 2, but validation rules, as well as data definitions, are stored and amended in one place, the DD. They are defined in a format intelligible to both human and machine. Thus, to display these rules on screen or print them out, the system takes them from the DD. The validation rules are copied into any application program that needs them, so that they don't have to be rewritten for each program. However, if the rules for a field in the DD are changed, the new version must be copied into each program that needs them.
- Gradation 4. **Dynamic integrated DD (ie using triggers).** As with Gradation 3, validation rules are stored and amended in one place, the DD. But they are kept centralised, not copied into the application programs. The very existence of a particular field in any update transaction anywhere in the system triggers the corresponding integrity rules into action. This is guaranteed by the DBMS. In this case the DD plays a full-time role when the system is operational, because every update of the database has to get through its centralised checking.

These four are gradation points rather than firm distinctions:

- You could use a Gradation 1 DD during the design stages of a project. When the design was firm you could use a facility that generated from the DD in a fairly automatic way the instructions needed to set up the actual database. After that though, any amendments would have to be made to both separately.
- In the Gradation 2 area some systems can be more convenient and automatic than others. One DD system might assume that if the name of a field changed from *last-inspection-date* to *previous-inspection*, without change of format (eg date format), then this was merely a change of name, which should leave the cross-references to screens and reports unaltered. But a different DD system might assume that the old *last-inspection-date* no longer existed and should be removed from all screens and reports.

• You can mix Gradations 3 and 4 together; eg treat most fields on a Gradation 4 basis except for a few special ones treated as Gradation 3 cases.
• At Gradation 4 the power and complexity of triggers can vary. A trigger handling **cascade deletes** might receive a transaction deleting a record from the *Protected-buildings* table, and then delete all records for that building in the *Outstanding-inspection*, *Tourist-attraction* and other tables of the database, without the need for any human intervention. Powerful, but disastrous if you haven't set the trigger up right to do precisely what you want under all circumstances. Again, a trigger can store some very complicated validation criteria (aka **business rules**); eg a check that newly updated toxicity data is acceptable, by calculating whether it lies within the limits of possibility set by the laws of chemistry.

Comparison of Classic Integrated DD with Stronger Forms

Within the area of Gradations 3 and 4 the possibilities are so powerful that they go far beyond the automatic record-keeping role of the DD. If the rules governing what input data is valid and what is not are kept in one place (call it for convenience the DD), as opposed to written separately in several programs, this does far more than guarantee that the DD documentation keeps automatically in step with the real system. It brings great advantages:
• **Consistency**. It avoids the danger that, in the event of a change to the rules, the change might not be made perfectly in all the separate programs affected.
• **Powerful rules.** Some kinds of validation rules may be complicated and entail checks for consistency between different parts of the database; eg before accepting the new value for *last-inspection-date*, look up the *Inspector* table to see if the inspector concerned was working or on holiday that day, and (though this is a little extreme) access data on other inspections by the same inspector that day and assess whether the set as a whole is credible. This kind of check that delves into many different parts of the database is easier to implement as one centralised piece of software, away from application programs, each mainly concerned with a particular part of the database.
• **More effective integrity and CRS.** Suppose the database contains several fields that must be kept consistent with each other; eg the field *hazard-code* in the record of each building and the fields containing the totals of buildings classed as moderately hazardous and extremely hazardous. As the code in the record for St Martin's

Church is changed, one of the total fields must be reduced by 1 and the other incremented. But all three fields can't literally be updated simultaneously. Suppose there were a hardware failure at the point where some but not all three fields had been updated. DBMS technology is there to deal with this kind of problem, but it can work more efficiently if the checking and updating all occur in one separate module.

• **New architectures.** Though it is most natural to discuss DD in the context of the established host architecture, the dynamic DD fits in well with the newer client-server approach. The trigger procedures can be stored centrally at the server, while the more specific application software is located at the clients.

All this seems to suggest that Gradation 3 or 4 of DD integration is always preferable to the classic Gradation 2. But what are the disadvantages? Gradations 3 and 4 call not only for sophisticated DBMS software but for skillful and dedicated people to set the DD up properly, with all the centralised rules properly defined, and to maintain it over the years. Another challenge is dividing procedures and responsibilities between four (or sometimes more) main parties: a database administration team taking an organisation-wide view of supply and demand; information analysts working on demand-driven business and data models; teams developing the detail of specific systems; and controllers of systems already operational.

Aspects of Repository

Some more inviting possibilities lie beyond the Gradation-4 DD, but it is important to remember that they are currently more talked about than implemented successfully in operational systems.

The idea of storing validation rules together in one place can be taken much further. With ingenuity, a large part of a system's functions can be expressed in rigorous forms such as rules and lists and tables. Suppose that whenever a new record about a protected building contains the *banned-material-code* (eg for a type of sandstone whose dust causes silicosis and therefore may no longer be quarried or worked), the building must be included in the weekly report for the Banned Material department. Normally, application programs would look after this, and the procedure might also be described in text within a DD. A much more advanced approach would be to hold the logic centrally as clearly structured rules, that could be both executed by the system and accessed for reference.

Progress away from mainly data definitions and simple validation rules towards more sophisticated rules leads to the storage of practically all kinds of descriptive information about the system and

Data Merges with Meta-Data

Classic Data Dictionary Approach:
There are Three Clearly Separate Things

META-DATA IN DATA DICTIONARY

record layout

building-number	name	last-inspection-date	hazard-code	etc	etc

field descriptions:

building-number is a unique identifier allocated for each new building by . . .
. . . . etc

ACTUAL DATA IN THE DATABASE

1438	St Martin's Church	5.5.94	E
1439	Bellevue Hotel	6.9.94	M
1441	etc etc		

UPDATE PROGRAM

```
IF HAZARD-CODE
    NOT = 'E' OR 'M' OR 'N'
    DISPLAY
    'INVALID HAZARD-CODE'
ELSE
    . . . . etc
```

Advanced Repository Approach
All in the Tables of One Database

TABLE OF STRUCTURE DEFINITIONS

146	Protected-building	must have non-blank	Hazard-code
147	Protected-building	may have non-blank	Banned-material-code

TABLE OF ACTUAL DATA

1438	St Martin's Church	5.5.94	E
1439	Bellevue Hotel	6.9.94	M
1441	etc etc		

TABLE OF EXPLANATIONS

5673	Hazard-code	E	The building is extremely hazardous. Any application for maintenance work must be passed to . . . etc

TABLE OF VALID VALUES

1885	Hazard-code	E
1886	Hazard-code	M
1887	Hazard-code	N

SUMMARY OF WARRANTS

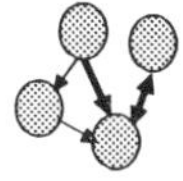
Chart of Data Dictionary Content: Data definition meta-data; Complex validation criteria; Explanations; Cross-references

Gradations of Integrated Data Dictionary: Separate DD through Classic-integrated-DD through Active-integrated-DD to Dynamic-integrated-DD

Comparison of Classic Integrated DD with Stronger Forms: Consistency; Powerful rules; More effective integrity and CRS; New architectures; Intellectual challenge; Organisational challenge

Aspects of Repository: Repository scope; Repository structure; Repository content

its purpose in a kind of super-expanded-dictionary. Although this is a qualitative rather than logical difference, it is convenient to use a different term: **repository**.

A repository can have two distinct roles: co-ordinating the development of new systems and databases; and controlling the use, particularly updating, of databases in operation. The main aspects of the repository concept *in operational use*, leaving aside its role in co-ordinating development, are as follows:

- **Repository scope.** The overwhelming bulk of all the design, logic and structure of the system is contained in the repository. Relatively little of substance is left in separate design documents or the documentation of application programs.
- **Repository structure.** The repository is itself a database, normally one using the same DBMS as the real database. Thus the operational database, containing data about protected buildings and inspections and health hazards and so on, has a relational schema and integrity control and CRS features and provides SQL or query-by-forms access; similarly, the repository database storing data *about* the database system has a relational schema, with SQL and CRS and so on.
- **Repository content.** The content is varied and thus can be analysed from numerous points of view, but there is an essential difference between that content which the automated system uses actively (particularly the rules and constraints for updating) where every quotemark and bracket must be absolutely precise, and that held for reference; eg if a text describing the purpose of a certain field contains a miskeyed ‘q’ instead of ‘w’, that will not have any effect on the operational system.

POSSIBLE DECISION-MAKING

For decisions about DD there are two classic problem situations. In one an organisation has a great installed base of systems, where the problem is to improve the DD support without jeopardising the operational systems. The other is Acacia's situation — a green-field opportunity, but one so challenging that it seems rash to aim for the ideal.

Some of Acacia's managers recognise this as an example of a very common problem in IT decision-making. It is relatively easy to sketch the outlines of an ideal solution — in this case, a comprehensive, highly integrated repository — and to spell out all the advantages this would have. But you also need to recognise how ambitious this goal is, what challenges it poses and what risks are attached. The sensible aim is for the best buy — the approach with the best balance of benefit and risk.

Strongly influenced by this maxim, the Acacia people spell out a number of plausible policy options:

- **Option 1**, the most straightforward: take the classic integrated DD route for all systems, and consider any more advanced ideas a few years later when a stable set of systems already exists;
- **Option 2**, which will take much longer, even if all goes well: develop all systems from the start using up-to-date CASE technology within a plan to arrive at a modern, sophisticated repository;
- **Option 3**, a more subtle one: set up a carefully chosen one-year project (not very demanding, but not too easy) and experiment with repository possibilities; at the same time get urgent systems developed in the least sophisticated way possible; review the situation after one year;
- **Option 4**, another subtle one: let one part of the organisation go ahead with classic integrated DD and another part (which has systems that could benefit) with dynamic integrated DD; after two years review the situation and, in the light of experience, make definitive plans for the organisation as a whole — anywhere along the gradations from classic integrated DD through to advanced repository.

Option 1 seems too conservative and Option 2 too rash. The choice between Options 3 and 4 probably depends on judging such things as how diffuse or interlinked the applications of Acacia's portfolio are.

CONNECTIONS

6. Database Integrity	About integrity options
27. Rules-with-Mainstream Systems	Storing rules in databases
29. Object-oriented Topics	Includes, among much else, the idea of storing both data and instructions together in the database

15. Development Tools and Languages

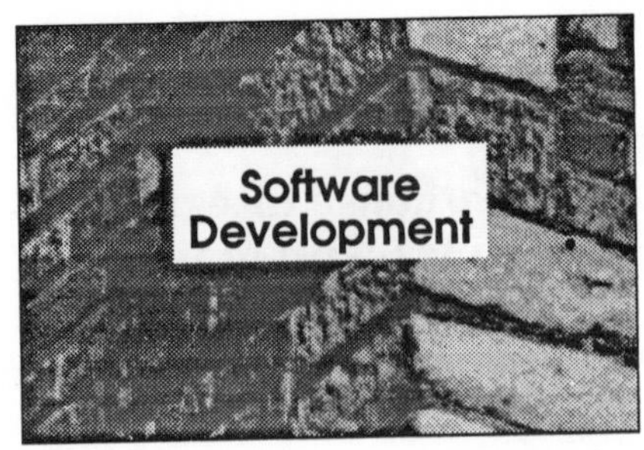

BEARINGS

Many DBMS products are commercially successful and bring benefits to the organisations using them because, in addition to CRS, deep design and other supply features, they provide a high-productivity programming language or similar tools for developing systems.

As noted in Briefing 5, the dividing-line between flexible, sophisticated access to an operational database and super-efficient software development is a judgement of convenience rather than fact or logic.

POSSIBLE CONTEXT

Yellow Carbeen manufactures vending machines. A project is planned to introduce new JIT (just-in-time) inventory systems. The new software will access some data already in the company's database, but for this system a whole new chunk of data will be added to the database. Discussion of this development project produces the following decision-making problem:

- Software development tools or languages have to be chosen for the project. At first glance, this may seem to be a matter of limited interest to most of the Yellow Carbeen managers on the project steering committee. Surely, it may be thought, the project manager should carry out whatever investigations are necessary in order to decide on the means most appropriate for carrying out the project efficiently.
- The project manager points out that things are not so simple: 'Suppose that, out of several languages, one was likely to produce a more efficiently running final system, but another made it easier to keep the eventual users of the system closely involved in development, and another produced a more robust system, easier to amend

in the future, while yet another would make it easier to run the system, if Yellow Carbeen should ever switch to different technology for its whole set of database systems. Would you want me to evaluate all those tradeoffs myself privately, without telling you anything about them, and simply announce that, on balance, language X was the best choice?'

• Plainly this question is a rhetorical one. But if they are to discuss tradeoffs, members of the steering committee need to make sense of the range of database-related software development products available — as far as possible by cutting through 99% of the detail to expose factors that have wide non-technical or semi-technical implications.

WARRANTS

This is another topic plagued by inconsistent use of terms and hazy language that merges related but different concepts. It is worth charting out the overlaps, interconnections, broad and narrow terms, distinctions without a difference and so on.

Charting Database Technology and Software Development

Why should the topic of developing software come up at all? Isn't technology for storing data a different thing from technology for developing application software?

A DBMS product is a piece of *general-purpose* software. It will store and access the database for any application in any industry, provided the constraints of a certain style of conceptual schema are observed. General-purpose features for data storage and access can assist software development in three main ways:

• **Data definition.** The DBMS possesses a definition of the database conceptual schema, specifying what data items exist and how they fit together. With that, it can relieve the programmer of considerable effort in defining data in various parts of the system. Tell the system to design a screen containing the data of the *Supplier* table, and it can generate a rough draft version, showing each of the fields with appropriate legends. Modifying this draft is far less work than designing a screen layout from scratch.

• **General-purpose tasks.** Generic matters such as concurrency control and the other CRS topics have to be contained in most systems to some degree. But they don't have to be programmed

Using a Development Tool

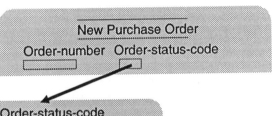

Developing the part of the system that will accept and validate new purchase-orders:

1. Tell the development tool you want a screen that will contain all the fields that make up a purchase-order.

2. Consulting the data dictionary, it knows which fields are in a purchase-order; thus it can suggest a simple screen design.

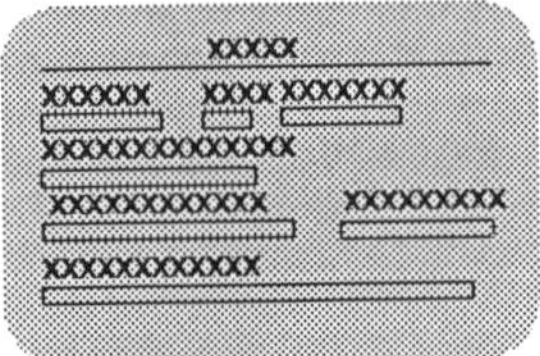

3. Using the screen-painter you rearrange fields and alter legends, according to taste.

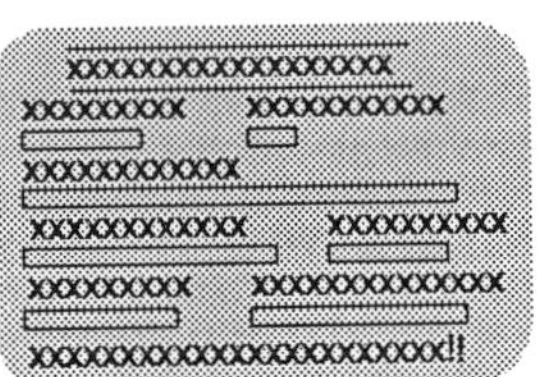

4. Then the tool helps you define validation criteria for each field. It offers simple generic options.

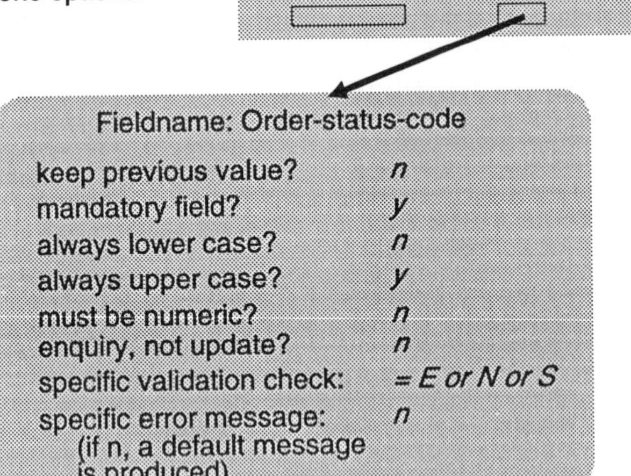

New Purchase Order
Order-number Order-status-code
Fieldname: Order-status-code
keep previous value? n
mandatory field? y
always lower case? n
always upper case? y
must be numeric? n
enquiry, not update? n
specific validation check: = E or N or S
specific error message: n
(if n, a default message is produced)

This is much less work than coding in a programming language:

```
IF ORDER-STATUS-CODE NOT = 'E' OR 'N' OR 'S'
        DISPLAY 'INVALID ORDER-STATUS-CODE'
        GO TO NEW-INPUT-ROUTINE
ELSE    etc etc
```

specially. It is simply a matter of choosing among the general-purpose options offered by the DBMS — a considerable saving of effort.
● **Data input and output.** A DBMS allows the programmer to issue instructions that input and output information from the database in a 'high-level way'; eg 'get all the *Delivery* records for this supplier', rather than writing a routine that reads in *Delivery* records one by one, examines the *supplier-number* in each and continues until all have been checked.

Distinguishing Languages from Tasks

The term 'language', as in (say) 'SQL can be used as a data definition language', often confuses by blurring some differences between computer and human languages.

To say that (eg) Pascal is a **language** means that Pascal is the name of a set of conventions for giving commands to a computer. The verbs and syntax and other details of the Pascal language can be looked up in a reference book, just as they can for the English or the Hungarian language.

Pascal, Fortran, C, Cobol and other well-known languages belong in the same category: general-purpose languages for computer applications that may produce invoices, control tanker fleets, forecast weather or a thousand other possibilities. Prolog and Lisp belong in a different category: languages used in artificial-intelligence applications and hardly any other. PostScript and PCL are in a more specialised category still: languages for commanding the processor inside a laser printer to format and print pages.

This way of categorising computer languages stretches the analogy with human language to breaking point. Whereas all natural human languages are essentially general-purpose, computer languages can be put in separate categories according to the **kinds of tasks** they are used for.

Distinguishing Development Language from Development Tool

Programming in a classic, command-based language involves keying commands in a language onto a blank screen. As the example in the diagram suggests, using a development tool can be quite a different experience. One way of capturing this distinction is to say that there are two distinct types of language (perhaps the first is a 'formal' language and the second some other kind) but it is better to avoid overworking the analogy with human language; distinguish:

• **Development language.** You formulate commands on a blank screen, using the conventions of a computer language.
• **Development tool.** The system finds out the commands required in some other way, eg, as in the example, by prompting and by assuming default options that can be amended.

This language-tool distinction can be consolidated with that drawn in the previous section:

• Distinguish development **languages** from development **tools**.
• Distinguish **tasks** you command the computer to perform from the language or tool used to express the commands.
• **Languages** and **tools** can be categorised by the kinds of **tasks** they command the computer to perform.

Charting Concepts around DDL (Data Definition Language)

These concepts help in clarifying ideas around several special types of language particularly associated with database; eg the DDL (data definition language).

One generic task is to set up the database with a certain conceptual schema, ie with a certain structure of tables, with tables containing certain fields, with each field having a certain length and format. Closely allied to this is the definition of the internal schema, ie saying which fields should be indexed, what kind of indexing and access mechanisms should be used and the like. What languages or tools handle these tasks?

One book gives: 'In many DBMSs . . . one language called the data definition language (DDL) is used . . . to define both schemas. The DBMS will have a DDL compiler whose function is to process DDL statements . . . to store the schema description in the DBMS catalog.'[1] These are statements of the type that can only be correctly understood by those who already possess the knowledge they convey. There are actually *three* main ways of setting up the conceptual and internal schemas:

• **DDL**. Some DBMSs (mainly hierarchical-network ones) have a special language for this purpose alone, applying only to that specific DBMS; such a language belongs to the category of **data definition language (DDL)**.
• **SQL**. But some DBMSs (most relational) provide for this same purpose a more general-purpose language, usually the powerful and widely used SQL. Instructions to set up databases are only a small part of SQL's repertoire; it can be used for many other tasks, eg updating an existing database with new data or making an enquiry.

SQL, moreover, is general-purpose in another sense: it can be used (though perhaps with minor variations) on many different DBMSs.

- **Guiding tool**. Or a guiding tool rather than a classic language may support the task of setting up schemas. A DBMS might offer several options, eg one based on display of a form to be filled in on screen and another that posed a succession of questions.

Different options suit different situations, but the most common approach for a substantial database is to use SQL. The database schemas are usually thought of as *designs*, so how exactly does the SQL *language* use them?

- The internal schema and conceptual schema are **descriptions** on paper of a database, analogous to the blueprint of a car. The schema neither is nor contains the data of the database — any more than a blueprint of a car possesses actual wheels.
- If you scrawl at the top of a blueprint 'make this car', the document becomes both a description of a car and a **command** to make a car. The **internal schema** for a relational database is like that. It is a set of SQL instructions commanding the DBMS to set up a number of tables, containing certain fields, with various indexes and other technical arrangements. In the SQL language, you write in effect 'make the following thing' and then describe what it is you want made; thus the instruction CREATE TABLE is followed by the description of the table you want to set up.
- The **conceptual schema** (or at least, the main part defining the structure of the database) consists of the same set of SQL instructions, but without those relating to technical matters, such as indexing, hashing and so on. There may be another version of the conceptual schema too, perhaps in diagram or list form, but this is merely a difference of representation; it contains exactly the same tables and fields as the SQL instructions.

Charting Concepts around DML (Data Manipulation Language)

Of DML the textbook says: 'Typical manipulations (of the database) include retrieval, insertion, deletion and modification of the data. The DBMS provides a data manipulation language (DML) for these purposes.'[2] This is misleading unless you already know about languages that manipulate databases.

The commands contained in a new application system will be a mixture of those that manipulate the database (eg add a new supplier record to the database) and those that don't (eg calculate the optimum stock quantity to order).

One approach is to use just one language, capable of specifying both manipulation and non-manipulation tasks. Languages in the general-purpose category, such as Pascal, Cobol etc, don't include adequate instructions for this approach, but there is a separate category of language specifically designed to combine the two types of instruction. For instance, the dBase language contains **database manipulation instructions** such as APPEND; DELETE; SKIP (followed by a positive or negative number), used to move forward or back a given number of records in the database; and FIND (followed by a character string) to find the first record in the database whose index key matches the string. The dBase language also has **non-manipulation instructions** such as SUM, to add up a number of fields; AVERAGE, to average them; IF, to test for conditions; and so on.

Some languages in this category are specific to just one DBMS product; eg PAL for Paradox and DQL for DataEase. Two particular languages have established a position as standards; ie they can be used with a number of different DBMS products from different suppliers: dBase (sometimes called Xbase to stress that it can be used not only with the DBMS known as dBase, but also with others: FoxPro, Clipper etc) and SQL.

But a language in this category is not always the best choice. Suppose the application was to optimise the scheduling of delivery vans. The bulk of the processing might lie in non-manipulation (eg heavy calculations of formulae based on queueing theory), and data manipulation might be relatively trivial (eg taking a record out of the database and putting it back updated). Here the natural approach is to use a language from the general-purpose category (eg Pascal, C etc) or perhaps even from some special category appropriate to the application, and then to *embed* the instructions that manipulate the database within the Pascal or C code. A pre-processor supplied with the DBMS converts these statements to make them compatible with the rest of the program.

Within this approach of embedding database manipulation instructions within a program written in a general-purpose language there are two main possibilities:

- **SQL:** embed standard SQL instructions for data manipulation within the code written in C, Pascal etc
- **Specific DML:** embed instructions for data manipulation specific to the DBMS within code written in C, Pascal etc; the definition of the verbs and syntax of these instructions can reasonably be called the DML of the specific DBMS (eg RDML is the name of the DML for the Supra DBMS). The DML is said to be 'hosted' by Cobol or whatever general-purpose language is used.

Charting Tools and Non-procedural Concepts

Application software that uses a database can be built with a **development tool** rather than a language. Here there are no instructions to key in. The tool normally generates the necessary instructions to process data and manipulate the database behind the scenes. This instruction-less characteristic is expressed in the term **non-procedural** ('declarative' is a near-synonym). But, though development tools are generally non-procedural, some languages are too. The overlapping concepts of tool and non-procedural need charting out.

The non-procedural concept is to tell the system *what* you want (as in the example given earlier, accept a certain input field only if its value is E or N or S), without saying quite *how* this is done. A procedural approach, by contrast, would be to define a sequence of commands, with a logic to it: eg first check for value E or N or S, then, depending on whether this is successful or not, go on to something else . . . Defining requirements in a non-procedural way is often less work and less error-prone, especially for generic tasks such as validating data or selecting records according to criteria.

The contrast between defining *what* and defining *how* is often expressed, but does it stand up to careful thought? Certainly, ordering from a restaurant menu is non-procedural (you say *what* you want to eat), while striding into the kitchen and telling the chef *how* to cook is procedural. But these are only the extremes of a continuum. To tell the waiter: 'I don't want any coriander used in that dish', or 'I want that one cooked five minutes less than normal' is getting a little procedural. In the kitchen, saying 'Cook the rice now' is procedural, but less so than 'Fill the saucepan with water, then boil it, then put the rice in . . .' There is really no absolute distinction between saying *what* and saying *how*. With computer languages too, there are degrees of procedurality; some languages are more procedural than others.

Development tools (as opposed to languages) are fairly non-procedural. Most general-purpose languages are fairly procedural, but some languages associated with database are fairly non-procedural. Using SQL entails formulating instructions on a blank screen in a language that calls for precise use of semi-colons, quotes, brackets etc. These instructions specify *what* data is to be extracted, without going into the detail of the operations to achieve it.

Sometimes SQL and similar languages are called query languages — a misleading term, since the languages can not only extract but amend and delete information from the database and even set up database tables and define authorisation constraints.

In practice, any complicated operation with a non-procedural tool or language entails defining *what* you want with considerable precision, using thought processes similar to those of a programmer in a procedural language. And testing mustn't be forgotten. To test a system by comparison of expected with actual results, it may be essential to think through the logic of the processing the computer ought to perform — irrespective of how procedural or non-procedural the programming was.

Chart of 4GL Components

4GL stands for 'fourth-generation language', but a 4GL isn't (or at least isn't only) a language in the sense of one where instructions are composed on a blank screen. A 4GL is really a *set* of development tools.[3] Brochureware for 4GL software is among the least informative in the whole IT industry, but three chief points help distinguish the dunes behind the sand-storms.

- A 4GL uses a **data dictionary**.
- It generates powerful **defaults** for standard functions.
- It allows easy **amendment** of its default choices or easy **choice** between options.

Suppose you tell the 4GL that the system needs to accept a new order transaction. From the data dictionary the 4GL knows which fields are probably needed for the transaction: those in the *Orders* table. It provides a draft, moderately intelligent screen layout as a starting-point. You can modify this layout by rearranging or adding fields according to taste. To help define the validation criteria, the 4GL offers generic options for each field (numeric, date, within some range etc). In effect, the 4GL helps you declare what you want and behind the scenes it generates the appropriate software to achieve it.

A 4GL software product usually provides a bundle of development tools, often together with a more conventional language. Here are its typical elements:

- **Data dictionary** — storing definitions of database content and structure; less as a good in itself than as the basis for most of the following tools.
- **Input validation generator** — for specifying data input and updating procedures in a non-procedural way;
- **Screen and menu generator-painter** — producing default draft formats of screens and menus and allowing easy redesign;
- **Report generator** — for designing the formats of printed reports

(including sort order, sub-totalling etc) easily in a non-procedural way;

- **Flow control tool** — to specify how certain menus lead to certain screens and certain data on screens trigger subsequent menus or screens;
- **Language** — for both procedural and non-procedural commands.

These things are related together in an interesting way, allowing different ways of working with the 4GL. In every case, the data must be defined in the data dictionary. Then there are two extreme alternatives:

- You develop the application by using tools and writing nothing in the language. The system translates what you specify through these tools into its own language, but that is all behind the scenes.
- *Or* you write part of the application in the language and develop part through the tools; then go to the language instructions that the system generated from the tools and amend them. A 4GL makes it easy to specify all the most common kinds of validation checks, but on occasion the validation criteria of a certain field might be so special that the only thing to do was define them in a procedural way, using instructions such as IF-THEN-ELSE or even an ENDLOOP within nested WHILE statements.

Chart connecting 4GL and DBMS

Another important link to clarify is that between the 4GL and DBMS. There are several possibilities:

- One 4GL may be part of the array of features of one particular DBMS; eg the DBMS Ingres comes with its own 4GL.
- Another 4GL may belong naturally with one particular DBMS of the same supplier (like Ingres above), and thus fit neatly in with its data dictionary and other tools — but also be usable together with other DBMSs too. Mantis and Natural are examples.
- Another 4GL (eg Focus or Nomad) may come with its own DBMS, albeit one relatively light in deep design, integrity and CRS features. Whereas most 4GL products in the other categories are usually regarded as tools to help professional programmers develop software more efficiently, a 4GL in this category is intended more for development of simple applications by non-experts, who might not otherwise develop software at all. For instance, the 4GL might be used by managers to access a decision-support database of data extracted from the main operational database.
- Another 4GL (eg PowerHouse) may not even require any DBMS to be used at all; the 4GL's data dictionary can be hooked up to access data stored in some more primitive way.

SUMMARY OF WARRANTS

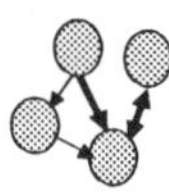

Chart connecting Database Technology and Software Development: Data definition; General-purpose tasks; Data I/O

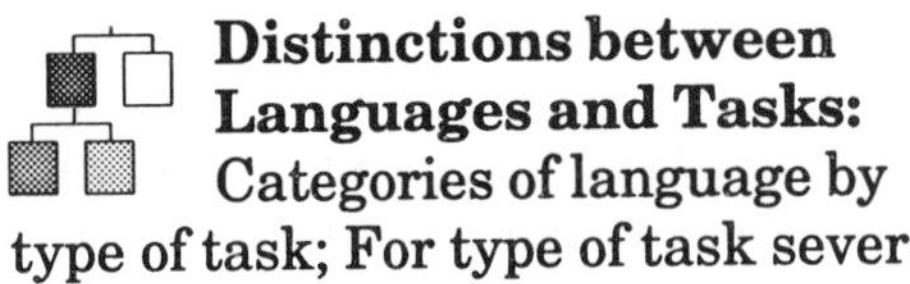

Distinctions between Languages and Tasks: Categories of language by type of task; For type of task several categories of language

Distinctions between Tools for Software Development: Development language; Development tool

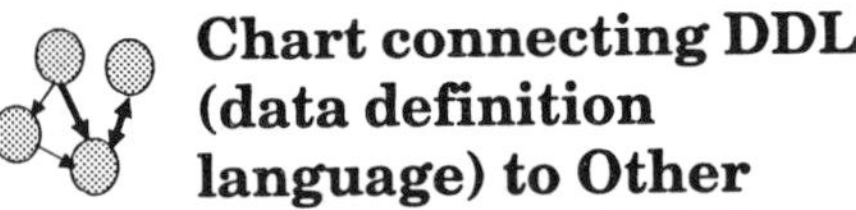

Chart connecting DDL (data definition language) to Other Concepts: DDL; SQL; Guiding tool; Description and command; Internal schema; Conceptual schema

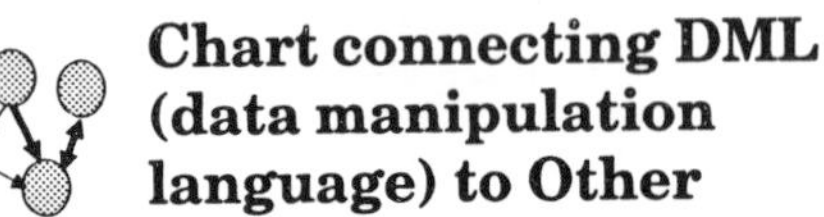

Chart connecting DML (data manipulation language) to Other Concepts: Languages including data manipulation instructions, standard and DBMS-specific; Embedded SQL; Embedded DML

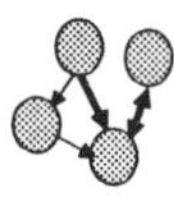

Chart connecting Tools and Non-procedural Concepts: Procedural, non-procedural and gradations thereof; Tools, SQL, query and other languages

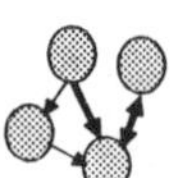

Chart connecting 4GL Components: Data dictionary; Defaults for standard functions; Easy amendment of defaults; Input validation generator; Screen painter and menu generator; Report generator; Flow control tool; Language

Chart connecting 4GL and DBMS: DBMS-specific 4GL; 4GL independent but with natural DBMS; 4GL with own CRS-light DBMS; 4GL with data dictionary, not DBMS

Distinctions between PC Development Features: 4GL-like tools; Own programming language; SQL; Interpreting; Compiling

Distinctions between PC Development Features

In the PC world development tools are often the main basis for deciding to use one DBMS rather than another. There is an initial straightforward distinction:

- Some DBMSs for PC provide a range of non-procedural **tools** such

as input validation generator, screen painter, menu generator and report generator — but without a language.

- Some DBMSs for PC provide a set of non-procedural **tools** but also a procedural **language**, eg Paradox has PAL, FoxPro has dBase etc.[4]
- Some DBMSs for PC providing a set of non-procedural **tools** and a procedural **language** also provide the non-procedural language **SQL**; eg Advanced Revelation has both R/BASIC and SQL.

DBMSs for PC also differ on the issue of interpreting and compiling:

- If the application software is **interpreted**, this means that the instructions written by the programmer are stored; when the program is run each stored instruction is read, translated from programming language into executable machine language and then executed. If the program has to calculate the inventory required for 10,000 parts, the same instructions may be translated 10,000 times.
- If the application software is **compiled** the instructions written by the programmer are translated into executable machine language once and the 'compiled' version of the program is stored; when the program is run, there is no need to translate the instructions repeatedly.

This seems to put interpreting at a disadvantage. Its main advantage is that program development is easier; when testing, the programmer can watch the progress of the program step by step, and see exactly where the logic starts to go wrong. With compiling, the whole program has to be run before expected and actual results can be compared.

This leaves three possibilities for a DBMS on PC: interpret only, eg DataEase; compile only, eg FoxPro; both interpret and compile options, eg Advanced Revelation.[5]

POSSIBLE DECISION-MAKING

The managers on the steering committee at Yellow Carbeen believe that the first issue is whether their aim should be above all to set up the software development arrangements that will best help professional programmers develop new software efficiently or — something different.

In many typical cases, sketched out in marketing brochures, it is advantageous for much of the software to be developed by users. If a system is confined to a small department or if it is to access management information from a special, separate database, then the advantages of user involvement, commitment, creativity, initiative, satisfaction etc can easily outweigh any loss of efficiency on the development project.

But that doesn't apply here. The JIT system is fundamental to the operations of the whole business. Therefore it is easy to decide that efficient professional software development must be at least one important objective.

The question then arises: are there *any* important considerations other than efficient professional development? Operational (as opposed to development) efficiency is one candidate. Using a 4GL rather than a language such as Pascal or C generally brings a tradeoff. In extreme form: software development work may be reduced by two-thirds, but the system itself may perform unacceptably, eg poor response time for users at terminals. In other words, the hand-crafted software in the regular language may cost more to develop, but at least it can be intricately designed to optimise operational characteristics such as response time.

Thus, there is usually a *potential* conflict between development efficiency and operational efficiency. But how grave is it *in practice*? There are really two main situations where a decision can be tricky:

- when the requirements of an application are particularly unusual and thus not well-suited to a 4GL style anyway, eg if linear programming and queueing theory calculations were needed in a purchase order system;
- when hardware resources are too limited for adequate performance; in principle, operational performance can always be improved by investment in more powerful hardware, but in some cases the marginal costs could be so high that the cost-justification of the project was ruined.

The Yellow Carbeen people quickly decide that the first of these doesn't apply, but the second very well could; the new system is intended to fit in with existing database systems on an existing configuration. If exceedingly resource-greedy, the new JIT system could force the whole installation into expensive upgrades.

Should the steering committee order that the software be developed as efficiently as possible, but subject to the overriding (indeed far-reaching) priority that operational efficiency should be maximised? Not quite; there is another consideration. It is no use optimising the operational efficiency of a system that turns out not to manage inventory in quite the way that the company needs. The question arises: Will managers in the Yellow Carbeen organisation be able to firm up the demand requirements clearly and surely and then turn them over to the technical people to supply?

In this case, the question answers itself: People agree that a new JIT system is sorely needed, but they are very uncertain about the fine detail: eg exactly which factors should determine restocking orders, what exactly should be the procedures to control the flow of material through the works, and so on. Yellow Carbeen therefore arrives at this policy:

- **Stage 1.** Develop a partial prototype as quickly as possible for the purpose of getting a better definition of requirements; ignore operational efficiency completely; use whatever tools for software development best meet this approach.
- **Decision point.** From the experience of Stage 1, get a better awareness of the scope of the new system, the operational constraints and the implications of different software tools. Make sensible plans for Stage 2.
- **Stage 2.** Develop the real system using whatever tools provide the best tradeoff between development efficiency and operational efficiency for this case.

CONNECTIONS

5. Accessing the Database	The access end of the Access-Development continuum, including the role of SQL
9. Client-server Architecture	SQL as intermediary in a client-server setup
17. Mainstream Software Products	Categories of software product

16. Mix, Match, Amend

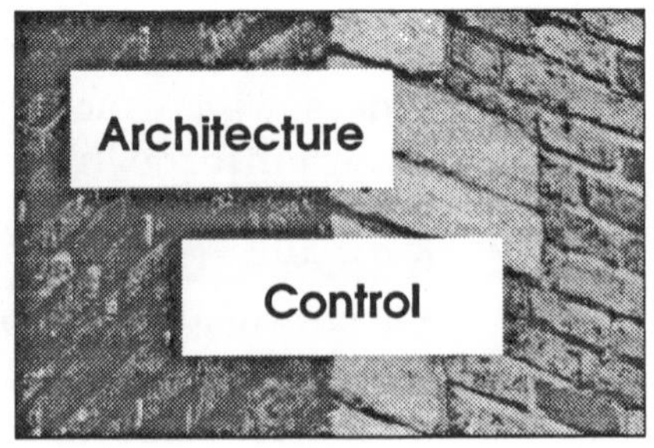

BEARINGS

One database system might be like a house of cards, standing but likely to topple if any component is ever altered; by comparison, another might be a sturdy lego model, whose parts could be interchanged without vexing repercussions throughout the structure. On the unifying chart, the system's capacity for interchange of components, for evolution and for flexible expansion is covered by both the control and architecture elements.

Such themes can be relevant to any technology at all, but they are particularly prominent in database technology. One fundamental characteristic of a database system is its mixture of the general-purpose (ie the DBMS) with the specific (the software developed for the application). Moreover, a great deal of thinking about relational databases rests on the underlying notion that a DBMS based on relational principles can be a very powerful, sturdy, general-purpose engine for managing data.

An extreme house-of-cards system is usually undesirable, but that doesn't mean that the most lego-like system is always the best, irrespective of its cost. In any case, decision-making about these matters should not rely on abstract terms and suggestive analogies. The concepts need to be made more concrete.

POSSIBLE CONTEXT

Blackbutt and Bloodwood (B&B) is a large legal practice. B&B is just finalising plans for a much-needed new database system to handle two core administrative functions. One is keeping track of time booked to different cases by different lawyers, something that can become quite complex when analysed in detail. The other is keeping the accounts, not just of fees due from clients, but also of clients' money in transactions the company is handling.

In planning these new developments of essential systems, one big theme is to maintain flexibility for further progress starting the day after the systems go live. Here are the main elements of the problem:

- First, most generally, the company wants to keep up with **new technology developments** in database software and software development techniques. B&B is happy to experiment with new ideas and technologies on a small project and, if all goes well, go on to use them more extensively. But B&B wants to do this kind of thing neatly, not to find that it often has to carry out huge conversion projects of software or database.
- Then, B&B has deliberately excluded the area of office automation (word processing, presentation graphics, electronic mail and so on) from its current planning. If the core database systems are built neatly and flexibly, then, so it is hoped, **office automation** data, whose scope is currently undefined, may be fitted in later.
- Another area where flexibility is desirable is integration of **other PC applications** of the type not generally called office automation. For instance, a B&B lawyer might set up a personal spreadsheet and load data into it from the main database.
- Finally, there is the strong possibility of B&B expanding by **acquisition**. It goes without saying that the new administrative systems must be able to cope with greater volumes, but there is another consideration. B&B might take over another company which had excellent, innovative systems; B&B might want to change part of its own systems to fit in with the others.

These flexibility requirements are easy to sketch in general terms. However, it is inconceivable that any system could be designed to provide *unlimited* flexibility in all these directions. So what are the realistic possibilities and which one presents the best balance of tradeoffs?

To resolve a case like this you first need to analyse the possibilities, limitations and options for this kind of flexibility with database systems in general.

WARRANTS

Terms such as 'independent', 'transparent' and 'modular' are often employed rather recklessly; analogies to houses of cards, lego models, frameworks, jigsaw puzzles, water-tight compartments and the like often lack precision. To get to grips with the issues and options it is essential to distinguish some related but different concepts.

Selective Description and Chunking

If this is the detail of a system: (computer system or transport system, social security system, banking system, ecological system etc etc)

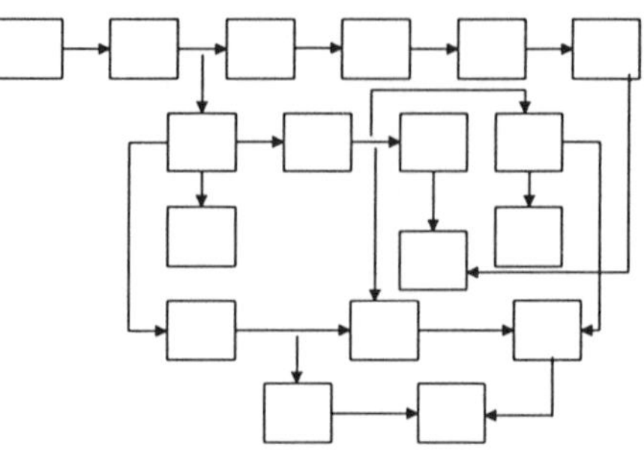

Then this is Selective Description

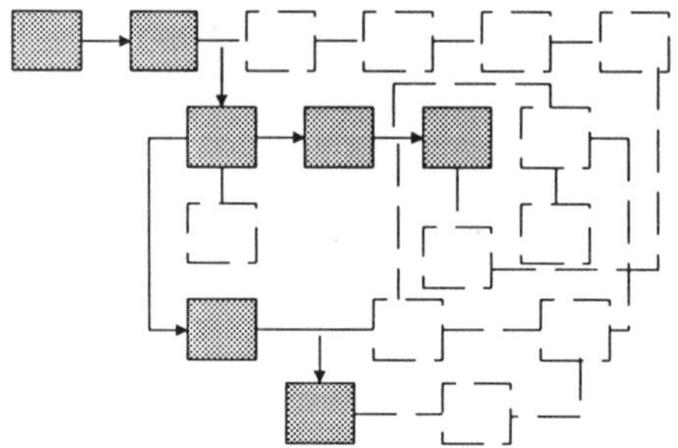

And this is Chunking

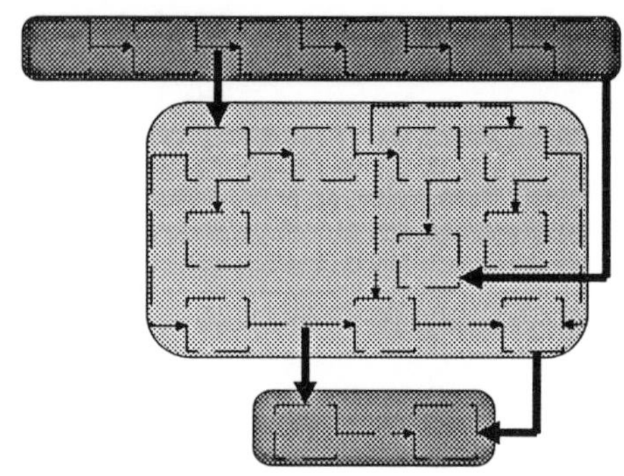

Distinction between Selective Descriptions and Chunks

Start by distinguishing two things whose overlap may otherwise cause confusion:

- **Selective descriptions**. Anything complicated can usually be described selectively in different ways. The famous map of the London Underground system is a selective description that concentrates on showing what stations, lines and interchange points exist. Other descriptions of the same system might use other bases for selection; eg ignoring stations but showing the depth of the tunnels and geology of the ground tunnelled through.
- **Chunks**. Complicated systems of any kind are often easier to understand and control or even to design when broken into convenient chunks. For example, in discussing the social security system of a certain country, it might be convenient to regard

unemployment benefit and old-age pension as different chunks that can be discussed or reformed separately.

These distinctions (illustrated by the diagram) become important with a database system that (as is usually the case) needs to allow flexibility for future change:

- **Selective descriptions** help in understanding something *in its present state.* To describe something complex like a database system it is useful to make several selective descriptions — particularly for different audiences, eg information analyst, technology expert, line manager etc. Then people can see what they need to know — no more, no less. But the fact that different selective descriptions of a database system or an underground railway system *can* be made does not of itself say anything about how easy or exacting it will be to make any changes or about how complex their implications may be. The only safe assumption is that well-chosen, neatly-made selective descriptions make it easier to *discuss* possible changes.
- **Chunking** affects flexibility for change. In one country, treating unemployment insurance and pension as separate chunks might be a good way of holding a coherent debate about the social security system. But in another country this chunking might be a dangerous over-simplification; eg discussing unemployment benefits in isolation is pointless, if many unemployed people also qualify for a variety of other benefits too. Other things being equal, it is attractive to keep any system cleanly chunked (since it is clearer for everybody), but awkward complexity may be unavoidable; eg if other goals such as fairness or cost-effectiveness are to be met. With a database system, as with any other, there is a prima facie case for establishing different chunks, separated as cleanly as possible. The cleaner the chunks and the simpler their connections, the more flexibility for change without complex repercussions. But this chunking may not be easy to achieve and other factors may drive in a different direction.

Gradations of DBMS-application Changes

Database technology provides a valuable division into two huge chunks fairly automatically:

- **General-purpose.** The DBMS typically handles matters such as CRS, integrity control and deep design and so on, where the same generic features are useful whether the database belongs to a lawyer, a florist or a chandler. There is no need to design and develop such things from scratch; the task is to choose from among the possibilities offered by the DBMS.
- **Application-specific.** Much of the detail of the processing in a

system is bound to be application-specific; eg the processing of a lawyers' accounting system will be strongly affected by the rules of the authorities on accounting for client funds, and the monthly reports on time booked to different types of activity will depend on the tastes of those partners who scrutinise them.

It is an attractive idea to divide the database system into two separate chunks of DBMS and application software, so that a change to one need not affect the other. But, no matter how neatly this is done, in practice things may not turn out to be so straightforward. Here are four main possibilities:

- **No corresponding change.** Often one chunk can be changed without any effect on the other. If the authorities decide that from now on certain sums must always go into certain escrow accounts, the application software chunk may be changed with no effect at all on deep design.

Conversely, if a new release of the DBMS offers improved indexing features, changes may be made in the DBMS chunk to exploit the new features with no effect at all on the functions of the system — except that response is faster.

- **Straightforward consequential change.** Sometimes a change in one chunk requires consequential changes to the other, but they can be straightforward. For example, new application software is written to support new enquiries on information that before was rarely accessed; adding one new index in the DBMS chunk is in practice essential to achieve adequate response time, but raises no wider problems.

Conversely, the new release of the DBMS offers improved integrity features that can now be used to trap certain possible errors; from the user's point of view something has changed, but only in the sense that new error messages will appear.

- **Complex but optional change.** Changing one chunk may mean that sweeping changes to the other, though not compulsory, are desirable. If certain new data and new analytical features are added to the application system, it may well be wise to take a completely fresh look at the security authorisation features.

Conversely, suppose the new release of the DBMS offers more advanced CRS features. Though it isn't compulsory to use them, this could be the opportunity to rethink the nature of the transactions themselves and thus the application software; eg instead of filling in timesheets that are then keyed in once a week, fee-earners might key in their hours as they go.

- **Complex and compulsory change.** A change to one chunk may force complex changes to the other. On taking over a new company, with new offices and working practices, it may not be possible to confine system changes to the application software chunk; the whole deep design or even the choice of DBMS may have to be altered.

Conversely, suppose the DBMS supplier goes out of business; in an unlucky case, an unavoidable switch to a new DBMS could force awkward changes in many parts of the application software.

These four gradations of awkward change help to firm up the notion of chunking DBMS and application software. The more cleanly chunked the two things are, the lower on this scale most changes will fall. Therefore, the more clean the chunking the better — other things being equal, of course.

Charting Concepts around Relational Theory

One great theme of relational theory is to chunk as neatly as possible — by fortifying the role of the DBMS to cover ever more general-purpose functions, in ever more rigorous ways, ever more cleanly separated from application programs.

Edgar Codd, the founding guru of relational database technology, has laid down a set of rules for a relational DBMS.[1] Statements such as 'DBMS X supports 10 of Codd's 12 rules and is therefore a more authentic relational DBMS than Y, which supports only 4' are common in marketing brochures. To assess the relevance of such claims, it is most important to know *what kind* of things these rules are, and how they are connected with other parts of relational theory:

- **Normal forms.** The normal forms are principles concerning the conceptual schema of a relational database. Codd's rules describe features that a DBMS might ideally provide for operating on a database that already has such a schema. But it would be possible (not necessarily wise) to have a database in perfect third normal form and use a DBMS that followed hardly any of the rules.
- **Nature of Codd's rules.** There are obvious advantages to storing integrity checks in one place as part of the definition of the database, rather than scattered over several application programs. But not all DBMS products permit this approach. Codd's Rule 10 (in rough summary) says that they should.

If the field *fees-year-to-date* stands at zero for a certain lawyer, that seems plain enough, but suppose it stands at zero because the figure is as yet unknown, since it hasn't been calculated yet. Anyone believing that the real figure was zero would very likely be wrong. Or perhaps zero stands for 'not applicable', because this lawyer, unlike the others in the table doesn't do chargeable work. Safeguards against this kind of imperfection could be devised by the analysts and coded into the application programs. But Codd's Rule 3 states that the DBMS should allow any field to hold either a value (which could be zero if that really was the true value) or an 'unknown' indicator or a 'not applicable' indicator.

As these two instances suggest, Codd's rules are essentially a list of features that would make a DBMS a robust, powerful engine performing general-purpose functions, as one chunk separated very cleanly indeed from the application software.

• **Status of Codd's rules.** The rules are sometimes treated as if they were definitive. But they are just a set of particular things that seemed important to one person at a certain time. Other relational authorities believe that some of them are not very practical and that all the items on the list are not necessarily more important than some others that are not included.[2]

• **DBMS and database system.** Codd's rules apply to *DBMS* software products; it would be imprecise to talk of a certain *database system* following the rules or not. Of course, there is scarcely any point having a Codd-ideal DBMS, unless its advanced features are in fact used with skill and diligence. Safeguards may be needed to ensure that people (perhaps hundreds of programmers in an installation) actually use the features, instead of following lazy, inferior practices, such as handling referential integrity checks or 'not applicable' codes within application programs.[3]

• **SQL and relational theory.** SQL is sometimes assumed to be a fundamental part of a relational DBMS, but this is not really so. Codd's rules stipulate that the language provided by the DBMS to operate on the database must have certain features, but not that it has to be SQL specifically. Comparable languages have been developed but SQL happens to have become the standard. A relational database can, of course, be accessed by other means too, eg QBF.

Examples of Changes in Client-server Architecture

There is another big case of chunking in database technology: the client-server architecture. In a client-server system the client-PC usually sends messages in SQL format across the network to the server-DBMS. This could work with messages in any format, but it is very convenient that there should be some industry-standard format, and SQL happens to have been adopted. This opens up possibilities for forming the system's architecture from clean chunks and gaining attractive advantages; eg:

• The chunk of software run on a client could be completely rewritten, perhaps to improve the quality of the user interface, but, provided it generated the same SQL requests as the old, there need be no consequential changes to the system at the database-server.

- A server-DBMS accepts SQL requests without any interest in the software on the client PC that produces them. Thus, one EIS software package could be replaced at the client by a different one that also generated SQL requests, without any consequential changes at the server.
- Similarly, software can be developed to run on a client and generate SQL calls for information from the server database, without making any assumption about which particular DBMS will manage that database. Thus one DBMS could be replaced at the server by another, without repercussions for the client software.

Unfortunately, SQL doesn't provide a perfect lingua franca in the client-server world. Some dialects offer extra verbs for particularly sophisticated types of data access. Though SQL offers a more-or-less standard way of requesting information from the server there is less standardisation of the format of the information that comes back, especially as regards error codes and the like. With that qualification, though, the client-server architecture allows a division into clean chunks and thus flexibility in altering or replacing chunks.[4]

Charting Models, Schemas and Logical Architecture

The other main area where ideas of chunks and selective description need clarification is that of data schemas and models. Here is a summary chart:

- Early on in development of database and system it is usual to have an **ER model**, describing data and relations in a format not specifically directed towards any particular DBMS.
- The ER model is input to further work to make the **conceptual schema** for the database. This schema is non-technical, without any explicit detail on how its demands will be supplied — except in one vital sense: it is cast quite rigorously in structures that the intended DBMS is known to support. If the intended DBMS is a relational one, the conceptual schema will consist of relational tables.
- The conceptual schema is input to further work to make the **internal schema**, that will include technical details; eg it will specify that various index and hashing arrangements are to be used.
- The term **external schema** is not symmetrical to internal schema. A database has one internal schema and one conceptual schema, but usually numerous external schemas. Each application system has its own external schema, a *subset* of the whole conceptual schema, showing only data that is relevant to the application; other data,

even though it may be physically or logically adjacent in the database, is kept out of the way to avoid confusion.

This outline isn't a recommended methodology, just an account of the approach most commonly taken, even though terminology varies. Schemas are sometimes called 'views'; 'global' is sometimes used instead of 'conceptual', 'physical' instead of 'internal' and 'user' or 'local' instead of 'external'.

Now for the three-schema architecture (for uninteresting reasons, sometimes called the ANSI/SPARC architecture). This is a recommendation that a database should have a logical architecture, whose three main components are conceptual, internal and external schemas. This notion of a logical architecture has great potential for generating confusion. Here are some preliminary clarifying points:

• The three schemas are not chunks of the database. Actual data (client details, accounts items etc) is stored just once — in the database. The schemas are different selective descriptions of one database — analogous to different selective descriptions of one underground railway system.

• Each external schema is a different subset of the conceptual schema. It isn't a subset in the sense of leaving out a certain *kind* of detail; it presents in full whatever the conceptual schema contains, but only in so far as it is of interest to a particular user or application. This is like a map of just the Northern line with the Central and other lines omitted.

Charting Concepts around the Three-schema Architecture

People often talk of the 'goal' of the three-schema architecture and imply that many DBMSs achieve it only to a certain extent. But this raises the questions: Why? What is so difficult?

It is not very exacting to require that a database should be describable in three different selective ways *at a certain moment*. The much stronger stipulations concern *changes* to these selective descriptions — but only certain types of changes:

• **External schema.** Suppose that the database itself (ie the thing that the selective descriptions describe), does not change, but one external schema needs to be altered, eg so that a certain program can use certain data that is already in the database. Then, the stipulation is, this should not entail any alteration of the conceptual schema.

• **Conceptual schema**. Suppose the database does change in ways that necessarily cause alteration to the conceptual schema; eg certain fields are removed from certain tables. Then, certain external

SUMMARY OF WARRANTS

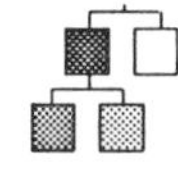
Distinctions between Selective Descriptions and Chunks: Describing the whole thing in different ways; Separating the whole thing into different parts

Gradations of DBMS-Application Changes: No consequential change; Straightforward consequential change; Complex but optional change; Complex and compulsory change

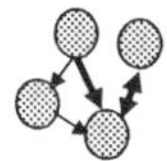
Chart of Concepts around Relational Theory: Normal forms; Nature of Codd rules; Status of Codd rules; DBMS; Database system; SQL

Examples of Changes in Client-server Architecture: Client software redeveloped generating same SQL requests; Client software package exchanged; Server DBMS exchanged

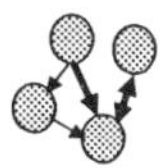
Charting Schemas, Models and Logical Architecture: ER model; Conceptual schema; Internal schema; External schema; Three-schema architecture

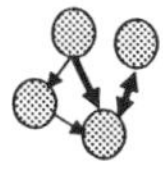
Charting Concepts around the Three-schema Architecture: Types of changes; Limitations of separation of conceptual and internal schemas

---

schemas (those that include the removed fields) are bound to require alteration too. The stipulation is that all the other external schemas need not be altered.

• **Internal schema and other schemas.** Suppose the database changes in certain technical ways. Then only the internal schema should need to be altered, but not the other two schemas.

Yes, but which kinds of technical changes are covered by this last stipulation? Is it true, for instance, that any changes made to the database solely to improve performance (eg in consequence of a stiff rise in data volumes) will, assuming good practice, always result in alterations to the internal schema, but not to the other selective descriptions, the conceptual and external schemas?

With the main relational DBMSs in use today the answer is no. Certainly, if you add an index or introduce hashing for performance reasons, then you change the internal but not the conceptual schema. However, you may well decide, purely for performance reasons, to denormalise and merge two tables into one. If so, you will have to change the conceptual schema as well.

With most current DBMSs, there is a one-to-one correspondence between the tables and their record layouts in the conceptual schema and in the internal schema. You can't have (say) a conceptual schema containing Table A with ten fields, and an internal schema showing how the data of Table A is split in three for performance reasons (eg the most frequently used records held in some location where they can be rapidly accessed etc). Neither can you have (say) two physical versions of Table A, of which one is stored for rapid access and contains only the four most commonly used fields.

It would be advantageous if you could define such technical arrangements neatly in a separate internal schema and alter them without touching the conceptual schema. Probably the people who conceived the three-schema architecture intended it to be so. But that is not the way most DBMSs currently work.[5]

POSSIBLE DECISION-MAKING

Every organisation (except perhaps some semi-government body due to be wound up shortly or some commercial joint-venture of fixed term) needs some degree of flexibility built into its database system. B&B believes, for reasons given above, that this should be an exceptionally important theme in its decision-making.

Perhaps strangely, it is not too clear quite what levers such a business has available to pull to reinforce its concern for flexibility. Adoption of relational database technology — a natural choice, anyway — necessarily brings with it scope for neat chunks and clear selective descriptions — especially if intelligent, thoughtful system designers are employed.

Should B&B show its concern for flexibility by choosing the relational DBMS that conforms best to Codd's rules or implements the three-schema architecture as powerfully as possible? Plainly, these criteria are important and it would probably not be sensible for B&B to choose a DBMS that lagged far behind its rivals. But real-life decisions are not so simple. Suppose DBMS A scores slightly higher than DBMS B on these criteria, but B has other qualities, less easily defined in abstract terms; eg better software development facilities, allowing certain types of new requirements to be programmed more quickly.

This sort of decision calls for more precision about why it is that you want great flexibility, sturdiness in the face of change and so on. One typical case is where the scope and boundaries of the database itself can be outlined fairly clearly, but flexibility is required because of uncertainties about how future systems will access and process the data, and because of the need for tuning the system to meet large volumes. Here fidelity to Codd's rules and purity of three-schema architecture should loom quite large in decision-making.

But B&B is motivated by rather different factors: possible large-scale extensions to the database system to encompass office automation and individual PC functions, together with very general requirements to be well placed to handle broad, currently unforeseeable changes, through technology developments or business changes.

In these circumstances, B&B should probably recognise one boring truth and one second-order policy recommendation. The boring truth is that, to a considerable degree, good quality design work (which almost everybody wants, whatever the more specific strategic themes) is equivalent to chunks and selective descriptions that are neat and sensible, and thus promote flexibility. Therefore hiring high-quality system designers and giving them the budget and climate to produce high-quality systems is important.

The second-order policy recommendation in this case is to have a bias towards client-server architecture, which facilitates a flexible design with interchangeable chunks. This doesn't mean assuming from the outset that all systems must be cast in that mould, even if some other approach is cheaper and easier. But if, for any given application, a reasonable, natural client-server approach is feasible, then there should be a presumption that, unless there are weighty counter-factors, the client-server approach should be taken.

CONNECTIONS

4. Conceptual Schemas	About the conceptual schema
8. Internal Schema Design	Nuances in the relations of internal and conceptual schemas
9. Client-server Architecture	The client-server setup with SQL as intermediary
31. Untangling Database and Wider Issues	Relation of mix-and-match objectives to wider issues of information management

17. Mainstream Software Products

BEARINGS

The preceding briefings have analysed mainstream database systems by looking in turn at the different elements set out in the unifying chart. They concentrate on the characteristics of actual systems, rather than on the software products that support the systems.

Most of the ideas outlined in the previous briefings on access to data, CRS, client-server, data modelling and so on are only options worth knowing about because standard software products already exist to provide them.

Different software products offer different possibilities, and at some point you will need to match up what you want to do with specific products that will do it. This briefing helps by analysing the market in software products such as DBMSs, client-server software, I-CASE systems and other related software.

The survey isn't comprehensive and it avoids value judgements as far as possible. The most useful knowledge here isn't knowledge about any particular software product. What is most worth knowing is how to distinguish between *generic types* of software product.

POSSIBLE CONTEXT

Within the Mahogany Motors organisation there are already some database systems in operation and several different DBMSs. The intention now is to standardise on software products — both DBMS and other database-related software, such as development tools, client-server software and so on. There are two different motivations:

- **to rationalise** what already exists; eg perhaps there is no good reason for different departments to use different DBMSs that each have much the same qualities;

• **to keep up to date** with technology, since, however desirable continuity and standardisation may be, it is also important that the software products used be somewhere close to the best currently available.

The obstacle in the way of clear discussion about these objectives is one encountered in many fields, that might be called the Uffizi Gallery problem. The 50 paintings of Virgin and Child may be masterpieces, but viewing them all in succession is a dull experience — unless you are primed to know what to look for, and in particular, to know what features are characteristic of the different schools and periods.

Primed with comparable insights into database products, the managers at Mahogany Motors should be able to make some useful statements fairly readily; such as:

'DBMS A and DBMS B are clearly competing products with similar scope. There is a prima facie case for standardising on one (after a careful study) and dropping the other.'

'DBMS C and DBMS D are of fundamentally different types. Any detailed comparison would be pointless. The real issue is: Have we two fundamentally different sets of demands, calling for separate DBMSs?'

'Leaving aside any judgement of quality, client software product E doesn't even claim to do the same job as client software product F. Therefore, instead of comparing E against F, it would be more sensible to compare E with its true rivals.'

But, unless they know what to look for, the Mahogany managers won't be in a position to argue in this way. They will experience nothing but a long succession of products, each in some ways similar to and in other ways different from all the others.

WARRANTS

The best way of organising this field is to make the three main architectures — host, PC and client-server — the basis for the first-order breakdown.

Host Architecture Distinctions

Within the host architecture there is an initial distinction between:

• The **host DBMS** that will store data structured as a conceptual schema and provide access, CRS, data dictionary and software development features etc.

• Software products primarily intended for **application develop-**

ment — mostly given the generic name 4GL — that will access data in a DBMS.

The rationale of the second category requires explanation. It would be absurd to say 'DBMS X is the main DBMS we use; however its deep design and CRS features are not ideal; therefore we supplement them with extra features from software product Y'. Deep design and CRS features are so fundamental to the whole DBMS product that you can't just replace them and leave the rest of the software untouched. But, on the other hand, you could very well complement DBMS X with another software product that provides exceptional software development features.

Some products in this category can work on a PC, but only as a kind of tactical measure; their end-purpose is to support databases within the host architecture.

At one time there was a real distinction between host DBMS products based on relational conceptual schemas and those based on hierarchical-network. Nowadays the great majority of available products are (or claim to be) relational. However, it is still worth making a distinction between:

- Straightforward **relational** DBMSs
- DBMSs that are either pure **hierarchical-network** or offer a combination of hierarchical-network and relational features.[1]

Aspects of Relational Host DBMSs

Host DBMSs are complex things. There are many different criteria for comparison, but there is no easy way of setting up sub-categories of DBMS. Here are some *aspects* that tend to differentiate these products:

- one scores high, when assessed on **Codd's twelve rules**;
- another has highly developed features for building in rules to guarantee data validity and **integrity**;
- another is particularly **portable** between many different hardware systems;
- another has powerful **fault-tolerance** features (ie ensuring that transactions will be correctly handled even in the face of technical breakdowns);
- another is designed to optimise speed and other **efficiency** factors;
- another is exceptionally strong in supporting **distributed database** requirements;
- another has unusually rich features for **software development**.

Thus, further detailed comparisons between actual products in this one broad category would be a formidable task.

PC Architecture: Application and Product Gradations

Some DBMSs for PC are intended to deal with quite complex applications, while others are far more limited. Complexity of application is really tantamount to complexity of interaction between database tables. Here are four hypothetical application systems in ascending order of complexity:[2]

- **Gradation 1.** There is just one table of (say) dealer information. The system's main task is to update this table, subject to simple validation checks.
- **Gradation 2.** As Gradation 1, but there is also another table containing orders, outstanding and recently completed. As well as maintaining the data in the two tables, the system has to *link* them. Thus for a given dealer, it displays all the data in the *Dealer* table, together with all outstanding orders for that dealer.
- **Gradation 3.** There are four tables: *Dealer, Order, Customer, Product.* When a new sales order is input, it is validated by reference to data in all four tables; the order acknowledgement document contains data items taken from all four.
- **Gradation 4.** As Gradation 3, but the system also produces a complicated report that extracts, analyses and summarises data from all four tables; eg it shows total sales, year-to-date, for a certain model car, analysed by customer *type* within dealer *type*.

This set of gradations is a useful tool for comparing DBMS products. Almost any product is likely to handle Gradation 1 adequately, but from then on capabilities differ. In practice, there is no even spread across the gradations; most (not all) DBMS products for PC belong in out of two clusters:

- **Flat-file.** Many products are primarily useful for Gradation 1 applications. Some of them can just about handle Gradation 2, but most do so only with compromises or considerable expert effort; eg perhaps the DBMS can easily be made to find the *first* outstanding order for a given dealer, but not all — though this problem might be soluble with tremendous effort by somebody who knew the DBMS inside out. These DBMS products are not contenders for systems at Gradations 3 and 4.
- **PC-relational.** The other cluster contains products that can handle Gradations 1 to 3 reasonably well. Probably all can handle Gradation 4 *somehow*, but in some cases it will be straightforward, while with others so much expertise and sheer effort might be needed that you would probably end up compromising on some of the finer points of the sales analysis.

The term PC-relational (invented for this book) needs clarification. These products are very far from following Codd's rules for a relational DBMS, but the term isn't totally misleading. If you draw up a conceptual schema in relational style, entirely in third normal form perhaps, the DBMS can store that data and provide the links between data items inherent in the schema. But the DBMS won't provide all the automatic checking mechanisms needed to guarantee that whatever data is added or amended, the database always remains true to the relational schema. Such safeguards have to be written into the code of the application programs.

Charting PC-DBMS Issues

Some other very important features differentiate DBMSs for PC. First, features for developing, not just running, database systems are a very big issue in this field. Almost every product (not every single one) corresponds to one of these two possibilities:

- **Tools-only**. With some products you define and develop systems completely using tools (eg for defining screen formats, validation criteria etc) rather than a programming language.
- **Tools + language**. With other products the tools are bolstered by a product-specific programming language, for the relatively demanding parts of systems.

In practice, most flat-file products are tools-only products and most PC-relational are tools + language products. This is a fact, but not a logical necessity.

Either type of product normally allows use of an industry-standard language, such as Basic or C, for programs that access the database. The point about a product in the tools + language category is that its product-specific language is designed to work particularly well with that DBMS.

Another issue that often confuses analysis is this: Who is meant to use this DBMS for development — a relatively unskilled end-user, writing small Gradation-1 systems for private or small-department use, or a professional developer, developing more complex Gradation-3 systems under contract? This antithesis is too simple:

- If the database system will only ever be used to develop simple programs for near-private use, then the natural choice is a flat-file, tools-only DBMS.
- If the system is for professional-level development of complex systems, then a PC-relational, tools + language system is the clear choice.
- But even a professional developer will probably make extensive

use of tools (rather than language) on certain parts of any system, where this saves work.

- Also, with a Gradation-1 system, the best choice even for a professional developer (not just an end-user) may well be a flat-file, tools-only DBMS.
- And again, not all systems built by end-users are Gradation 1 or 2. If developing a Gradation-3 system for personal use, they will probably need a PC-relational DBMS.
- *Corollary of the above points:* People often suggest that a flat-file DBMS is easier to learn and easier to use than a PC-relational DBMS. This is true in the general sense that any instrument simpler and more limited than another will be easier to learn — but only if used for a task that suits it. A toothbrush is easier to master than a vacuum-cleaner — in general, but not if the task is to clean a carpet. A flat-file DBMS is only easier than a PC-relational, if the applications for development are Gradations 1 and 2 — not if they are Gradations 3 and 4.

A different issue altogether is the ease of use of the database system when used operationally, ie after it has been developed. For a sophisticated interface that is intuitive and pleasant to use, certain DBMSs are better choices than others. But differences between DBMSs here don't correlate with the distinction between flat-file and PC-relational. Here are some of the factors:

- Any DBMS, whether flat-file or PC-relational, that runs in the Macintosh or Windows **environment** has a huge start over one that runs under DOS — since many of the sophisticated interface features come ready-made.
- Interface quality doesn't come free. Some DBMSs are relatively weak in this area because they deliberately concentrate on some other variable, eg **efficient, fast processing**.
- For a really ingenious interface with original features, even a Gradation-1 system may demand the more advanced programming resources of a language attached to a PC-relational database.

A couple more issues do fit the two main clusters of products fairly well:

- Some DBMSs (most, though not all flat-file DBMSs) support only **one user** at a time. Some DBMSs (most, though not all, PC-relational DBMSs) also allow the database to be shared on a **multi-user** basis.
- PC-DBMSs are in general far more limited than mainframe DBMSs on **supply-side elements** such as recovery, integrity, security and deep design. Most flat-file DBMSs offer very little; most PC-relational offer slightly more.

Client-server Architecture Distinctions

The client-server architecture contains a kaleidoscopic variety of software products. Here is an initial breakdown:

• **DBMS server.** The DBMS software manages the server database. It offers features to cover most of the elements of the chart of database technology, but there is less need to provide easy access or software development features; in this architecture such things are more appropriate to the client.

As with the host DBMS, these products are huge pieces of software that may be differentiated in many ways. One product may offer an array of CRS and deep design options that an expert can tune for very efficient performance; another may have far fewer options, but it may be far easier to install to achieve adequate performance. One product may have very sophisticated CRS features for 'mission-critical' or 'fault-tolerant' applications; another may have less overhead and thus be a better buy for applications with less stringent demands.

• **Client software.** A great variety of products provide software to run on the client. They are analysed further below.

• **Middleware.** There are two main potential problems with the concept that client software issues SQL requests for data, which server software accepts and meets. First, the client and server may not use identical dialects of SQL. Second, if the client and server are remote from each other (ie not linked on the same local area network), messages will have to pass across a wide-area network, using its protocols — message formats, error recovery procedures etc. A middleware software product aims to alleviate these complications. The claim is roughly: 'Given any of the following dialects of SQL generated by the client . . . and any of the following DBMSs as server . . . and any of the following main types of network . . . this middleware software will handle all the interface problems.'

As with other translation tasks, a middleware product may adopt one of two main strategies: literally translate any of the supported SQL dialects into any other (eg dialect A straight into dialect Z) *or* use an intermediate dialect, perhaps that of some particular well-known server product (dialect A into intermediate dialect, then intermediate dialect into dialect Z).

Client Software Distinctions

SQL is the lingua franca tying together the different components of a client-server architecture, but few application systems require the user at the client PC to express access requests in SQL itself. The language is too tedious for that. Most client software products have one thing in common: they allow requests to be made at the client PC in some easy way, eg clicking with the mouse on an item in a list, and they translate this request into SQL instructions sent across the network to the server. Within that general definition there is quite a variety of software products:

• **Application development** tools and language. This software enables the development of application software to run operationally on the client. There is a labour-saving way of defining general-purpose functions (input validation criteria, screen layouts and so on), while minimising programmer involvement in the detail of interaction between client and server. One useful concept is to allow data items to have special names: if there is (say) a field, *Dealer-no* in the database, but one department prefers to call it *Showroom-code*, then the software may remember that preference and automatically translate it whenever an SQL statement is generated. A big issue in this field is whether the SQL generated should be hidden or open to amendment.

• **Enquiry facilities.** This software provides ad hoc *access* facilities to the server database; ie it is not for development of regular system functions. The aim is to make it very easy to extract data according to selection criteria and display it conveniently, perhaps with a moderate degree of analysis, eg calculating totals and averages. Some products concentrate on screen display, others on printed reports, and others are strong in both.

• **Analysis tools.** This software differs in emphasis from the previous category. It typically has more powerful 'drilling-down' and business graphics features; it might display a pie-chart analysing sales, allow selection of one slice of the pie, then display another pie-chart analysing that slice, and go on drilling down through further levels. The stress is on allowing the busy manager to analyse quantitative data from the corporate database *in the kind of way such analysis is typically done* — as opposed to providing a general-purpose facility to select any data by any criteria. These products are usually regarded as tools used by programmers to develop an EIS (Executive Information System) for their senior managers. However, computer-literate managers may find the software convenient enough to serve as ad hoc access facilities, without the intervention of programmers.

• **DBMS hooks.** This software allows a standard PC software product, a spreadsheet (say), to access data stored externally in a server database. To the user the spreadsheet may seem to function in the normal way, but behind the scenes, the extra piece of software

SUMMARY OF WARRANTS

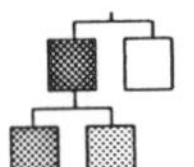
Host Architecture Distinctions: Host DBMS (relational); Host DBMS (hierarchical-network); Application development

Aspects of Relational Host DBMSs: Supporting Codd's rules; Built-in data validation rules; Portability; Fault-tolerance features; Optimised efficiency; Distributed database; Software development

PC Architecture: Application and Product Gradations: Processing: Single-table through two-linked-tables through many-linked-tables to analysis-of-many-linked-tables. Product: Flat-file through PC-relational

Chart of PC Architecture Issues: Application complexity; Development tools and language; Ease of development; Ease of use and interface; Data sharing; Other CRS factors

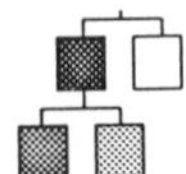
Client-server Architecture Distinctions: DBMS server; Client software; Middleware

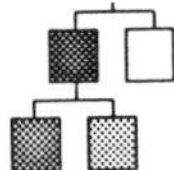
Client Software Distinctions: Application development; Enquiry; Analysis; DBMS hooks

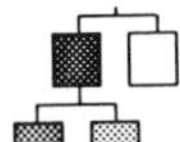
Distinctions between Products Preceding Architectures: Upper-CASE; I-CASE

is interacting with the server. Leading spreadsheet products, such as Lotus 1-2-3 and Excel, generate SQL requests for a server database, in classic fashion; they can also send requests to DBMSs, such as Paradox, dBase IV and Access, that are not accessed through SQL.

Complications arise when the PC product provided with hooks is itself a DBMS. The user of (say) a Paradox database, with DBMS hooks attached, need not care whether the data extracted comes from the local Paradox database or (say) the Oracle server database across the network. This facilitates that refinement of client-server architecture, where a small database is held at the client too. Some of the products in the other categories of client software given above also permit this client database possibility. However, this area is too murky to be clarified in a brief space; eg some application development products encourage use of a client database — but only for *testing* until the system with a server database goes live.

Products Preceding the Architectures

Most products associated with modelling data and designing systems can't really be associated with one architecture or other because they tend to operate at a pre-technology level of abstraction. In other words, a software product that helps with data modelling isn't necessarily based on any assumption about which architectures subsequent systems will run in. The main categories here are:

- **Upper-CASE** — for modelling at one particular level;
- **I-CASE** — for modelling at several levels, linking models and making them consistent.

POSSIBLE DECISION-MAKING

This breakdown of types of product can help any debate about products for Mahogany Motors, especially if the empty categories are filled in with the names of some representative products.

As the resulting table shows, one annoying complication has to be resolved in any broad review of specific products. Suppliers of host DBMS software products often compete in other categories too. On the whole, a supplier of several products will try to make them compatible. In fact, some (though not all) products are specifically intended to work only (or normally) with others from the same supplier. Sometimes relations between these products are apparent from their names and sometimes they are not: Oracle Data Browser is a product in the client enquiry category from the makers of the Oracle DBMS; and ViewPoint is a product in the same category from the makers of Informix. To avoid tedious detail, the table lists some items only as 'also from suppliers of'.

The table should make debates and decisions more disciplined:

'I think we should decide first which of the two main categories of PC DBMS we need, and only then go on to look at individual products.'

'From this glossy brochure nobody could tell whether Product P was similar in role to DataEase or PowerBuilder or SequeLink. Question the salesman far enough to assign the product to just one of the categories.'

'If you want to use software product Q to develop software to access the database managed by DBMS product R, you must be able to show how the development features provided by Q are superior to those of R itself in some way. Otherwise, using product Q seems a pointless complication.'

Mainstream Products: Categories and Examples

Category	*Representative Example Products*
Host Architecture	
DBMS	
Relational	*DB2, DEC Rdb, Empress, Informix, Ingres, InterBase, Oracle, Pace, Supra, Unify*
Hierarchical-network (maybe with some relational features)	*Adabas, Allbase, CA-Datacom, CA-IDMS, DEC DBMS, IMS*
Application Development	*CA-Ramis, Focus, Mantis, Natural, Nomad, PowerHouse*
PC Architecture	
Flat-file DBMS, without programming language	*AceFile, FileMaker, PC-File, Q&A, Reflex*
PC-relational DBMS, with programming language	*4th Dimension, Access, Advanced Revelation, DataEase, dBase IV, FoxPro, Paradox, R:Base*
Client-server Architecture	
Server DBMS	*Gupta SQLBase, Microsoft SQL Server, NetWare SQL, Sybase SQL Server, Watcom SQL also from suppliers of: DB2, Informix, Ingres, Oracle*
Client Software	
Application Development	*JAM/DBi, ObjectView, PowerBuilder also from suppliers of: Gupta SQLBase, Informix, Ingres, Oracle*
Enquiry	*Business Objects, ClearAccess, DataPrism, Intelligent Query, ReportSmith also from suppliers of: Gupta SQLBase, Informix, Oracle*
Analysis	*EISToolkit, Forest and Trees, InfoAlliance, LightShip*
DBMS hooks	*for spreadsheets: Lotus 1-2-3, Excel for PC DBMSs: Access, DataEase, dBase IV, Paradox*
Middleware	*Database Gateway, EDA/SQL, SequeLink*
Pre-Architecture	
Upper-CASE	*ER-Designer, ER-Modeler, ERwin, PC Prism*
I-CASE	*Excelerator, Foundation, IEF, Teamwork*

'To be honest, our CASE investigations haven't got very far yet. We haven't even decided whether we want an upper-CASE product such as ERWin or an I-CASE product such as IEF.'

'Forest and Trees is a good example of the analysis category of client software product. Let's think about the kind of things it might do for us. That should stimulate some ideas that might not arise if we tried to define our requirements in the abstract, or maybe help us discover that we have requirements that this kind of product can't meet. After that, we shall be well placed to compare Forest and Trees with LightShip and the other main competitors in its category.'

CONNECTIONS

15. Development Tools and Languages	This analyses approaches to software development and, along the way, mentions some random examples of actual products
28. Non-Mainstream Software Products	Software products for non-mainstream databases; possibly competitive with mainstream products in some border-line cases

18. Untangling Text Systems

BEARINGS

This is the first briefing concerned exclusively with non-mainstream database systems. Text and keyword are different from mainstream data, as Briefing 2 describes, but then so are spatial data and bit-mapped images. Why should text and keyword data be taken together?

A database storing *texts* (eg the texts of laws or of articles in legal journals) provides information useful in itself: you satisfy your requirement for knowledge by reading the text from the database. This seems a very different thing from the library database containing *keywords* that describe hundreds of thousands of texts (of laws or articles); there you only discover what texts *outside the database* are likely to be relevant or interesting, and you have to find them elsewhere.

Nevertheless, as the account in this briefing shows, the two apparently distinct categories turn out to overlap considerably. It is best to think of a continuum of possibilities extending from pure text across to pure keyword data. This briefing marks out the main variations within this field and thus provides a programme for further analysis in Briefings 19, 20 and 21.

WARRANTS

The briefing examines the subtleties of this field from five different angles.

Comparison of Text and Mainstream Database Systems

The most fundamental issue of all is whether text or mainstream database is the right technology for the application. If the requirement is to store nothing but long texts, the answer is obvious, but not all cases are clear-cut. A typical **mainstream database system** has the following traits:

- exclusively or predominantly mainstream (ie atomised, consistently patterned) data;
- segregation of logical from technical design, each with its own well-established principles;
- plenty of on-line updating, hence need for strong CRS and integrity features;
- substantial software written for the application, going with the DBMS software product to make the whole system.

A typical, large-scale **text database system** has the following traits:

- text and/or keyword (ie less atomised and consistently patterned) data predominant;
- logical design less clearly separate from technical design, with no equivalent of relational conventions and widely-taught principles of technical design;
- mainly accessing rather than updating information; integrity and CRS demands much reduced — a vast saving;
- relatively little application software; reliance on capabilities of the text DBMS software product.

This comparison has a double purpose. It helps in fundamental decisions on which way to go in a certain case. It also shows why certain issues are very important in text, while others need far less attention. [1]

Chart connecting Text and Keyword Data

The analysis just given begs an important question: Is it justifiable to put text and keyword data together in one class to be contrasted with mainstream? There are several reasons to regard pure text and pure keyword data as different points on a continuum:

- Though some databases are all text and others largely keyword data, many combine the two kinds of data, perhaps in complex ways. Often the real challenge in designing a new system is to choose the mix that will best meet people's needs for information.
- Some techniques are common to both; a search for all items in the database where the two terms 'law of the sea' and 'whales' appear together, can be done either on keywords describing texts or on the content of actual texts.
- Many non-mainstream software products are equipped to handle both text and keyword data.

In this book 'text database system' is used rather than a more precise but cumbersome expression such as 'text and/or keyword database system'.[2]

Distinctions between Access Techniques

Though text database is best taken as one field, it is useful to distinguish between the main access techniques it provides. Here they are, without nuances, in bold, primary colours:

- **Text-search.** The search request is a command, eg find all texts in the database containing the word 'devil'. The system searches the whole database. If it finds (say) 2000 items meeting the search criterion, a new command can narrow the search; eg within that set of 2000, find those that also contain 'sulphur'.
- **Keyword**. As with text-search, but the system only searches within the keywords that have been carefully chosen to describe each item.[3] Thus the complete texts of documents need not be present in the database. Moreover the keywords need not describe documents at all; the items described could be people or museum exhibits or real estate properties etc.
- **Hypertext**. Texts not keywords are stored, but the idea of *context* is used. The user of a system based on text-search or keyword access typically undertakes a number of searches, each starting afresh on the whole database. With hypertext the items of the database are arranged in a certain structure; you move around this structure; what you can access next depends on where you are at the moment; you may spend several hours with the system and never go back to the beginning and start again. In a simple hypertext database, the items might be arranged in a hierarchy; when you are looking at any particular item, the system offers you the chance of jumping to other items that are close to it in the hierarchy structure — and probably just by clicking with a mouse, rather than keying in a command. Within the general category of hypertext much variety is possible, because a simple hierarchy is only one of many ways to structure a database.

Some other access variants differ significantly from the three main cases. Here are two representative but much less common examples:

- **Text-search in context.** Text-searching can be provided without the need to formulate commands and with a small element of context. A search can be launched by clicking with a mouse on a word already present on the screen — in some systems any word on the screen, in others any word marked as a possible useful search term.
- **Dynamic keyword hierarchy.** A keyword search is done in the usual way, but after all the items meeting the search criteria have

been found, the system arranges them in the neatest, most convenient hierarchy it can devise. It takes account of all the keywords attached to the items — including those not part of the original criteria. Thus, after a search for items with keyword 'church', it might organise those items found into a hierarchy: all those whose other keywords include 'Norman' in one branch, all with 'Gothic' in another branch and so on. This creates a temporary context for browsing, analogous to that of a hypertext system.

Aspects of Advanced Text Systems

In terms of this book's unifying chart, the three main elements of concern with a database system based on text-search and keyword techniques (but leaving aside hypertext) are structure, access and deep design.

In comparison with a relational mainstream database, the conceptual schema of most text databases shows a rather simple structure. But with some of the more advanced features of text database the situation is different. A variety of possibilities can be grouped under two main aspects:

- more sophisticated access possibilities, largely through advanced ways of **indexing** material in the database; eg using a thesaurus of approved terms for searching, or letting the computer system assign keywords automatically;
- more explicit structure to hold material in a **multi-purpose form**; eg so that a text can be accessed in the database through a terminal, and also, without any reformatting, used selectively as the basis for a nicely printed book (such requirements are much more demanding than they may at first appear).

Chart connecting Hypertext to Text and Hybrid

Hypertext is a more recent technology. Its application sometimes overlaps classic text database, ie it is a rival way of doing things. It is also applicable in some areas where text database is not so relevant. Things need to be charted out with some care:

- Hypertext offers a **different way of structuring and accessing** text data from more established text-search techniques. Even in relatively simple systems, hypertext uses a more detailed and explicit structuring of items. Sometimes text-searching is the natural choice for an application and sometimes hypertext, but in many cases there is a difficult choice between the two approaches.
- There are **software products** to manage a text database and software products to manage a hypertext database. But some text

SUMMARY OF WARRANTS

Comparison of Text and Mainstream Database Systems: mainstream or text data; separation of logical and physical design, and associated techniques; updating with CRS and integrity or just accessing; application and packaged software

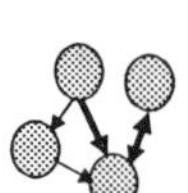

Chart connecting Text and Keyword Data: Mixture of data as best way of meeting requirements; Overlap of techniques; Overlap of software products capabilities

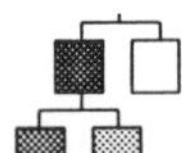

Distinctions between Text Techniques: Text-search; Keyword; Hypertext; Text-search in context; Dynamic keyword hierarchy

Aspects of Advanced Text Systems: Sophisticated indexing; Material in multi-purpose form

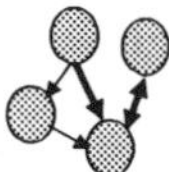

Chart connecting Hypertext to Text and Hybrid: Semi-overlap of demands met; Semi-overlap of characteristic access features; Hypertext handles graphics

---

software products offer relatively crude hypertext features as a kind of extra resource. Similarly, some hypertext software products offer some text-searching features as extras.

- Hypertext and text database are often in contention for the organisation of databases that store only text, but hypertext (despite its misleading name) is also a strong candidate for a different task: managing a database that stores a combination of **texts and graphics**.

CONNECTIONS

19. Classic Text Systems	Outline of main characteristics of classic (ie non-hypertext) text database systems; mainly, but not only, issues of structure and access
20. Advanced Text Systems	Concentrating on more advanced techniques for indexing and searching (ie accessing) text database systems, and for structuring information in a multi-purpose form
21. Hypertext Systems	Outline of main characteristics of text database systems built on hypertext principles; main attention: structure and means of access
26. Text-with-Mainstream Systems	Hybrid database systems where both text and mainstream data are prominent; range of possibilities, but integrity can be a difficult issue

19. Classic Text Systems

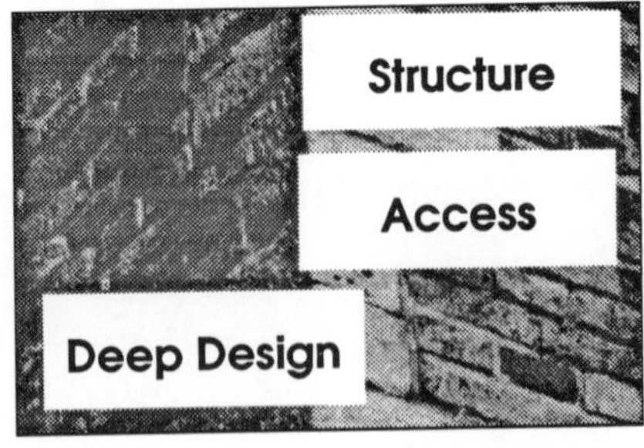

BEARINGS

In many previous briefings mainstream database systems are discussed, taking an element at a time from the unifying chart. This briefing pinpoints several elements that expose the main issues with one particular type of non-mainstream system — the classic text database system, based on text-searching and/or keyword techniques.

Since this field is large and complex, the briefing concentrates on the most classic features; the more advanced are kept back for Briefing 20.

POSSIBLE CONTEXT

Hill Banksia is a large firm of accountants. It offers clients a wide range of complementary professional services, such as management consultancy, executive search, relocation planning, market research, project management and so on.

The idea has been launched of setting up a database of texts — primarily CVs of professional staff and descriptions of projects they have done, but also other texts such as marketing material about experience in particular industries, research reports, articles published by professional staff and so on. Such a system will have two main advantages:

- People within the company can find out what experience the company possesses and use it most effectively in doing their work on assignments.
- They can assemble material to be marshalled into proposals for selling professional services to clients.

This sounds attractive, but Hill Banksia has a decision-making problem. The people — technical and non-technical — assembled as a steering committee for this project are quite knowledgeable and experienced enough to make sensible decisions about mainstream database systems. But nobody has experience of text databases. This causes them to lack confidence in grasping the true potential and limitations of the technology, distinguishing issues with far-reaching implications from less critical issues, recognising tradeoffs and so on.

They need a concentrated overview of the main possibilities arising within the technology. Then they will be able to recognise the decisions that face them and the options they have.

WARRANTS

This briefing contains eight warrant sections. The first is concerned with the chart element kind of data, the second with structure, the next four with access, the last two with deep design.

Distinctions between Roles for Information

Text and keyword are different *kinds* of information, but it is useful to analyse something slightly different — the *roles* such information can play:

- **Text-in-itself.** The database consists largely of text data, eg the text of the Bible, and the purpose of the system is to allow people to read that text.
- **Bibliographic.** The database contains data mainly concerned with describing and pointing at texts (eg books or journal articles) that are not themselves contained in the database. The kind of data it contains is typically some combination of keyword, mainstream (eg numeric classification codes) and text (eg a 100-word abstract of the ideas in a journal article, to summarise what the article is about).[1]
- **Indicative**. The database also describes and points at things outside the database, but things other than texts — eg exhibits in museums or real estate properties or people. As with a bibliographic system, there may be a combination of keyword, mainstream and text data. In this case, though, the brief texts are descriptions of things, not abstracts of other texts.

This analysis[2] allows another important distinction to be made:

- With most mainstream database systems **exact answers** are desirable and possible: 'the current quantity in stock of that product is . . .' So too with many uses of text-in-itself systems: 'yes, there is a precedent for a judge ruling that an individual could not be deported solely to a ship, as opposed to a country . . .'[3]

• But usually with bibliographic and indicative systems only **possible (not certain) answers** are appropriate; eg 'these fifteen medieval texts seem most likely to help me learn more about the Templars . . .' or 'these eight criminals seem particularly relevant to our enquiry';

Issues of role are of the first importance when a possible new system is under discussion since different roles call for different styles of conceptual schema.[4]

Distinctions between Styles of Conceptual Schema

Within the broad class of text database there are many varieties of logical structure or conceptual schema:[5]

• **Simple texts.** The database is a simple collection of texts, none of which are sub-divided any further or related to each other; eg essays by anonymous school children. This conceptual schema could hardly be more simple: the database is just a heap of items.

• **Simple texts with other data.** The database is a collection of texts, none of which are broken down any further, but each text has mainstream and keyword data fields attached to it; eg texts of news items, each accompanied by mainstream data (eg name of newspaper and date) and keywords.

• **Organised texts with other data.** The database consists of one or several texts, that are broken into sub-texts, each with mainstream and keyword data fields attached. A database storing the text of an economics textbook would be a (relatively) simple example; one storing texts of the minutes of meetings, broken down into points that are cross-related, would be more complex.

• **Records including text fields.** The database consists of records, which in turn are made up of fields, and some of these fields are texts. A database about windmills might have a record per windmill; within each record there would be mainstream fields such as *name* or *construction-year*, keyword fields for specially interesting features (eg 'mustard', 'snuff', 'vertical grinding stone', 'Fauël wings' etc) and text fields such as *history* (several hundred words, if necessary) and *state-of-repair* (another text).

• **Records without text fields.** The database consists of records, which in turn are made up of fields; none of the fields are text, but some are keywords. A library catalogue often takes this form.

Comparison between Types of Access

There are three principal ways of accessing information in a classic text database:

- **Text-search.** The system seeks out nominated search terms within the words and sentences and paragraphs of real texts.
- **Keyword.** The system seeks out nominated search terms within the keywords stored as individual fields in records.
- **Mainstream search.** As the analysis above shows, a text database may still possess mainstream fields that are useful for searching; eg a windmill's *name or construction-year* or even some numeric code devised to classify different types of windmill. But mainstream coding often has great limitations: in many areas it isn't feasible (eg try it with sociology or philosophy); also, there is no point in making an intricate breakdown of a subject into categories, unless the people who will use it are content to make the effort to master it.

Keyword access often has one clear advantage over text-searching: it gives the system far less work to do in its searching because there is less material to search; therefore it may provide faster response and/or be feasible on a cheaper computer.

Sometimes a keyword search may find useful information more effectively, even irrespective of cost. A list of 10 articles, all described by the keyword 'concrete' may be more useful than a list of 1000 articles all of whose texts contain the word 'concrete' somewhere.

On the other hand, the keyword approach often exacts a considerable cost in intellectual work: somebody has to decide on the most appropriate keywords for each item. If the database is to be accessed mainly by text-searching, the texts can be loaded in with much less indexing work.

Also, the person allocating keywords has to take a view on what labels are most likely to help a later user find relevant information efficiently. Sometimes this is difficult:

- Take a text entitled 'Paradoxes in Game Laws Relating to the Use of Automobiles in Fishing on Frozen Lakes'. What keywords should be assigned to it? Only an expert taking the time to study the text carefully could decide the most appropriate keywords to choose, and even an expert might not be able to predict who might search for the item under what circumstances.
- To extract from a database all CVs of management consultants with keywords such as 'Costa Rica' or 'pharmaceuticals' might be easy, because countries or industries are natural candidates for choice as keywords. But suppose the search was for something less predictable, eg all consultants who have done any work concerned with bassoons or with epilepsy. It probably wouldn't be safe to expect that those terms, if applicable, would be among the keywords attached to the CVs.

Examples of Boolean Searching

Retrieve all items indexed with **keywords** both *agriculture* **and** *development agency*

Retrieve all items whose **full text** contains both *agriculture* **and** *development agency*

Retrieve all items whose **full text** contains *financ** **and** **culture* **and** *wom?n*

NB * stands for any characters (however many) and ? for any one character

Retrieve all items with **keywords** meeting **any one** out of the following three conditions:

agriculture **and** *development agency*
trade **or** *trading* but **not** *urban*
finance **and** *development agency* but **not** *urban* and **not** *infrastructure*

Retrieve all items whose **full text** meets **any one** of the following four conditions:

rural **and** *trade* **within three words** of each other
agriculture **and** *trade* within the **same paragraph**
finance coming **before** *development agency* in the **same sentence**
trading **or** *development agency* but **not** *urban* in the **same sentence**

NB This shows the *logic* of typical search commands. Formulating these commands to an actual system may call for great patience in getting all the required brackets and quotation marks and full stops etc exactly right.

For cases like these, keyword access tends to fall short and full-scale text-searching may be more fruitful.

Examples of Boolean Access Facility

Boolean search is the term for the clever searching used in a text database. The representative examples in the sidebar provide an impression of the possibilities. As the example suggests, most Boolean searches can apply equally well to keyword and text access, but **proximity** criteria (eg one word in the same paragraph as another) are only relevant to text-searching.

Different systems provide this kind of access to different degrees. Some restrict search criteria to just a pair of words; others accept quite complicated expressions. Diminishing returns can set in: flexibility in defining search criteria is desirable, but beyond a certain point, people may find it just too demanding to work out how best to frame their searches.

Aspects of Interface Facility

Here are some aspects affecting the rather vague area of interface.

First, **user-friendliness.** Many systems offer a plain interface to the searcher without the pull-down, pop-up menus, split-screens and mouse-guided selection familiar to the Apple Macintosh or Windows user. Intricate Boolean searches may be done through arcane commands such as 'C 10 NOT 6', meaning 'take the set of items containing the keywords used in step 10 of the search, but excluding all those found by the keywords specified in step 6'.

One reason for old-fashioned interfaces is that many large-scale text software products were developed for use within huge organisations or even on a public service. Therefore they had to be able to work with a wide range of terminals, including the most primitive.

Second, **industry standards**. There are none. To search for texts containing (say) 'Burmese' and 'harp' together in that order, the command in one system is 'Burmese adj harp', in another 'Burmese harp', and in another 'Burmese(w)harp'.

Third, **presentation**. Systems can vary dramatically — particularly on PC. One might show one record of information on the screen at a time in a conventional plain-vanilla format. Another might put each record into a standard graphic frame resembling an index card, and permit several cards to be displayed in different screen windows. Another might frame each record as if it were notes on a scrap of paper (whose size depended on the amount of text), with the scraps presented on screen piled as an untidy heap. But, despite these differences, all three systems might have identical structuring and text-searching capabilities.

Fourth, **Type of user**. There are three main cases:

- Some systems are so powerful and intricate that they are normally used by somebody with highly developed skills in information science; very often they act as **providers** of information for others in the organisation.
- Some systems are meant to be used without any special intermediary, but they are appropriate for people who are **used to working with computers**: ie who understand how important it is to format requests precisely, who can think of explanations if the results are surprising etc.
- Some systems are meant to provide facilities simple enough for use

by **practically anybody** — perhaps including members of the public.

Aspects of Access Techniques

Learning how to formulate searches by putting logical operators ('or', 'and', 'not' etc) around the terms is only the start of using a large-scale text database system. There are associated skills and techniques:

- Sometimes a kind of **logical chaining** can be a good technique. Having used certain keywords to pick up useful items, you can see what other keywords are attached to them, then use those keywords in turn to find new items.[6]
- Sometimes it is necessary to make a judgement on the **generality** of the search. In one case, it might be wrong to limit a search to 'pizza' when a broader term like 'fast food' could throw up valuable items. Another time, 'solar energy' might be too broad and the narrower 'solar heating' might be better.
- Then again, the skillful searcher recognises instinctively when **truncation** is needed (eg 'pollut?' finds 'pollute' and 'pollution') and when there is a danger of missing things through variants of proper names (eg 'NATO' or 'N.A.T.O.' or 'North Atlantic Treaty Organization').
- The use of **key phrases** rather than keywords is another issue. A search under 'Prague' might never find items indexed under 'Prague Spring'. This is only a problem in searching keywords rather than the text of an abstract or complete document.
- **Expansion** is a relatively crude extra resource. If the searcher gives a term such as 'bankruptcy', the system responds by giving those access words it can find in the database that are close to it in spelling eg 'banknote, bankrupt, bankruptcies, bankruptcy, banner'. This is done simply on the basis of spelling; the meaning of the terms could be unrelated.
- If the **complete text** of a document is available on-line and searchable, that doesn't mean it has to be used as the target for all searches. It may be far more efficient to stick to keywords, because the text-search gives too many hits, many of which turn out to be useless. Again, this is an area where searching experience and skill are needed.
- With an **SDI** (Selective Dissemination of Information) facility, the user of a service can store whatever collection of codes, keywords, author names etc best define a profile of interests (the term 'clippings folder' is also sometimes used). Then the system itself can automatically monitor all new items added to the database and match them

against the profile; it can either send a bulletin of relevant new items at regular intervals automatically or else provide all the new items next time the user signs on to the system.

It is also possible to set up a sort of home-made SDI facility: keep an interests profile stored as a set of search commands on your own PC; then, from time to time sign on to the system and 'upload' the set of search commands.

Comparison between Main Design Possibilities

In the classic approach to the large-scale text database system, text data is loaded into the system's own database, ie a database separate from the original source of the texts. Then the system indexes this information. However, some software products don't index the information at all, and others don't even load it into the system's database. There are four possibilities to distinguish and compare:

- **Own database; indexed** — often the only feasible approach for a large-scale, complex system.
- **Own database; not indexed** — most common in low-volume, personal applications; eg a manager's personal information system (with address lists, to do lists, reference knowledge etc).
- **No own database; indexed** — can be a useful way of providing access within an office automation system to a body of documents in (say) WordPerfect format; perhaps perform the indexing at the end of each day.
- **No own database; not indexed** — like the previous case but not indexed; tradeoff: no need to spend time on separate indexing run, but searching takes longer (put another way, the volumes of text that can be searched within an acceptable response time are lower).

Example of Deep Design Choices

Systems with hundreds of millions of characters of text are invariably pre-indexed. If somebody keys in a request for all the documents in which the word 'rural' appears, it is not really acceptable for a system to start looking at the first character of the first document and work all the way through to the end, noting all the occurrences of 'rural' along the way.

When every word in any document (other than a set of trivial 'stop' words such as 'the', 'at', 'however' etc), is indexed, the resulting huge index is called an **inverted file**. The system can go to this index, look for 'rural', and there find (say) the five documents where that word appears.

But there are many different ways of designing such indexing

Text Database: Very Detailed Indexing

	document	*paragraph*	*sentence*	*word*
rupture	121	6	1	4
rural	**5**	**6**	**2**	**1**
rural	**16**	**8**	**3**	**5**
rural	**67**	**2**	**1**	**3**
rural	**70**	**3**	**6**	**21**
rural	**68**	**23**	**3**	**6**
rust	73	15	6	17
rust	2	6	2	2
rustic	45	9	8	14
toy	91	16	4	19
trace	132	63	6	4
trace	127	2	2	5
trade	**8**	**7**	**3**	**8**
trade	**16**	**8**	**3**	**11**
tramp	34	14	3	15

Using this enormous index, the system can handle a proximity search such as:

find all the documents where 'rural' occurs within the same sentence and within three words of 'trade'

In this example there is a near miss.
The two terms do appear in the same sentence in document 16, but 6 words apart.

arrangements and much scope for skill and expertise. Here is an example to give a flavour of the kind of issues involved.

Suppose the indexing is detailed enough to record that 'rural' appears as word 1 of sentence 2 of paragraph 6 of document 5, and again as word 5 of sentence 3 of paragraph 8 of document 16, and so on, as in the diagram. This makes the system very efficient at handling proximity searches. Most of the search processing can be done on the index, without even looking at the real text itself.

An alternative is to index each word only down to the level of document and paragraph — not sentence or word within sentence. Now a proximity search could still be handled, but it would take longer. The system would carry out some processing on the indexes and then carry out further checks at sentence and word level on the text itself. There are tradeoffs:

- The first approach is faster on the tricky **proximity searches**, because its indexes are more detailed. But this means that it takes longer to construct new indexes (when new data is added), and that

SUMMARY OF WARRANTS

Distinctions between Roles for Information: Text-in-itself (precise answers); Bibliographic (possible answers); Indicative (possible answers)

Distinctions between Styles of Conceptual Schema: Simple texts; Simple texts with other data; Organised texts with other data; Records including text fields; Records without text fields.

Comparison between Types of Access: Text-searching; Keyword; Mainstream code

Examples of Boolean Access: Combination, truncation and proximity refinements

Aspects of Interface: Friendliness; Standardisation; Presentation; Type of user

Aspects of Access Techniques: Logical chaining; Search generality; Truncation; Key phrases; Expansion; Text; SDI

Comparison between Main Design Possibilities: Database indexed or not; Separate database or not

Example of Deep Design Choices: Indexing strategy: tradeoffs between access refinement, access speed and overhead

---

it bears an extra index-processing overhead on all its accesses, even the simple ones.

- The second is less efficient on the proximity searches, but, being less elaborate, it is **more efficient** in other ways: constructing simpler indexes means less work and a simple access (eg find any document with the word 'rural' anywhere in the text) bears less overhead.

Plainly, choice between such options should take account of the types of search expected and their relative frequency and importance. This is not *the* important tradeoff in the deep design of text databases, merely a representative example, giving an *impression* of the kind of issues that arise as supply interacts with demand.

POSSIBLE DECISION-MAKING

The members of Hill Banksia's steering committee soon realise that the field of text database is vastly more complex than they had expected. Most of the issues aren't really technical ones, in the sense that people normally think of the term, and yet they are issues calling for some fairly powerful abstract thought.

One natural starting point seems to be the mesh of distinctions between kinds of data and structure and access. But, it soon becomes plain, there are any number of possible combinations of choices on these matters — far too many for well-organised decision-making.

To deal with this perplexity the Hill Banksia committee sketches out the following plan of approach for investigating the demand and supply options:

- Sketch the outlines of the most natural, plausible system imaginable, and define this system in terms of the warrants of the briefing: On the conceptual schema issue this system takes the 'simple texts with other data' option; on the issue of types of access . . .' etc.
- Then consider plausible variants: eg a system exactly the same except with a different choice on the issue of types of access . . .
- By considering many such variants develop a whole set of possible combinations of choices. Along the way knock out those that seem less relevant or inferior.
- End up with (say) four different options — possible systems each defined in terms of the warrants.
- Get an expert to study each of the four in detail to contrast drawbacks, costs, risks and so on.
- Insist that the expert reports in a format that clearly describes the four main options in terms of the warrants in the briefing and contrasts them in business-like terms.

Once that material is available well-informed decision-making can begin. . .

CONNECTIONS

20. Advanced Text Systems	More complex problems and approaches
21. Hypertext Systems	A rival technology
26. Text-with-Mainstream Systems	Systems where text is mixed with mainstream data
28. Non-Mainstream Software Products	Software products for text database

20. Advanced Text Systems

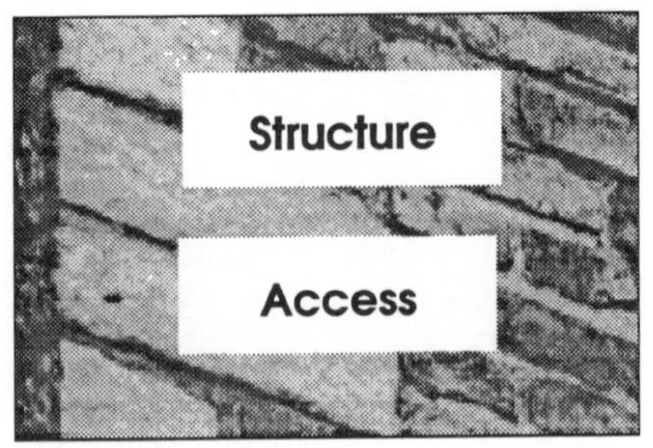

BEARINGS

For all the complications of transaction processing with distributed databases, many people who know both mainstream and text database systems find text database the more fascinating. In a sense, every database system is a means of imposing order on the slippery complexity of things and events out in the world, but with an advanced text system the sense of fashioning an incisive instrument to master treacherous information is at its most striking.

The previous briefing sets out the most fundamental themes of text database, and this one goes on to explore more advanced features in two particular directions: sophisticated indexing of information for better access; and structuring text information to make it reusable for different contexts and purposes.

POSSIBLE CONTEXT

The Yertchuk Documentation Centre is a combined library, museum and art gallery about the history and culture of the Yertchuk region. The centre already has a computer system that stores information helping people to use the collection.

Every book, document or object has brief information defining it (eg name, author etc) and describing it (eg 50-word abstract of a document's content) and indexing it (either a subject code or several keywords or both). The information can be used in searches; eg to find every item with the word 'gold' in its descriptive text; to find all items with both 'windmill' and 'corn' as keywords etc. But the system falls short in two main ways:

- **Access**. The search facilities are less useful than expected. Beginners often search on (say) 'gold' and never realise they miss many references including the word 'golden'. Also, sophisticated users become infuriated, knowing only too well that unless they can think up all the synonyms and near-synonyms of 'corn' ('wheat', 'grain', 'maize' etc), they may miss useful items.

- **Multi-purpose information.** Recording all the information in the database was a large data-encoding task but a greater intellectual one (writing the brief descriptions, thinking out the keywords and codes etc). The hope was that, once in the computer system, the information could also be used for many spinoff purposes; eg print out an attractively formatted catalogue of all the Centre's pre-1900 paintings. A simple selective listing of database contents is indeed possible, but a great deal of typographic, editing and other intellectual work is still needed to make an acceptable document.

Yertchuk is therefore interested in exploring opportunities for making a text database more sophisticated in two main directions: one is more subtle forms of indexing, the other multi-purpose use of content.

WARRANTS

The first three warrant sections are about access: issues in the indexing and associated organisation of text. The other four are about structure: permitting the multi-purpose use of document content.

Distinctions between Thesaurus-like Approaches

Practically every text database system raises the problem of using terminology consistently. Even a manager in the electrical industry keeping a small database of personal jottings may search in vain on 'GEC' and 'General Electric' and 'G.E.' for an item that is indexed as 'GE'. In a larger database it may be vital to search on 'CAD', rather than 'computer-aided design'.

Different but associated is the point that some words or phrases are **broader terms** than others. To use a database of geological information you may need to know that 'lava' is a broader term than 'volcanic rocks' (ie all volcanic rocks are lava, but not all lava is volcanic rocks); but 'lava' is a narrower term than 'andesite' (all lava is andesite, but . . . etc).[1] If you don't know these things you may search on 'lava', be disappointed at not finding all the information you wanted and not think to search on 'andesite'.

It is probably even more important to know that the people who set up the keywords have standardised on the term 'dolerite', rather than its **synonym** 'trap'. There are various ways of coping with these and similar issues. First, distinguish these four:

- **Open source**. This is the do-nothing option: no particular guidelines on search terms.
- **Controlled vocabulary**. This is normally a printed document laying down preferred terms; eg 'dolerite' should be used instead of 'trap' or 'GE' instead of 'General Electric'. Consulting this document can help in formulating search requests efficiently. The content of this document can also be stored in the computer system itself and referred to on screen.
- **Thesaurus**. This controls vocabulary but goes further. It structures the terminology; eg by saying that 'lava' is a broader term than 'volcanic rocks'. It can be a printed document or available on-line. A thesaurus in this usage is a richer, more ambitious thing than the book *Roget's Thesaurus*; that merely lists words of similar meaning, without showing how they overlap.
- **Active thesaurus**. Here the thesaurus is stored in the system and can take an active part in the search process. Thus if a search asks for items with the keyword 'andesite', the system can automatically search for the narrower terms 'lava' and 'volcanic rocks' as well. Also, if a search is made on 'trap' it can automatically search on the preferred term 'dolerite' as well.

Actually there are more possibilities than four: eg access to a certain database might be open source for text-searching but active thesaurus for keywords. There are more options still, because **setting up** keywords is different from **using** them in searches; eg:

- Keywords might be set up very carefully using a controlled vocabulary, but the people accessing the data might habitually ignore the thesaurus and frame open source requests.
- *Or* keywords might be set up using a sophisticated thesaurus, but the people accessing the data might work from a simpler controlled vocabulary.
- *Or* keywords might have been set up inconsistently in the past or by people with disagreements about vocabulary (thus effectively open source), but searchers might use a thesaurus to find their way around the subject.

For clarity, note that with any keyword approach the indexer may set up keywords that don't exist in the actual text; eg a scientific article might mention 'bio-engineering' in nearly every paragraph, but the indexer might still assign the keyword 'bio-technology' as the most helpful (with open source), or (with controlled vocabulary) because that is the preferred term for the database as a whole.

Example of Automatic Indexing

Within a keyword approach there is another issue: whether to use automatic indexing. Suppose the computer system could examine the texts of new documents added to the database and then decide automatically what keywords to allocate. This would avoid the need for a human indexer — potentially a great advantage, since otherwise the indexer may have to be an expensive, knowledgeable person, doing rather tedious work and yet still making mistakes. Here is an example of the way a representative system for automatic indexing can be set up.

First, decide on say 30 category names, with the intention that it should be possible to give every article in a certain journal one of the thirty as a keyword. Then assign the categories yourself to a representative set of articles. Store the titles and abstracts of these articles, together with your assigned category names, in the computer. Then make the computer process this material as follows:

- delete from the titles and abstracts common ordinary words such as 'the', 'of' etc;
- delete also any specialised words that crop up very frequently in this set (eg 'species' if all the articles were from a journal about evolutionary biology);
- to the residue apply intricate maths techniques that measure how well particular words in the titles and abstracts cluster within a certain subject category; eg the word 'Mendel' is almost only ever associated with those articles about 'genetics' (one of the 30 category names);
- end up by identifying an optimum set of about 100 terms associated most clearly with the 30 categories.

After this intensive work you have a set of 100 terms which provide a basis for automatic indexing. Whenever a new journal article comes in, the system can search the title and abstract for any of the 100 terms, and, on the basis of its findings, automatically allocate the article to one of the 30 categories.

There is no need to know a great deal about the mechanics of automatic indexing. The purpose of this example is to give an *impression* of what is typically involved. Plainly, automatic indexing is likely to work better in some situations than others.

Automatic and manual indexing may be combined; eg have somebody check the automatic keywords, or add new keywords in subject-areas where the automatic facility is known to be less effective.

Example of Best Match Searching

Another approach rests on the following idea. If you know exactly what piece of knowledge you want, then it is often easy to frame a search request for it, but suppose you know only roughly what might be of interest. You can extract all items containing (or indexed by) plausible search terms, but there could be thousands of items. Suppose the software applied criteria for *ranking* the likely value of items found. Then you could examine (say) the top twenty, or perhaps work down the list until diminishing returns set in.

Here is an impression of this **Best Match Searching** technique. A database stores anthropological field notes and related documentation about the culture of a certain tribe. Rather than formulate a Boolean search, you key in a phrase or sentence describing your interest eg 'How do village chiefs behave on feast days — wear feathers, paint their bodies, take drugs?' The system ignores the grammar of the phrase and picks out all the significant words to search on (village chief, feather etc). In these searches many items in the database get at least one hit, some more. The system ranks the value of all these hits, according to its criteria; eg:

- Other things being equal, the **more hits** any document gets from the keyed-in terms, the higher it ranks.
- Other things being equal, hits on **words that are rare** in the database (eg feather 78 appearances) are more valuable than hits on more common words (eg feast day 511 appearances).
- The above two criteria interact; the ranking algorithm might assess a document with hits on two rare words as more valuable than one with three hits all on less rare words.

Working this out behind the scenes, the system produces a list of items in descending order of likely interest. You might work carefully through twenty or thirty *or* quickly decide to try again with a whole new group of terms *or* study a few items, focus your interest better and frame a more precise Boolean search.

In its most sophisticated form, such a system can use feedback. The users tell the system which items they actually did find most useful; this data can automatically adjust the weights of the ranking criteria applied in future searches.

Gradations of Text Availability

With a mainstream database system, information is presented on the screen and can also be printed out. With a text database system, things are not so simple; several cases have to be distinguished:

- Gradation 1 is the classic **bibliographic** database system. This system only holds data — titles, abstracts, keywords and the like — about books, journal articles and other documents, whose texts are not in the database. The system may print out lists of references, but you have to order the document itself from a library, or go and make a photocopy of it.

- Gradation 2 is the case where the database system itself will **accept an order** for documents. Having obtained bibliographic information about (say) ten relevant articles, you place an order with the system for copies. That order is sent by the system, perhaps over a telecoms network, to an appropriate library or perhaps to the publisher of a journal, and in due course the copies arrive.
- With Gradation 3 document pages are held as bit-mapped **images** on high-capacity storage such as optical disk. They need not be accessible on-line. From the user's point of view, the ordering service is the same as with Gradation 2, except that document images could be printed out from the disk and delivered faster — in hours rather than days.
- A Gradation 4 system does store the **complete text** of documents and make it available, albeit within certain constraints. Having used bibliographic data to track down likely documents, you can display their text on the screen. This could have two different purposes: you find precisely the information you were looking for; *or* by looking at the texts on the screen of ten promising references, you know which three are the important ones and you order copies of them. But there is an important constraint at this gradation. What is displayed on the screen is generally a more primitive version of the printed document: photos and drawings may be missing; diagrams, wordcharts, tables and formulae may be missing or presented in a crude form; typographic detail (italics, different point sizes etc) may be flattened out.
- Gradation 5 arises when the system stores not only the simple characters of the text of the document, but sufficient additional **formatting detail** to reproduce the original document (or at least close to it) on screen or printed out.
- Though important conceptually, Gradation 5 by itself is rarely a good buy. Having paid the substantial price of storing formatting detail, it is usually worthwhile to go a little further to Gradation 6 by adding the ability to **dissect documents**. Thus, you could ask the system to print out in the original form ten documents but only certain portions of them: say, the introduction and conclusions sections of each. A related feature at Gradation 6 is to store formatting detail in such a way that a document can be printed out again as close as possible to the original in different technology environment, ie with a different type of printer or a printer where the original fonts are not available but close substitutes are.

Examples of the Complexity of Text

To understand the technology underlying Gradation 6 systems it is best to have a good impression of where the difficulties lie in recording a text's **logical structure**. Everything stems from the fact that — as the example shows — a document, even if mainly straight text, is more than just a string of characters and spaces arranged in paragraphs.

- **Format and structure.** Usually, some parts of a document are in a different format from others: eg some words are in italics, some whole lines are bold, some in larger type. One format device may serve several purposes; eg italics may convey stress on important or surprising words or may indicate a foreign word (eg *echt*) or may play a structural role, eg in a heading. The reader is assumed to grasp that the use of italics in one place is an important signpost to structure, though in another place it is not. But a computer can't tell; it needs some more explicit coding of structure.
- **Format and content.** There is a distinction between the content of the text and its formatting (typeface, type size, page design etc) in any particular production. It would still be natural to say that two productions were presenting the same content, even if differences of formatting were dramatic. On the other hand, if any minor changes were made to the text itself (eg '*echt*' replaced by 'authentic'), it would be natural to say that the content had changed. If a document contains tables and diagrams the distinction between content and document-format becomes more striking. A table of tides might be printed out in quite different formats (different column widths, different type face, different page breaks, different vertical and horizontal rules etc) in two almanacs, but it would still be natural to say that the same content had been printed in both.
- **Format-independent structuring.** As soon as the idea is accepted that a database might record the structure and content of a piece of document in some way independent of its formatting, a new possibility arises. Why not structure the text in a more explicit and rigorous form than it would normally take on the page? You could distinguish (say) material at a summary level from detail-level material. If it fitted the subject, those parts of the text about theory and principle could be distinguished from other parts containing facts and examples of actual practice.

Examples of Using Documents' Logical Structure

If a database system can make proper sense of the distinctions

Text: Format and Structure

Italics used for structure (headings) and foreign words and random stress on important words

Social Security Systems
There are two main models for a national system of social security: the *Bismarck* (or *Continental*) and the *Beveridge*.
No state operates a pure version of either model. Most advanced European countries have a Bismarck system, though each deviates from the pure model to some degree.

The Bismarck Model
One characteristic of the Bismarck model is its stress on the analogy to conventional insurance. Just as you insure against your house burning down, so you insure against being unable to work through illness.
An *echt* Bismarck system applies the principle that an insurance premium should be related to the risk it covers. If workers in one industry are sick more often than those in another, then *ceteris paribus* their compulsory insurance contributions should be higher. *Thus, a construction worker might have to pay more than a bank clerk with a similar salary.*

Same text, same structure, different formatting

Social Security Systems
There are two main models for a national system of social security: the *Bismarck* (or *Continental*) and the *Beveridge*.
No state operates a pure version of either model. Most advanced European countries have a Bismarck system, though each deviates from the pure model to some degree.

The Bismarck Model
One characteristic of the Bismarck model is its stress on the analogy to conventional insurance. Just as you insure against your house burning down, so you insure against being unable to work through illness.
An *echt* Bismarck system applies the principle that an insurance premium should be related to the risk it covers.

Same text — as stored in database, with format-independent structuring

main heading	Social Security Systems
summary theory	There are two main models for a national system of social security: the *Bismarck* (or *Continental*) and the *Beveridge*.
summary facts	No state operates a pure version of either model. Most advanced European countries have a Bismarck system, though each deviates from the pure model to some degree.
sub-heading	The Bismarck Model
summary theory	One characteristic of the Bismarck model is its stress on the analogy to conventional insurance. Just as you insure against your house burning down, so you insure against being unable to work through illness.
detail theory	An *echt* Bismarck system applies the principle that an insurance premium should be related to the risk it covers. If workers in one industry are sick more often than those in another, then *ceteris paribus* their compulsory insurance contributions should be higher. *Thus, a construction worker might have to pay more than a bank clerk with a similar salary.*
detail facts	In the Netherlands, the economy is divided, for the purposes of

between formatting, structure and content, then all kinds of useful multi-purpose functions become possible:

- You could easily bring together the introduction and conclusions sections of each of ten documents and thus **make a new document**.
- If the originals were in a variety of typefaces and used different conventions for indicating headings, you could give them a **consistent format** in a new document — simply by adjusting a few codes.
- By adjusting a few other codes you could ensure that the same content printed nicely in **different productions** of the document; eg as camera-ready copy for the pages of an A5-size paperback book or as A4 pages on a home laser printer with a limited range of fonts.
- Without having to key in all the data over again you could change some codes in order to print out a complex table in an **improved format** over the original.
- More interesting than any of the above from the database point of view — you could hold pieces of text on **different planes**. Portions of texts marked structurally as 'notes for experts' might only be displayed on screen to a person choosing to call himself an expert; there could be 'explanations for beginners', suppressed for those who were not beginners; some texts on geography could be marked as suitable only for those who also had a strong interest in geology; and so on. This kind of thing can be done to only a moderate degree in the formatting of a book, but with a database the possibilities are endless.
- A similar concept can govern **customised publishing** of text. Suppose a certain product, eg a combine harvester, has numerous features, for each of which numerous options exist. Ideally each customer would receive supporting technical documentation exactly tailored to the particular options chosen. But this would be hopelessly expensive and error-prone to achieve by normal technology. If some coding system exists to mark out all the discrete logical elements and their variants that make up the master documentation, then it becomes at least feasible, though still tricky, to tailor each set of documentation. A similar application is the production of different editions of a magazine, with advertising and editorial content varied according to subscribers' location, age, business sector and so on.

Chart of SGML, Other Standards and Concepts

SGML (the letters stand for nothing very meaningful) is a set of conventions for placing tags (ie codes) within documents to record the logical structure. A tag can record (say): 'this paragraph, whatever typographic format it may be given, is a chapter name' or 'this paragraph is a sub-heading' or 'the following set of numbers is the data of a table which, however it may be presented within an actual book, logically has 268 rows, each of 1450 columns'. The tags say nothing about format. One print program may format every piece of text tagged as a sub-heading in italics, Avant Garde font, 12 point with a space of 16 points above and 8 points below; another program displaying the text on a screen may adopt some completely different format.

As well as this, the *relationships* between the tags are contained in a separate file defining a document's general structure: eg a section (which starts with a <SECTIONHEADER> tag) may contain any number of sub-sections (which always start with a <SUBSECTIONHEADER> tag) etc. This is a meta-file *about* the document. A program for customised publishing or one to display only information on certain planes from the database can use this meta-file as its guide to the structure of the texts.

Here is a chart of some industry standards and related things around this SGML concept:

- **SGML** is a set of conventions: tags, such as <CHAPTERTITLE>, can be included in a document, independent of formatting details; and a separate meta-file can describe how the components marked by the tags fit together in the logical structure of the document.[2]
- **Software** products that handle documents — eg word-processing or text-database software — are beginning to support the SGML standard, ie to put documents into SGML format and to recognise and use them.
- **CALS** is a broader standard, which says in effect: use SGML for text; use various other standard formats for other things (eg CGM for business graphics, IGES for more complex engineering graphics) and fit those different components together to make up one document in the following standard way . . .
- CALS is sometimes called a **compound document architecture**; ie a standard for bringing together in one document information of distinct kinds, while retaining logical structure.
- **ODA** and **CDA** are other such architectures with their own adherents too. They are relatively less concerned with the refinements of logical structure and more with the challenge of combining genres in compound documents in the office: say, a memo text with a piece of spreadsheet, a bar chart and voice commentary — delivered by electronic mail, perhaps to different recipients in different versions. But with this stress they just slip away across the border from database into other technology domains.

SUMMARY OF WARRANTS

Distinctions between Thesaurus-like Approaches: Open source v controlled vocabulary v thesaurus v active thesaurus; Text v keyword; Setup v usage

Example of Automatic Indexing: Correlate terms in titles etc with pre-defined subject categories

Example of Best Match Searching: Searching an anthropology database with rambling phrases, and ranking those items found

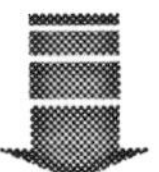

Gradations of Text Availability: Bibliographic only; Bibliographic + order facility; Bibliographic + images; Bibliographic + simple text; Bibliographic + formatted text; Bibliographic + multi-purpose text

Examples of the Complexity of Text: Formatting, structure, content and new opportunities for format-independent structuring

Examples of Using Documents' Logical Structure: Dissect and combine documents; Make composite documents consistent; Print on different hardware; Reformat tables; Data on different planes; Customised publishing

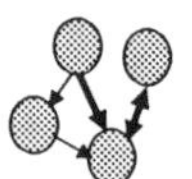

Chart of SGML, Other Standards and Concepts: SGML (tags and meta-file); SGML software; CALS; Compound document architecture; CDA; ODA

POSSIBLE DECISION-MAKING

From all this knowledge the Yertchuk decision-makers spot one particular point that seems important:

- The matter of **general-purpose data** is a high-commitment one. A lot of quite difficult (and therefore risky) design and coding work has to be done upfront. The benefits flow later. Also it is probably awkward to go back and amend the original design and coding of such a database. Thus, however great the eventual benefits, a large commitment is required.
- But matters of thesaurus and indexing seem to permit more flexibility; eg you could start with a very small thesaurus and extend

it gradually. You could, within some limits, replace one thesaurus by another without having to redesign or recode your database.

It is tempting to adopt a masterplan strategy to set up both advanced general-purpose data and comprehensive thesaurus and indexing facilities. Perhaps that really is the best decision, but it shouldn't be taken unless other strategies have been considered too. Yertchuk looks at four strategy options in detail; this range of four is best understood as offering a range of commitment and flexibility possibilities:

- **Strategy A.** Ignore the matter of general-purpose data for now; review it in a few years time; meanwhile concentrate on building extensive new thesaurus facilities.
- **Strategy B.** Ignore the matter of general-purpose data for now; review it in a few years time; meanwhile experiment with a variety of access techniques in different knowledge areas — controlled vocabulary, active thesaurus, automatic indexing, best match searching, perhaps others; learn from this experience, before strong commitment to any particular technique.
- **Strategy C.** Concentrate on the problem of general-purpose data. Keep it as simple as possible, and within just one part of the database. See how successful that is before deciding whether to extend it to other parts, or to concentrate on thesaurus and related matters instead.
- **Strategy D.** Make a five-year step-by-step master plan now, that firms up an integrated design for general-purpose data and thesaurus and automatic indexing and the other access techniques.

Other strategies are possible too of course; the main point is that setting out and comparing the strategy options in this style provides a reasonable chance of finding the best-buy or least-bad choice.

CONNECTIONS

19. Classic Text Systems	Basic text issues and approaches
21. Hypertext Systems	A rival technology
26. Text-with-Mainstream Systems	Advanced systems that combine text data with mainstream data

21. Hypertext Systems

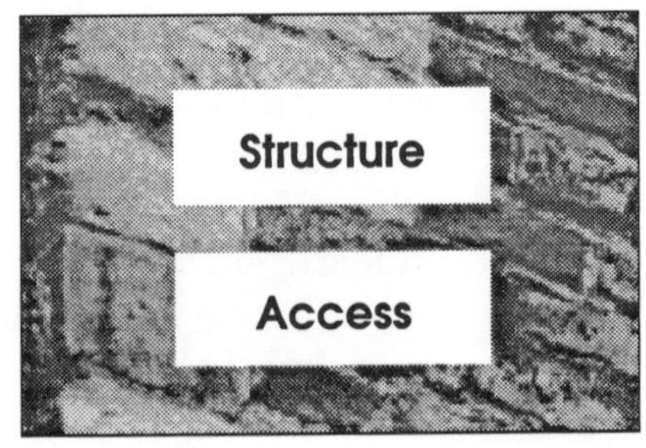

BEARINGS

Hypertext is a relatively new addition to the range of practical options for organising a database. It differs fundamentally from the longer-established approaches to text database of the previous two briefings. With hypertext the items of the database are arranged in a certain structure and you move around this structure. As with the rooms of a museum, the information you can see next depends on where you are at the moment. For some applications this may make hypertext a better choice than classic text database; for others the reverse will be true.

A hypertext database is also more adept at storing images and other kinds of data along with text. (For this reason hypertext is a rather confusing name for the technology.)

This briefing concentrates on the fundamentals of the *hypertext style* of structuring and accessing information. This can be discussed best with reference to text data alone, without the distractions of images or other data. Briefing 23 is about picture database systems and there hypertext plays a very prominent part.

POSSIBLE CONTEXT

Red Box Data Services (RBDS) was once an ordinary computer services bureau, but it has formed a new business strategy — to develop new types of electronic publishing product. One of RBDS's projects is based on the idea of reviving the *Red Sallee Guide to India and the Sub-Continent*. This is a well established, rather old-fashioned guidebook. It is extensive (800 pages of small print); there are hardly any photos, maps or drawings; its information is organised as 50 railway-based routes; knowledge is provided about the cultural and historical associations of the places to be visited, rather than practical matters (eg about hotels or museum opening times).

Why not store the content of this book as a database? This should allow people to access its knowledge in ways not feasible with a book. Take a simple example: while reading on the screen about a certain Parsee temple in Bombay, the reader might call up information about the Parsee religion in general, read it, and then continue reading about the temple.

There is one immediate strategic choice in designing such a knowledge product;

- *either* make a lavish **multimedia** product; supplementing the book's text in the database with many colour photos, and (probably to a lesser degree) music, other sounds, animation and motion video; *implications*: supply database on CD; restricting potential market to people who have fairly powerful PCs, and making the database rather difficult to use on a portable PC;
- *or* make a less glamorous, **text-only** product; *implications*: supply database on normal magnetic diskette; can be used with less powerful PC; could reasonably be used on a portable PC taken on a journey through India.

Since RBDS already has other projects experimenting with multimedia database products, it seems a good idea to opt for an experimental product based on the second, less glamorous approach. The following chain of reasoning now arises:

- As the example of the Parsee temple shows, a database system clearly can offer *some* extra ways of navigating around textual content that are not easily possible with a book.
- Moreover, it is fairly well accepted that the technology of hypertext is the natural one for this kind of application.
- The real question is whether a hypertext database is *so very much better* as a source of knowledge than a book, that people will want to incur the extra costs and complications of using a computer rather than a book.
- To debate this question, RBDS decision-makers need to obtain a clear analysis of the possibilities for organising knowledge that are available in hypertext technology.

WARRANTS

The warrant sections in this briefing are largely concerned with showing how a hypertext system differs from text or keyword systems, on the one hand, and from a conventional printed book on the other. Most attention centres on issues of information structure and access.

Comparison of non-Hypertext Possibilities

The best approach to the possibilities and limitations of hypertext is to see how the more traditional approaches fare in structuring information.

With **keyword and text-searching**, you frame the search command and the system searches the whole database. If it finds a great many items, you may narrow the search with additional criteria. Eventually you have the items you need. To get new information you start the process over again, with a search of the whole database. Here the database is really structured as a heap of items, to be accessed by combinations of search terms in any number of possible ways.

Searching in this way through information about Indian architecture may work well if you want to know about some particular building, but a search on some general term, eg Mughal, may yield hundreds of hits; how do you know which are most relevant to your needs? Or suppose you want a beginner's overview of the main styles of architecture, or a list of the most important examples of a certain style to study, or of the important temples fairly near Madras? What words can you search on to find that kind of knowledge? It would be far easier if the database had some clear structure that showed how all its material was arranged — as a book might.

By comparison, a **printed book** has a very clear structure; the pages are in sequence and (if it is non-fiction) the content is usually organised in some natural hierarchy. But this is often too rigid:

- Suppose a guidebook is organised in alphabetical order of place. The first major body of information might be about Agra: the Taj Mahal, Agra Fort and other buildings of classic Mughal style; and nearby Fatehpur Sikri, 16th century, built by a Mughal emperor, but experimenting in Hindu, Buddhist and Persian styles. But it seems very odd to start learning about a country's history and architectural styles in the 16-17th century and come to early periods later as alphabetical chance determines. Moreover, if you do want to get up to speed with the Mughals first, it would be better to find out about Delhi and Jaipur at the same time, rather than wait for their turn in the alphabet.
- Of course, the book could be organised chronologically by architectural style, rather than alphabetically, but that would make it difficult to find individual places. And what about religion and history? Many but not all buildings of interest are temples, some associated with important historical events and some not. A book can't be organised primarily by alphabetical location *and* by ar-

Example of Hypertext Access

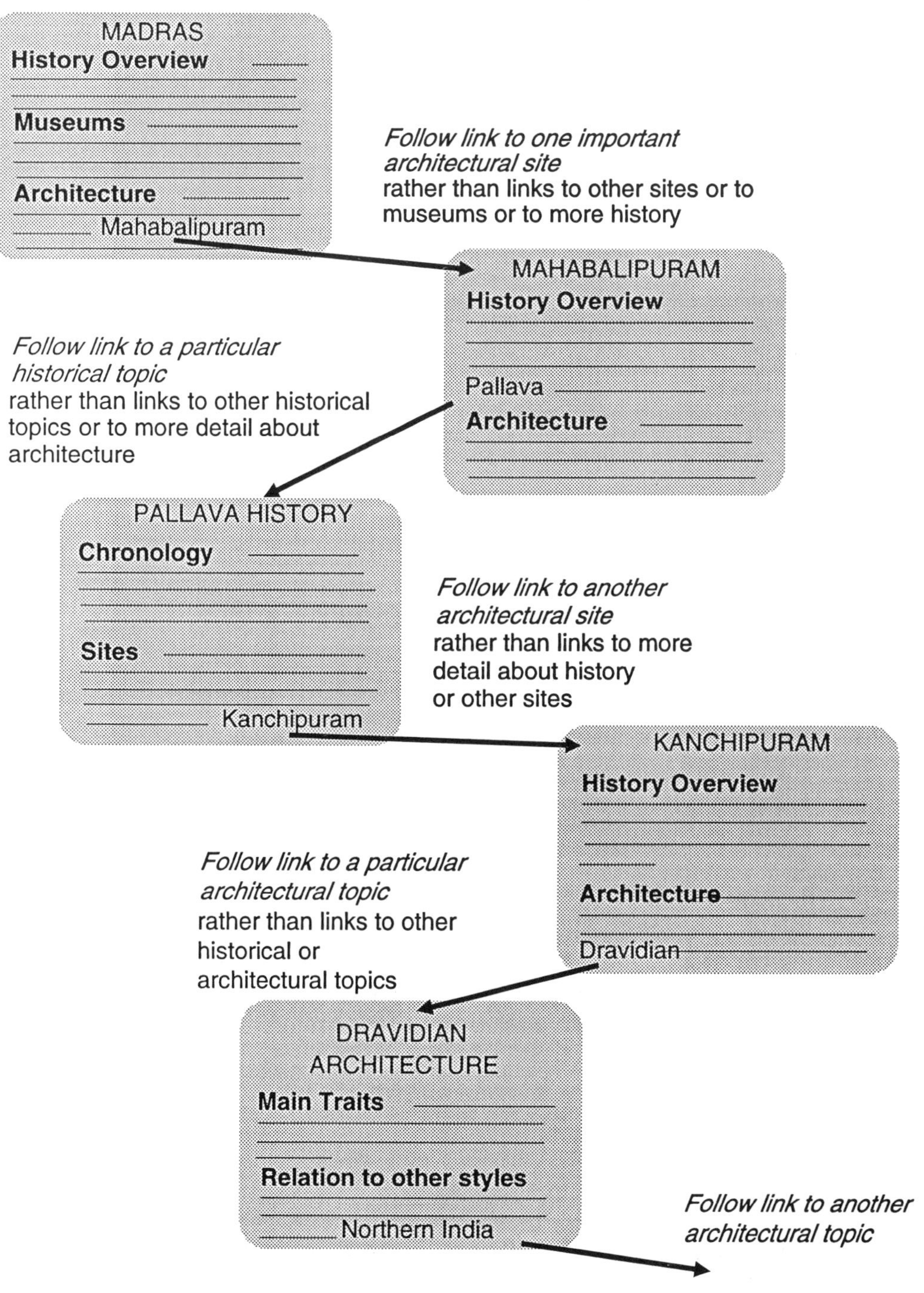
MADRAS
History Overview
Museums
Architecture
Mahabalipuram
Follow link to one important architectural site
rather than links to other sites or to museums or to more history
MAHABALIPURAM
History Overview
Pallava
Architecture
Follow link to a particular historical topic
rather than links to other historical topics or to more detail about architecture
PALLAVA HISTORY
Chronology
Sites
Kanchipuram
Follow link to another architectural site
rather than links to more detail about history or other sites
KANCHIPURAM
History Overview
Architecture
Dravidian
Follow link to a particular architectural topic
rather than links to other historical or architectural topics
DRAVIDIAN ARCHITECTURE
Main Traits
Relation to other styles
Northern India
Follow link to another architectural topic

chitectural style *and* by religion *and* by history. One dimension or another must be the primary one and the others must suffer to some degree.

At some point any book format becomes inadequate if its information exists in several different dimensions, each needing a different structure.

Example of Hypertext

Hypertext, unlike keyword and text, holds its information in a certain structure — perhaps a simple hierarchy like a book's, but perhaps something more complex than any book could support. You move around this structure; what you access next depends on where you are at the moment. When you are looking at any particular item, the system offers the chance of jumping to several other items close to it in the structure — and by clicking with a mouse, rather than keying in a command. The diagram illustrates a session with such a system.

Most users may not think it out in detail, but such a system may be based on quite an intricate structure, carefully designed to bring together information on different subjects (architecture, history, museums and attractions etc) in a coherent way.

Distinctions between Hypertext Structures

Hypertext is based on the concept of database items (typically chunks of text) being held in a certain structure, and accessed by a reader moving around that structure. So far this briefing has not been very explicit about the exact structure a hypertext database has. How would it compare to the conceptual schema of a mainstream database? The schema of a mainstream database may be in relational or network or some other form, are there analogous established forms for hypertext?

Hypertext is still an immature field; no concepts or approaches yet have the clout of relational theory in the design of mainstream databases. Still there seem to be four main different styles for the schema of a hypertext database:[1]

- **Simple hierarchy style.** The database consists of a large number of conveniently-sized chunks of text (or other data). It is easiest to imagine each chunk as a card, but instead of being kept in a tray, the cards are as if spread out in the shape of a hierarchy on a table. For example: every card might describe a tourist attraction; those about buildings might be in one main branch of the hierarchy tree, museums in another branch, natural attractions in another; the buildings branch might be sub-divided further between cards about temples, mosques, palaces, forts and so on. With this approach, it is usually best to help the user understand and move about the structure by showing the hierarchy as a list of indented headings or graphically as boxes in a diagram.

- **Multi-hierarchy style.** The structure implied by the example with Madras, Mahabalipuram etc is more complex than a simple hierarchy. The database consists of cards, arranged in a hierarchy — but in several hierarchies in different dimensions. Thus a card describing the Kanchipuram temples occupies a certain place in one hierarchy (Hindu temple within temple within building within tourist attraction), but it also has its place in other hierarchies; eg Dravidian architecture within Southern Indian architecture within Hindu etc; and also Kanchipuram temples within Kanchipuram City within Seven Sacred Cities within Hindu religion etc. Talk of cards structured in multiple hierarchies in different dimensions sounds very abstract, but the user of the system need not visualise it that way. The point is really that access possibilities become far richer, because you can both go up and down a hierarchy and jump from one hierarchy to another.
- **Free card style.** Here the database is still a set of cards but it is no longer possible to describe its structure clearly as made up of several hierarchies. A miscellany of information items are linked together in a complex web; eg about Indian history, buildings, religions, painting, food, sport, jokes, politics, personal experiences, television, landscape, agriculture etc — and not treated systematically as separate hierarchies.
- **Book style.** Unlike the other three, this style doesn't divide its information into separate card-like chunks. The database is subdivided into pieces, perhaps very intricately, but the resulting structure is like a continuous book (though without any equivalent of pages), albeit organised electronically in ways impractical with print on paper. Many jumps are offered to and fro; connections are made between items of information that defy the sequential constraint of a normal book. Much of the text is 'tucked away' out of the main-line. If you are studying a topic in detail you can 'fold out' the detail tucked away; if not, you continue reading at a synoptic level.

Aspects of Access

However intricate its underlying structure of items, a hypertext system stands or falls by the quality of its access features.

Having to key in 'Mahabalipuram' in full within a complicated **command** syntax, where various commas and apostrophes have to be exactly right is just unacceptable. A good hypertext system allows selection of Mahabalipuram by clicking on a mouse — or something equally simple, eg touching the screen.

Another aspect is screen **presentation**. It is less pleasant to read text on screen than in a nicely printed book. To compensate, a hypertext database has to offer advantages that the print medium cannot. Two things with no obvious equivalent in 99.9% of books are varying the size and shape of the screen windows that contain the text, and varying the colour of the text and the background of its windows.

If the designer of a hypertext database can use windowing and colour variation in a consistent way, that reinforces the meaning of the content and helps to clarify the structure of the whole body of knowledge — then the resulting system has the chance of being something more than just a curious, alternative version of a book.

The third access aspect is **navigation and orientation,** and this embraces a great variety of possibilities.

Aspects of Navigation and Orientation

Hypertext is a fine way of meeting certain kinds of information needs, but a design problem arises: how to help the person using the system to keep a sense of direction in travelling about the hypertext database. There are three main aspects: knowing where you are in the database, knowing where you have been and knowing where to jump to next.[2]

Here are some typical techniques under the heading of **knowing where you are**:

- In addition to the screen's main content, two small **overview diagrams** are always present. Their sole purpose is to preserve the reader's orientation. One overview always presents the structure of the whole database; the other presents in more detail the structure of the portion of the database that the reader is currently navigating.
- **Graphics** can suggest the character or status of the information presented; eg some text is in an oil-painting frame, other text on pages of a spiral-ring notebook; references to other works are presented as book spines on a shelf.
- A **scroll bar** indicates how much of that particular piece of information at that point in the structure is currently on the screen; perhaps the 100 words on the screen are approximately the middle 20% of a five-screen essay on a certain topic.
- **Inter-screen effects** help in a different way; eg a slide-projector effect suggests that you have come to information on the same logical level as the previous screen; a closing iris effect suggests movement

to high-level and more general information; an opening iris suggests the reverse.

Here are some typical techniques under the heading of **knowing where you have been**:

● The system records **footprints**. If there is a possible jump from one screen to another, but there is a tick against the option, this means that you have already been to that screen.

● Eventually, the whole database could be covered in footprint ticks. Therefore the footprints can be made to **decay automatically** with time; eg get fainter or change colour to approach the colour of the main text.

● Similar information can be shown graphically as reduced **images of past screens** arranged in the order they have been visited.

● The system can show on each screen: **time since you were last here**; eg 40 minutes, 5 days, never. It can also generate summary lists of screens visited and times.

Apart from straightforward concepts such as offering options for moving up or down the levels of a hierarchy, a variety of other techniques can be put under the heading of **knowing where to jump to next**:

● If a screen offers a variety of possible jump options, some can be given **more prominence** than others; eg presented in larger letters or at the top of a list.

● In many hypertext structures some links are to **popups**; choose the option marked 'mahayana' and a brief definition of mahayana pops up on the screen. After reading this, all you can do is go back to the previous screen. This is quite different from jumping across to a different part of the database. A popup can be marked with some graphic convention, so that the reader knows what it is.

● Another idea is to **display the structure** of the database (or part of it) graphically, as a diagram with boxes and arrows, and allow the reader to get from one place to another by selecting the appropriate box.

● Another interesting feature is **random jumps**. From some screens there may be a variety of plausible jumps. The reader can ask the system to decide at random which one to take.

Comparison of Hypertext and Classic Text Database

By building in links between different items of text, the hypertext approach allows the reader to move around a structure of information. There is a price to be paid: the up-front effort of forging the links.

How does the system know that somebody reading about the

SUMMARY OF WARRANTS

Comparison of non-Hypertext Possibilities: Limitations of keyword or text database and of printed book

Example of Hypertext: Indian guidebook

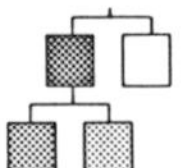

Distinctions between Hypertext Structures: Simple Hierarchy style; Multi-hierarchy style; Free Card style; Book style

Aspects of Access: Commands; Presentation; Navigation and orientation

Aspects of Navigation and Orientation: Knowing where you are; Knowing where you have been; Knowing where to jump to next

Comparison of Hypertext and Classic Text Database: Up-front effort; Different types of texts

temples of Mahabalipuram may well want to switch to information about the Pallava dynasty? Why does it offer this link for the reader to choose rather any of thousands of other possibilities? A hypertext system is not normally context-sensitive in the sense of making intelligent guesses about which information is likely to be of interest to a reader in a certain context. The technology merely allows a human author or editor to build in links from one item to another that, *so it is expected,* will probably be most useful to the reader.

Thus there can be far more intellectual work in setting up a hypertext database than one where access is through text-searching. In the latter case, the necessary building of indexes is more or less automatic; with hypertext, the work of setting up the links that define structure is less amenable to automatic procedures.

But the keyword approach also carries the burden of up-front indexing activity. How do hypertext and keyword compare on this issue? A great deal depends on the style of hypertext:

- With a hypertext database in **simple hierarchy** style, it may be relatively easy to set up some automatic mechanism to forge the links between the cards loaded into the database. This will probably be less trouble than choosing keywords for each card.
- With a hypertext database in **free card** style, there may be no alternative to taking each card at a time, visualising all the links that need to be forged and then setting them up. This is usually more demanding than setting up keywords.
- A hypertext database in **multi-hierarchy** or **book** style will fall somewhere between these two extremes.

The other major factor in any comparison of hypertext with text and keyword is whether the information will benefit from the structure that hypertext provides; eg:

- In a database of Indian religious and mythological texts, there might be little scope for useful hypertext links; keywords might be a more useful way of helping you to find texts in the *Mahabharata* about particular heroes and events.
- For a database of 1000 learned articles about Indian culture from many different sources, the best approach is probably to use text-searching or keyword for access. Building in hypertext links would probably be extra work for scant advantage.

POSSIBLE DECISION-MAKING

A hypertext database has certain unquestionable advantages over a book. The real issue facing the Red Sallee Project is whether the advantages of a hypertext database about India are so great that people will incur the extra costs and complications of using a computer rather than a book.

This can't be resolved either way by mere debate. An experimental project is needed. The interesting challenge now is designing an experimental system that will yield clear answers on vital points without making an extravagant investment. Here is one set of plausible judgements that could shape further work:

- The database ought to be designed specifically to use the multi-dimensional structuring of knowledge possible with hypertext. Otherwise the experiment will be largely pointless.
- Those designing the experimental system should define its structure by choosing explicitly between the four styles — simple hierarchy, multi-hierarchy and so on — and define its access in terms of the three navigation and orientation aspects. That is much the clearest way of understanding what the hypertext system does and doesn't do.
- On the command and presentation aspects of access: do what is possible with the moderate hardware capabilities (in terms of screen technology and memory) of the PCs most potential buyers will possess. But, in case it turns out that this approach falls short, build in the possibility of switching over to something more sophisticated that will only run on a relatively upmarket PC.

With an experimental knowledge product designed in this way there is a good chance of gaining insight into the strengths and weaknesses of hypertext technology for this application, thus preparing the ground for decisions about larger investments.

CONNECTIONS

19. Classic Text Systems	Text database, a rival technology — basic problems and approaches
23. Picture Database Systems	Hypertext structure and access principles as basis for a database of pictures
28. Non-Mainstream Software Products	Software products for hypertext

22. Untangling Hybrid Systems

BEARINGS

A hybrid database system brings together two or more different kinds of data.[1] A great variety of hybrid databases can be imagined: mainstream and photos, mainstream and texts, texts and maps and so on. How do you keep a sense of direction amid such variety?

In any situation where many plausible combinations of options exist, a listing of the combinations rarely delivers much insight. It is more worthwhile to set up a simple framework, based on a few cardinal issues. That at least enables you to judge how any particular possibility you come across is related to all the others. This briefing proceeds in that way, and thus provides an outline view of the content of Briefings 23 to 27.

WARRANTS

The warrant sections of this briefing are largely devoted to showing what factors cause hybrid database systems to vary greatly in their complexity.

Gradations of Hybrid Systems

The greatest challenges of hybrid databases arise largely from needs to *integrate* different kinds of data. Many different degrees of integration can be envisaged. Here are some useful points to mark out along a continuous scale.[2]

- Gradation 1: **Pseudo-hybrid**. The database is in essence a mainstream or text database, but it includes another kind of data as a supplementary feature: eg a database of consultants' CVs might include their photos as well.
- Gradation 2: **Semi-hybrid.** The database is primarily a set of data of the less tractable sort (bit-mapped graphics, audio etc), but

keywords (or perhaps mainstream or text data) serve as a kind of index or table of contents; eg a database of cartoons might be searchable through keywords, such as 'politics', 'yuppy', 'feminism', 'pun', 'exaggeration', 'catch phrase' etc.

- Gradation 3: **Simple-hybrid.** Two or more kinds of data fit together closely and it can't be said that the database consists primarily of one kind or another. But updating is not a major issue. An art gallery might store photos of its collection together with descriptive and analytical texts. Plainly, the photos and texts have to be kept consistent whenever any update occurs, but updating is a small part of the system; pictures don't flow in and out of a gallery at the same rate as the goods of a supermarket.
- Gradation 4: **Complex-hybrid.** Two or more kinds of data fit together closely and *updating* is important and challenging. If data of one kind is updated, then data of the other kind may have to be kept consistent, and this may be a tricky thing to guarantee. A database containing maps, photos and factual data about a town could be an example.

Aspects of Complex-hybrid Systems

With complex-hybrid systems, a further range of issues exists. The example of a town's database could be relatively demanding, but a case on the border between simple- and complex-hybrid could be a market research database, where numbers quantifying the results of surveys (mainstream data) were mixed up with texts such as 'I found the product very awkward to use' or 'because of bad weather at the time of the survey, responses in this village may be untypical'.

Rather than pursue finer gradations, it is better to identify separate aspects that determine the issues and possibilities for any particular complex-hybrid system. The aspects are really areas for complication, each of which will tend to make the application more demanding:

- two or more out of the three **heavyweight kinds** of data — mainstream, text/keyword and spatial — interlocked;
- **update** of interlocking data **intricate and vital**; eg if map data is updated to show that a certain street in a town is now one-way, it is crucial that another part of the database, containing rules data for fire-brigade routes, be updated too;
- **frequent updating**, probably imposing heavy hardware requirements if it is intricate too;
- **multiple users** of the same database — as opposed to each user having a separate copy of the database on a PC;
- **volumes** both absolutely high (in terms of eg disk storage) and

high in terms of items (ie numbers of distinct records, images, soundbites etc)

• **access** facilities open-ended, ie the user isn't restricted to following certain paths; many combinations of different pieces of data may be displayed together on the screen.

Charting the Main Combinations of Kinds of Data

With this preparation, it is worthwhile to mention a few combinations of kinds of data that are particularly important in practice. As the list shows, there are usually choices to be made about how complex a hybrid the system should be:

• Combination of **photos with text and/or mainstream data.** Choices: usually in the range of semi-hybrid to simple-hybrid.

• Combination of **document images with mainstream and/or keyword data.** Choices: usually in the range of semi-hybrid to simple-hybrid.

• Combination of **geographic (ie spatial) data with mainstream data.** Choices: either simple-hybrid or complex-hybrid; these two options are often fairly stark. Most people reserve the term GIS (geographic information system) for those database systems (and also software products supporting them) that integrate geographic with mainstream data in a complex-hybrid way. A complex GIS may be *very* complex.[3] Business mapping is a useful term for the simple-hybrid case.

• Combination of **text data with mainstream data.** Choices: anywhere from pseudo-hybrid through to complex-hybrid, though rarely as complex as a complex GIS.

• Combination of **rules-based data with mainstream data.** Choices: simple-hybrid or complex-hybrid, though rarely an extreme case of complexity.

Chart of Multimedia and Object-oriented

An analysis of hybrid database has to take some account of the loose term 'multimedia', and a discussion of multimedia frequently arrives at the elastic 'object-oriented'. These fashionable terms need to be demystified. First, notes on **object-oriented**:

• Many innovative ideas about the development of database technology are based on object-oriented concepts. Note: it is quite important to distinguish between the following: object-oriented concepts, object-oriented programming, object-oriented modelling and object-oriented DBMS. These are all sorted out in the briefing on the subject.

SUMMARY OF WARRANTS

Gradations of Hybrid Systems: Pseudo-hybrid; Semi-hybrid; Simple-hybrid; Complex-hybrid

Aspects of Complex-hybrid Systems: Several heavyweight kinds; Complex interlocking; Frequent updating; Multiple users; High volumes; Open-ended access

Chart of the Main Combinations of Kinds: Five combinations of data kinds related to possible gradations of hybrid systems

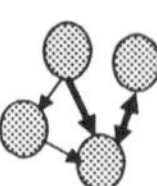

Chart of Advanced Concepts: Object-oriented; Multimedia; BLOB

• Object-oriented concepts (it can plausibly be argued) can offer advantages in any kind of database system at all. Thus, object-oriented concepts could be appropriate even for the dullest of mainstream applications.

• But object-oriented concepts (so the argument goes) are particularly advantageous for relatively complex systems, eg those with hybrid databases.

Second, notes on **multimedia**:

• Sometimes the term multimedia is a synonym for hybrid (ie *any* combination of different kinds of data). Sometimes it stands for the combination of three particular technologies: computer, telecoms and television. But in perhaps its most useful sense multimedia describes knowledge products that: include not only graphics but animation and/or motion video; provide numerous paths through this material; are made in many copies and published; and are meant be explored but not updated. An encyclopaedia published on compact disk is a typical case.

• An essentially mainstream database system may be said to provide multimedia because it includes a **BLOB** (binary, large object) feature. This means that its relational records may include fields of the BLOB type, ie one consisting of many thousands of bits that make up one image or piece of audio or other kind of awkward data. However, this in itself only provides a pseudo-hybrid system. A database of consultants' CVs might store their photos as BLOBs, but this is still a long way from applying integrity checks (eg noticing that photos of the same person are stored in two different records) or searching their content (eg selecting from the database all red-haired people with glasses).

• Multimedia databases — in almost any sense — are challenging to build, and (many people think) object-oriented concepts are currently the most promising approach.

CONNECTIONS

23. Picture Database Systems	Combination of photos with text and/or mainstream data; main concerns: structure and access
24. Document Image Systems	Combination of document images with mainstream data; range of possibilities, for some integrity is tricky
25. Geographic Information Systems	Combination of spatial (specifically map) data with mainstream data; if complex hybrid, GIS; if not, business mapping system
26. Text-with-Mainstream Systems	Combination of text data with mainstream data; range of possibilities, but integrity can be a difficult issue
27. Rules-with-Mainstream Systems	Combination of rules data with mainstream data; surprising range of possible problems *and* solutions
29. Object-oriented Topics	New concepts, potentially relevant, in a general way, to any hybrid system

23. Picture Database Systems

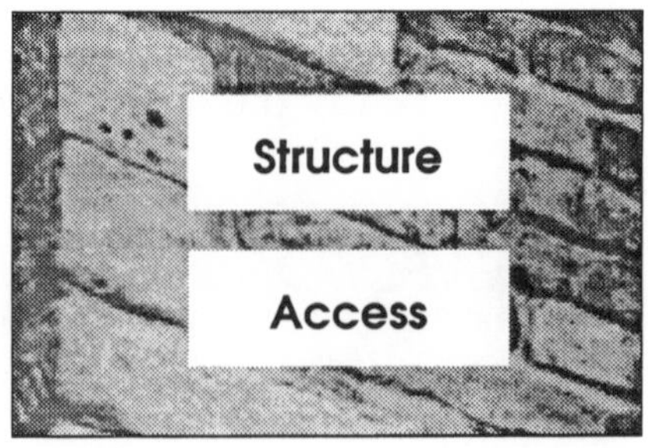

BEARINGS

Picture databases are inevitably hybrid; a system that stored pictures only, without any other kind of data to help in finding and understanding the pictures, would be too primitive to be called a database system.

Most picture database systems are for people to search through and refer to, but *updating* the database is a relatively unimportant matter. The challenges of really complex hybrid systems, that have to maintain integrity in the face of updates affecting several different kinds of data, are avoided.

This briefing concentrates largely on different ways of structuring and accessing a picture database. One of the most important styles discussed is hypertext, whose general approach to structure and access is the subject of Briefing 21.

POSSIBLE CONTEXT

Mountain Blueberry is an upmarket department store. It is more ready than most to employ innovative ways of using IT that are visible to the customer. This is partly because a detail of superior service that might be considered a silly gimmick in a supermarket could be well justified as a way of reinforcing the business's luxury image. For example, the following idea is under serious consideration:

- The National Gallery in London has a picture database system that displays reproductions of paintings on a screen, together with explanatory text. The system can also print out a map of the gallery showing which rooms to visit to see selected paintings.
- Why not have a picture database for customers at Mountain Blueberry? It would show pictures of the store's goods, with descrip-

tive text, including prices. It could also print out a map showing how to get to the part of the store where chosen items were on sale.

The decision-making problem is this: How do you progress from vague discussion of the broad-brush idea to actual decisions about whether, and in outline how, to set up such a system? Mountain Blueberry could organise a team of people for an expensive, large-scale feasibility study of the matter. The trouble is that such studies often take on a life of their own, don't necessarily examine issues and options in a cold-blooded way, and sometimes produce documents so detailed that they are unreadable at any speed. Isn't there some more incisive approach that will produce better decisions more efficiently?

One essential is to get an overview of the main issues that typically come up with picture database — possibilities and limitations, problems and choices. The most efficient way of doing this could be the following:

- Make a description of a representative application — eg the National Gallery system — summarised to bring out its main features.
- Move on from this by seeing how that example application relates to picture database systems in general; ie which possibilities it takes and which it ignores.
- From there, identify the options that seem most plausible for a Mountain Blueberry system.
- In that way, get a firmer idea of what a Mountain Blueberry system would be like, its pros and cons and perhaps some big issues where choice between alternatives seems crucial. If, after this, the idea still seems attractive, proceed to more detailed feasibility studies.

WARRANTS

This briefing uses an account of the picture database at the National Gallery in London to develop a more general view of issues and options in this field.[1] Most of the issues are those of demand — kind of data, structure and access — and these require careful analysis. But it is also necessary to get at least an impression of some tricky supply issues too.

National Gallery Example: Main Points

Visitors to the National Gallery can go to the 'Micro Gallery' computer room and use one of the PCs there to display images of paintings and notes about them. Here is a rough account of the

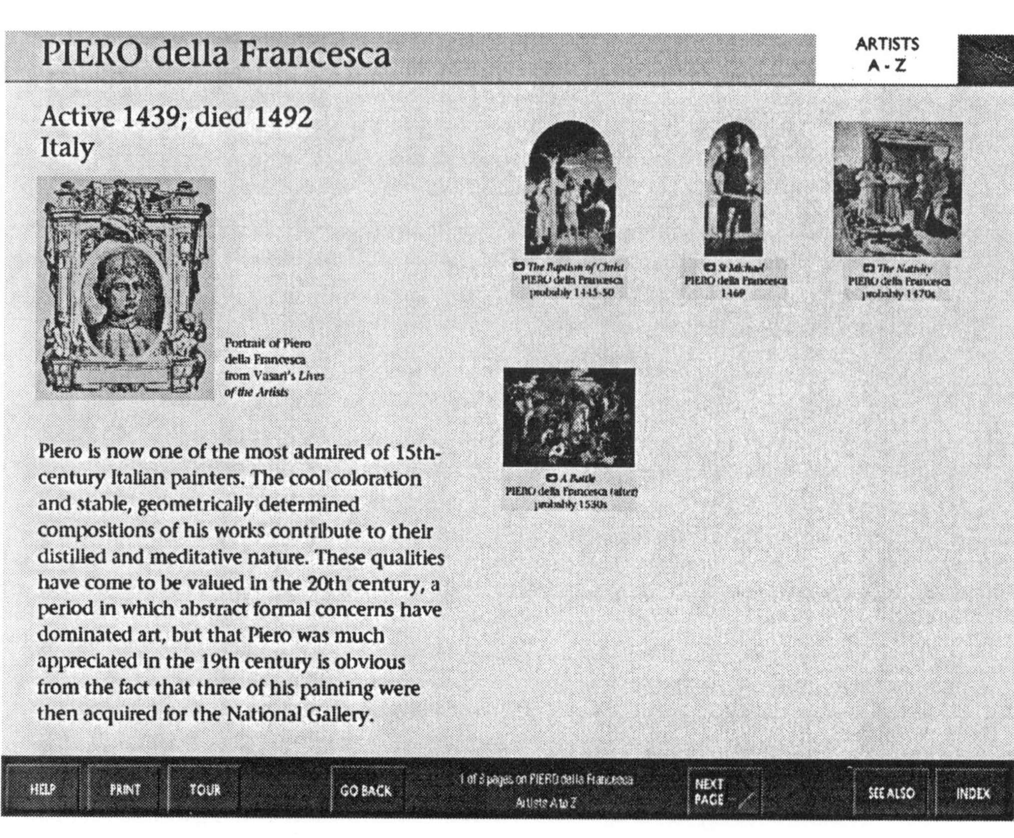

Reproduced by courtesy of the Trustees, The National Gallery, London

Painter card: notes on the painter and his work in general; thumbnail images of his works; select any one and you jump to its Painting card.

system's scope in terms of the first three elements of this book's chart of database technology, kind of data, structure and access.

The system stores several **kinds of data**. There are colour images of over 2000 paintings from the collection (including those there is no room to exhibit). Also, there are about 1000 supplementary graphics of various types: eg maps, artist portrait (usually monochrome) and (a few) pictures from other collections. There are also texts to accompany the images; eg pointing out details about the content of a painting or an artist's technique or an artist's life.

The logical **structure** of this database is best thought of as a collection of 'cards', each containing a combination of image and text: 4500 cards in total. These cards are arranged in hierarchical structures. Here is a simplified account of how this works:

- **Main hierarchy**. For each painter, there is a card (see first

St Michael

PAINTING CATALOGUE

PIERO della Francesca
1469

Full title 'Saint Michael (Panel from a Polyptych)'
*Inscribed on the armour: *angelvs* potentia dei*lvcha*
Wood, pointed top was originally rounded, 133 x 59.5 cm
No. 769, Purchased, 1867.

On 4 October 1454 Piero was contracted to paint the high altarpiece of S. Agostino in Sansepolcro. It was apparently completed by 14 November 1469.

On pictorial grounds the following panels, placed from left to right, are associated with it: *Saint Augustine* (Lisbon); this *St Michael*; a missing central panel, perhaps a *Virgin and Child enthroned*; an unidentified saint (Frick collection, New York); and *Saint Nicholas of Tolentino* (Poldi-Pezzoli Museum, Milan).

Room 66

Reproduced by courtesy of the Trustees, The National Gallery, London

Painting card: image of one painting with notes about it; for some paintings (not this one) you can go a level deeper to cards with images and notes of particular details of the painting.

illustration) of notes on his life, general style and importance, that also includes thumbnail images of the painter's works. Then, at the next level of the hierarchy, there is a separate card for each painting (see second illustration). Then, at the next level down — for some paintings only — there are further cards that show and discuss details from the painting.

- **Extra hierarchy level.** Many people using the system probably think of the three-level hierarchy just described as the main organising principle of the database, but there is an extra level too. There are cards above the level of painter, each referring to a whole school of painters (eg Venice, Florence, Rest of Italy etc), showing which painters belong to which school.
- **Separate hierarchy**. The cards are also arranged in another hierarchy based on a different dimension altogether, the subject of

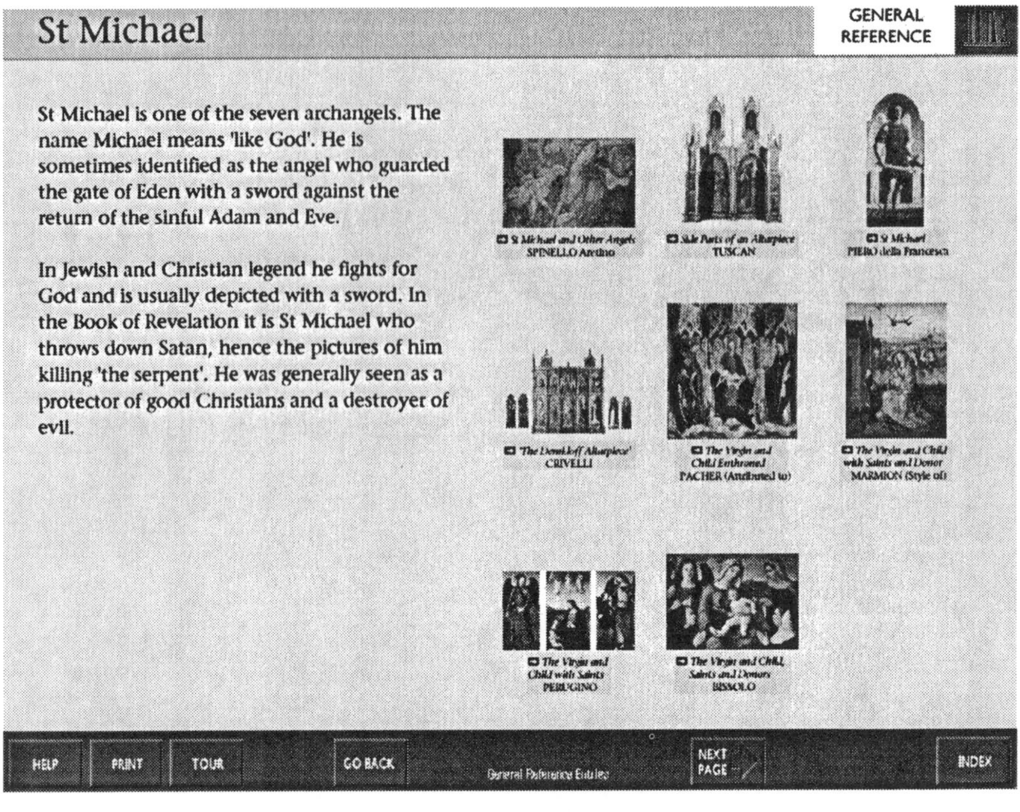

St Michael
GENERAL REFERENCE
St Michael is one of the seven archangels. The name Michael means 'like God'. He is sometimes identified as the angel who guarded the gate of Eden with a sword against the return of the sinful Adam and Eve.
In Jewish and Christian legend he fights for God and is usually depicted with a sword. In the Book of Revelation it is St Michael who throws down Satan, hence the pictures of him killing 'the serpent'. He was generally seen as a protector of good Christians and a destroyer of evil.
TUSCAN
CRIVELLI
HELP
PRINT
TOUR
GO BACK
NEXT PAGE
INDEX

Reproduced by courtesy of the Trustees, The National Gallery, London

Specific Subject card: notes on the subject of St Michael; thumbnail images of paintings of that subject (including that by Piero); select any one to jump to that Painting card.

the painting. There are six cards at level 1 of this hierarchy, corresponding to: religious, portrait, view, everyday life etc. At level 2 within (say) everyday life there are cards for music, drinking, work etc. (See the third illustration for a subject card within the religious part of the subject hierarchy.)

In this database system, **access** corresponds to structure very closely indeed. You access the logical units of the database's structure, the cards, one at a time and each card fills one screen. The information in the database is planned so that (on the whole) the content of each card is complete in itself; you don't have to go to a following card to complete a sentence or a chain of thought.

You move around the database by following its unifying hierarchical structure; thus:

- **within the main hierarchy:** from the card of Piero della Fran-

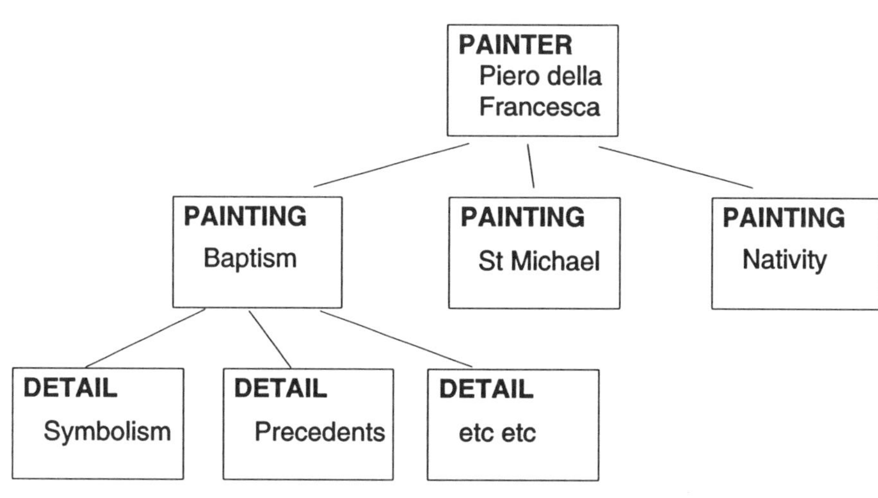

cesca himself jump a level down to the card of one of his paintings and from there, perhaps, a level down to a card describing a detail of that painting (as suggested by the first diagram);

- **from one hierarchy to another:** from the card of Piero's St Michael (reached via the main hierarchy) jump across to the card for a painting of St Michael by a different painter, which exists in the separate hierarchy of subjects of paintings (as suggested by the second diagram).

Commands to the system are expressed entirely through a touch-screen device. The design of interface and screen are excellent, meeting the twin objective of being self-evident when you are getting to know the system, without being tedious when you are already familiar with it.

The system will also print out a standard map of the gallery on which the locations of certain paintings are marked — those paintings you selected while going through the database.

Chart of Structure Issues

The National Gallery system is designed so neatly that it makes a good starting-point for exploring some of the more tricky concepts associated with database *structure*:

- **Simplicity and second-order detail.** It is desirable to keep the database structure as neat as possible, but in practice complications arise. The National Gallery system has one card for each painter, containing thumbnails of his paintings — in principle, that is. In

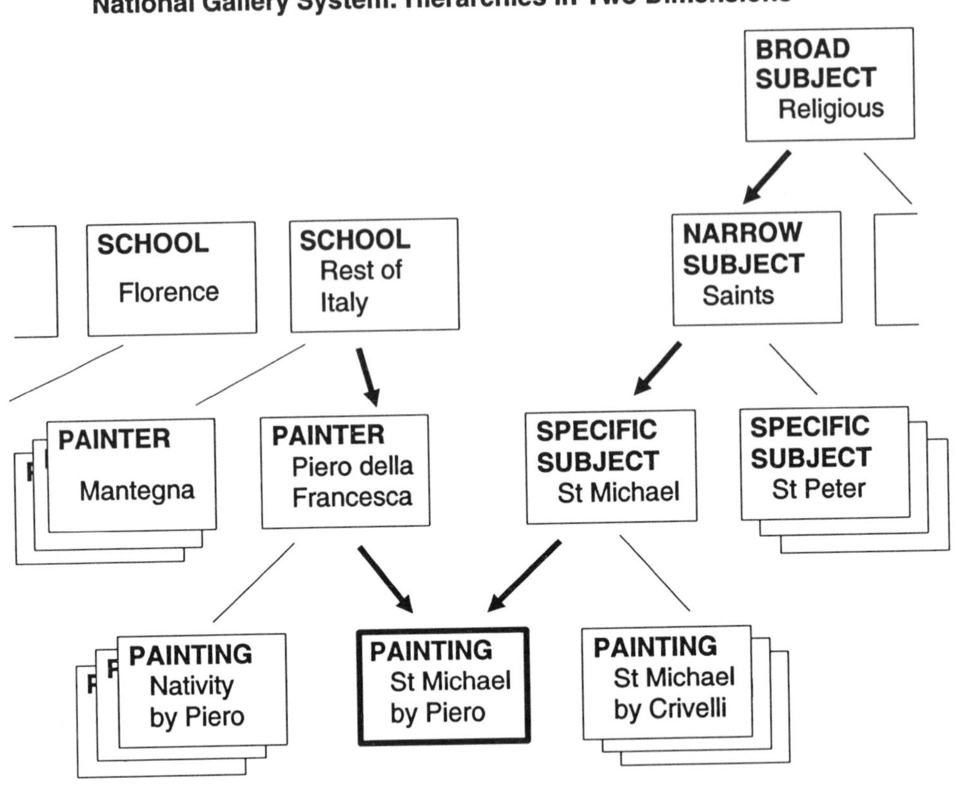

practice, overflow cards are needed for some painters to accommodate all the paintings. Moreover, some painters are so important that, irrespective of the number of paintings, continuation cards are used to hold extra detail about life and style. Thus, a properly detailed account of this database's conceptual schema would have to record that for each painter there is always one master biography-card, whose text is complete in itself, but contains an arbitrary number of thumbnails; there is then a variable number of following cards — some holding both overflow thumbnails and more text, others holding more text with no thumbnails, others more thumbnails but no text.

- **Hierarchy constraints.** Hierarchies impose order on the material of a database, but however carefully devised, order is usually bought at a price: certain types of information may not find a home anywhere in the hierarchy. Suppose you wanted to add a card to the National Gallery system to contain details from four of the Rembrandt paintings in order to compare and discuss the signatures. There is no good place in the structure to put that card: it doesn't belong with the detail cards of any one painting, but it can't go at the level of Rembrandt either, because the cards at that level don't contain details, only thumbnails of whole pictures. Or suppose you wanted to compare Rembrandt's *general style*, illustrated by details from several paintings, with that of Vermeer, also with several details. There is no place in the hierarchy for cards on that particular plane. (Though a card describing how *one particular* painting by Rembrandt is related in some way to work by somebody else can be fitted in.)

These are logical not technical constraints. It would be quite possible to fit the new types of cards into the database — but only at the price of transforming its neat, classical hierarchy into a somewhat more baroque network.

• **Tradeoffs between simplicity and constraints.** There are tradeoffs. First, it is good to keep the logical structure of the database as simply hierarchical as possible; this makes things easier for everybody, developers and users alike. *But*, even if you design things very carefully, a structure may be just too simple and constrain you from organising information with the subtlety you need. *But again*, if you make the essential hierarchical structure (and its second-order detail) more sophisticated, it may soon become unmanageable *and yet* still impose some residual constraints that prove irksome. You have to weigh things up to find the best-buy solution in the particular case. The designers of the National Gallery system have probably come close to achieving that.

• **Complexity of information.** The National Gallery collection has arguably the best selection of all Western painting 1200-1900 anywhere in the world, but suppose its scope was narrower; eg mainly Impressionists. Then intense analysis of picture content, styles, techniques, influences between artists and so on would have a higher priority. This might become the determining factor in reaching quite a different decision on the tradeoffs in database structure.

Aspects of Access

In a similar way, the National Gallery system helps expose some aspects of *access* where different choices are possible:

• **Structure-access correspondence.** There is a close correspondence between the unit of information you extract from the database at a time — a screen-full — and the units that make up the logical structure of the database — a painter card, painting card etc. This makes for neatness, but it does rule out some access possibilities that another system, even though based on the same structure, might conceivably offer. Thus there is no scope for zooming in on image details within one card at your own initiative. Also you can't split the screen to display two cards (or parts of two cards) at the same time.

If there are (say) six cards at the same level, (say) details of a certain painting, you must go through them in order; you can't jump from the card at the level above, the whole painting, straight to (say) the fourth detail card.

You can't jump straight from any card to any other (say from Piero's St Michael to a painting by a Zurbaran); you have to follow the logic of the system's hierarchies and that can entail passing through several intermediate cards at different levels.

• **Interface device.** Commands to the system are expressed entirely through touch-screen not mouse or keyboard. Touch-screen is the least forbidding to the novice, but most people find the mouse ergonomically superior even for very simple interaction with a system. The more complex the operation or command the more necessary the mouse: eg ticking several choices on a menu, zooming in and out of images, resizing windows etc.

• **Non-structural searching.** The advantage of allowing access through the keyboard is that words can be keyed in for keyword or text-search. You might want to search for all pictures in whose accompanying text a certain word or phrase appears; eg 'Benedictine' or 'geometry' or 'Duke of Urbino'. This style of access ignores hierarchies, but could be a useful extra resource for those accesses where normal navigation around the database structure seems inadequate.

• **Tours.** A system normally allows the user to navigate around its data structures at will, but you might also build in some standard tours through the database that have nothing to do with its essential structure; eg the top 20 must-see paintings in the collection or children's favourites or pre-1500, all schools, similarities and contrasts etc.

• **Modes.** Another access refinement is to offer several modes of use: eg straightforward mode; power user mode (extra facilities for the computer-literate, such as keying in terms for text-searching); connoisseur mode (providing access to information too arcane for most people to bother with).

None of this is meant to suggest that the more of these things you include in your system, the better it will be. Tradeoffs apply here too, and if the system is primarily intended for a wide public, that is a formidable argument for keeping things simple.

Distinctions between Styles of Structure

The essential structure of the National Gallery's database is a set of cards — with a defined format, flexible though not totally free — arranged in several intermingled hierarchies. Call this the **Multi-hierarchy style**. For other picture database systems, other styles may be worth considering:[2]

- **Simple hierarchy style.** Again the database consists essentially of a set of cards, but there is only one hierarchy; eg school-painter-painting-detail with no hierarchy based on the subject of the painting. This may sound a weaker option, but could be best if the hierarchy had many levels and the branching at each level was complicated; eg if a gallery had a collection from a narrow field that could be sub-divided in great detail.
- **Slideshow style.** The system is just a means of displaying images on the screen one by one; the only other things on the screen are some simple identifier and command buttons, such as 'next', 'end' etc. Access is rudimentary — sequential or by image reference number. An example might be a system for viewing the pages of a medieval gospel too fragile to be handled.
- **Cardtray style.** The database cards are really records in a database table, all in a standard format. The image is just one field of a special kind among the fields making up the record; the others are mainstream data and perhaps keywords. The cards are arranged in some natural order but can also be accessed by field value (eg all cards where a certain field is greater than 57). There are no hypertext-like jumps between cards. The system usually has just one table of records, but a more advanced possibility is to enable data from several different tables to be combined in a semi-relational way. However, movement in this direction really makes use of the mainstream data more sophisticated, not the picture data. This might be the style to adopt if the main aim of the system was to store financial and administrative data about a collection (valuations, insurance details etc).[3]
- **Retrieval style.** Each picture has descriptive text and/or keywords associated with it. A typical access request might be all pictures with keyword 'fruit' and whose descriptive text contains the word 'orchard'. With this approach the full panoply of advanced indexing and search techniques for access to the pictures is possible: thesaurus, best match searching and so on. A possible application might be a database of many pictures, not necessarily masterpieces, for use in researching iconography and the use of certain symbols in Western art.

• **Free card style.** Here the database is still a set of cards but there is no straightforward structure; you can't say that there are several different types of card (*Painter, Painting*, say) and that a card of a certain type is always linked to cards of certain other types. The content of any given card and its links to others are determined one at a time according to the judgement of the designer of the database. Any diagram of the structure would be a huge, tangled network.

This has a very low rating for simplicity but still has merits. Suppose you wanted a system about a collection of objects that were widely different but richly interconnected. A museum might have a collections of paintings, furniture, porcelain, books, historical objects etc of the seventeenth-century Netherlands. A database system might link all these things together coherently yet flexibly: '*This painting* by De Hooch shows a man smoking a pipe. Here is a *photo of a pipe*. Tobacco was first imported from the West Indian colonies shown on *this map* of trade routes. And here is *a model* of the kind of ship used for importing tobacco. Compare it with *this other model* of a ship designed for the Baltic trade. Now here is *a painting* of Amsterdam harbour . . .'

• **Book style.** Now the concept of a database of many cards arranged in a structure disappears. Instead there is one continuous piece of text with embedded illustrations like a book — maybe still divided into chapters, sections etc, but not cut into standard card-sized chunks. You can go through sequentially but numerous jumps from one place in the book to another are built in; also much of the material is 'tucked away' out of the main-line, to be 'folded out' if required. The content of a coffee-table book on the history of art might be loaded into a database in this style, and given added value by the possibilities for jumping about for acute comparisons of the art of different periods.

Of these seven styles, multi-hierarchy, simple hierarchy, free card and book are really different forms of hypertext; they are all based on the concept of the database items being held in a certain structure, and accessed by a reader moving around that structure.

Supply Aspects

The analysis of picture database so far is entirely in demand terms. The National Gallery system helps expose some important supply issues too:

• **Update, integrity and CRS.** The National Gallery system is concerned with allowing people to *access* information, but not to *update* the database. This means that issues such as concurrency control, integrity control and so on don't arise. Of course, there must

SUMMARY OF WARRANTS

Example of National Gallery System: Kind of data; Logical structure; Access

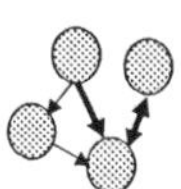

Chart of Structure Issues: Simplicity; Second-order detail; Hierarchy constraints; Tradeoffs between simplicity and constraints; Complexity of information

Aspects of Access: Structure-access correspondence; Interface device; Non-structural searching; Tours; Modes

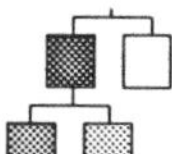

Distinctions between Approaches to Picture Database Structure: Multi-hierarchy; Simple hierarchy; Slideshow; Cardtray; Retrieval; Free card; Book

Supply Aspects: Update, integrity and CRS; Purpose and image quality; Image acquisition; Architecture

be facilities to add new pictures to the database or to add more detailed notes on a picture — but this is to prepare a new edition of the database that will then last for months, rather than to update a database in the usual sense.

• **Purpose and image quality.** System purpose interacts with supply choices, because storage of high-quality, detailed images is so expensive in disk storage and other technology. Your purpose may well not call for anything like perfect image quality. Take two different cases. First, a picture database system shows images of objects that can't otherwise be seen, because they are held in store for lack of room in the gallery. Second, a system is primarily intended to keep control of which work of art is located where for a wealthy family whose collection is spread over many different residences. In the first case, high quality is probably essential. In the second, it would be pointless to pay for technology to achieve superior quality, since 'recognition-quality' images, not even in colour, would be adequate for the purpose.

• **Image acquisition.** With a picture database there is a problem that hardly arises with any other type of database system discussed in this book. It may be very difficult to get the content loaded into the database satisfactorily: it is a far from trivial task to photograph a set of objects and arrange for their images to be stored on a disk, in such a way that they look marvellous when displayed on a screen.

In some situations, there may be little practical choice but to seek out specialists who are experienced and successful in this field, and rely on them to cope with all the photographic equipment, image-editing software, data compression techniques, graphics format standards and other tradeoffs and variables that affect image quality. But, in cases where superb quality is not essential, Kodak's Photo-CD service may be a much more straightforward alternative. You take the photos with an ordinary camera; hand the roll in at a shop and receive a CD back a few days later, containing the photos stored in a format that can be read by HyperCard or some other software product for PC.[4]

- **Architecture**. In the National Gallery system each PC has its own complete copy of the database. This is a natural way of doing things. If great quantities of image data had to be transmitted to PCs across a network from a central database, response time would suffer. For a different system, perhaps with less detailed or lower quality (and thus more economically stored) images, the calculus of cost and performance might turn out quite different.[5]

POSSIBLE DECISION-MAKING

There are several differences between the requirements at Mountain Blueberrry and the National Gallery. First, with the National Gallery, a painting's room location is not all that important; many users never bother to print out a map. At Mountain Blueberrry the location of a product in the store is vital, because the main purpose of the system is to send people off to see and buy the goods. Thus, keeping data about the location of goods up to date is vital.

Second, updating requirements for text and images are different:

- The National Gallery database must occasionally be updated (eg if a picture is sent away on loan to an exhibition), but this is a very limited form of update.
- At Mountain Blueberry, updating is much more important, since the range of goods and their prices are changing all the time.

Nevertheless, there are important similarities between the systems too. Just as with the National Gallery, the costs of high image quality must be borne: customers must be seduced by the striking images of desirable purchases.

Out of the different approaches to picture database structure — multi-hierarchy, simple hierarchy, cardtray and so on — it seems that the multi-hierarchy structure, as at the National Gallery, is most appropriate for Mountain Blueberry too. This is a major decision — only to be taken if it is reasonable clear how the information might be arranged usefully in that structure. Thus:

- At the National Gallery the main organising principle is a three-level hierarchy, painter-painting-detail.
- Mountain Blueberrry can adopt a hierarchy too: eg chess set is a sub-category of games, which is a sub-category of leisure goods.
- At the National Gallery there are extra possibilities of access through a different hierarchy: eg all paintings of St Michael.
- Similarly, at Mountain Blueberrry there must be possibilities of access through hierarchies other than the main product-category hierarchy: a source hierarchy (eg all the goods from a certain prestigious manufacturer) or association hierarchy (eg all the goods associated with television programmes or pop-stars).

The National Gallery example is much richer in issues than this. By going through these and a number of other similarities and differences the decision-makers of Mountain Blueberry can proceed to take reasonable decisions about the main outlines of a possible system.[6]

CONNECTIONS

4. Conceptual Schemas	Hierarchy in the mainstream world
21. Hypertext Systems	Hypertext structure and access principles — a basis for many picture database systems
28. Non-Mainstream Software Products	Possible software products for picture database
29. Object-oriented Topics	Relatively complex databases that store pictures and other information may well benefit from the object-oriented approach

24. Document Image Systems

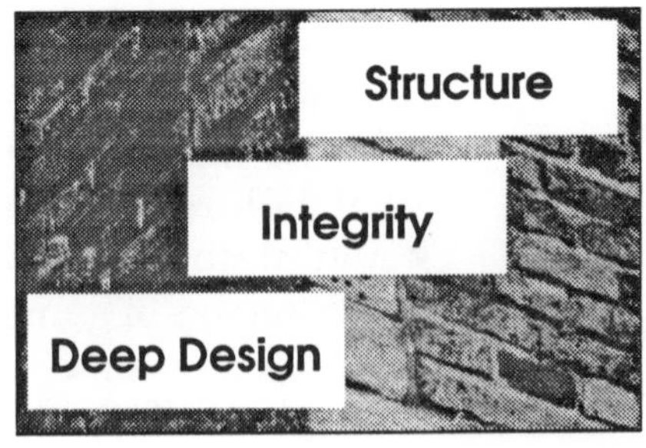

BEARINGS

Document imaging is the technology of scanning document pages and storing them as bit-mapped images on high-capacity disks (typically, though not necessarily, disks using optical storage technology). The pages can later be called up and displayed on screens, without necessarily any translation or rekeying of their content into normal, computer-readable characters.

From a technical point of view, the image of a document, an aircraft inspection report or a customer's complaint letter (say), is an item of bit-mapped graphics like any other image — of a face, a brain-scan, a galaxy or anything else. Some management consultants hold that document-imaging technology offers rich opportunities for radical redesign of procedures within many businesses. However that may be, the fact that the bit-mapped image is an image of a *document*, rather than some other article, does raise some interesting issues of database supply and demand.

Document images alone are of limited use. Any genuine database system is a hybrid combining document images with mainstream data and perhaps text or keyword data as well. This hybrid characteristic makes the topic interesting and rich in options.

POSSIBLE CONTEXT

Alpine Ash Airlines already has experience of the technology of imaging. As an experiment it set up a system that stored the images of certain hand-written reports of routine aircraft inspections (advantages: saves keying in the hand-written comments; provides psychologically vivid evidence in cases of disputes about what was inspected and what was found; allows things to be described in sketches rather than words).

Now Alpine Ash wants to go further with imaging. In the

inspection reports application the image of the document remains an image. The computer system cannot read or interpret its content. If the document implies that something is wrong and action has to be taken, then new data is keyed into a separate mainstream database system that guides all further actions. Whatever a report's content, its image remains no more than an item in a crude electronic archive: you ask to see the document with a certain reference number and it is displayed; that is all.

What about applications in other areas of the business where an image could be *to some degree integrated* with other types of data in a database system? Storing additional keywords describing the content of each inspection report would be a small step in that direction; you could then search the archive for all reports described by a keyword, such as 'metal fatigue' or 'rust'. A more ambitious application might have the system store images of airline tickets, *automatically* read their content (name of passenger, flight number etc), and store these fields in the parts of the mainstream database for accounting and load planning and so on.

These are just arbitrary examples, drawn from a survey that identified a dozen vague possibilities. Nobody at Alpine Ash really knows enough about the essential issues of the subject to tell whether they are the best applications and to find the right questions to ask about them. This leads to a tough decision-making problem:

- Integrating different types of data generally calls for plenty of planning. Moreover, the hardware of imaging technology is quite expensive (an adequate workstation to display a document image costs much more than the average PC) — another argument for methodical planning.
- On the other hand, it is silly to draw up careful plans on a subject where your ignorance is great. As soon as you start to implement the plans, you will probably discover that they are based on wrong assumptions, gloss over certain problems, overestimate certain difficulties, ignore important options and so on.
- So what should Alpine Ash do? Set up a taskforce to make a masterplan for a document-imaging infrastructure — selecting preferred suppliers, deciding which document images should be linked to which other pieces of data in which ways, outlining appropriate new working practices etc — even though this will very likely turn out to be naive or futile? Or avoid doing that and allow anarchy to prevail?

Deciding whether or not to have a masterplan now is the most fundamental of all decisions to be taken in this situation. It sets the scope for everything else. It is plainly a management decision to which technology knowledge is one input, rather than a technology decision on which managers may be consulted. Before resolving the dilemma, Alpine Ash managers need a briefing to help see the range of options with the use of document images in a database system.

WARRANTS

At the start of the nineties many consultants and gurus began to associate imaging technology with radical re-engineering of working practices in most organisations.[1] This briefing doesn't aim to cover all such possibilities and implications; it concentrates on the issues of data structure and integrity that arise in systems that use document images. You *can* re-engineer a business without knowing any of this, but then so can anyone. To do it *successfully*, on the other hand, some knowledge is needed.

Distinctions of Roles

One good entrance to this field is to draw distinctions between the different roles document images may play. There are four main possibilities:

- **Pure archive.** Documents are held in image form mainly to be accessed *after the event*, just in case they should ever be needed — eg for use in a legal case or for random checks by auditors or to track down some suspected fraud. Thus the great majority of stored images are probably never accessed.
- **Live archive.** Documents are held in image form mainly to be accessed *while the transaction or matter they concern is still live* — but only on a just-in-case basis. For instance, all letters of complaint from customers can be stored as images, even though for the great majority, the image is never accessed, since a simple letter in response closes the matter. However, about 5-10% of complaint cases develop a real life of their own; for these, the document images are likely to be accessed several times by several people.
- **Matter-handling.** Documents are held in image form to be accessed while the matter they concern is still live — and all are certain to be accessed, since this is an *integral part of the workflow*. For instance, whenever there is any dispute with a travel agent or airport or regulatory authority, the airline stores all relevant documents as images. There are standard (albeit complex) procedures (eg for handling a travel agent's disagreement about commission calculations), which ensure that the right document images are routed to the workstations of the right people at the right points in the cycle.

• **Reference.** The document images don't refer to any particular matter or transaction; they are to be *referenced when needed.* They could be facsimiles of the small print of an airline's standard contractual arrangements with travel-agents or the pages from a legal report about some case setting a precedent in disputes between airlines and travel agents.

Distinctions between Types of Associated Data

Another way of analysing the scope of different imaging applications is to ask: Some data associated with the document images must surely be stored; what kind of data?

A system storing the images of letters may well store the name of the sender as mainstream data so that the letter images can easily be found. Since the sender's name appears in the letter, it can be said that here the **associated data** is also part of the image itself. But a system might also store (say) a *worry-code*, assessing the seriousness of each complaint on a scale from 1 to 9; this associated data is not part of the image (unless perhaps an ex-employee writes in: 'I know your system and I think my complaint is worth at least an 8').

As the diagram illustrates, the distinction between associated data which is and that which is not part of the image can be taken further to produce six categories of associated data:

• **Key data.** This is mainstream data serving as keys to identify the document image in a unique or close-to-unique way; eg *correspondent-name, letter-date* etc. This data is often contained in the image, but not necessarily; eg a letter probably won't quote the identifying *customer-number* that the database system uses.

• **Data for processing.** This is mainstream data contained in the document image that is taken out and held separately, for mainstream processing rather than for identity, eg within a customer complaint letter: *flight-number, flight-date, ticket-price, travel-agent, cabin-attendant, airport* etc

• **Alternative form data.** Some systems take all (or the bulk) of the content of the document image and hold it in another form too: eg a letter may be stored as an image, but its entire text (except the letterhead and signature) is stored as characters too. Either form can be accessed; perhaps one is more convenient than the other in different cases or in different procedure steps.

• **Keyword data**. This is data that doesn't form unique keys for identifying an image specifically, but helps in finding *likely* relevant items — eg keywords describing the main features of a certain

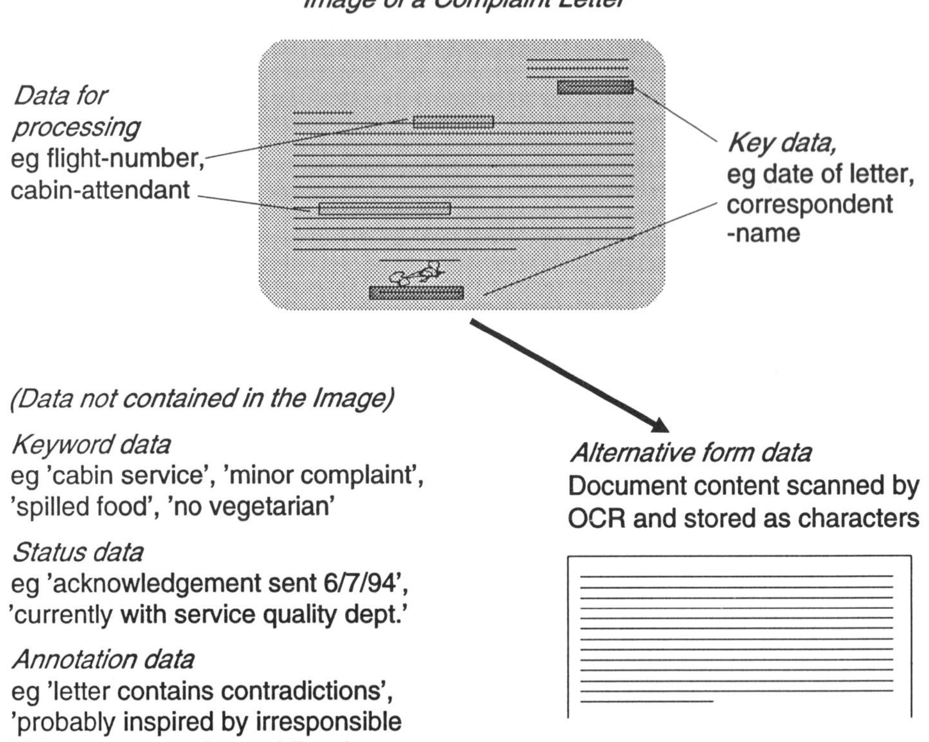

matter or the trickiness of a case. This kind of data is very unlikely to be a clear element of content within the image.

- **Status data**. This is data showing where a document currently stands within the standard processing cycle: eg for this complaint, procedure-step 3 has been completed, but the unusual step 3a is needed before step 4 can begin. This data typically consists of status codes, dates and step-identifiers. It is dynamic, and by its nature will not be contained in the image.
- **Annotation data**. This is usually text, though it can be stored voice. It covers a great variety of free-form comments such as 'We stand to lose $158,356 on this one, if the claim is valid, which I doubt' or 'If she invokes article 137 (a) (iv), inform the MD and settle out of court at any price' or 'the second and fifth paragraphs of this letter are contradictory'.

Gradations of Data Structure

For this briefing call the images together with the associated data — whether mainstream, keyword, voice or anything else — the database. This database can have structures of greater or lesser complexity. Here are the main gradations:

- Gradation 1: **Simple flat set.** One image and its associated data correspond to one document. The database is just a set of one-image documents, each with its own simple, associated data. There is no more subtlety than that to its structure.
- Gradation 2: **Paged flat set.** One document may have several pages and thus several images and there will be data associated with the document (as opposed to with individual document pages). Otherwise the structure is as simple as with Gradation 1.
- Gradation 3: **Three-level hierarchy.** There is a three-level structure: case-document-page. Thus, one document normally consists of several images (ie pages); but one case (or matter or transaction, depending on the application) normally has several documents. Perhaps the standard procedure for handling a dispute over travel-agent's commission means that there *must* be certain documents on file before the case is closed: original letter, internal auditor's report (signed), comment from travel-agent-liaison department (signed)... acceptance of revised commission (signed by travel agent) etc. Associated data probably has to be held at two levels, case and document. The database maintains this structure; eg given a certain case-identifier it can extract all the relevant documents and associated data, and also, to some degree, state whether any documents are outstanding.
- Gradation 4: **Complex hierarchy.** This is more complex than Gradation 3, but still definable. Perhaps more than three levels are needed: if there are numerous disputes with a certain travel-agent, perhaps images and associated data are needed also at a top travel-agent level. Or a pure hierarchy structure may be inadequate: though documents are structured by case, they may sometimes be organised into other hierarchies too: eg complaint-type within complaints-clerk-responsible within document-type.
- Gradation 5: **Flexible hierarchy.** Some hierarchy structuring similar to Gradations 3 and 4 is used, but in fact no one pre-defined structure will meet the requirements, except possibly one far too complex to be workable. For instance, Customer A makes three separate complaints in separate letters, then sends a letter making a fourth complaint that contradicts the grounds for the second and third complaints; but then a quite separate complaint by Customer

B is resolved by the courts in a way that seems to have implications for A's first and third complaints. If this kind of thing is typical or frequent it may be foolish to define an explicit structure so complicated that it can record all possible ways in which items can conceivably be linked together. The combination of a simple hierarchy with keyword techniques may be more appropriate.

Aspects of Imaging and Data Organisation

The three main pieces of analysis presented so far in this briefing can be combined with three more points to make a set of six aspects of imaging and data organisation.

- **Role.** As already described, it is useful to draw some very broad distinctions between the main roles and purposes of documents in image form.
- **Associated data.** Coherent use of document images calls for sensible decisions about the kind of associated data and the way it is used.
- **Data structure.** Even with relatively non-tractable data such as document images, complexity of data structures is an issue.
- **Data capture.** In so far as the associated data contains data already present in the document image, decisions are needed on how to capture it. The main two possibilities are: either key the data in, or use OCR (optical character recognition) to scan the document and translate the text (or part of it) into characters that a computer can process.
- **Data consistency.** If some data is both in the document image and in associated data, then there is a potential for inconsistency. This may be merely theoretical, but it may be a major concern, requiring specific measures.
- **Deep design.** Storing, transmitting and displaying substantial quantities of document images is relatively extravagant in hardware resources and thus costly. Therefore any system should be competently designed by someone who understands the technology. Of course. But there can be cases where technical competence at supplying the agreed demands is the wrong goal. Sometimes awareness of technical supply-side design should feed back and lead to alterations to what has been demanded.

Consistency and deep design need discussion in more detail.

Gradations of Consistency

Document images are usually stored on optical (as opposed to the usual magnetic) disks, which have a high capacity but can't be amended. This latter trait leads to some interesting issues in maintaining data consistency.

The gravity of issues of consistency between image content on optical disk and associated data on magnetic disk depends in large part on how much data is common to both. Other relevant issues are how *likely* it is and how disastrous it would be for data to become inconsistent.

Any inconsistency is undesirable; on the other hand, it can be foolish to make systems very complicated in order to guard against inconsistencies that will almost never occur and which will not matter very much anyway. Solutions to the consistency problem have three main gradations:

- Gradation 1. **Don't bother.** Characteristic situation: only a small amount of key data is common and needs to remain consistent so that the image can be found in a pure archive system. Perhaps there *is* some possibility of inconsistency arising; eg *name* might be a key field and a woman's name might change by marriage. But is it sensible to spend hundreds of thousands of dollars on building in extra system features to cover this, just in case a woman wishes to reopen some long-dead complaint and doesn't tell you she has changed her name in the mean time? If all the consistency problems of a system are similar to this, it probably isn't worth investing in a completely rigorous system.
- Gradation 2. **Annotation adequate.** As Gradation 1, but the image plays a live-archive or matter-handling role. Perhaps the key includes the name of travel-agency A that initiates the dispute but A is taken over by travel-agency B and the latter's legal department is now handling the case and sending further letters. A subtle data structure is needed to keep this straight, but still nothing can alter the fact that the original letter from A is now filed by the system under B — something that, at a hasty glance, could be a mistake.

This is different from the first case. Apparent inconsistencies in data relating to a live matter can cause confusion among staff working under pressure and that confusion can lead to mistakes that cause genuine inconsistencies or other errors. Probably it is necessary to record explicitly that identification data preserved in the document image is no longer valid; but, important though this is, a special annotation entry may be an adequate, simple solution.

- Gradation 3. **System design required.** Fields susceptible to frequent updating shouldn't normally be chosen as key fields at all, because of all the complications it can cause. But suppose the system takes other data — for processing, not as keys — out of the document image, stores that in the mainstream database and subjects it to updates.

First of all, this is no great problem if the data, by its very nature, is not something that need retain consistency. The customer's letter may estimate that the cost of replacing the suit ruined by the cabin attendant's sloppy service is $2,000; but if the mainstream field *compensation-reserve* has $500 rather than $2,000, there is no great reason to suspect a mistake; it is just a shrewd guess of what the customer will settle for.

Suppose the letter of complaint from a customer contains data such as *ticket-price, travel-agent, cabin-attendant, airport* etc. These become fields in the mainstream database. But later investigation shows that the customer was mistaken: it was a different travel agency with a similar name, a different cabin attendant etc. Now if you update these fields in the database with the truth it will be inconsistent with the image. Which do you want: truth or consistency?

If this kind of case is at all common, probably the solution is to design the system to store two sets of fields (*travel-agency, cabin-attendant* etc) in the mainstream database — one recording the customer's version or claims, consistent with the document image and not normally amended, the other recording the current assumption of the truth. But this can be a very tricky piece of systems analysis. Suppose a letter arrives: 'I hereby revise some of the facts I gave in my letter of complaint last month. . .' That kind of case has to be accommodated too.

Deep Design Examples

Whatever technology is used for whatever purpose, the people doing the deep technology-related design work need to be competent. Sometimes there is one natural, straightforward way of doing things, that anybody competent is likely to find. Other times there are two or three different approaches that a competent person might find, but in practice the third-best isn't all that much inferior in financial and other business terms to the very best. But there can be cases — and they include some, not all, imaging systems — where a really *clever* technical design may be greatly superior to a merely competent one. To give a brief taste, not a proper analysis, of how this can be, here are two examples of design issues that can make a big difference:

- **Client-server architecture.** Most imaging systems use some version of client-server architecture. A powerful server manages great volumes of data in the central bank of optical disks, and the client work-station must be quite a powerful device too. It accepts images that arrive from the server in compressed form (to minimise the burden on the network), and decompresses them for display on a high-definition screen — something that may call for considerable processing power.

But there is scope for choice on how the workload is split between client and server. Should the client do decompression and display, but leave most other intelligent processing to the server? Or should the client do more; eg apply workflow rules to decide for itself when to ask the server for which documents? This kind of design decision arises with all client-server systems, but the stakes are higher here, because the volumes of data are greater.

- **Optimising image storage and access.** Besides having very high capacity and making data, once written, impossible to amend, optical disks have a third salient difference from magnetic disks: access to them is much slower — perhaps in some cases too slow to provide acceptable response time. There is scope for ingenious design to mitigate this disadvantage according to the characteristics of a particular application.

One resource is use of a magnetic disk as a temporary, high-speed cache. Document images likely to be requested by a workstation in the near future (eg other documents of the same case as the document already requested) can be automatically written to the magnetic disk, just in case they are called for. (The contents of a magnetic disk can, of course, be over-written time and time again.) Again, document images are normally stored over a whole bank of optical disks, but the hardware may well retrieve (say) five images that are next to each other on a disk quicker than if they are scattered over the disk or over different disks. Shrewd decisions about which images to store where can be very important.

Thus, investment in the effort of clever design of magnetic disk cache usage and allocation of images to disks can pay large dividends. Moreover, a general awareness that such supply issues exist can be useful in formulating realistic demands.[2]

POSSIBLE DECISION-MAKING

Six warrants for imaging and data organisation have been spelt out. The different parts of this analysis are interrelated to some degree. If an imaging system has a pure archive role, then probably consistency controls and clever optimisation of deep design will be less substantial issues than if the role were (say) matter-handling. Again, a system holding a considerable amount of status data and annotation data will probably (though not certainly) be quite high on the gradations scale for data structure.

SUMMARY OF WARRANTS

Distinctions of Imaging Roles: Pure archive; Live archive; Matter-handling; Reference

Distinctions between Types of Associated Data: Key data; Data for processing; Alternative form data; Keyword data; Status data; Annotation data

Gradations of Data Structure: Simple-flat-set through Paged-flat-set through Three-level-hierarchy through Complex-hierarchy to Flexible-hierarchy.

Aspects of Imaging and Data Organisation: Imaging role; Associated data; Data structure; Data capture; Data consistency; Deep design

Gradations of Consistency: Don't-bother through Annotation-adequate to System-design-required

Examples of Deep Design Issues: Client-server architecture; Optimising image storage and access

However, these interrelations between warrants are not all-determining. Though the pure archive role is the simplest in many respects, a system with this role might still contain much keyword data and annotation (at the case level) and call for a relatively complex data structure. Matter-handling with complex status data seems the most exacting type of system in general, but that doesn't mean that such a system will *always* call for very skillful deep design. It may; but perhaps, given the characteristics of the application, the natural, straightforward design can't be varied with any great advantage.

One thing the Alpine Ash managers might do is have this briefing's *general* analysis of imaging systems expanded into a document perhaps five times as long, by mapping out these interactions in more detail: Which particular factors in complex matter-handling, as a general rule, lead to significant deep design choices and which do not? How can the general category of pure archive cases be broken down between those requiring complex data structure and those that do not? And so on.

This would be an excellent investment of intellectual effort within a business that had already recognised dozens of likely imaging applications, or perhaps for some consultancy company aiming to purvey expertise on imaging systems. But Alpine Ash managers take a more direct, less generalised approach. They sketch out the logic of their decision-making as follows:

- We are currently aware of seven or eight plausible imaging applications within the organisation.
- We will define the scope of each fairly well in terms of the six warrants. This will help us to see, perhaps, that two applications superficially very different are, when analysed in terms of the warrants, rather similar. Also, we may see that some large areas of the possibility-space are unoccupied: ie some gradations or distinction-categories that are obviously important in the general analysis of imaging are untouched by any of our applications.
- But the above is a simplification; it implies that it is easy to see where each application should stand on each of the six warrants. In practice, there will be plausible alternatives; eg a matter-handling system might be done in an advanced way with sophisticated status data and data structure, or in a simpler way, and both options may seem plausible. Therefore, where relevant and exercising some self-discipline, we should use the six warrants as the basis for defining two or three *variant approaches* to certain of our applications.
- The result of this will be a kind of map, with the warrants (and their breakdown into distinctions and gradations) as a grid or framework, on which individual applications and application-variants are plotted.
- Where will we go from there? This exercise *may* get us to the position where our imaging requirements seem quite clear and firm. If so, the natural strategic decision will be to work out plans for one coherent imaging infrastructure to meet all our needs; the map can be the starting-point for that planning work. On the other hand, it may be that our feelings and the evidence of the map will produce a different situation. Perhaps we shall decide that the possibilities are too varied to be assessed without practical experience. Perhaps setting up an infrastructure would be premature; a better strategy might be to pick from the map a few inexpensive applications as experiments and learn from them. Or perhaps our strategic decision will be somewhere between the pure-infrastructure and pure-experiment options . .

CONNECTIONS

8. Internal Schema Design	Deciding disk allocation and the like for mainstream systems
9. Client-server Architecture	Deciding on the split between client and server functions
19. Classic Text Systems	Accessing text or keyword, often a part of a database including document images
28. Non-Mainstream Software Products	Software products for document image database

25. Geographic Information Systems

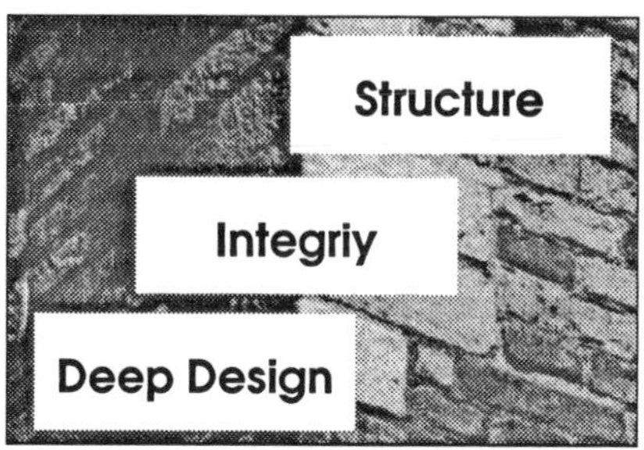

BEARINGS

Briefing 2 explains how spatial data can be used in two different ways: as if it were pure graphics data to produce graphics, and as if mainstream data for processing such as selection and calculation. When the spatial data is geographic (as opposed to engineering, astronomical, medical etc), then the graphics are maps and the processing is calculation of distances along roads, selection of buildings within a certain proximity of canals and the like.[1]

To count as a database system, rather than just a system for producing maps, a system generally combines geographic data with mainstream data; ie it is hybrid. A hybrid system that crosses a certain threshold of complexity is generally called a GIS (geographic information system). In some cases, though, a simpler form of system — called business mapping in this book — may be a more favourable match of supply and demand.

POSSIBLE CONTEXT

The village of Eucalyptus is being developed as a new city. Its public transport system will integrate metro, high-speed tram and bus services; facilities for tourists will be planned from the start; and civic administration systems will make full use of database technology.

It soon becomes clear that a GIS should be seriously considered. Here is a simple example of what it might do:

- use mainstream data to produce figures for each district about crime (or population profile or retail outlets etc etc);
- then display a map of the city, with districts coloured differently according to crime-rate, population density, types of shops etc.

And here is a more complicated task:

- use data — both mainstream and geographic — about tourist

attractions and also about public transport routes and frequencies, in order to work out the best way to get to the attractions;

- then print out information sheets for tourists, showing both in words and as simple maps that (say) to get from central station to the art gallery it is best to take the metro to the harbour and then change to bus 35.

Moreover, the really attractive feature of a city's GIS can't be shown in a few examples: a system that meets a few specific purposes — illustrate statistics on a district basis or do clever things with public transport data — is one thing, but a *general-purpose* system would be far more valuable. Ideally a system would use the same basic geographic data to plan public transport and schedule sewer maintenance and control the licensing of businesses and match schools' capacity to pupil numbers and monitor pollution and so on.

The planners at the Eucalyptus development agency see that a GIS, though plainly a valuable thing, could easily become a very ambitious undertaking. They also know that most ambitious computer systems, whatever the technology, share a certain property: The marginal cost of supplying some of the most sophisticated demands may be far greater than their marginal benefit. If 90% of the demands can be supplied at 60% of the cost, risk and timescale, it may not necessarily be a good thing to invest in the last 10% of demands as well. Put another way, the essential problem is to find the best-buy combination of supply and demand.

It isn't reasonable to expect all the planners at Eucalyptus to become experts on GIS technology, but they need to be adequately briefed on the most basic tradeoff possibilities. Otherwise they won't be able to take any useful part in debates about possibilities, implications and best-buy decisions.

WARRANTS

This is another technology where marketing brochures and magazine articles often obscure the shape of the continent by describing its capes, bays and fjords.[2] Fortunately, GIS yields quite readily to the technique of sketching out gradations of complexity as a framework for understanding. This briefing begins with gradations and then develops the main concepts they expose.

Gradations of GIS (Demand)

First concentrate as much as possible on what kinds of thing a system may do, leaving aside how it does them. There are a few main gradations:

- Gradation 0: **Pure mainstream.** Fields such as *district* or *postcode* are plainly concerned with location, but they may still be used as straightforward mainstream data. Analysing crime totals by district is no different from analysing by type of crime or age of criminal or time of crime. The geographical facts that district 3 is in the north of the city and shaped like a salamander while district 13 is in the south and shaped like an orange are irrelevant.

Probably the records in the *Crimes* table will show the address where the crime was committed — not the district; to arrive at the district, the system might look up a large table, showing for every postcode (many thousands) the corresponding district. This is still mainstream processing — no different from using a table of times of sunrise and sunset to see whether a crime committed at a certain time on a certain day occurred in daylight or not. The geographical facts that postcodes 3055 and 3089 are right next to each other within district 13, while 3091 is over in the opposite corner are irrelevant.

- Gradation 1: **Thematic mapping.** Just as a piechart can show a city's crime figures broken down by district, so a map can show districts coloured differently according to their crime figures. Here the map feature of the system is purely a display technique; it generates no extra information, since the same crime analysis could just as well be printed out as a list of figures.

This may sound a rather trivial presentation technique, but suppose the information is shown at a very detailed level, such as postcode area. The mosaic of thousands of tiny areas, coloured in many shades from pale pink through to magenta, might convey a message that few people would discern from a long list of figures. A related presentation technique is to colour in only those areas with (say) twice the average rate of crime and leave all the others blank, without even drawing their outlines.

- Gradation 2: **Business mapping.** Many business application systems, particularly those concerned with sales, combine thematic mapping with just one other feature: selecting (say) buildings that meet the criterion of being within a 300-metre radius of the town hall. This *within-a-certain-radius* feature can't really be handled by straightforward mainstream processing; using districts and postcode areas (or even block-codes within postcode area) is just too awkward. For each item that may be accessed through this feature, the system needs to hold spatial data, enabling both map display and calculation of distance between points for selection purposes. As

'Business Mapping' Possibilities

Display all buildings of architectural interest, within a 300-metre radius of the town hall, using shape to indicate status, and shading for age

□ protected building (grade 1)
◇ other protected building
○ other notable building

less than 15 years old
15-50 years old
more than 50 years old

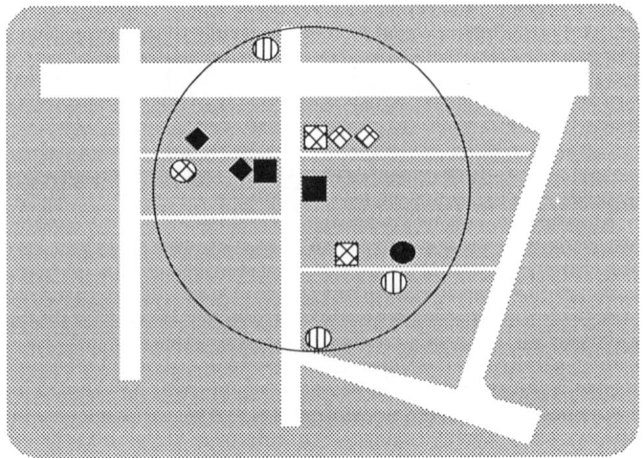

The next enquiry could select buildings by some other criteria, or analyse status and age differently, or base shape and shading on some other mainstream data

the first diagram suggests, the resulting system may be powerful enough to meet quite a range of demands.

• Gradations 3 and beyond: **GIS.** Systems beyond Gradation 2 store more spatial data and use it in more sophisticated ways, but their most striking feature is **layer management**. As the second diagram shows, this concept allows you to produce a map of all the streets of a city and nothing else, or to add an extra layer of detail about public transport routes or to show any other combinations of layers; systems often have dozens. It is easy to see, at least intuitively, that layer management is a foundation for much more complex and varied uses than those of Gradation 2.

A system that can select (say) all buildings within a *buffer-zone* of 200 metres along the length of a motorway is more sophisticated than one that can only select those within a certain radius of one given point. A system that can calculate the percentage of all children in the city that are within 20 minutes travelling distance of a suitable school is advanced too, though in a different way. Any number of such features could be set out, but this is unnecessary. The main point is that systems at Gradation 3 (and however many

Map Layer Management

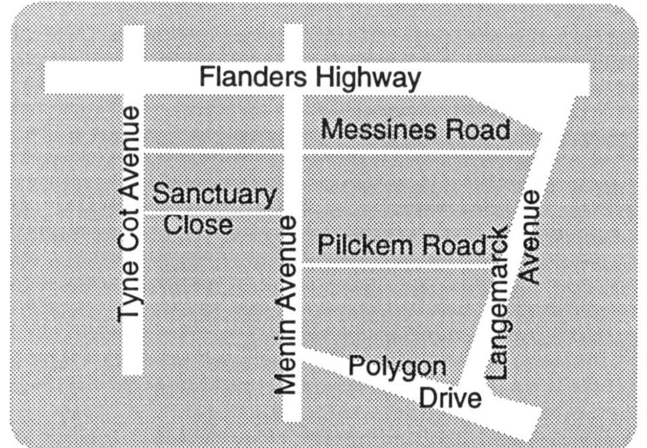

Street Layer only

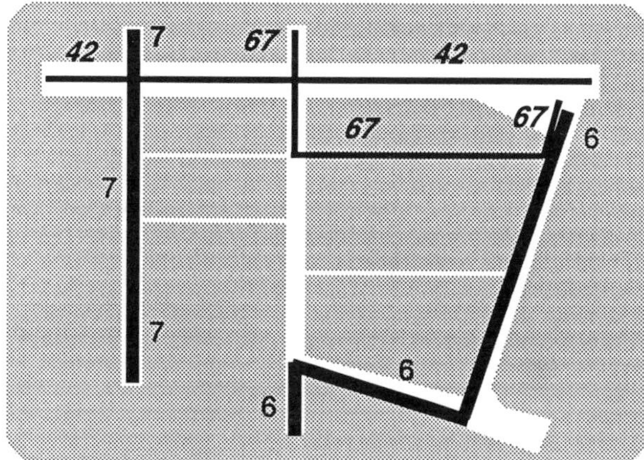

Street Layer combined with Public Transport Layer

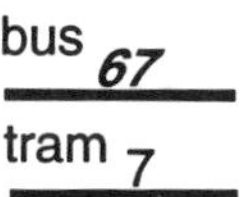

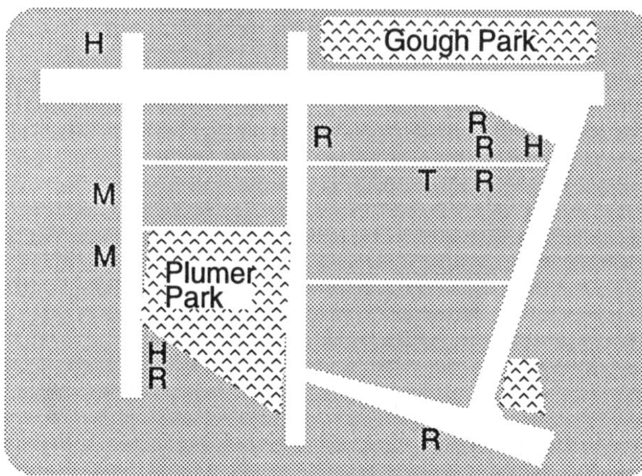

Street Layer combined with Parks Layer and Tourism Layer

H Hotel
M Museum etc
R Restaurant
T Theatre etc

more gradations you care to make) share the vital characteristics of using genuine spatial data and managing data in layers.

Gradations of GIS (Supply)

To see why these gradations of demand take the shape they do, see how they are likely to be supplied:

- Gradation 0: **Pure mainstream.** This is a mainstream database like any other.
- Gradation 1: **Mainstream with graphics.** There are two bodies of data: a pure mainstream database and a separate collection of data in vector graphics format, defining the shapes (eg districts and postcode areas) making up the map. Provided each shape has an identifier (eg district 13 or postcode 3055) that also exists in the mainstream database, the system can meet its demands. With the link between the two bodies of data so simple, technical design can be concentrated on storing the graphics shapes, redrawing them and fitting them together as *efficiently* as possible. Issues such as making it easy to alter individual shapes, or providing detailed checks for consistency between the graphics shapes and the mainstream data don't really arise.

  The detail of *how* the system fits together all its shapes into a map is hidden. It might store a co-ordinate of the top left corner of the shape of every postcode area, relative to the top corner of the whole map; or it might store a co-ordinate of every postcode area relative to the top corner of the district to which it belongs or it might adopt any number of more complicated but perhaps more efficient approaches. But this is of no interest to the user of the system.
- Gradation 2: **Mainstream with graphics plus.** This is best seen as a modified Gradation 1 approach. For certain (not all) shapes on the map, the graphics format also contains enough data to permit the *within-a-certain-radius* feature to operate. This is a pragmatic way of meeting a certain set of relatively modest demands, but it is a dead end.
- Gradations 3 and beyond: **Explicit, objective co-ordinates.** From here on a completely different approach is needed — one that stresses general-purpose use of data over mere efficiency in handling graphics. In a genuine GIS every point on the map — every building, every point defining the shape of a district, every twist and bend in every road — is given its own explicit, objective co-ordinates (ie a pair of numbers), on some simple, consistent basis: often, but not necessarily, latitude and longitude on the earth's surface. The content of the map is said to be **geocoded**. The stored co-ordinates can

be as detailed (ie lengthy) as are needed for the accuracy of map-drawing and calculation required.

For some operations this approach may be far less efficient than mainstream-with-graphics-plus. Also, the task of capturing all the co-ordinate data may be onerous. On the other hand, beyond this threshold, many powerful possibilities open up. If you need to select all schools that are at least 0.7km from any postcode-area with higher than average crime, and not within 1km of any point on a motorway, and no more than 0.5km along a well-lit road from a metro-station, then, in principle, this approach has the data organised to handle that.

Again, if the database has 27 layers, but you want to merge layers 2 and 25, while shifting some of the items in the old layer 25 over to layer 24, that can all be done methodically without anxiety about perplexing repercussions on the rest of the data.[3]

Examples of Structure of Data

With the thematic mapping and business mapping gradations, two separate bodies of different kinds of data are held and linked together in a simple way. But with true GIS it is worthwhile to think of the whole database having one coherent conceptual schema. Such a schema might be something like this:

- There are many items of graphics data corresponding to all the different things on the map, but they are grouped into (say) ten sets, each corresponding to one layer of information required on the maps: street layer, public transport layer, tourism layer etc.
- There are (say) forty tables of mainstream data, each table associated with one and only one of the layers; eg one table contains a record for every metro station that exists on the public transport layer and another table has a record for every tram-halt. The key of each mainstream record also identifies each shape among the graphics data.

This arrangement for a schema seems attractively neat and convenient, but things often get more complicated; eg:

- There might be no one-for-one correspondence between one shape on the map and a record in a table. In the public transport layer some mainstream data might be held in a *Tram-line* table, with one record for each service, but the graphic corresponding to the service on the map isn't one item such as a circle or a tetrahedron; it is a concatenation of many short stretches of lines corresponding to the streets passed through.
- The layers might not be cleanly separate; eg mainstream tables storing directions to tourist attractions might exist at the tourism

layer, but part of the data they derive from may be the routes of public transport services that are held on a different layer.

• GIS layers are normally thought of as transparent layers, to be arranged in any combination, without concern for any structure or hierarchy. Thus, no layer is more important than another; no layer is dependent on another; no layer is an alternative version of another. But this concept can't always be kept entirely pure. Often, one of the layers (the street layer in the case of a city) has a special status as the base layer on which all others are overlaid; the information at the public transport layer may be difficult to use, except in combination with the street layer — but the reverse is not true.

• The simplicity of separate layers might be undermined in other ways, particularly by layers that really contain the same information as others, but to different degrees of detail. As well as having ten main layers you might want to have several variants: eg layer 1A shows major roads, 1B all roads, 1C all roads and cycle routes, 1D all roads, cycle routes and footpaths.

Distinctions of Integrity Requirements

It is difficult to keep heterogeneous data consistent. Suppose the boundaries of certain districts are to be redrawn. This should happen graphically on the appropriate layer of the map, but some fields in the tables of mainstream data may have to change too. If there are fields showing the surface area of each district, or the population of each district, they will presumably be out of date once the boundary changes are made. If all mainstream fields affected are not changed, the database will become inconsistent — a poor state of affairs. For most GISs the question arises: What safeguards are needed to avoid inconsistencies between graphics and mainstream data and maintain the integrity of the database? Four main types of integrity control case need to be distinguished:

• **No update, no safeguards.** Many modest systems include no regular facility for any update that might cause inconsistency between graphics and mainstream data. A system might perform thematic mapping at the level of city districts and the district boundaries, without any defined facilities for handling changes to district boundaries. Perhaps the boundaries *do* change about once a decade, but, when that occurs, there is always plenty of time to work out all the implications and prepare for a special one-off operation.

• **Simple consequential change.** To maintain integrity, a system might refuse to accept a change to its mainstream data (eg deletion of the record about a certain glass-disposal container from the *Waste-container* table) unless some obvious, consequential graphics

Graphic Shape and Mainstream Table

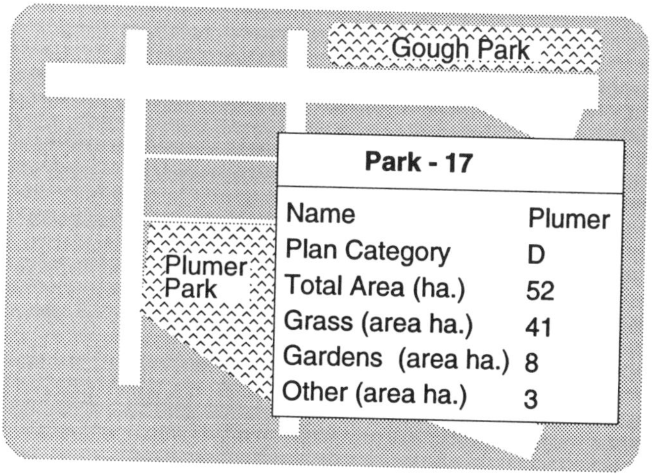

Gough Park

Plumer Park

Park - 17	
Name	Plumer
Plan Category	D
Total Area (ha.)	52
Grass (area ha.)	41
Gardens (area ha.)	8
Other (area ha.)	3

Click with a mouse on the shape of Plumer Park and the system shows the record of mainstream data held about the park

Suppose you alter the shape of the park on the map.
Then some of the mainstream data (eg about area) will no longer be consistent with the map.
The system needs integrity control features to ensure that graphic and mainstream data keep in step.

change was also made (eg removal of the shape from a map) — either explicitly or perhaps, as a default, automatically. Automatic integrity control for this kind of update is usually essential. Having to *remember* to amend the map data after the mainstream data will almost certainly be unacceptable.

- **Simple, non-automatic change.** Suppose that a corner of Plumer Park is to be lopped off for use as a supermarket (see the third diagram). The shape of the park can be altered on the screen, using a mouse or similar device. Since there is a mainstream record for Plumer Park, the system will display that too. Plainly, the field *total-area* must be updated. The system could safeguard consistency by examining the revised graphic to recalculate and update this field automatically. But what about the other mainstream fields that break down the park's total area by use? That data can't be derived from the graphics of the map, so the system can't work out any new values. The best it can do is to *insist* that *some* update of this data be keyed in and to check the resulting fields for consistency.
- **Pragmatic integrity.** Sometimes it may not be feasible for a

system to preserve consistency in either of the two ways described above. Suppose there is a *Tourist-information* table, recording which public transport to take for each attraction. Bus 35 used to stop right outside the art gallery, but now that its route has been altered on the map, it no longer does. Should the system change a piece of mainstream data in the *Tourist-information* table automatically? Or insist on input of some change and validate it stringently?

Suppose bus 35 now stops just 20 metres from the art gallery; or 200 metres; or 400 metres? Does it matter that bus 35 still stops nearer than any other, except bus 178, a two-hourly service? Suppose bus 178 were a half-hourly service; would that make a difference? There is a dilemma here: If the system has no integrity safeguards for changes of bus-route, then, however diligent the users of the system may be, the *Tourist-information* table will probably contain data sooner or later that is incontrovertibly false. But defining a set of rules for the system to apply rigorously seems an impossibly complex task. The only answer may be to build in features to combat inconsistency in a pragmatic rather than rigorous way; eg printing out lists of data that ought to be examined to see if *perhaps* some inconsistency may have arisen.

Comparison of Deep Design Approaches

Definition of the layers and tables of the GIS's conceptual schema may still leave open a choice between two fundamental options of deep design:

- **Loose hybrid.** The mainstream data is kept in a relational database (or perhaps a PC-relational database such as dBase) and the graphics data is kept separately as a set of files in some standard graphics format. Appropriate keys and indexes mesh the two bodies of data together to effect the structuring into layers defined by the conceptual schema.
- **Tight hybrid.** All the data, mainstream and graphics, is kept in one relational database. Though it seems rather unnatural, vector graphics data *can* be stored in this way; the lines and shapes and colours on the map can be decomposed into tables and records and fields.

The tight hybrid approach facilitates those controls on integrity that can be rigorous. It provides the CRS features characteristic of a powerful relational system. Also, some intricate spatial calculations may be done very efficiently if all the relevant data is stored in one relational database; eg work out a revised timetable for tram-line 7, given road-works and changed traffic-lights priorities at certain points of the route.

Disadvantages of the tight hybrid approach arise because relational organisation of geographic data can be unnatural and inefficient in some circumstances. If each record in a relational table represents one halt on a bus route, the only way to record the sequence of these halts is to include a field *sequence-number* in each record; merely *storing* them in sequence is not relationally correct. This may not sound a great hardship, but suppose the data has to be updated: to add a new halt between halts 2 and 3 will mean updating the *sequence-number* of the old halt 3 and of all the following (say) 30 halts on the route.

This rather trivial example is emblematic of the unnaturalness of the tight hybrid approach. Most designers of systems and software products to date have preferred to use the loose hybrid approach and store each of the two kinds of data in the way that suits it best.

Some suppliers of GIS software products aver that in the long term all-relational GISs will prevail, since this is inherently the cleanest approach. Others are more interested in waiting until other approaches, such as object-oriented DBMS, come to maturity.

Chart of Data-combination and Practical Matters

The gradations of demand and supply at the beginning and the subsequent discussions are largely concerned with the issues in *combining* different kinds of data in the database. This data-combination theme also interacts with certain practical matters of technology supply:[4]

- **Map-drawing.** This is concerned with the output medium, quality and complexity of the maps displayed or printed by the system. Sophistication can vary considerably: to display on the screen a map of a city as different-coloured districts is a less demanding task than to print out a detailed relief map with contour lines, subtly shaded according to the elevation of the ground. More or less infinite gradations of map quality are possible, depending on such variables as the resolution of the output device (printer, plotter or screen) and the range of colour supported.
- **Map-drawing and data-combination.** You could have a system to produce graphically sophisticated maps that scarcely combined geographic with mainstream data at all or, at another extreme, a system that combined mainstream and geographic data very cleverly to optimise tram-routes but printed its results as a very crude map or, thirdly, a system powerful in both map-drawing and data-combination. In other words, the two elements of map-drawing and data-combination are in free variation.
- **Map-acquisition.** This is concerned with getting the data into the

system ready for use. It covers both simple things like the use of clip-art outlines of a state or province, and complex ones, such as processing photos of the earth taken by satellite.

- **Map-acquisition, map-drawing and data-combination.** Map-acquisition is related to the other two elements as supply is to demand. That is, if you want sophisticated graphics or spatial calculations, it is a necessary but not sufficient condition that geographic data be acquired that is adequately clean and detailed.[5]

Gradations of Map-acquisition

In planning the map-acquisition element of a system much depends on whether the geographic data required is already available from some source, such as a semi-government body, not-for-profit organisation or commercial business. If so, the only issue is the cost and conditions of acquiring the data; there is no need for such feats as turning bit-mapped images from satellites into maps with lines and points. Here are the main gradations of map-acquisition functions likely to be relevant:

- Gradation 1: **External graphics.** Acquire whole maps or map elements (eg shapes of regions, states, districts etc) externally as vector graphics images, without explicit, objective co-ordinates.
- Gradation 2: **External geographic data.** Acquire externally the geographic data of maps in some special defined format — either industry-standard or specific to a certain software-product — including explicit, objective co-ordinates.
- Gradation 3: **Address tables.** Generate the co-ordinates of geographic data from mainstream data. Typically, the postal addresses of (say) all the buildings in a city are easily available in mainstream files, but not their co-ordinates. One common approach is to use a table that gives the co-ordinates of the *midpoint* of each postcode area; then every building in the city is given the co-ordinates of the midpoint of its postcode area. For many purposes this may be an adequate approximation; if not, more complicated tables can be used, eg storing several sets of co-ordinates within each postcode and recording for each the corresponding streets (or portions of streets by range of house number).
- Gradation 4: **Digitised maps.** Capture data by using a digitising tablet to trace over existing paper maps and thus input their shapes into the computer system, for storage in an appropriate vector graphics format.
- Gradation 5: **Enhanced external data.** Acquire geographic data externally (as Gradation 2), display it as a map and use a digitising

SUMMARY OF WARRANTS

Gradations of GIS (Demand): Pure-mainstream through thematic-mapping through business-mapping through GIS

Gradations of GIS (Supply): Pure-mainstream through mainstream-with-graphics through mainstream-with-graphics-plus through explicit-objective-co-ordinates

Examples of Structure of Data: Graphics and tables held in layers; Table record, but multiple graphics; Information crossing layers; Base and other layers; Variant layers of different detail

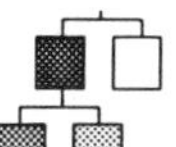

Distinctions of Integrity Cases: No update, no safeguards; Simple consequential change; Simple, non-automatic change; Pragmatic integrity

Comparison of Deep Design Approaches: Loose hybrid v Tight hybrid: Performance; Integrity

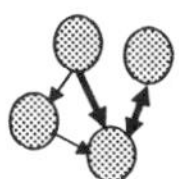

Chart connecting Data Combination and Practical Matters: Data combination; Map-drawing; Map-acquisition

Gradations of Map-acquisition: External graphics through External geographic data through Address tables through Digitised maps through Enhanced external data through Image processing

---

tablet to modify it (as Gradation 4), not just by changing details, but by making certain parts more detailed.

- Gradation 6: **Image processing.** Acquire photographic images (eg from satellite or at any rate as bit-mapped images) externally; then, use a digitising tablet to trace over the image to generate geographic data in an appropriate vector graphics format.

Projects where map-acquisition is handled through one of these higher gradations may incur costs on this essential but mundane task so great that all else pales into insignificance. As with most matters that fall into gradations of increasing complexity, it is usually most rational to take the lowest feasible option, unless there is some good reason for going higher.

POSSIBLE DECISION-MAKING

After all this, some of the Eucalyptus City planners feel that it might be better to leave the supply gradations, integrity safeguards and so on to technical experts. Surely users of the system shouldn't need to worry about such things.

This point is absolutely valid, but it doesn't follow at all that the *people who make the decisions* that set the scope of the systems, the degree of risk, the level of ambition, the amount of investment and so on should all ignore the options raised by the technology. If they are rational they want to choose the best-buy match of supply and demand; that may mean discarding some demands whose supply is too expensive or disadvantageous for some other reason. Moreover they may find that, through familiarity with the available options for achieving a GIS, some relevant demands, hitherto vaguely apprehended, become more attractive and tangible.

It is possible to imagine Eucalyptus City having one super relational database, integrating considerable bodies of mainstream data and graphics data, with very slick, automatic integrity. Perhaps this really is the best approach. But it is a very ambitious one, particularly if strong CRS and integrity features are also needed for high-volume mainstream transactions such as billing and payment of local taxes as well. Therefore, before assuming that the most elaborate ideal system is the appropriate one, Eucalyptus planners explore some possibilities that may lead to better buys:

- Suppose there were two main database systems — one all mainstream with no use for maps and one graphics-driven — and the simple links between them supported thematic mapping but no more. This would reduce the risk of one ambitious project, but at what price? What demands would have to be sacrificed? How many important demands really call for heavy integration of graphic and mainstream data? Which of them justify a large marginal risk?
- *Or*, perhaps a perceptive analysis of all plausible demands would show that some form of genuine GIS was essential and that some, but relatively few, of the updating requirements posed difficult problems of integrity control. By curtailing some of the more extravagant demands, perhaps these integrity problems might be greatly reduced. Thus the GIS might perform a great quantity of useful functions, but still be in essence relatively simple.
- *But* perhaps there really is a formidable set of non-negotiable demands that unavoidably entail a GIS supply of considerable complexity.

How do you evaluate the tradeoffs to decide on the right policy in this kind of situation? By summarising possibilities in a careful way that makes it easy to grasp how straightforward or formidable the more detailed implications will be — in other words, by debating demand and supply factors together.

CONNECTIONS

6. Database Integrity	Integrity in the mainstream world
26. Text-with-Mainstream Systems	One of the other main categories of complex hybrid systems
28. Non-Mainstream Software Products	GIS software products

26. Text-with-Mainstream Systems

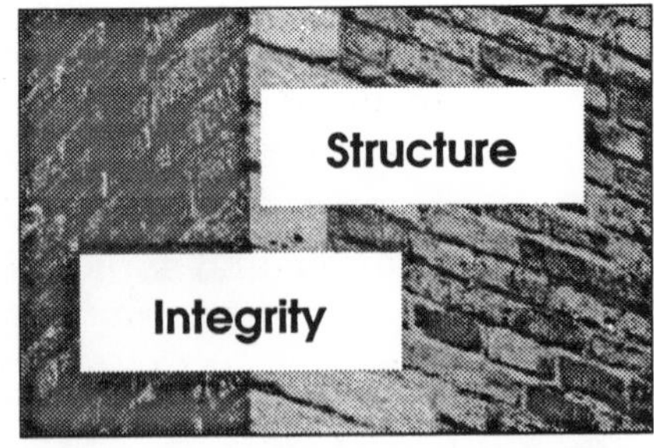

BEARINGS

This briefing tackles the case of the database that combines text and mainstream data — partly because of its intrinsic importance, but also as a representative example to expose some generic issues with complex hybrid database systems.

With a relatively demanding case like this one it becomes less appropriate to lay out generally applicable issues and options in any detail. The important thing is to gain a realistic impression of the kinds of options that you may have to decide between, and of the kinds of factors and complexities that come into the deliberations.

POSSIBLE CONTEXT

The go-ahead mayor of Cedar Wattle City is determined to upgrade the quality of civic administration through imaginative use of information technology. Here is one idea out of many:

- As in any large bureaucracy many paper documents are produced internally. Focus on two main categories of document: first, those that are, in some sense, plans (including discussion documents, strategy papers and the like); second, those in the broad category of progress reports and minutes of meetings, that essentially describe how plans on particular projects, problems and issues are progressing and what actions are due to be taken. Naturally, such documents will be produced with word processing technology and printed out. But why not go further and load them into a text database, so that they can be easily accessed?
- But this seems to be an application of text database where keyword or text-searching may not be sufficient. There is a need for stronger links between certain documents or between certain items of information. For instance, somebody looking at discussion point 7 of a meeting of a certain committee needs to jump easily and reliably to

other relevant material (eg the same issue discussed at the previous meeting, or the planning document that is referred to in point 7 or the overall policy on this issue defined at a meeting of some other committee). This might be done by hypertext links, but another attractive approach is to store relational tables of mainstream data, in addition to the texts themselves, to maintain a careful record of the entire structure of all the documents and parts of documents.

- This idea of holding a body of mainstream data is reinforced by another consideration. The text in many documents may contain things that need to be processed in a pure mainstream way: eg the budget figures contained in planning documents or the action points (person responsible, estimated completion date etc) defined in minutes of meetings may be used to produce lists of budget variances or outstanding actions that are late. Taken to an extreme, the documents might be strongly integrated with an accounting application and with a critical path analysis application for project control.

Probably then text and mainstream data will need to be combined *to some degree*. But to what degree? Not necessarily the extreme. Presumably, the more elaborate the integration of these inherently different kinds of data, the more powerful the system's functions, but the more expensive, risky and time-consuming it will be to implement. If so, there are very likely tradeoffs to be weighed.

You could spell out ideal requirements in purely non-technical terms, and leave a technical person to combine whatever data in whatever way seemed best to supply your defined demands. But that seems unsatisfactory because it really allows the central issue to go by default. If demands are defined in isolation from supply tradeoffs, then the central question of the *degree of integration* will never be explicitly discussed.

The challenge then is to discuss options in this area in a way that does justice to the main tradeoffs without losing sight of the desert for the dunes.

WARRANTS

The four warrant sections here deal specifically with hybrid databases of mainstream and text data. Even so, many of the themes that emerge in the discussion (eg consistency issues, loose and tight coupling etc) are relevant to other varieties of complex hybrid database system.

Gradations of Mainstream-Text Hybrids

To home in on the possibilities, imagine a database of information about meetings of work-groups on one huge development project — a great variety of meetings on different matters at different levels of policy and detail. A set of gradations helps to clarify the possibilities:

- Gradation 1: **Pure text.** The texts of minutes of all the meetings are held as documents for text-searching; thus you could search for each paragraph from any meeting's minutes in which both the words 'sport' and 'health' appear. There is no provision for mainstream data.
- Gradation 2: **Hybrid, but mainly text**. Minutes of meetings are held as documents for text-searching, but as an additional feature the system allows some mainstream data fields to be embedded in the text. If a text contains '#work-group=121', then the special character # signifies that work-group is not merely a word in the text, but also the name of a mainstream field. Thus you could search on 'sport' and 'health', but with the additional restrictive criterion that you were only interested in the meetings of work-group 121 or (say) work-groups 120-135.
- Gradation 3: **Complex hybrid of text and mainstream.** This is the most challenging; it divides into tight and loose hybrid, discussed in detail in the next section.
- Gradation 4: **Hybrid, but mainly mainstream.** Another approach is to reduce and regularise what is said and decided at meetings as far as possible into mainstream data fields that can be held in relational tables. A table might perhaps contain records with fields such as: *work-group, meeting-date, point-number, subject-code, department-responsible, person-responsible, priority-code, deadline-date* etc. But each record might also contain one field of text, called *minuted-text*, variable in length up to several hundred or thousand characters, containing the actual text from the published minutes.

Even if the text part of such a database turns out to be greater in volume than the mainstream data, it is still best thought of as a kind of adjunct. The idea is to search on the mainstream data; having tracked down the combination of work-group and subject-code of interest, you then display the full record and see the text. It is not the intention that searching on words contained in the text field should be the primary means of access. Even if allowed, this access facility is primitive: inefficient, since it goes against the underlying design and limited, since you can't search for (say) the combination of 'sport' and 'health' within one text.

- Gradation 5: **Pure mainstream.** The database follows standard relational principles for a mainstream database. As with Gradation 4, the meaning of the text of a document is translated as far as possible into codes and other mainstream data. No variable length text field is stored — just a reference identifying the document in some filing system, either paper or electronic, but in any event outside the database system.

A large Gradation 2 system (hybrid, but mainly text) may embed a substantial amount of mainstream data within text, without the advantages of organisation in a normal mainstream database. Conversely, Gradation 4 (hybrid, but mainly mainstream) may hold too much valuable information in the text fields with inadequate opportunity to use it for searching. There is a large gap to be filled by a genuine complex hybrid of text and mainstream.

Example of a Tight Hybrid Approach

With Gradation 3, the complex hybrid choice, two fundamentally different approaches are possible. The essence of a **tight hybrid** approach is to use a DBMS that is essentially relational, but has been given special extended facilities for storing and accessing text. Here is an outline example of the way this might be done:

- As well as allowing any field in the conceptual schema to be numeric or date or one of the other mainstream types, the DBMS allows an additional type: searchable text.
- The format of a record is allowed to contain any number of these searchable-text fields, provided they are of fixed length — as are all fields in any table of relational form.
- But the DBMS allows a deviation from the relational form; one and only one searchable-text field per record may be variable in length, up to (say) 64,000 characters.
- The DBMS includes an extra variant of the SQL language, so that the criterion for selecting information from the database can include the presence of a certain word anywhere within a certain searchable-text field.

Thus, assuming such an extended DBMS is available, one table of the database might hold in each record: the mainstream data fields *work-group, meeting-date, point-number* and so on; some fixed-length, searchable-text fields such as *action-point-description* (say 200 characters) and *implications* (say 500 characters, to allow for notes on the wider effects on other parts of the project); and the variable-length, searchable-text field *minuted-text.*

Text-with-Mainstream: Alternative Approaches

Tight Hybrid Approach

Relational record including special text fields

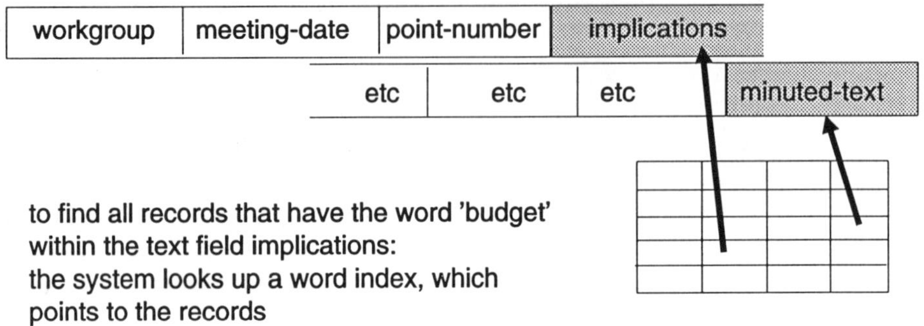
workgroup
meeting-date
point-number
implications
etc
etc
etc
minuted-text
to find all records that have the word 'budget' within the text field implications: the system looks up a word index, which points to the records

Loose Hybrid Approach

Ordinary relational record

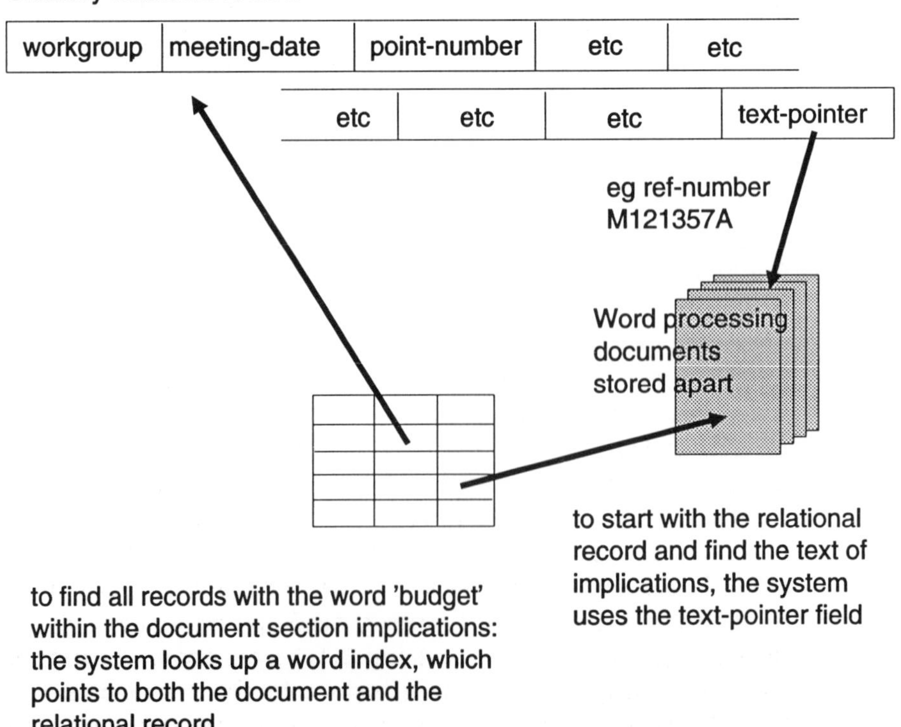
workgroup
meeting-date
point-number
etc
etc
etc
etc
etc
text-pointer
eg ref-number M121357A
Word processing documents stored apart
to start with the relational record and find the text of implications, the system uses the text-pointer field
to find all records with the word 'budget' within the document section implications: the system looks up a word index, which points to both the document and the relational record

Then an SQL instruction could select (say) all records for work-groups 120-135, during 1994 (normal SQL criteria), and also (extra variant of the language) where *implications* contains the word 'budget' and *minuted-text* contains the words 'sport' and 'health'.

For such a system to work effectively the DBMS needs to maintain special indexes not needed for a normal relational database. For each of the words 'budget' and 'sport' and 'health' and in fact all words entered in any of the searchable-text fields (other than 'of', 'the', 'in' etc), it needs to keep index records such as: 'budget' occurs in the *implications* field of records 127, 138, 145, 1354 . . . and in the *minuted-text* field of records 86, 127, 129 . . . The system needs a facility to update this indexing automatically whenever new text is added to the database. Thus, to the person using the system there seems merely to be one extra possibility for searching and selecting data (one more expression in the SQL language), but behind the scenes a large amount of extra DBMS software and extra processing and storage is entailed.[1]

Example of a Loose Hybrid Approach

Call the above a tight hybrid approach. The other plausible approach is to maintain links between mainstream and text data in a looser way: keep the mainstream data in a relational database; keep the text data itself separate, eg as a word processing file; but maintain whatever links and indexes are necessary to integrate the two.

This might be done in a variety of ways different in detail. A relational table might contain records made up of the mainstream data fields *work-group, meeting-date, point-number* and so on, together with one additional field: *text-pointer*.

Text-pointer contains the name of a document outside the database, eg a word processing document in WordPerfect format, with text in three sections — action-point-description, implications and minuted-text. Thus there could be a record in the relational database for work-group 121, meeting-date 4/4/94, point-number 7. This record contains in its field *text-pointer* the value M121357A, the name of the WordPerfect document holding the text.

Indexes are maintained for the words ('budget', 'sport', 'health' etc) that appear in the word processing documents. Given this, it should be possible for the system to provide exactly the same search facilities as with the tightly integrated approach; eg find all records for work-groups 120-135, during 1994 where *implications* contains the word 'budget' and *minuted-text* contains the words 'sport' and 'health'. Thus, in principle, the person making such a search request should not need to know or care whether the text actually resides within the relational database proper or is fetched from a pile of word processing documents stored elsewhere.

Comparison of Tight and Loose Hybrid Approaches

The two approaches are contrasted in the diagram. One great advantage of the tight hybrid approach is that it permits better control of **integrity**:

• With the loose hybrid approach somebody could delete the WordPerfect document M121357A or change its name to something else. The pointer field in the main database record will remain at M121357A — a false value. It is practically impossible to build in automatic mechanisms to prevent this kind of inconsistency arising. With the tight approach the issue doesn't arise.

• Also, somebody could revise the text of M121357A. At that point the indexes of words like 'sport' and the rest would no longer necessarily be correct. The system administrator ought to start up the database system to carry out reindexing, but there is no way of forcing this to happen. With the tight hybrid approach it is easier to ensure that the indexes keep in step with the text.

The other main advantage of the tight approach is often **performance**. Since everything is held within the database, there can be shorter, or at any rate, more efficient, sequences of indexes, pointers and the like to retrieve text. This difference could be decisive. On the other hand, the characteristics of particular cases could change things; eg if a certain system requires some enormous chunks of text in some records, but not in others, then it becomes difficult to make prima facie judgements about relative performance.

The loosely coupled approach has its claims too:

• **Format**. If the original text contains much typographic variety (text that is bold, italic, in different point sizes, laid out in tables, several different paragraph indentations, footnotes etc), much of that variety will be lost when the text is stored by a DBMS. DBMSs simply don't hold that richness of format. This might not matter in the case of minutes of meetings, but for other documents (eg management consultancy reports, PR releases etc) it might.

• **Revision**. Once the original text has been stored in the database it is relatively awkward to revise. When working on successive drafts of a text with a word processor the author has many useful facilities: search-and-replace, spelling checker, collapsible outliner, macros for frequently done operations, viewing different parts of text in different windows etc. These aren't available in a DBMS. This may not matter in the case of minutes of meetings, which once agreed aren't meant to be altered, but it could be relevant to other kinds of texts,

SUMMARY OF WARRANTS

Gradations of Mainstream-Text Hybrids: Pure-text through Hybrid-but-mainly-text through Complex-hybrid-of-text-and-mainstream through Hybrid-but-mainly-mainstream to Pure-mainstream

Example of a Tight Hybrid Approach: All data in a non-standard 'relational database', with specially extended DBMS software

Example of a Loose Hybrid Approach: Mainstream relational database, text of documents stored separately, but database holds pointers and word-indexes

Comparison of Tight and Loose Hybrid Approaches for Mainstream-Text: Integrity; Performance; Typographic format; Revision; Variety

eg contracts that go through many iterations of negotiation or publicity brochures that have to be discussed with many different people.

- **Variety**. Suppose the database system is to store a great range of types of mainstream data and texts, not just action-points of meetings. The tight hybrid approach would have a different table with a different format of text fields for every type of document, even if there were hundreds of types, many quite rare. With the loose hybrid approach, the relational database design can be simpler, storing only mainstream fields and pointers to documents. The variety of text structure and content can then be handled more flexibly within the word processing document.

POSSIBLE DECISION-MAKING

How does this affect the mayor and administrators of Cedar Wattle City? Why can't they leave the technical people to worry about the choice of supply — complex hybrid, loose or tight, or whatever suits the requirements?

Rational decision-makers will aim to find the best-buy match of supply and demand. It follows that they have to be prepared to discard some demands, whose supply is too expensive or too complicated or too ambitious for some other reason. Moreover, they may well find that, through familiarity with the broad supply alternatives, they discover that other relevant demands, hitherto vaguely apprehended, become more tangible and attractive.

Cedar Wattle City could aim to integrate considerable bodies of mainstream data and text data, and perhaps even graphics data as well, in one database. There could be powerful text-searching facilities and rigorous integrity control of the different types of data. Perhaps this really is the best approach. But it is quite an ambitious one. Therefore, before assuming that the ideal system is necessarily the appropriate one, mayor and colleagues consider a few possibilities that will either lead to better buys or, alternatively, strengthen the justification for the most ambitious approach:

- Suppose there were two entirely separate database systems — one conventional, relational mainstream and one conventional, text database. Admittedly, this approach would not integrate text with mainstream data in any sense at all, but then it would probably be cheaper and simpler. There would be drawbacks, but what drawbacks exactly? Are they serious enough to make a more expensive system without the drawbacks a better investment?
- Suppose there were two main database systems: one hybrid but mainly text (Gradation 2) and, as good as separate, one pure mainstream (Gradation 5). This avoids the risk of one monumental project, but at what price? Are there really any important demands that can only be met sensibly through one massive database? Will there really be important integrity problems that undermine the credibility of the systems? If so, do these things justify the marginal risk involved in the more ambitious approach?
- Or suppose that two database systems each stored both mainstream and text data. One might be a high-volume database supplying demands of access to information for the sole purpose of reference, so that the issue of integrity was down-graded. The other, lower-volume, would allow updating of live texts, albeit with reference to old ones for comparison and copying. If that is a fairly clean breakdown, why not have two separate database systems along these lines?

The only way to generate such options and arrive at rational decisions about them is to develop an understanding of the kind of demands these different approaches are good and bad at supplying.

CONNECTIONS

19. Classic Text Systems	Fundamentals of text-only database systems
20. Advanced Text Systems	Advanced access and structure possibilities in text database systems
29. Object-oriented Topics	Ideas widely regarded as particularly helpful with complex hybrid databases

27. Rules-with-Mainstream Systems

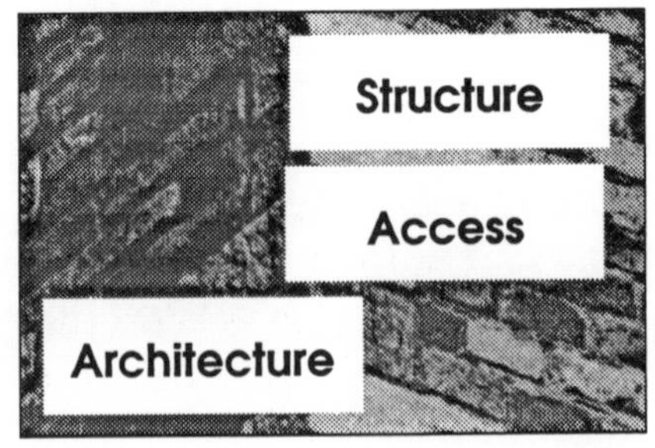

BEARINGS

If a hybrid database system is one that uses two or more radically different kinds of data, then there are many varieties of hybrid system. Sometimes distinctions between them have to be drawn with some delicacy, but this briefing discusses one particular case, whose edges are relatively clear — even if the options within it are complicated: the database system that combines rules data with mainstream data.

POSSIBLE CONTEXT

Angophora is an international mining company. Its head office legal department is considering the idea of a database to store information about important contracts with joint-venture partners or with governments. Though small in the whole scheme of things, the notion of such a database has one very interesting property: a great variety of options exist, differing widely in both demand (what contractual information and how used?) and supply (what kind of technology?). The project team pieces together the following line of reasoning:

- One possible system might be mainly concerned with answering such enquiries as: 'On what date was contract 137 signed?' This is a request for a piece of mainstream data. A system might also access text data, in response to, say: 'What is the wording of the *force majeure* clause of contract 137?'
- A more sophisticated system might help with questions such as: In what essential way does the *force majeure* clause of contract 137 differ from our standard *force majeure* clause? Or even conceivably: How will the revolution in Bolivia affect contract 137? For the latter, a system would have to decide, among other things, whether the revolution triggered the *force majeure* clause.

- A system capable of handling such questions would do far more than store mainstream and text data. It would hold the content of contract clauses in the form of rules that could be used by expert system technology.
- Such features would probably entail considerable marginal cost and risk. Would they be justified? Perhaps not, but, before settling for a straightforward mainstream or text database, it seems worth spending a little time on the idea of storing rules in a database as well.
- In any event, asking whether or not to include rules data in the database is too crude a question. Presumably rules data could be *integrated* with mainstream and text data in various ways, some simple and some intricate; this difference too would surely have implications for the cost and risk of the system.

Before going further the members of the team have to face up to a dilemma. It is tempting to ignore awkward questions of technology supply, to go ahead defining system demands and leave the supply to be settled afterwards. But then you may find that the supply's cost-estimate is five times greater than you ever intended to invest. Alternatively, you can bring supply issues into the debate at an early stage, but then there is a grave danger of getting lost in a technological labyrinth.

This briefing shows how, in a case like Angophora, the second approach is really essential, since some awareness of supply issues can help focus debate on such fundamental demand issues as the real purpose of the system. The trick is to see the whole archipelago rather than the straits, bays and isles.

WARRANTS

As with many hybrid systems, the most fundamental question is: How complicated and integrated should the combination of several kinds of data be made? Discussing this in an entirely abstract way is hopeless. Certain demand and supply options go well together, and others don't. After clearing some ground, this briefing presents some varied, representative examples.

Aspects of Databases

What grounds might justify talk of knowledgebase rather than database? Here are three aspects of 'database' in its wide sense of *any* organised body of data. Most mainstream databases possess them to some degree, but the more pronounced they are, the more it makes sense to talk of a **knowledgebase**:

- **Facts.** Databases normally store facts, in the sense of data meant to be true rather than false. A narrower, though still impressionistic, definition of the idea of a fact might stress two points: facts are permanent (eg the atomic number of manganese is 25), rather than changeable like the data of business transactions; a fact is a small piece of knowledge made up of a few interdependent items (atomic number, manganese and 25), whereas mainstream data usually identifies one thing (eg a contract) and gives any number of data items that are *all about* it (eg the contract-number, its title, the contracting parties, the date of signature, the language of the contract, the country whose legal system applies . .)[1]
- **Rules.** Most database systems use rules in their processing; eg 'If the contract-number keyed in is not numeric, reject it' and 'If there are any contracts in the database, where the language of the contract is Spanish, display their contract-numbers on the screen'. In most systems, rules are no more than the essential logic of basic tasks such as accessing data from the database and avoiding the storage of false data. But in some systems, rules play a far more central role than this; eg the system uses stored rules to guide somebody through the process of negotiating a contract ('use the standard wording for the *force majeure* clause, unless the region has a history of volcanic activity, in which case . . .)
- **Problem-solving.** In a sense, any database solves problems by providing you with information you need: if your problem is that you don't know which contracts are in Spanish, the database system can solve the problem by telling you. But a system may solve problems in a stronger sense; eg prompting you for data and calculating the maximum price it would be rational to pay for a certain joint-venture to extract manganese.

These three aspects are all defined in demand terms (ie what the system does for the people using it) as opposed to supply (ie the type of technology supplying them). As the above notes suggest, even the most mundane database system possesses the three aspects to some degree — so mainstream database technology is an appropriate supply to some degree. But a database whose demands were dominated by the facts, rules and problem-solving aspects might deserve the distinctive term knowledgebase and be best supplied by technology other than mainstream database.

Though these extremes may be clear, a sharp cutoff point is not. Certain demands may be feasible with mainstream database technology, but rather awkward; others just possible, but extremely awkward, and so on. Judgement is needed to gauge the point at which a given set of demands is best met by using knowledgebase technology. To develop that judgement, it is best to clarify the differences between the possibilities, and after that to examine a few representative examples.

Chart of Knowledgebase Technology

This briefing uses the term 'knowledgebase' because it is the least bad term available. To see why, the relations between several commonly found terms need to be charted out.

A **knowledgebase** is a body of facts and rules. An **expert system** is usually regarded as a system which accesses the content of a knowledgebase and draws inferences from it. But some questions arise:

- Does an expert system necessarily use facts and rules provided only by **experts**, as opposed to facts and rules from other sources? Some writers say so, but this seems arbitrary.[2] One system may be a distillation of the knowledge and intuition of an expert, such as a cancer specialist, but another may use rules and facts which *anybody* with sufficient patience could extract from publicly available material, eg the conditions for payment of unemployment benefits, or other content from the texts of laws, timetables, tourism guides, high school textbooks, encyclopedias and so on.
- Is an expert system normally concerned with **probabilistic** problem-solving, informed guesses, rules of thumb and the like, as opposed to the exact processing of most other IT systems? Some writers say so. But few systems have a knowledgebase where every single item is a best guess; at least some are likely to be facts. Conversely, few systems include *only* simple facts; even one based on railway timetables might well include some approximations and rules of thumb, to reduce unmanageable complexity. This is all a matter of degree.

For economical discussion, one term is needed for all those systems that possess a knowledgebase of facts and rules, and that draw inferences from them, irrespective of the second-order issues just noted. This briefing uses the term **knowledgebase system**.

For mainstream systems, the distinctions between the three things database, DBMS and database system are fundamental. A knowledgebase is roughly (only roughly) analogous to a database. An actual knowledgebase *system* (eg one for diagnosing infectious diseases) is then equivalent to an actual database *system* (eg one for planning mining production). What then is the equivalent of the DBMS (eg DB2 or Sybase or Pace etc), providing generalised facilities to manage a database?

The usual name for a software product providing generalised facilities to use a knowledgebase is **expert system shell**. The most important facility it provides is an **inference engine** — general-purpose logic that can compare facts and rules to generate conclusions that form the starting-point for following new rules, and so on. Prolog is generally regarded as an **AI (artificial intelligence) language** rather than an expert system shell. In essence, though, they differ only in degree: Prolog has a more general-purpose inference engine than most shells — in some ways more spartan, in others more flexible.

Comparison: Database or Knowledgebase

Here is a more detailed comparison of the two types of system:

- Within a **mainstream database system** there is: a database specific to the application — not only in content but in structure (subject to being in the format and general structure required by the DBMS); application-specific software (ie programs developed specifically for the system); DBMS software, providing general-purpose facilities for managing data.
- Within a **knowledgebase system** there is: a knowledgebase specific to the application — containing both facts and rules (subject to being in the format and general structure required by the expert system shell); expert system shell, providing general-purpose facilities for reasoning through rules, in particular an inference engine.

Thus, with a mainstream database system, there is a clear distinction between application-specific data (in the database) and application-specific software; but with a knowledgebase system there is not. The knowledgebase contains both facts — a kind of data — and rules that can be thought of two ways: either as data, because they are stored together with facts, or as software, because, in combination with the inference engine, they determine the course of the processing.

The other important difference is data structuring. The structure of a mainstream database is designed with great care and may be quite intricate; skill invested in optimising structure may bring rich rewards. The structure of a knowledgebase is a less important issue. Often it is no more than a list of statements expressing facts and rules. The order is often not very important because the inference engine is capable of noticing without any prompting that the conclusion reached by following rule 49 is relevant to evaluating the conditions that govern rule 23; therein lies much of the power of this type of software. Ordinary word processing software is used to prepare and amend the statements of the knowledgebase; these are read in by the shell and converted into some internal format.

From this outline comparison, some points become clear:

- The pure knowledgebase approach to rules is more convenient if the critical factor of the system is above all getting the rules right.[3]
- The pure knowledgebase approach to data is adequate if the data is mainly facts (in the sense of things that don't get updated), and they are not structured in any complicated way, and there is no need for intricate checking that different facts are consistent with each other.
- The less weight the above points have in a given case, the less advantage pure knowledgebase has over mainstream database.

Distinctions: Database, Knowledgebase or Hybrid

Sometimes the decision to use either pure knowledgebase or pure mainstream database technology is clearcut. But in many cases where facts and rules are relevant several distinct decisions are at least plausible. Here are the main possibilities:

- **Mainstream database only.** Facts are stored in a relational database; rules are coded as conventional software.
- **Pure knowledgebase.** The technology is used to the full, but the complexities of data structuring and integrity are ignored.
- **Knowledgebase, pre-loaded with mainstream data.** All mainstream data that the knowledgebase system may need is loaded from a database into the knowledgebase, which can run independently of the database thereafter. If this mainstream data is subject to update in its home database, a new version of the whole set of data is loaded into the knowledgebase from time to time (once a day, once a month etc).
- **Knowledgebase, accessing mainstream facts**. When a knowledgebase system needs certain facts (eg about the properties of manganese), ie data of a fairly permanent character, it retrieves them from a mainstream database, which is on-line, either for this sole purpose or (more likely) for access by other operational systems. To do this, access statements pre-written in SQL may be stored in the knowledgebase. The knowledgebase system never updates the mainstream database.[4]
- **Knowledgebase, accessing mainstream operational data**. A knowledgebase system accesses, without updating, non-fact data, such as names of joint-venture partners, operational plans etc. This kind of data is inherently more changeable than the narrow class of fact data. It is subject to update in the database by some other

operational system at the same time as the knowledgebase system is running.

- **Complex hybrid.** As with the previous gradation, a knowledgebase system accesses a mainstream database for data, but it also *updates* the mainstream database. This raises problems of CRS and integrity.

As a general rule, it is inherently more tricky to combine technologies than to use a pure form of just one. Of the mixed approaches, knowledgebase with facts is less ambitious than knowledgebase with operational data. Both are less ambitious than a complex hybrid approach.

The possibilities exposed here are options of architecture, ie ways of fitting knowledgebase and mainstream database together. Deciding the appropriate architecture for a given case usually entails clarifying the *purpose* of the system. The different generic purposes are best shown by examples.

Monarchs: a Mainly Reference Example

Imagine a system to store the dates of monarchs who have reigned in European countries. These are facts all in the same form: a certain monarch (eg Carol I) reigned over a certain country (eg Romania), from a certain date (eg 1881) to a certain date (eg 1914). This can be held quite well in a relational table, *Reigns*, with in each record the four fields: *country-name, monarch-name, reign-start, reign-end.*

To ask a question such as 'Who was King of Romania in 1910?', you could use SQL to select from the table only those records with country-name 'Romania' and excluding those where *reign-start* was later than 1910 and also excluding those where *reign-end* was earlier than 1910. This should narrow it down to one record, that containing the *monarch-name* Carol I.

It would be more laborious, though still possible, to handle the request 'Who was the longest-reigning monarch whose reign occurred (at least in part) in the seventeenth century?' or even 'Which countries (if any) have had at least one monarch named John, none named Peter or Charles since 1700, and at least two named Louis that reigned longer than 50 years?' The data is structured in the database in a way that permits these kinds of enquiry; it is just a matter of carefully spelling out the criteria, step by step, for accessing certain records from the table.

But what about this? 'Which year between AD500 and 1918 was the one where the fewest changes of monarch took place throughout Europe?' In principle the facts held in the database are sufficient to answer this question, but it would be extremely onerous to spell out in SQL all the criteria for accessing and comparing records from the table to arrive at the answer. This problem just *doesn't fit the structure* of the data at all well. Now consider knowledgebase technology. As well as facts, the knowledgebase would contain rules such as:

> **If** *monarch-name* reigned in *country-name* between years A and B
> **and if** year Z falls between A and B,
> **then** *monarch-name* was reigning in *country-name* throughout year Z

Using this rule, the inference engine can deduce that in Romania there was no change of monarch in 1882, nor in 1883 etc. This takes it a long way towards answering the question posed.

In practice, even the most relationally correct designer of a mainstream database of facts has to make some assumption about the needs for information likely to arise. Any requests for information that don't fit the structure at all well, however feasible in theory, may be impossible in practice. By contrast, a knowledgebase system offers far more scope for making use of the facts stored from *any* angle.

Suppose the data to be stored is a variety of historical facts — not just reigns, but battles, civic charters, plagues and so on. With the mainstream approach a new type of table with its own format is needed for each kind of fact, a *Battles* table, a *Charters* table and so on. If there are many kinds of fact, some of them with only a few cases, this can be quite onerous. By contrast a knowledgebase for Prolog could easily contain hundreds of kinds of fact — just a line for each fact:[5]

```
reign(carol_I,romania,1881,1914)
charter(gouda,1272,floris_V)
capture(antwerp,spanish,1585)
life(dante_alighieri,1265,florence,1321,ravenna)
```
and so on

Thus, for a simple reference database on monarchs' reigns, relational database is a natural choice. But as the reference enquiries become more involved (eg very demanding accesses and/or many other facts besides reigns), it becomes plausible to consider knowledgebase as an alternative, and after a certain point pure knowledgebase may become the *only* sensible choice.

Train Tickets: a Mainly Problem-solving Example

Sometimes the balance of difficulties is quite different: the rules may be easily defined, but complex, and they have to be applied to solve a definite problem.

Imagine a complicated rail journey: a group of fifteen people

Train Ticket Rules (In Outline)

A family (ie parent(s) with children) of three or more persons travelling together gets a certain percentage reduction — in 14 (not all) of the countries of Europe (in France, the minimum family is two, though the reduction is less).

A group of a minimum of six people, not necessarily part of a family, can also get certain reductions — in any of 17 countries.

If under 25, you can invest in a special ticket for unlimited free travel in 19 countries for a month (can be worthwhile, even for one long journey).

If over 60 or 65 (depending on sex), you can invest in a special ticket, providing reductions on all journeys in any of 22 countries for a whole year.

If a family or group contains old and/or young people possessing the special tickets just mentioned, they may either waive their rights and be counted as part of the family or group, or else . . . *and so on*

from Brussels to Rome and back via Copenhagen. How much should the tickets cost? There is a normal price for any rail journey based on the number of kilometres travelled, but there are myriad special pricing schemes that lead to reductions. The sidebar shows very impressionistically some of the rules that might apply.

Once carefully defined, such rules can be used by a knowledgebase system to work out the most advantageous price for the travellers. This is a soluble problem with a definite answer.

A clever system might also draw a customer's attention to other possibilities: eg paying only slightly more for this specific journey in order to end up with a special ticket providing cheaper travel on future journeys. (This kind of thing can be expressed as rules too, if 'only slightly more' is replaced by (say) '10%'.)

Like the Monarchs system, this one needs to hold a body of facts (eg the distances in kilometres between the main nodes of the European rail network), but rules are more prominent here. There are options: the complicated rules seem best held in a knowledgebase, but facts about distances might be held either in the knowledgebase or in a separate mainstream database. Also, some rules can be defined more elegantly if certain facts are kept in the database rather than embedded in the logic of rules themselves. A rule could say (roughly):

If group is at least 6 people
and country is Belgium or France or . . . (for all 17 countries)
then consider the group ticket

But it would be neater to record which countries participate in which schemes as *facts* in the database. Then the rule can be:

If group is at least 6 people
and country is a group-scheme-country
then consider the group ticket

If the facts about countries, reduction schemes and so on were subject to frequent change and if any update of one piece of data had to be checked carefully for consistency with the rest, these would be further good reasons for storing the facts in a database rather than embedded in knowledgebase rules.

With this sort of case, the maxim applies: the more complicated the system gets, the more advisable it seems to make full use of the respective strengths of both knowledgebase and database technology. However, there is probably no need to go as far as a complex hybrid system: the process of problem-solving need not entail *updating* the data in the mainstream database.

Side-effects of Drugs: a Multi-role Example

A printed book containing information about drugs and their side-effects contains facts in the sense of fixed knowledge, but these facts, unlike those about history or train tickets, are arranged in quite a detailed structure. The book may be primarily organised according to some classification of drugs into types and sub-types; then within sub-types of drug, parts of the body affected; for each part of the body, types of side-effects and so on.

If all this is stored in a relational database, many useful possibilities for combination and cross-reference arise; eg:

- The patient has been taking four different drugs and is now coughing blood; which of those four drugs is known to have that side effect?
- Given three undesirable side-effects suffered by the patient and the combination of four different drugs in use, can any of the side-effects be eliminated by replacing any of the drugs with another for the same purpose (eg replace one type of sleeping tablet by another)?

Such questions can be handled by using a language like SQL to select and combine sets of records that meet defined criteria. This applies even to the extreme second question, though the problem would have to be broken down into a number of steps. But there must

Medical Rules (In Outline)

If the situation is unsatisfactory, check whether substituting one drug with a generic purpose (eg sleeping-tablet, pain-killer) for another is feasible.

If a certain side-effect is associated with the combination of two of the drugs being taken, replace one of them.

If two drugs being taken are both known to cause a certain side-effect, even when taken alone, either replace both drugs or neither.

If considering replacement of drug A by drug B, check for the following allergies . . .

---

be a practical limit to this approach. The database remains a passive reference source. The person accessing it has to break the problem down into pieces and decide what searches to make and how to fit them into the whole problem. At a certain point all this will become just too complicated.

Perhaps the system should take a more active role. It could ask which side-effects the patient suffered from, and ask which drugs were being taken. On the basis of the answers, it could decide that a different sleeping tablet might on balance be preferable, but, before suggesting it, ask certain questions about the patient, eg about allergies.[6] In other words, perhaps knowledgebase would be more suitable than relational database here. The facts and rules used by such a knowledgebase system are only those contained in (or implied by) the original medical text.[7] Typical rules are given (impressionistically) in the sidebar.

In this case a variety of architectures corresponding to a variety of different purposes for the system might be considered:

- *either* **mainstream database only** — for reference (like the monarchs example), but ignoring problem-solving (like the train tickets);
- *or* **pure knowledgebase** — allowing both problem-solving and reference, but making it difficult to *manage* the highly structured data, ie difficult to update with new or altered information about drugs and to ensure that it is all consistent;
- *or* **knowledgebase** for the rules, but also **accessing mainstream facts** about the properties of drugs stored in a mainstream database;
- *or* **knowledgebase** for the rules, also **accessing mainstream**

SUMMARY OF WARRANTS

Aspects of Databases: Facts; Rules; Problem-solving

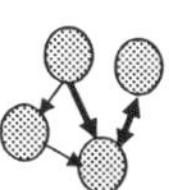

Chart connecting Concepts in Knowledgebase Technology: Knowledgebase; Expert system; Rules-based system; Knowledgebase system; Expert system shell; Inference engine; AI language

Comparison between Database and Knowledgebase: Data and software v facts and rules; Complex or list structure; Criticality of rules; Structure, integrity and updating of data

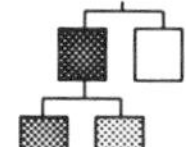

Distinctions of Architecture: Mainstream database; Pure knowledgebase; Knowledgebase, pre-loaded with mainstream data; Knowledgebase accessing mainstream facts; Knowledgebase accessing mainstream operational data; Complex hybrid

Mainly Reference Example: Monarchs: how awkward the search, how varied the facts

Mainly Problem-solving Example: Train tickets: how complex and changeable the facts

Multi-role Example: Side-effects of drugs: reference only or problem-solving and guidance or prescription and updating of patient records

---

operational data, the clinical records of specific patients (as well as accessing facts about drugs);

- *or* **complex hybrid** — knowledgebase for the rules, data about drugs and about patients accessed from a mainstream database, but also with updating of patient records in the database as decisions are made about the prescription of drugs.

POSSIBLE DECISION-MAKING

Why should decisions about integrating mainstream database and knowledgebase merit so much attention? Shouldn't the Angophora project team be most concerned with defining demand — the kind of information to be stored and the kind of access required and the kind of problems the system should solve? Only when that was settled, it might be thought, should a smaller group of more technical people decide what the supply factors ought to be.

But this would probably not be a sound approach. The most rational thing to aim for is the *best-buy match* of supply and demand and there is no guarantee that finalising demand first will achieve that. 99% of the demand might be met quite well by a mainstream relational database, but the remaining 1% might force you into a system that combined mainstream database and knowledgebase in an awkward, complicated way. If so, the straightforward system meeting only 99% of the demand might well be a better buy.

A more interesting point is that a system cleverly linking mainstream database and knowledgebase might support demands hitherto not thought of or assumed impractical, and as a result turn out to be a good buy. Awareness of supply possibilities and implications may *stimulate* awareness and help firm up more imaginative demands.

Seeing things in that light, the Angophora team decides to identify the most promising available options in both demand and supply terms. If left unchecked, work on defining options can easily lead to unmanageable proliferation of possibilities. Therefore the team decides to work out and compare five strategies, each based on a certain approach to supply:

- **Strategy A**: store mainstream contract data in a relational database only;
- **Strategy B**: store mainstream contract data in a relational database and contractual texts (not rules) in a separate text database;
- **Strategy C**: store the content of contracts in a knowledgebase system with no relational or any other form of database;
- **Strategy D**: have a knowledgebase *and* a relational database;
- **Strategy E**: have a knowledgebase and a relational database and a database of texts.

For each strategy, the intention is to outline the most attractive system available within the supply-side constraint. That will show which types of demand can be readily met by which strategies. No doubt Strategy E will be shown to meet most demands and Strategy A least but the interesting thing is to see which demands can only be met by which supply factors.

Quite possibly, the result will be a judgement such as: The two most attractive strategies are Strategy A — easily the simplest, but it meets a surprisingly large proportion of the important demands expressed — and Strategy D — much more sophisticated than A, but less complex than Strategy E, whose large marginal costs deliver relatively little in return.

Suppose, for the sake of argument, things were narrowed down in just that way, the Angophora team could then go further in refining the comparison of Strategy A — a mainstream database system, albeit, within that limitation, carefully designed to handle some relatively intricate access requirements — with Strategy D — coupling knowledgebase and mainstream database.[8]

CONNECTIONS

5. Accessing the Database	Access options, including the role of SQL
14. Data Dictionary Control	Storing business rules in a data dictionary
28. Non-Mainstream Software Products	Software products for knowledgebases
29. Object-oriented Topics	Techniques that may well be useful for integrating rules and mainstream data

28. Non-Mainstream Software Products

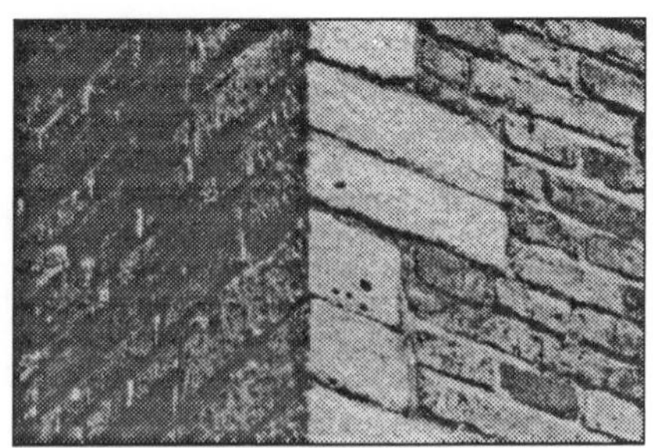

BEARINGS

This briefing surveys a range of software products whose purpose is to manage a database of non-mainstream data — whether on PC, minicomputer or mainframe.

Knowledge about any particular software product has little merit without knowledge about the place of the product relative to others: With which other products does it share the same category? How do products in its category differ from products in neighbouring categories?

The class of 'everything outside mainstream' is quite heterogeneous. This briefing aims to set up some broad categories for non-mainstream software products, while minimising gross distortion through simplification.

POSSIBLE CONTEXT

The board at Ribbongum, the pharmaceuticals company, is familiar with the concept of a portfolio of innovations: out of a number of possible new drug products one or two will be winners that justify the cost of the whole portfolio. It has now decided to apply the portfolio concept to IT.

A fair number of small-scale prototype or experimental projects will be set up: a project to offer large customers product information in hypertext form, a project to apply expert system rules to streamline product ordering procedures, a project to give the R&D department a picture database, and so on. The projects will apply a variety of different technologies; almost all will use some kind of non-mainstream database. It is hoped that at least some will show convincingly how the technology tried can produce large-scale advantages for the business, perhaps in several areas.

A true portfolio approach entails a balanced coverage of the main possibilities rather than an accumulation of separate hunches. Therefore, to keep things clear, those on the Ribbongum board most interested in IT want to map out the different varieties of system; eg distinctions can be drawn between mainstream and text and keyword systems, between basic features of text database and advanced features and so on. Having that clear view is essential to choosing possibilities that give a balanced portfolio.

To carry out most of these projects software products are needed. It might seem that for each category of system there should be a certain category of software product. But this is true only in a very superficial sense. In practice, some software products can serve several categories of system and some others only a sub-category; in other cases again the relation between type of system and product is even more confusing. Therefore, to pursue its innovation portfolio policy, Ribbongum also needs an analysis of the main types of non-mainstream DBMS software.

WARRANTS

This can be a most perplexing area. One software product is described by its suppliers as 'a high-performance information retrieval system that provides instantaneous access to text files or documents, as well as associated images', another as 'a software solution for manipulating, storing and retrieving multimedia objects from client applications that work with DEC Rdb databases' and a third as 'a document management and retrieval system for textual, image, graphics and alphanumeric information collection, organization, access and delivery'. Are these three all much the same in scope, but described in different words? If so, perhaps hundreds of others are too; if not, how can they be assigned to clear and separate categories?

The first warrant section establishes a few broad concepts necessary for charting out this whole field. The other sections break things down further.

Distinction between Simple and Composite Products

The only way forward is to establish the notion that any software product falls into one of two classes:

- **Simple**. The product is primarily concerned with managing one particular kind of data in a certain way. It may perhaps be encrusted with additional features for managing the same kind of data in a radically different way or for managing other kinds of data, but if so, these things can be regarded as second-order.

• **Composite**. The product handles one kind of data but in alternative radically different ways and/or it manages several different kinds of data. For this product, it would be quite misleading to tame the diversity by calling some of it second-order. The variety is the very essence of the product.

Two products may appear to have similar features — each provides storage of document images and text-searching facilities (say). But one may be *essentially* a powerful instrument for storing large quantities of text and allowing very sophisticated and highly efficient text-searching; being able to store document images as well is a useful extra. The other may be *essentially* intended for storing and displaying document images, with relatively straightforward text-searching facilities as one means of finding a certain document. Both of these are simple products, but of two different kinds. A third product may be a composite product, largely relevant to applications where images and text are to be intertwined in quite complex ways.

Distinctions between Types of Products

With this simple-composite distinction available for use, it is possible to set out five main categories of non-mainstream software product:

• **Text**: products primarily concerned with managing text, but including a few composites that are strong in text-with-mainstream hybrid applications.

• **Hypertext**: products that organise information in hypertext style. Despite its confusing name the hypertext style is well suited to managing a mixture of kinds of data, particularly text and graphics. Most products here are therefore composites.

• **Document images**: mainly simple products that manage document images. Some manage other kinds of data as well, but whether they go far enough to count as composite products is debatable.

• **GIS** (including the simpler business mapping system): products that manage both mainstream data and geographic data. They are composite by definition.

• **Expert system shell**: products that store and use facts and rules in a knowledgebase. Simple.

Most of these five can then be broken down further. To help analyse the **text** category of DBMS software products, leave products aside for a moment and distinguish two well-established types of *systems* (as opposed to products):

• **Document database system** — Documents are stored and their content is copiously indexed to permit access through text-search. The quantities of text may be enormous.

• **Library database system** Textual material is stored within records as opposed to in free-form documents. There are text-search facilities, but much of the access is through keyword. The typical application, though not the only one, is the library catalogue.

This helps to break down the field of *software products* that support text database systems:

• **Classic text** — simple product, used for both the document and library types of system, but really comes into its own with a heavyweight document system;

• **Semi-structured text** — simple product, used mainly (but not only) for the library category of system;

• **Text-with-mainstream** — composite product, with both text and relational features, supporting hybrid systems.

Among **hypertext** products there are two main styles:

• **Card style.** The essential structure is a set of card-sized chunks — with a defined format, flexible though not totally free — arranged in hierarchies, enabling the reader to spring between cards around the structure of the database.

• **Book style.** There is one continuous piece of text, like a book (or a very long scroll) rather than organised into standard card-sized chunks. Images may appear anywhere in the text as required. Hypertext jumps can be made up and down the book.

For management of document **images** there are two main types of product:

• **Classic image**. Simple product: images of documents are stored for access through mainstream identifiers and keywords.

• **Image-with-text**. Composite: images of documents are stored, but documents are also read by OCR; their text is also stored and accessible through text-search.

Products to manage geographic and mainstream data in hybrid systems are always composite, but split into two main types:

• **Business mapping.** The data for generating maps is kept in graphics files, and mainstream data is held in a relational database or spreadsheet. Combination of these two kinds of data is limited to a few relatively straightforward possibilities.

• **True GIS.** As well as pure graphics and pure mainstream data, the system holds extensive spatial data as well, to define as co-ordinates the locations of points on the map and items in the mainstream database. This produces a much more powerful, general-purpose system for combining and manipulating data.

SUMMARY OF WARRANTS

Distinctions between Simple and Composite Products: One style (though perhaps with second-order features); Composite style

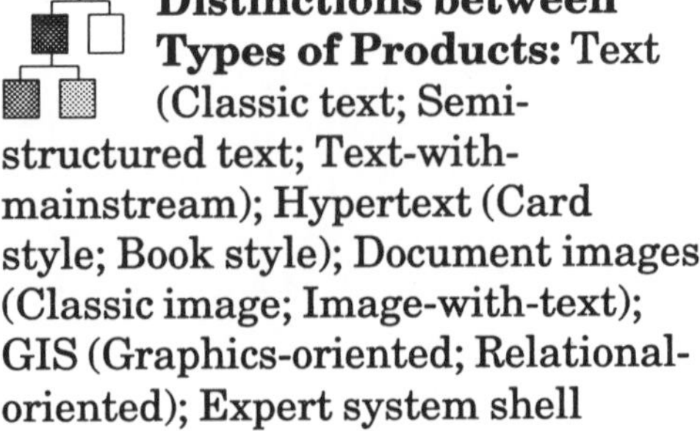

Distinctions between Types of Products: Text (Classic text; Semi-structured text; Text-with-mainstream); Hypertext (Card style; Book style); Document images (Classic image; Image-with-text); GIS (Graphics-oriented; Relational-oriented); Expert system shell

POSSIBLE DECISION-MAKING

This rough breakdown of the field provides the Ribbongum board with a useful planning document. To bring to life the distinctions it draws, an analyst is asked to fill in the categories of software product with representative examples. The resulting table can make debates and decisions more disciplined:

'From this glossy brochure I can't judge whether Product V is essentially concerned with storing text organised in the classic text way with indexes for text-searching and so on, or whether it is a hypertext product. Please clarify that point, straight away.'

'If you want to use software product W rather than X for storing the document images, you must be able to show that its facility to store and search on text is actually needed. Otherwise X, being simpler, is surely the better buy.'

'Do we need a GIS software product as a general-purpose tool for all manner of processing of spatial and mainstream data? Or are we looking for fairly straightforward business mapping facilities? We should decide that point first, and only after that, start choosing between individual products.'

'Product Y seems inappropriate because it is based on a card-based style of hypertext, whereas the content of our proposed database seems to fit a book-style much better.'

'Product Z is a good example of the text-with-mainstream type of software product. Let's think about the kind of things it might do for us. That may stimulate some ideas that might not arise if we tried to define our requirements in the abstract or, conversely, it may persuade us that we don't need that kind of product at all.'

Non-Mainstream Products: Categories and Examples

Category	***Representative Example Products***
Text	
Classic Text	*BasisPlus, BRS/Search, Stairs, Status,*
Semi-structured Text	*askSam, Assassin, Cairs, Tinman, Trip*
Text-with-Mainstream	*DM, Info-DB+, Inquire*
Hypertext	
Hypertext-Card	*ArchiText, FolioViews, HyperCard, SuperCard*
Hypertext-Book	*Guide*
Document images	
Classic Image	*DECimage, Keyfile, PixSure, Plexus XDP*
Image-with-Text	*Sonar Image, ZyImage*
GIS	
Business mapping	*GeoQuery, Harvard Geographics, MapLinx, MapViewer, Tactician*
True GIS	*Arc/Info, Atlas GIS, GIS/AMS, GisPlus, Intergraph IMAP, MapInfo*
Expert System Shell	*Exsys, Guru, KEE, KES, VP-Expert*

CONNECTIONS

17. Mainstream Software Products	Mainstream software products that may be competitive in border-line cases

29. Object-oriented Topics

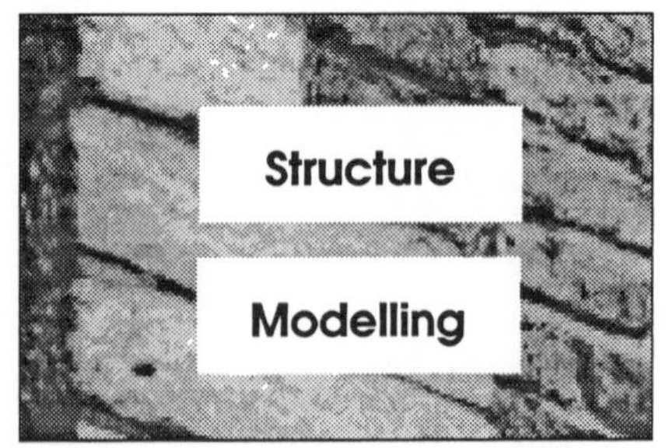

BEARINGS

'Object-oriented' has become a plastic status-symbol adjective, like a security pass that opens all doors. But beneath all the hype are some stimulating insights that are likely to be of enduring value.

This briefing aims to demystify object-orientation by sorting through a variety of intermingled terms and examining those ideas relevant to database technology.

This is a rare briefing in that object-oriented ideas are relevant to all kinds of data, mainstream and otherwise.

POSSIBLE CONTEXT

You might expect a management consultancy business such as Coachwood Consultants to have a particularly well designed organisation structure, but this isn't necessarily true. It seems desirable to break the business down into parts so that different parts have their own budgets and consultants have some loyalty to close colleagues, but what is a sensible breakdown? By type of client or by type of work? What about office location? What about assignments needing multi-disciplinary teams? And since the company's portfolio of assignments is at the mercy of the market, an organisation structure that seems ideal on paper may not suit the mix of work that actually occurs.

Coachwood Consultants decides to reorganise itself yet again. Here are the main points of the new scheme:

- There are two types of people — those who earn fees from providing consultancy services to clients, and those such as secretaries and clerical personnel who stay in the office keeping the administration going.
- Each fee-earner and many non-fee-earners belong to a 'skill-group', led by a partner. Each group specialises in a particular genre of

consultancy, eg consultancy in human resources or the oil industry or total quality management. Each group has its own budget and profit-and-loss account.

- The terms of reference of the skill-groups are deliberately defined with some overlap; eg one assignment might be to recruit a total quality manager for an oil company. This overlap is meant to encourage healthy competition between groups, but also to encourage groups to hire consultants with skills they need from each other at published internal-transfer fee-rates.

The IT management committee at Coachwood decides that for this new scheme to work properly a new database system will be needed. In essence, the new system will keep the accounts, but that task may be quite complicated; eg work done by consultants temporarily hired by another skill-group has to be accounted for; these transfer charges may have to be recharged if the work of a consultant hired by another group turns out inadequate; commissions may be paid between groups (one group may secure an assignment which it then gives to another group in return for a commission); and all kinds of other subtleties are needed to encourage the concept of keen, commercially-minded skill-groups.

These commercial procedures pose quite severe requirements for a database system, but Coachwood also wants to go further — perhaps not immediately but certainly in an easy, smooth manner before very long. The intention is to store information about the actual skills within the skill-group, not just to maintain sophisticated accounts about it. For example, the different assignments done within the oil-industry skill-group and the experience possessed by its consultants (some of it gained before joining Coachwood) should be analysed. This will (probably) be done by devising codes, breaking down (say) the oil industry further into types of company and types of assignment.

The most important requirement of all is that the whole database system should provide flexibility, particularly in three main dimensions:

- There are dozens of skill-groups. The intention is that **new groups** should be constantly emerging, while existing ones are withering or more likely merging. The system should cope with this as a normal event without any technical strain or skilled work by expensive experts.
- The **internal commercial rules** must be amenable to change. If it were decided that an entirely new internal transaction should be allowed — say, purchase of an *option* on the future use of a certain consultant from another group — then it should be possible to introduce that cleanly without months of extra programming.

• Some trial and error will doubtless be needed in the process of **codifying skills** that comes later; it must be reasonably easy to abandon some styles of analysis that prove too tedious to justify themselves and to try out other styles.

The partner who manages the skill-group for database consultancy advises that, given the demands already explicit and the vaguer requirements for flexibility, there is a prima facie case for applying object-oriented concepts. To see the mountain range rather than confusing crags and boulders the members of the IT management committee need a briefing.

WARRANTS

Why are 'New Zealand' or 'electron' called what they are? It really doesn't matter; those names are best regarded as arbitrary labels. Similarly, it is best to start out treating 'object-oriented' (from now on usually OO) as a mere label, without going into its derivation. Picking out different overlapping areas within the OO field and contrasting them with non-OO ideas is the next step.

Object-oriented: First Chart

A number of related but different things all bear the OO label:

• **OO concepts.** There are some relatively new ways of thinking about the use of computers to tackle problems, about how to structure systems, design software, organise storage etc. This body of general ideas is made concrete by the next three things in this list.[1]

• **OO programming language.** A programmer who favours OO concepts will find it irksome and to some extent impossible to apply them in an established language such as Cobol or Fortran. Some newer programming languages are specifically intended for programming in OO style; two such are Eiffel and C++.

• **OO modelling.** OO concepts can also be applied to technology-independent modelling. An information analyst might choose to model in this style in preference to the classic ER approach. Various authorities have put forward appropriate modelling conventions; eg Shlaer-Mellor or ODT (by Rumbaugh et alia). For these and similar approaches to modelling the term **EER (Enhanced ER) modelling** is probably the best (even though the context sometimes makes use of the term OO modelling more natural).[2]

• **OO-DBMS.** None of the well-established DBMS products was designed with OO concepts in mind. Certain newer DBMSs are specifically intended to permit database access and storage in OO style; two such are GemStone and Ontos DB.

- **Relations between the above.** OO doesn't pose an all-or-nothing choice. You could use an OO programming language, but a relational DBMS; EER modelling doesn't compel you to use an OO programming language; etc.

Example of EER Modelling

The quickest way to get insight into EER modelling and its underlying concepts is to start from the classic ER model. It distinguishes different types of relationships between entities, in the sense that some are one-to-many, others are one-to-one optional and so on. Apart from these rigorous distinctions, a model also contains verbal descriptions of the relationships. Thousands of different relationships are possible; here are six:

- **Works on.** A *Consultant* works on one or more *Assignments*.
- **Manages.** One and only one *Partner* manages each *Assignment*
- **Fosters contacts with.** A *Partner* fosters contacts with one or more *Clients*
- **Is paid for by.** Each *Assignment* is paid for by one and only one *Client*
- **Is one kind of.** A *Partner* is one kind of *Fee-Earner*
- **Is one part of.** A *Consultant* is one part of a *Skill-group*.

There is no special notation, no special use of shapes or lines, to distinguish (say) a 'works on' relationship from a 'manages' relationship or 'a fosters contacts with' relationship. That would need more variations than Chinese has characters and, besides, what purpose would it serve?

The diagram presents an example of EER modelling.[3] In EER modelling, two of the above relationships are singled out for special treatment: the relationship where one entity 'is one kind of' another entity, and the relationship where one entity 'is one part of' another entity.

The presence of the verb 'to be' in the verbal description is an intuitive clue that these two relationships have a special kind of status. To see more clearly why they are special, turn to the analysis of attributes. If a *Partner* is one kind of *Fee-Earner*, it follows that these two entities will share some attributes. *Standard-fee-rate* will apply to all fee-earners (ie consultants as well as partners); on the other hand, other attributes (eg *profit-share-percentage*) will apply to partners but not to other kinds of fee-earner. *Standard-fee-rate* need not be repeated for several entities in the model; if it is recorded once against *Fee-Earner*, the 'is one kind of' conventions will show

EER Model: a Management Consultancy Company

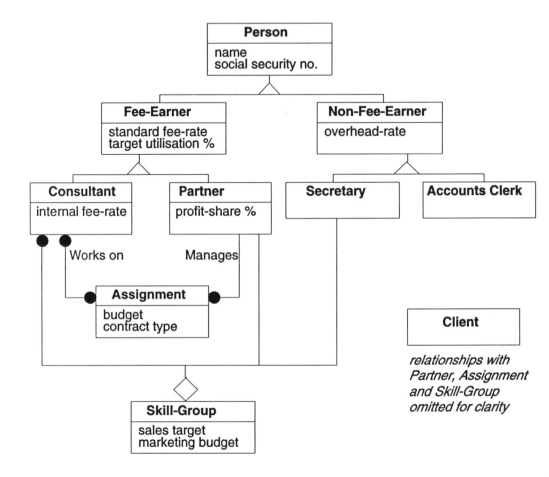

Person
name
social security no.

Fee-Earner
standard fee-rate
target utilisation %

Non-Fee-Earner
overhead-rate

Consultant
internal fee-rate

Partner
profit-share %

Secretary

Accounts Clerk

Works on

Manages

Assignment
budget
contract type

Client

relationships with Partner, Assignment and Skill-Group omitted for clarity

Skill-Group
sales target
marketing budget

Symbols Used

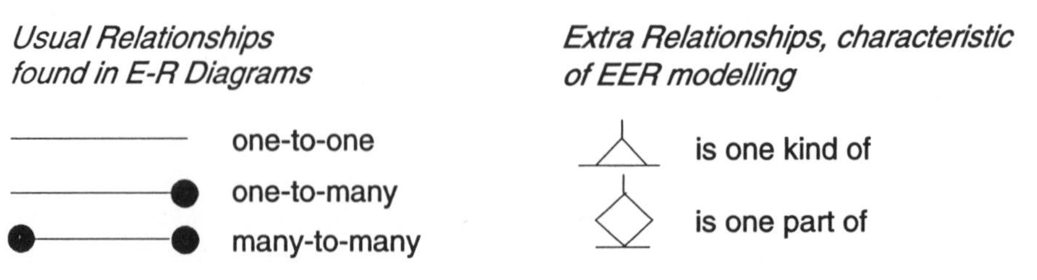

that this attribute is common to *Consultant* and *Partner*. A similar approach is taken to the attributes of entities in an 'is one part of' relationship.

Since it has extra conventions to record these relationships, EER modelling is inherently more complex than ER. However, once you get used to looking out for these two special kinds of relationship and taking advantage of the way they structure attributes, the price of more complex conventions may buy a more elegant and richer model.

The difference between the two types of relationship special to EER modelling is of the first importance:

- A *Consultant* is **one part of** a *Skill-group*. There is a thing called a skill-group, which is made up of consultants and other things.
- A *Consultant* is **one kind of** *Fee-Earner*. There is *no such thing* as a fee-earner, of which consultant is just one of the parts.

This example is meant to give a flavour of the basic concepts. Reality being awkward to reduce to models, any robust methodology needs numerous further refinements. Suppose some attributes are common to all *Consultants* and *Secretaries* but not to *Partners*; or certain people have all the status of consultants and do some fee-earning occasionally, but are really high-grade, non-fee-earning administrators. Extra techniques and conventions are needed for such cases and others that crop up in real-life modelling.

Aspects of OO-DBMS

If that is an EER (ie OO) model, what is an OO-DBMS? Talking, as some do, of 'a DBMS with the ability to manage object data types' isn't very illuminating. OO-DBMS is rather an immature field of technology. There is currently no such thing as a well-established, industrial-strength OO-DBMS product, already used in hundreds of high-volume systems. But there could easily be before long, and it is reasonably clear what the main characteristics of such a DBMS would be. Here are the main aspects:

- Above all, the OO-DBMS supports a **conceptual schema** in EER form. With a relational DBMS, typically you first make an ER model and then change it into a collection of relational tables making up the conceptual schema. With an OO-DBMS, you make an EER model and that is the conceptual schema. Thus this conceptual schema is two steps removed from a relational schema: the relational schema is (at least mainly) in third normal form, an ER model is less rigorous than that, and an EER model contains more meaning than an ER model. A CASE tool may convert the EER model defined as diagrams automatically into language instructions defining the schema of the

OO-DBMS, or there may be manual transcription work, but the point is that no further *brainwork* is required, as it is in converting ER diagrams into relational tables.

- The OO-DBMS can control the **integrity** of the database organised in EER form. Since this is a richer structure than a relational database, there is more scope for adding new data or amending data in ways that subtly undermine the structure. Therefore integrity control can be a formidable task.
- The OO-DBMS, like the relational, offers powerful, robust features and options for **concurrency control, recovery, security and deep design** for a database organised in EER form. Since the structure of the database and the nature of typical accesses are radically different, quite different techniques are needed to provide these facilities.[4]
- The OO-DBMS provides an appropriate **language** to access data held in EER form. Just as the form itself is more complex than relational tables, so the language must be more complex than SQL.
- The OO-DBMS provides **access and development features** such as query-by-forms, query-by-example and the usual 4GL tools for use with a database in EER form. To cope with the data's more complex structure, facilities are more sophisticated and make greater hardware demands (eg large screens and the computing power to drive graphic interfaces).
- As a somewhat separate point, an OO-DBMS allows storage in the database of software for **operations** associated with each entity in the schema. The software to validate a certain field can be stored in the database rather than contained in a number of different application programs. This concept can be taken further too; eg the software needed to assemble and format all the data needed to produce an item such as a customer invoice can be stored.

  Storage of software in the database is already supported by certain relational DBMSs. Of course, that in itself does not justify calling them OO-DBMSs.

OO: Second Chart

The opening chart separated and related four things: OO concepts, OO programming language, EER (or OO) modelling and OO-DBMS. This is only a start; further charting out of ideas is needed.

Can you have OO programming without using an OO programming language? And if you have carried out EER modelling, can you then use the model as the starting point for programming in a non-OO language?

Yes to both questions. One of the best books on OO topics[5] shows for each of the (non-OO) languages Ada, C and Fortran, how you *can* (if you have to) make the best of the language in order to program in a style that uses OO concepts. It isn't the case that an OO language can make a computer do things that a non-OO can't. The important point is that, after using OO concepts to define requirements, it will be easier to program them using an OO language; there should be less work, fewer errors and more scope for easy amendment later on.

If you have carried out EER modelling, can you then use the model as the starting point for defining the schema of a database that is based on other principles, relational, say? This is a more interesting and important question.

The great problem is the qualification preceding the list of OO-DBMS aspects in the previous section. OO-DBMS is far from being a mature product category.

Relational DBMS products such as DB2, Oracle, Ingres and so on have developed over a decade or more, improving in efficiency and reliability all the time. Even so, writers on relational database still make comments of the sort: 'unfortunately most commercial DBMSs provide no adequate support for null values (or for X or Y or some other refinement).' OO-DBMS products are still a long way behind, in that the fundamentals, let alone the refinements, are still open to debate.

Trying out an OO language or an EER modelling technique on a particular project need be no great risk; the worst that can happen is that after six months you decide that it has all been a waste of time. If things go well, you can increase use of the language or modelling technique fairly smoothly. But a DBMS is more of an all-or-nothing choice. Using an immature product as the basis for an application system could, in the worst case, have disastrous business consequences.

This leads to the question: Suppose you carry out an EER modelling exercise, believing its extra richness of insight and elegance of style to be well worth having; to avoid use of immature OO-DBMS software, could you convert the EER model into the tables of a relational conceptual schema and use a relational DBMS? This issue is likely to remain important during the years while OO-DBMS products are growing to maturity.

Example of Different EER-to-Relational Conversions

An EER model is inherently richer than an ER model or a relational model. You can convert an EER model into the tables that form the conceptual schema of a relational database, and usually there are

Converting an EER Model to Relational Tables

Part of an EER Model

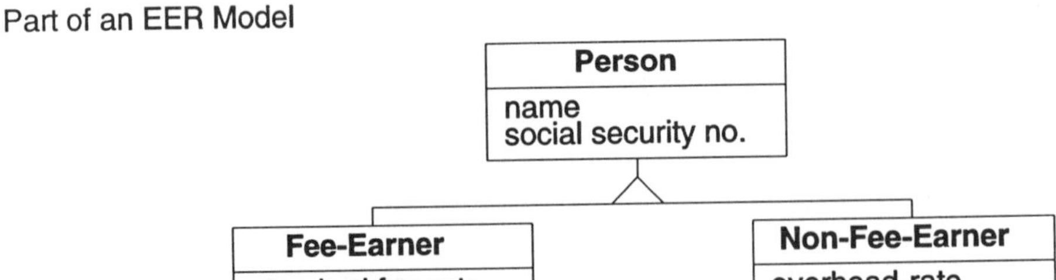

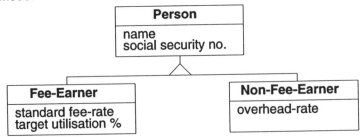

How to convert this into relational tables?

Three possible solutions:

A

PERSON table

name	social security no.	fee-earner code

FEE-EARNER table

name	standard fee-rate	target utilisation %

NON-FEE-EARNER table

name	overhead-rate

B

FEE-EARNER table

name	social security no.	standard fee-rate	target utilisation %

NON-FEE-EARNER table

name	social security no.	overhead-rate

C

PERSON table

name	social security no.	fee-earner code	standard fee-rate	target utilisation %	overhead-rate

Is it best to set up three, two or one relational tables?

several different ways of doing it, each bringing certain disadvantages. Thus, in the example, shown in the diagram:

- **Solution A**, if followed through consistently, will lead to a great proliferation of tables, with negative effects on system performance. Moreover, there is an integrity problem: with a schema designed this way, a relational DBMS won't prevent the same person being added to both the *Fee-earner* and *Non-fee-earner* tables. Special application programming would be needed to prevent it — something generally agreed to be less than ideal.
- **Solution B** has ugly repetition of the fields at *Person* level and has the same integrity drawbacks as Solution 1.
- **Solution C** is against the principles of relational design, since not all the fields can apply to all the records (eg for a non-fee-earner, *target-utilisation-%* will always be blank). Put another way, this also has integrity drawbacks: all application programs updating the table must check that *target-utilisation-%* is never updated for a non-fee-earner.

This unrealistically simple example shows that, however you go from EER to relational, some sacrifice or compromise will be needed:

- **Performance** — through proliferation of tables;
- and/or **Design elegance** — relevant because it promotes relatively error-free software and ease of amendment;
- and/or **Integrity** — in the sense that the DBMS can't enforce all the necessary rules; they will have to be embedded (in perhaps several places) in application software; this costs work and is less reliable;
- and/or **Storage space** — if, to reduce the number of different tables, great volumes of records, mostly containing blank fields, are stored.

Different situations will call for different approaches. If the two types of person have 20 fields in common and only two different, Solution C may be the least bad. At the other extreme, if only two fields are common and twenty different, Solution B becomes more attractive. Again, if the pattern of common and distinct fields were less skewed, it might be relevant to consider the kind of accesses expected. Solution A might be best if many accesses could be satisfied by retrieving data from just the *Person* table, without touching the other two tables.

The above analysis shows three generic solutions, with their generic pros and cons. In real life mixed solutions may have to be considered. The best buy in a certain case might be essentially Solution A — except (for the sake of performance) with some fields located in the *Person* table that (if elegance of design were all) ought really to be in the other two tables.

As this suggests, there is no alternative to getting an expert to spend a considerable time studying the factors and possibilities to arrive at the least-bad design.

Comparison of OO and Conventional Approaches to Database Systems

People sometimes talk as if certain types of application are *inherently* OO applications. Multimedia or engineering drawing or graphic user interface applications are frequently mentioned as examples to illustrate OO concepts. Sometimes it seems that any system to do with anything that in normal English can be called an object (eg objects in a museum or objects on a map) is to be regarded as an obvious candidate for OO technology. Two simple points help sweep such confusions away:

- OO concepts are so general and abstract that they can be applied to **any application** — sales order entry as well as animated design for a nuclear power station.
- Since OO concepts are rather more sophisticated than previous system design concepts, they bring the greatest advantage in an application that is more complicated in its detail than average or one that is more intellectually exacting than average.

To develop these points in more depth first make the distinction between systems that deal with mainstream data in typical business applications, on the one hand, and all other types of development on the other.

If done successfully, **EER modelling** offers two main advantages in **mainstream** applications: more insight into the system being modelled and a more robust base for future system changes. But there are two disadvantages:

- However great the value of an EER *model as product*, the EER *modelling process* can be quite a challenge. Normally you need to take along with you line-managers and others who supply knowledge and check that the models made of the organisation are correct. They need to become reasonably fluent in the concepts of whatever modelling method is adopted. If most of the departmental managers are impatient with the intricacies of ER modelling, they are unlikely to take to the extra complications of EER very happily.
- When the time comes to implement the model as a database, you must either use an OO-DBMS, an immature class of technology, or lose much of the model's subtlety by setting up a conceptual schema for a relational DBMS.

In short, there is a balance to be struck between the extra insight and the extra effort. For relatively simple systems this balance may be unfavourable to EER, but things move in EER's favour as the application becomes more complex. It is possible for a pure mainstream application to be so complex that EER modelling is far more cost-effective than straightforward ER, since it reduces the expensive back-tracking caused by late discoveries of hidden subtleties and confusions.

Analogous tradeoffs arise with the **database** and the **DBMS**:

- **Efficiency.** Relational may be the sensible choice if the application calls for 100 tables, most with tens of thousands and some with hundreds of thousands of records. But suppose the application needs 1000 tables, many with only tens or hundreds of records, and suppose many of these tables are frequently joined to numerous others, giving a great number of possible combinations. Then relational may have no advantage of efficiency over OO, and the danger of the relational conceptual schema becoming just too intricate for anyone fully to comprehend may be considerable.
- **Flexibility**. In any system, but particularly a very complex one, it should be easier with OO to support future system changes, at least in principle, since many revisions can be restricted to one part of the schema without wider implications. For instance, several years after setting up the database, it is decided that instead of the two-way split between *Consultant* and *Partner*, there should be three possibilities: *Consultant, Managing-consultant* and *Partner*. Probably this change can be made without disturbing the definitions of *Fee-Earner* and *Person* at higher levels in the schema. The value of this extra robustness in the face of change will vary from case to case. In some situations, setting up a durable foundation for undoubted future changes may be the fundamental objective; in others, it may just be something that, other things being equal, is worth having.

Outside the mainstream, things are rather different, particularly in a hybrid database system — whether an apparently modest one that still raises awkward issues of integrity or an extreme case with a mix of five or six kinds of information. Here there is no straightforward comparison to be made between a well-established way of doing things and the innovative OO approach.

You *can* use established relational database technology to store texts or rules or bit-mapped images along with mainstream in a hybrid database. Very often this is the best way of doing things — but that is because the powerful relational DBMS already exists as the product of enormous investment for the mainstream market; it is not because relational DBMS is the natural tool that anyone would invent for the specific task of managing a hybrid database. It is quite plausible that EER and OO-DBMS are inherently superior ways of

SUMMARY OF WARRANTS

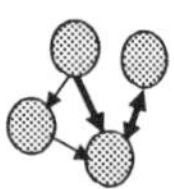
Chart connecting Object-oriented Things: OO concepts; OO programming language; OO modelling; EER modelling; OO-DBMS

Examples of EER Modelling: Two special types of relationship: 'is one kind of', 'is one part' and ensuing complications

Aspects of OO-DBMS: Conceptual schema in EER form; Integrity; Concurrency control, recovery, security and deep design; Language; Access and development features; Stored operations

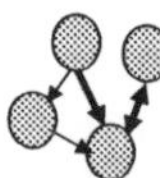
Chart connecting more OO Things: OO programming and OO programming language; EER modelling; OO-DBMS; Relational DBMS

Example of Different EER-to-Relational Conversions: Factors: Performance; Design elegance; Integrity; Storage space

Comparison of OO and Conventional Approaches: Increased demands on modelling participants; Loss at conversion to relational; Extra insight; Better basis for changes; (Non-mainstream and hybrid) inherently superior concepts but still early days

tackling many non-mainstream and hybrid database systems. The trouble is that there is a long road to travel from attractive concepts to successful application systems based on powerful, well-established software products.[6]

POSSIBLE DECISION-MAKING

The partners on Coachwood's IT management sub-committee decide very quickly that, though advanced technology may sometimes be a good bet on minor projects, they are not prepared to experiment with OO-DBMS as the basis for a system so fundamental to their business.

But this doesn't mean that *EER modelling* should be rejected. The argument in its favour is that the complexities of the system they want for billing and analysing professionals' time within a complicated organisational structure are greater than appear at first glance. Moreover, everyone agrees that the flexibility requirements are very demanding. Therefore, so it can be argued, extra investment in a more subtle data model is likely to be justified in the long run.

The counter-argument is that converting the EER model to fit the constraints of a relational database is so uncomfortable. Even if the meaning-rich EER-model is preserved on paper, the schema of the database itself will necessarily lose much of the extra meaning. Secondly, there is a problem of principle. A conceptual schema is supposed to show the data to be stored in a logical, non-technical form. But if making the conceptual schema entails appraising a large number of practical tradeoffs in order to find the least bad out of many different possibilities, that seems to undermine its whole basis. It will no longer be the most natural and logical way of describing the database, within the context of relational conventions; it will be the design that, on balance, is least bad in practical terms.

It does seem difficult to decide whether to invest in an EER model and then convert to relational, or whether to stick to the well-tried ER model with its clear route to relational database. However, another factor comes into things at Coachwood.

Once the database system is set up to handle the commercial procedures, Coachwood intends to extend the database with as yet vaguely defined information about skills. This won't be pure mainstream information; there will quite possibly be keywords or rules or texts accessible by searching. It seems plausible that a system which integrates this type of data with the relatively complex mainstream data really does call for the extra keenness and insight supplied by EER modelling. So, on balance, the Coachwood partners decide that is the way to go.

CONNECTIONS

13. Data Modelling Method and Process	Basic ER modelling
25. Geographic Information Systems	Complex hybrid — a good target for the OO approach
26. Text-with-Mainstream Systems	Another complex hybrid

30. Untangling Adjacent Technologies

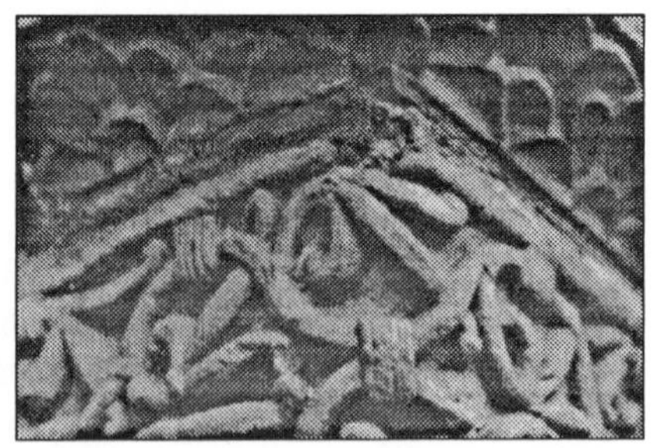

BEARINGS

This briefing has a different purpose from those preceding it. They explore the field of database technology fairly thoroughly. This one merely points things out, rather than exploring them. The sights pointed out are the regions of information technology adjacent to the normally accepted territory of database.

POSSIBLE CONTEXT

As a thought experiment, take Blue Gum, manufacturers of cigar-making machines. Its computer-literate managers have a good knowledge of database technology — how it can be broken down into different elements, the demands it can supply, the different types of system etc. But they still need to know about the areas that border database technology, because:

- To study any field you have to draw boundaries around it. But knowing what lies just outside the boundaries, and why it is there, can help strengthen your command of the subject.
- Plainly, Blue Gum should be ready to consider using *any* technology possibilities that may further its commercial success. It would be irrational to focus only on those that happen to fall within database technology. Perhaps, for a certain application, no characteristic form of database technology quite meets the needs, but some closely related, non-database technology does.

Therefore, at a minimum, the Blue Gum managers need a chart sketching out how various other technologies, not normally counted as database technology, are nevertheless related to it.

WARRANTS

The first warrant section presents a very broad-brush chart to help focus on the problem. The warrant sections after that identify specific boundary cases.

General Chart of Database and Other Technologies

The opening briefing of the book suggests a ten-element chart that helps break down and fit together the main elements of database technology. The first six — kind of data to deep design — describe features of a certain database system at a certain time. The next — architecture — is about how things fit together as a whole. The last three — modelling to control — describe the processes and activities of setting up and controlling a database system.

Consider these elements as together making up just one thing called **database technology**. Then all the other technologies adjacent to database technology can be swept into three groups:

- **General-purpose.** The architecture of any database system needs to include certain technology components that are not themselves part of database technology because they are too general-purpose. PCs and printers and telecoms equipment can be used for many tasks outside database systems: for word processing, sending faxes, solving weather forecast calculations, controlling pumps and sluices etc.
- **Organised data, but not database**. Database technology organises data in a structure and permits certain types of access. Some other technologies not usually regarded as database do structure data in their own way with correspondingly different access and other features. Spreadsheet is an example. A definition of database that was both broad and strictly interpreted ought perhaps to encompass spreadsheet and some other things, but in practice they are normally regarded as outside the boundary.
- **Database but specialised.** Some technologies are undeniably versions of database technology, in terms of data structure and the other demand elements — albeit perhaps with extra twists. Yet they are usually kept outside what is considered to be database, for a reason that is purely pragmatic rather than logical: they are too specialised to be relevant to the average organisation. Publishing many copies of a database on compact disk is an example.

System Aspects met by General-purpose Technologies

Here is an outline of general-purpose technology components found in a database system, broken down from five different aspects:

- Any database system needs to **run on computers**. PCs, workstations, minicomputers and mainframe can be used for much else besides database systems. Perhaps the closest boundary case is the exceptionally powerful PC or workstation, specifically designed by its manufacturer to be a powerful server in a client-server database setup.
- Many database systems need to **send data across networks**. Telecoms hardware and software are not themselves part of database technology because they can be used for many other things besides. Again there are boundary cases, eg telecoms software products whose main use is likely to be in providing the telecoms facilities within a client-server setup.
- The data in any database system needs to **be captured** somehow. The data captured by a hardware device or by software can be used for any purpose. Besides keyed input, scanned or bar-coded input may capture data for a database. Some data capture technology includes software. Thus, scanning a graphic to capture it in bit-mapped form is largely a hardware task, but scanning text with OCR (optical character recognition) requires sophisticated software to recognise the characters.

  An example of software-only technology is software that accepts texts prepared with a certain word processor and automatically converts and stores them in a different format. Analogously, software may be used for conversion of graphics from one format to another. Pattern recognition software attempts the arduous task of making sense of bit-mapped data input; eg analysing voice data to pick out the words contained in the utterance, or scrutinising images of cars to decide which part of the image is the number-plate, and within that, what the number is.
- The data in any database system needs to **be stored** somewhere. Magnetic (ie normal) disks can store data for any purpose. So can the different varieties of optical disk (WORM, CD-ROM, videodisk etc), though these tend to be most suitable for high-volume, database-like applications, perhaps with distribution of multiple copies. A related technology is software that manages the compression (and decompression) of data; this is particularly relevant to the storage of graphics, where important tradeoffs arise between storage requirement and image quality.
- The data in any database system needs **to be output** somehow;

ie printed or displayed on screens. Data output devices are general-purpose technology. If the database itself contains colour or high-resolution images, this will call for appropriately sophisticated output devices.

Examples of 'Organised Data, but not Database' Technologies

Earlier briefings have dealt with database issues in expert system and imaging technology — but with particular reference to hybrid systems. In each of these, there are lower gradations of complexity where the database is scarcely hybrid, if at all. Then the data is certainly organised (as opposed to chaotic), but not as a database in the usual sense. It is simply in the format most convenient for the specific purpose: drawing diagrams, making inferences etc.

Here are five more examples of other technologies that do organise data, but in structures not usually considered to be database structures:

- **Spreadsheet.** Data (mainly numeric) is stored in the cells formed by the rows and columns of a matrix. Some of the cells store formulae defining how they are derived (eg A19 = A17 + A18). The emphasis is on performing calculations, as opposed to providing access to stored data. However, as if to show that this is really just a difference of emphasis, many spreadsheet software products provide a so-called database facility; eg allowing a search to extract all rows where the cell at column 16 is greater than that at column 4.
- **Outliner**. An outliner is essentially a software tool for *developing a document*. A long report usually has a hierarchical structure: chapters, headings, sub-headings etc. An outliner tool allows you to 'collapse' (ie remove from view temporarily) the text under a certain heading or under all headings or all those of a certain level. This makes it much easier to find your way around and also to switch blocks of text from one place to another. Little to do with database perhaps, except that an outliner can also *manage a permanent document*, as a rival to text-DBMS software. The document might consist of hundreds of references to magazine articles, all arranged under subject headings in a collapsible hierarchy.
- **Personal information manager (PIM)**. A PIM is meant to help a manager keep ready to hand useful information such as appointments diary, names, addresses and phone numbers, to-do lists, scraps of text (eg ongoing list of bright ideas for new products etc) or chunks of reference information (eg notes on government safety standards for cigar-making machines) or items midway between the last two (eg notes on hobbies of customers and of other people

meriting flattery). For handling notes and scraps of text a modest text-DBMS is the natural choice, but the PIM as a separate category usually combines a facility for text-searching with other features to handle the more structured data of diaries, address lists and so on.

• **Revisable documents.** If somebody sends you a document file produced using (say) Microsoft Word, you can normally display it and even alter the text on your own PC, providing you have the Microsoft Word software too. But suppose the document was prepared with some more sophisticated page makeup software that you don't use; then it can't easily be displayed or amended. It is a rather esoteric field, but work is going on to develop standard structures to hold the content of documents with complex formats, so that they can be displayed and amended, even without the originating software. This problem of data organisation is loosely connected with the issues of SGML and similar advanced developments in text database.

• **Animation.** Some picture or spatial databases offer a modest amount of animation; eg displaying a colour photo of a cigar-making machine, on which, during a two-minute sequence, lines and arrows gradually appear to show the processes it carries out — perhaps with a synchronised commentary. But if the body of data is stored *primarily* for the purpose of generating animated graphics, then since the data structures, access and other elements are so different, it is not really to be regarded as a database.

Examples of 'Database but Specialised' Technologies

A number of technologies can be described as containing a specialised extension of database technology — particularly of the access element of the unifying chart:

• **Electronic forms**. A fairly new type of software product aims to replace paper forms by displaying an electronic facsimile of a form (sales order forms, stock requisition forms, employee address change forms and the like) on the screen. The clerk can fill in the form on the screen from the keyboard, and the data goes off to update the database — without the need for writing on a printed form at all. This approach could prosper at the expense of 4GL-like tools currently used to design input screens for most database systems.

• **Groupware aka workflow.** Some of the current jargon most perplexing to pin down hovers around ideas for helping people work together better — whether by facilitating tasks that can be structured (eg preparing a manufacturing schedule) or improving communications between people engaged in tasks that cannot (eg designing a new cigar-making machine). Sometimes 'groupware' is nothing but a halo-name for a system based on client-server or distributed database architecture, very likely using middleware (ie software that resolves all the problems of incompatible DBMS and network technologies). In more interesting cases, the term denotes some neatly contrived combination of disparate functions; eg electronic mail, mainstream database and text database may all be made accessible to the user, through an interface that is both convenient and standardised.

• **Database publishing.** A DBMS can store large quantities of information in a defined format but is usually limited in subtlety of presentation in printing it out. Desktop publishing (DTP) software, by contrast, is concerned with providing flexible, subtle typographic options: different typefaces, point sizes, paragraph formatting and so on. A software product for database publishing bridges the gap. It allows you to prepare a script for production of a complex document by passing data from the database to the DTP software. You can specify (say) that the *product-name* field from the database record should be printed in a certain column of the product catalogue document and that it must be in Helvetica bold, 11 point and that any break over two lines should be between complete words. The *product-description* field, by contrast, might be printed in the Palatino font, not-bold, 10 point, with hyphenation for line-break if necessary; and so on. (Note: Database publishing is not to be confused with CD-ROM publishing, below.)

• **On-line database service.** A few organisations such as Dialog or Dow-Jones make a vast range of databases available for anyone to access through any PC equipped for telecoms. In this sense, the database service is a public one (not public in the sense of being run by a government or monopoly utility). These are mainly keyword and text rather than mainstream databases. You can access the data as a customer or perhaps do a deal with the 'host' organisation to supply a database of your own to the information supermarket.

• **Videotex**. There are several contradictory definitions of videotex. A broad definition is a host-based database system allowing people to use a low-cost terminal through a simple interface to access the database (any type of database). On this basis, some people regard the on-line database service just mentioned as a form of videotex. Others do not, because they prefer a narrower definition, restricting videotex to two particular forms of technology invented by the British and French post offices.

• **CD-ROM publishing.** Though it may be used loosely (as in 'desktop publishing'), 'publishing' really ought to be kept for cases where information is distributed in many copies — either to the world at large or at least to a variety of recipients within an

SUMMARY OF WARRANTS

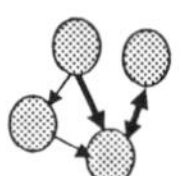

Chart of Database and Other Technologies: Database technology; General-purpose technology; Organised data, but not database; Database but specialised

Aspects for General-purpose Technologies: Run on computers; Send data across networks; Capture data; Store data; Output data

Examples of 'Organised Data, but not Database' Technologies: Spreadsheet; Outliner; Personal information manager (PIM); Revisable documents; Animation.

Examples of 'Database but Specialised' Technologies: Electronic forms; Groupware aka workflow; Database publishing; On-line database service; Videotex; CD-ROM publishing.

---

organisation. The CD-ROM version of compact disk is an important enabling technology for the distribution of multiple copies of databases. Its advantageous characteristics are: high capacity, thus providing room for images in addition to mainstream and text data; low marginal cost of disk copies; fairly consistent technology standard.

POSSIBLE DECISION-MAKING

As usual, this kind of knowledge enables managers to participate in decision-making about IT, rather than just accept whatever the technical experts tell them. They can ask useful questions such as:

'You say it will take three months work to produce those reports from the database in the format we want. Haven't you considered use of a database publishing package?'

'Why not load that information into a spreadsheet rather than access it in the server database?'

'There are at least three ways of capturing text for a database — keying, OCR and conversion of word processing documents. Have you compared all these options fully?'

'Isn't it worth investing three days work just to see if we might possibly have a potential application here for publishing information to our customers either on CD-ROM or through a public database service?'

CONNECTIONS

The section *How to Be Your Own Guide* suggests a set of general-purpose tools for keeping afloat in the technology maelstrom. The companion book *Information Management Decisions, Briefings and Critical thinking* goes into much more detail.

31. Untangling Database and Wider Issues

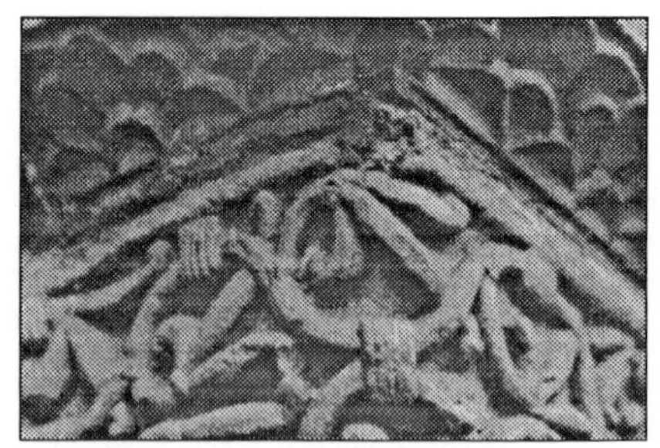

BEARINGS

This briefing has a different status from all the others. They are about technology and take the following form: Here is analysis of some particular area of technology, organised to promote well-warranted decisions in that area.

But the ramifications of certain decisions about database technology can influence an organisation's policies on wider matters, beyond particular systems and technologies. Conversely, some high-level decisions that may seem far removed from database can in practice close off important options for decisions about database technology.

Pursuit of such connections and interactions between decisions would lead ever further away from material about technology towards the general principles of the management of information technology. This briefing merely provides signposts — from within the territory of database technology out towards adjacent regions of management.

POSSIBLE CONTEXT

The executive committee of the board of Black Ash Bank, suspecting that the company's use of database technology is weak and behind the times, commissions a study from consultants. They produce extensive proposals: a phased plan to redevelop essential systems using both client-server and, to some degree, distributed database technology; a new project to set up a large text database containing texts of banking laws and regulations, and standard terms and conditions governing all types of accounts; a picture database project for the bank's real estate subsidiary, etc etc.

All these things are really suggestions for *matching supply and demand.* This matching may involve taking a more or less clear demand (eg running customers' current accounts) and finding a way to supply it better (eg with distributed database) or the matching may be a recognition that a certain supply technology (eg picture database) can serve demands not hitherto articulated (eg showing prospective purchasers photos of properties on a screen in the office).

Is it true that the most important decisions about using IT within the bank all belong to this general type? Are they all, however strategic, ultimately matching decisions? No. Some important IT decisions are not matching decisions:

- Suppose the bank decides to set up a separate innovation group within the organisation charged with recognising, spearheading (evangelising even) the use of new technologies. That decision is an important one about IT, but it isn't a decision that matches supply and demand in any particular way.
- Neither is a decision that the central IS department should be run as a profit centre charging departments commercial rates for its services.
- Neither is a decision that the organisation should have a five-year (as opposed to a three-year or six-year) plan for IT.

These three non-matching decisions belong, along with matching decisions, within the broad class of **information management (IM)** decisions.[1]

Now a question arises. Will decision-making be more methodical and manageable if matching decisions are taken separately from non-matching? Or should some decision-making concerned with matching database supply and demand interact with (as opposed to follow from or determine) that about other IM matters that are not matching?

The second of these must surely be right. Take a crude example: the matching decision to redesign major systems (with certain demands), using client-server and distributed database techniques (a certain supply), has fundamental and long-term implications; it is inevitably bound up with the IM decision that there should be a detailed, five-year IT investment plan — as opposed to (say) a detailed three-year plan or outline five-year or separate, loosely related plans for different departments or any number of other forms of plan. This decision about the nature of the planning will probably be based on assessment of factors such as how settled or turbulent are business conditions, and where to strike the balance between freedom and control of planning in different departments. If business conditions are turbulent, it may follow that detailed long-term planning is not sensible, and from this, it may follow that a large-scale demand-supply match is not wise.

If at least some matching decisions about database can interact in this kind of way with some other IM decisions, dangers emerge. A bank might take a matching decision without fully appreciating the implications and thus drift into some other IM decision (eg detailed, five-year, integrated plan), without fully assessing it.

Almost any kind of matching decision might have wider IM implications under some conceivable circumstances, but certain interactions are more common than others. To attack this problem the executive committee of the board needs some general chart to show how certain areas of decision-making about database are frequently associated with other IM issues.

WARRANTS

Discussion of the general question of how decisions that match supply and demand are related to other types of decisions in managing IT takes a book in itself.[2] This briefing is restricted to issues that arise with database technology in particular — and it merely points them out, rather than discusses how to resolve them.

General Chart of Database and Information Management Decisions

The opening briefing of the book suggests a ten-element chart that helps break down and fit together the main elements of database technology. The first six — kind of data to deep design — describe features of a certain database system at a certain time. The next — architecture — is about how things fit together as a whole. The last three — modelling to control — describe the processes and activities of setting up and controlling a database system.

Now here is a chart of wider scope: it proposes five categories for IM decisions:

- **Matching decisions:** deciding how to match supply and demand; eg 'We will allow people in the branches to refer to the clauses of banking laws (demand) through terminals accessing a host text database system (supply) — as opposed to distributing texts in print form or on CD-ROM (other supply options).'
- **Scope decisions:** deciding the terms of reference within which matching decisions will be made and projects will take place; eg 'We will set up three separate limited projects to try out different uses of document imaging (ie each having a different match of supply and demand) — as opposed to having one coordinated master-plan for all our imaging projects (ie matching one whole set of demands against one whole supply).'

- **Context decisions:** deciding on the management environment within which other types of decisions will take place; eg 'Each of the five divisions of the bank will have its own IT director and make its own IT decisions (including, but not only, decisions about matching supply and demand); if some facilities, such as database, telecoms network etc, are shared between divisions, this will be arranged through bilateral treaties — as opposed to through one central authority, such as a CIO or a planning group or a sub-committee of the board.'
- **Approach decisions:** deciding how to structure the process of taking decisions of any of the above types; eg 'We will follow the standard methodology for strategic information planning (which is itself a way of defining demand and deciding how to supply it) of an established consultancy, yet to be selected — as opposed to devising an approach of our own, or using a consultancy that shuns detailed standards.'
- **Agenda decisions:** deciding the broad outlines of policy that will affect decisions of all the other types; eg 'We will introduce IT-based facilities for our back-office workers at least as good as those of our most sophisticated competitors — as opposed to finding the leanest, most cost-effective way of organising the offices.'

This is a start towards showing how certain elements of database technology can have strong links to certain types of IM decision. The rest of this briefing points out for each of the four types of IM decision, other than Matching, the most common examples of interactions with elements of database technology.

Chart of Scope Decisions and Database Technology

Here are some of the most important links to Scope decisions:

- **Physical architecture**. Certain forms of architecture imply different degrees of scope for projects and systems using the database. For instance, a certain variety of client-server architecture might make it very easy for separate projects of limited scope to be developed independently in a prototyping style. This could cause you to prefer this architecture over some other architecture that might be superior when viewed only as a way of supplying the demand currently defined.
- **Logical architecture**. The concepts of chunks and selective descriptions that run through database technology are relevant to the tradeoff between commitment and flexibility often found with IM decisions of scope. In general, commitment to large-scale, integrated plans can bring economies of scale at the expense of flexibility. Flexibility to respond to future changes and new require-

ments, may be bought at the price of incoherent developments and unnecessary costs. The opportunities for chunks and selective description in database technology don't abolish this tradeoff, but, used carefully, they can permit a more favourable balance of advantage.

• **Modelling**. Many books and other authorities explain how to make data models of various kinds, but glide over a huge issue of scope that can be vital in practice. Before you start you have to decide the scope of the modelling. Otherwise how can you determine what the rough boundaries of your model should be and what kind of details can be left out? Reaching a sensible decision on this can be trickier than actually doing the modelling. A model of moderate quality based on a sensible scope decision is likely to be far more use than a perfect model based on a misguided scope decision.

Chart of Context Decisions and Database Technology

Two of the most important links to Context decisions:

• **Architecture**. Questions of database architecture are often related to context policy. A strongly integrated database setup, with much sharing of data between departments may fit badly with a management context that encourages a great deal of independence between departments — or perhaps not in every case; at any rate this is an interaction that should be recognised and explored.

• **Access to data** and **software development**. Database access features can go through various gradations of sophistication, providing different degrees of initiative to the user of the system. After a certain point on this scale, it becomes more accurate to say that the user is carrying out new software development rather than accessing the database in new ways. End-user computing is an IM topic whose issues frequently reduce to finding the context that provides the best balance of user initiative and central control. Plainly, decisions on end-user computing will need to be consistent with choices of database access and development tools.

Chart of Approach Decisions and Database Technology

There is a general problem. It is attractive to organise IT decision-making, planning and design in a methodical, multi-level structure, where more fundamental things are settled before more trivial, where decisions at one level lead on naturally to decisions at the next, and the final product is a detailed document, bringing coherence to the organisation's different projects, systems and databases. But there are some typical pitfalls with this concept: the enterprise model so detailed that it is 'unreadable at any speed' is the most common.

One particular problem exists on the frontier between two distinct cultures. Many information analysts devote themselves to detailed, rigorous ER **modelling**, that they regard, reasonably enough, as a vital part of the process of designing databases. But others, particularly management consultants, develop models of the business, its essential processes, its information requirements and so on. Terms such as information engineering and strategic information systems planning may be used. These products can become quite detailed, but they are more impressionistic than ER models and thus quite far from database technology. In fact, their proponents may insist, in some cases sensibly, that a business view unfettered by technology practicalities is exactly what the organisation needs.

Both approaches have some merit. The problem is to find an overall approach that mixes them successfully. A necessary but not sufficient condition is that the two types of work actually can be fitted together. It is undesirable for the ER modellers to start from scratch, because the strategic information architecture developed by others with several workyears' effort is too hazy or too idealistic to be a sound basis for development. To be more precise, you need to judge the level of detail at which impressionistic business-oriented modelling should turn into rigorous data modelling. Where this point comes will differ from case to case.

Chart of Agenda Decisions and Database Technology

An agenda decision can be about anything, provided it is so fundamental that it sets the agenda for decisions of other types — matching, context etc. This makes it difficult to point to any specific elements of database technology particularly related to agenda decisions.

At the start of the eighties, the decision to shift from earlier technology and get up to speed with database was a commonly found agenda decision with extensive implications.

For the first half of the nineties it seems plausible to single out the topic of **kind of data**. For many organisations, database systems are still nothing other than mainstream database systems. The realisation that many other types of data (text, geographic, bit-mapped image and the rest) can be organised in databases too may be sufficiently powerful to produce genuine, far-reaching agenda decisions.

SUMMARY OF WARRANTS

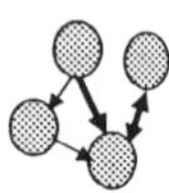

General Chart linking Database and Information Management Decisions: Ten elements of database technology; five types of IM decisions

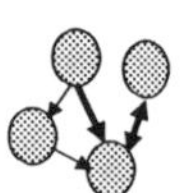

Chart of Scope Decisions and Database Technology: Links between scope decisions and architecture (physical and logical) and modelling

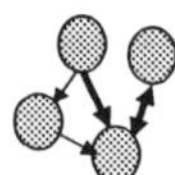

Chart of Context Decisions and Database Technology: Links between context decisions and architecture, access to data and software development

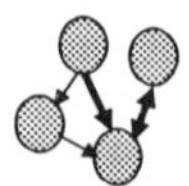

Chart of Approach Decisions and Database Technology: Links between approach decisions and data modelling

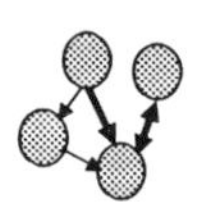

Chart of Agenda Decisions and Database Technology: Links between agenda decisions and kind of data

POSSIBLE DECISION-MAKING

Through this charting members of the executive committee at Black Ash Bank can see how decisions about matching database supply and demand fit together with other kinds of decisions about information management. This enables them to get better value from their consultants:

'Why should we commit ourselves to a large client-server-based project now, based on requirements that will be carefully defined for the whole company and then frozen? Why not give the project a more flexible *scope*? With the software development tools now on the market, you can run an experimental or prototyping project quite cheaply and nimbly. Different departments might even be allowed to try out different ways of doing things. In fact, perhaps the whole concept of one large project to build one company infrastructure is questionable.'

'Granted distributed database is a relatively advanced technology, but the crucial issues in our case seem not so much technical as *contextual*. Will this technology fit in well with the distribution of responsibility we already have? For instance, suppose the IT director of one operating unit isn't happy with the decisions of the administrator of the distributed database. What then? If we have real problems here, should we change the context or consider a different technology supply or even alter the demands?'

'Investing in sophisticated CASE technology to produce ER and other models sounds attractive, but we need to be clear about the place of data modelling in our whole *approach* to decision-making. Are the models meant to help us build databases and systems better — provided we already know roughly what databases and systems we need? Or are they meant to help us make the decisions about what systems we should have, which should have priority, how elaborate or simple they should be, and so on?

'Unquestionably, new kinds of database — hypertext, photos, maps and such like — are interesting. But are they just things to bear in mind when a new system comes up for discussion? Or should this be a real *agenda-setting* theme? If so, maybe we should set up a special centre of expertise in GIS, subsidise from central funds half the costs incurred by any department in capturing colour images, insist every department has a text database policy and so on.'

CONNECTIONS

This briefing operates on a higher level of abstraction than the rest of the book. It is about questions of principle that affect the whole IM decision-making process.

Demands and Decisions, Briefings on Issues in Information Technology Strategy is a companion book of briefings on strategy issues. All the IM issues signposted in this briefing are discussed in detail in that book.

The other companion book, *Information Management Decisions, Briefings and Critical Thinking* discusses the different types of IM decision in detail. It surveys the whole subject, summarising some well established concepts and discussing them — sometimes sceptically.

How to Be Your Own Guide

Each of the warrants presented in the briefings is fashioned into one out of a small number of forms: a *comparison* of a small number of possibilities with their pros and cons is one form; a breakdown exposing important *distinctions*, but without pros and cons is another; and so on.

These warrant forms are generally applicable intellectual tools. If you had to explore some narrow sector of database technology in much more detail, you could use these tools to whip the content of books, articles, technical documents and the pronouncements of specialists into a shape that permitted clear decision-making. If you had to get to grips with some other area of information technology than database, you could use these same tools to discern the facts that should affect decisions.

A companion book, *Information Management Decisions, Briefings and Critical Thinking*, develops these ideas in detail with many examples. It suggests a repertoire of six warrant forms:

- In practice, the most forceful form of warrant is the **comparison**. It exposes two or more mutually exclusive options and compares their pros and cons in general terms. By seeing how these factors weigh in your specific case, you can arrive at a decision (eg which technology option to choose for your system).
- The **distinctions** warrant also exposes distinct possibilities but contains little or no detail of their pros and cons. Thus, it helps you establish what the main generic options are for consideration in your case, without explicitly helping you choose between them.
- The **gradations** warrant plays a similar role to a distinctions warrant in establishing options — but in areas where the possibilities fit naturally into ascending degrees of complexity.
- An **aspects** warrant is less decision-forcing, but can be very valuable nonetheless. It doesn't go as far as separating options out; it is an orientation device that helps you get a grip on the whole debate.
- A **chart** warrant occupies the same point on the decision-forcing scale as an aspects warrant. Its purpose too is orientation, but it is more complicated. It charts out (logically, not necessarily as a diagram) how certain concepts are related to each other.
- At the bottom of the decision-forcing scale but still invaluable at times are **example** warrants. A good example warrant isn't just anecdotal; it has general relevance. Moreover, it does more than

Typical Matching Warrants for Other Technologies

Warrant Form	Representative Warrant	Representative Matching Decision
Comparison	The tradeoffs between CD-ROM and WORM as storage media for high-volume data storage and distribution are . . .	We will use CD-ROM (rather than WORM) for this particular application system using a high-volume database.
Distinctions	This table classifies the different ways of using expert system technology to support different styles of computer-assisted instruction . . .	The broad category of computer-assisted instruction we need is . . .
Gradations	Here are four main varieties of ATM systems, in ascending order of sophistication of technology and facilities . . .	We choose to have a new banking system, using advanced ATMs to provide the following new facilities for customers . . . (but not these other possible facilities . . .)
Aspects	Word processing packages have five main aspects, under which all the more detailed features can be bunched: Presentation, Content, Manipulation, Essential Interface and Advanced Interface . . .	We will choose our word processing package primarily on the quality of its Presentation features (as opposed to the other aspects).
Chart	Videotex is a technology with several variants. Prestel is one particular videotex service. Some other services use the same variant of videotex as Prestel; others don't . . .	We will consider videotex, but not the Prestel variant.
Example	Here is how a bank's expert system can authorise or block a cash payment from an ATM . . .	With that understanding of expert system we can define the use of an expert system in our mining company . . .

exemplify some idea that could be expressed more economically as the text of some other form of warrant. It helps form an instinct about some concept that will have some influence on debate.

The *WARRANTS* segments of the 31 briefings of this book contain 181 warrants, broken down as follows:

Comparison 20
Distinctions 35
Gradations 19
Aspects 26
Chart 42
Example 39

In summary: example warrants help form instincts about matters likely to be relevant to your debate; aspects and chart warrants help you organise the debate in directions across the most important ground; distinctions and gradations help you establish what the options are in a given area; comparison warrants help you evaluate specific options. The table shows how these six forms are general tools, applicable to technologies other than database.

Notes and Arguments

Introduction

1 For a roundup of definitions offered by many different authorities see *Database and Data Communications Systems: A Guide for Managers*, Myles E Walsh, (Reston, 1983); or *Information and Data Modelling*, David Benyon, (Blackwell Scientific, 1990).

2 One book that brings together both mainstream and other database technologies is *Intelligent Databases, Object-Oriented, Deductive Hypermedia Technologies*, Kamran Parsaye, Mark Chignell, Setrag Khoshafian and Harry Wong, (Wiley, 1989): useful, but advocates new directions more than it reviews current technologies.

How to Use This Guide

1 Any book explaining technology or science raises the question: Why this content? Why should X be fully explained, but Y only lightly sketched? Why this particular mixture of facts, general principles, examples, advice, theories and forecasts, and not some other? If the reader can sense the rationale for the selection of material, the book is likely to convey a good understanding of its technology; but if not, not. This is also a good test of books about (say) the history of time or other large subjects.

2 The term *warrant* is used by Stephen Toulmin in his books *The Uses of Argument* (Cambridge University Press, 1958) and *An Introduction to Reasoning* (with Richard Rieke and Allan Janik), (Macmillan, 1979). Toulmin puts forward a generic format for arguments, with six standard components: claim, warrant, backing and so on. However, the format is not a great success. This book ignores the format, but uses the word *warrant* in a way analogous though not identical to Toulmin.

3 These warrant forms for holding technology knowledge — comparison of generic possibilities, analysis into aspects, chart to sort out overlapping concepts and so on — are general tools for fashioning warrants to support sound decisions. A companion book to this one — *Information Management Decisions, Briefings and Critical Thinking*, Bart O'Brien (Pitman, 1994) — pursues this theme in some detail and suggests a repertoire of warrant forms that help make sense of any technology, not just database.

4 A fabricated example is generally more incisive than a real case. Real-life, situation-specific details usually blur the general points illustrated by the example. And if the case is edited drastically to avoid this, then it is no longer a real case.

Management gurus usually cite real not imaginary examples, but if a book's aim is to discuss generally useful ideas, this preference has no logic. The problems in geometry books are no less meaningful because their triangles and spheres are imaginary. Technical books about database use made-up examples of data modelling, database design etc, and nobody finds them any the worse for that. Why should examples of problems and techniques in IT *decision-making* be any different?

1. Untangling Database Technology

1 Chart is a better term than map. A map follows well-defined cartographic conventions. One important thing about an intellectual chart, whether graphic or textual, is that it relates things in a provisional, impressionistic way.

2 Examples of confused usage: R Elmasri and SB Navathe, *Fundamentals of Database Systems*, (Benjamin/Cummings, 1989) p622; also, *Database System Concepts*, HF Korth and A Silberschatz, (McGraw-Hill 1986), first sentence on page 1.

It is best to avoid 'database management system'. For the software product that manages the database, say 'DBMS'; for the whole system, say 'database system'.

3 This poses a certain problem of scoping. A system that uses database technology may be called a database system, but not every component of the system counts as database technology. For example, the technologies of colour screens or telecoms networks or document scanners are not database technology.

Fortunately 'database technology' is like 'game'; the precise definition may be elusive, but the term can still be used with little or no confusion. Even so, it is useful to know where the main frontiers with other technologies and topics lie; the last two briefings of the book perform this demarcation task.

4 These ideas about supply and demand are presented in more detail in the briefings of a companion book, *Demands and Decisions, Briefings on Issues in Information Technology Strategy*, Bart O'Brien, (Prentice Hall, 1992).

5 A more stringent test, it might be thought, could be whether the chart was true. But this kind of chart can't really be proved to be 'true', in the sense that there are really ten elements rather than (say) eight or thirteen. The chart is justified only by being convenient.

6 Constraints can generate creativity. As Lord Clark of *Civilisation* used to say in a different context: 'How often has a difficult rhyme led to a beautiful thought'.

7 Chapter 1 of Elmasri and Navathe, one of the most recent and widely used textbooks. Here is a mapping of the elements of this briefing's chart against the content of the chapters of that book: kind of data: chapter 22; structure and access: chapters 6, 10, 11, 12; integrity: chapter 20; CRS: chapters 19, 20; deep design: chapters 4, 5, 14, 18; architecture: chapters 2, 21; modelling: chapters 3, 13, 15, 16; software development: chapters 7, 8, 9; control: chapter 17.

In *Data Base Management Systems*, (Allyn and Bacon, 1985), A Cardenas gives a very typical list of nine 'objectives': 1 data independence; 2 data shareability; 3 non-redundancy; 4 relatability; 5 integrity; 6 access flexibility; 7 security; 8 performance and efficiency; 9 administration and control.

Walsh gives five main 'considerations': 1 data independence; 2 non-redundancy; 3 flexibility in handling online retrieval transactions; 4 flexibility in responding to ad hoc requests for information; 5 security.

2. Untangling Kinds of Data

1 The two most common uses of spatial data are for maps and for engineering design (aka CAD, computer-aided design). Engineering data can be used both to reproduce a drawing and as the basis for calculations: of the weight of a certain component, whether it will stand up to a certain stress etc. Unlike mapping, CAD applications are relevant only to limited areas of industry, and are therefore not covered in this book.

2 This section presents some general arguments about the relevance of technology knowledge to non-technical decision-makers. The corresponding section in subsequent briefings is usually shorter — but only to avoid going through similar arguments each time; they apply just as well when transposed to the contexts of other briefings too.

3. Untangling Mainstream Systems

1 People don't always break down integrity, concurrency control, recovery and security in exactly the way given here. This may not matter very much, as long as the breakdown used in any discussions is reasonably sensible and everyone understands it the same way. The real danger is that two people may not notice that they are using (say) recovery or integrity to cover different things.

4. Conceptual Schemas

1 It would surely be better if the technology allowed the internal schema to be more independent of the conceptual schema than this, so that data could be arranged in an entirely different structure, if that were desirable technically. But as a general principle, this book describes the way the technology currently is, rather than how it ought to be or what it may become.

2 Some books (eg Elmasri and Navathe or Korth and Silberschatz) give separate chapters on hierarchical and network database, as if they were important alternatives. In practice, few *databases* of any great scope are pure hierarchy. Also, there are relatively few hierarchical *DBMSs*, and most of them have special features allowing you to turn the database structure into a rather messy network.

3 Watch out for statements that are not exactly false, but potentially misleading: eg 'The conceptual schema does not take into consideration how the data and processes will be implemented on the computer'. When you order goods from a mail-order catalogue, you don't take into consideration how your order will be implemented — checked, put with other orders, sent down to the warehouse etc. But you do place the order by filling in a form in the exact required format, with the product code, choice of colours out of those offered in the catalogue etc. So you do consider the mail-order company's internal procedures to the extent of recognising that they depend on receiving an order expressed in a certain format. Similarly, when you make a conceptual schema you do so in a format that takes into consideration what kind of data and structures a DBMS is capable of handling.

4 Few writers pay much attention to the rather fundamental assumptions and constraints associated with modelling and schema-drawing. One

worthwhile book that persistently asks the awkward questions is *Data and Reality*, W. Kent, (North-Holland, 1980).

5 Most specialists in the field talk of the 'relational model'. But then 'model' comes to be used confusingly in different senses: eg 'This model (ie description) of Sycamore's data is based on the relational model (ie conventions)'. In this briefing and the rest of the book 'form' or 'conventions' is normally used instead of 'model' for the latter sense; eg 'This model of Sycamore's data is made in relational form.'

6 Following through the table analogy, records are often called rows and fields columns. Still, some of the leading relational authorities do talk of records and fields.

7 Some DBMSs offer more intricate possibilities; eg from a Hewlett-Packard brochure: 'Allbase includes both network and relational technologies under one umbrella . . . The dual interface feature allows users to choose the most appropriate technology for each database application.' As with any promise to deliver all the advantages of two different approaches, you need to check carefully for any minor disadvantages there may be too.

8 Elmasri and Navathe, p. 376 (for the algebra) and Tom Kemm, 'A Practical Guide to Normalization', *DBMS*, December 1989, pp. 46-52. The latter gives a good jargon-free account of the normal forms, with neat, vivid examples and pragmatic comments.

9 Robin Bloor, 'The End of Relational?', *DBMS*, July 1992, p. 8.

5. Accessing the Database

1 The briefing discusses styles of interface but not *quality*. Good interface quality usually comes from avoiding bad practice, rather than by applying great creativity. One generic example of bad interface is offering options on a menu that in the user's current situation are meaningless or not available (instead they should be shown greyed out). Another is inconsistency in the simplest functions; eg to exit from a menu sometimes you have to press 'Esc' and other times F7 and sometimes 'q' for quit. Another arises with operations requiring successive menus: you select an instruction (eg quit) and the program has further questions for you (eg save or not?); in this second or later step, you might change your mind; the interface should offer you the option of cancelling at every step, rather than forcing you through to the end.

2 '. . . two men appeared to be checking computer printouts, one by one, by hand . . . Sharlett Underhill smiled. 'That's our VIP anti-goof squad. Many public utilities have one.' Arthur Hailey, *Overload*, p. 411 (Pan Books edition, 1980).

3 These considerations apply *a fortiori* when a view is not a subset of the conceptual schema, but makes a different schema altogether that is not even relationally correct. A view might present selected fields from different tables together in one 'virtual' table, in (say) second normal form. This is regarded as quite acceptable, provided that the real conceptual schema follows the relational norms and updates affecting the database are subject to appropriate safeguards. See Chris Date, *Database A Primer*, p. 237-8 (Addison-Wesley, 1984).

7. Concurrency, Recovery, Security

1 For more impressions of the complexity of CRS and of how different DBMS products offer different options: Frank Sweet 'Optimistic Concurrency Management', *Database Programming & Design*, November 1989, p. 34-42 and Steve Bobrowski, 'Protecting Your Data', *DBMS*, July 1993, pp. 55ff. Neither of these consist of material it is vital to know. Rather, they are clearly written accounts of the detail of some representative issues. They help you sense *the kind of* issues, factors and solutions that can come up.

8. Internal Schema Design

1 Database textbooks don't usually describe things that way. They often leave the general impression that the mapping of conceptual schema to internal schema can be a good deal more subtle, since the deep designer has (or at least ought to have) great scope for making design choices and changes independently of the conceptual schema. Nobody could deny the desirability of this aim, but what is most worth *knowing* is how things actually are in current database systems that use the main DBMS products. This briefing and this book concentrate on that.

2 Some books discuss in great detail how to achieve the most logical possible design, and then how to choose the technical options: indexes, hashing etc. The massive book by Elmasri and Navathe does mention the possibility that you may perhaps denormalise a logical schema for practical reasons — but only in one mild paragraph on page 477. The book by Korth and Silberschatz (546 pages, much in algebra) leaves out the idea altogether.

However, there is a useful article 'Denormalization: Why, What, and How?' by Ulka Rodgers, *Database Programming & Design*, December 1989, pp. 46-53.

9. Client-server Architecture

1 There is a common variant to the classic host architecture. People use ordinary PCs for word processing and spreadsheet and business graphics etc, but equipped with a special device, allowing the PC to function also, whenever required, as a terminal to the database system on the minicomputer. This doesn't mean that the PC, when used as a terminal, can access data or software or hardware that it normally accesses as PC; nor vice versa. It is simply more convenient than having both a terminal and a PC on almost every desk.

2 You can get round the concurrency limitations of file-server by breaking a database artificially into files, bearing in mind that one file can only be updated by one PC at a time. For example, a publisher might make the data concerning adverts in each of 50 magazines a separate file, and have certain people at certain PCs responsible for certain magazines. However, this kind of kludge has its limits.

3 For completeness: analogous problems and opportunities for optimisation occur also with large systems based on the host architecture — but with client-server the stakes are higher.

4 Some (not all) who use the three-way breakdown of client-server work promote a fallacy. This is that presentation and interface, business logic and

data management are like three successive stretches along a road and the question is where along the road the frontier should be drawn between the province of Client and the province of Server. This is a false view of the matter because it excludes certain plausible mixes; eg having all presentation and interface at the client, splitting business logic between client and server and also splitting data management between two.

10. Special Architectures

1 The term 'distributed database' is sometimes misused to stand for *any* database that can be accessed from more than one location. But this is true of nearly all large database systems. A database only counts as distributed if its data storage (not just its access) is spread over more than one location.

2 For some sturdy common sense about distributed database: Martin Butler and Robin Bloor, 'Distributed Database', *DBMS*, September 1991, pp. 16-17.

3 For more detail on an involved topic: Steve Bobrowski, 'Parallel Oracle 7.1', *DBMS*, December 1993, pp. 89-93; and Colin White, 'Processing in Parallel', *Database Programming & Design*, January 1994, p. 21-22. As these articles illustrate, ingenious new software and hardware products are appearing in this area — but that has been true for many years, and the techniques haven't made a great impact. On the other hand, as solutions to the most fundamental database problems become established, attention is likely to shift to more advanced matters, such as these.

11. Untangling Models, Tools and Control

1 If there must be a distinction between data dictionary and repository, probably the least bad criterion is this: the data dictionary only describes the system's data, whereas the repository describes more, in particular the system's processing. But this distinction is difficult to sustain. As you describe data in more and more detail you inevitably describe more and more about the whole system: eg 'This data item may take the values A, B or F. Value B shows that this policy is co-insured; ie other companies bear part of the risk. Co-insured policies are treated differently in the processing of monthly agency accounts . . . etc etc.'

12. Data Modelling Method and Process

1 The example diagram is based on conventions suggested in chapter 3 of the book by Elmasri and Navathe. Other conventions for drawing ER models exist; eg Chen, Bachman, Howe etc. All model the same sort of items and relationships; where one uses (say) a double line to define a certain kind of relationship another uses an arrowed line. Such differences of notation are unlikely to pose dilemmas with far-reaching implications and are not pursued in this book.

2 The diagram conventions are a simplified version of those suggested by DR Howe and used in chapter 7 of Benyon's book. They differ from those of Elmasri and Navathe, but that is a superficial point; they represent the same kind of content. Distinguishing the *content* of a model from the *conventions* used to represent the content is a fundamental tool in making sense of

the variety of modelling methods that people propose.

Benyon's book (chapters 7 and 8) is a good place to find out more about ER modelling. It describes some insidious traps modellers can fall into. Seeing the traps and limitations is vital to understanding any modelling method. Mark down texts that don't mention them.

3 Wayne Harris, *Databases for Business Users,* (Pitman, 1992), chapter 3. The service in that case study is actually computer-based dating, but the portion of its ER model discussed in the briefing could just as well apply to a library.

4 For a briefing-length discussion of this problem: Briefing 22 of the companion book *Demands and Decisions, Briefings on Issues in Information Technology Strategy*.

5 This example needs notes on four different planes:

First, in a real library the situation would be more complicated because some of the most popular CDs would be held in several copies. However, this need not affect the general point made in the briefing.

Second, relational theory definitely calls for choice of one and only one primary key for a table, even when several fields would be equally effective in conveying unique identity. But this point worries some authorities. See 'The Primacy of Primary Keys: An Investigation' by Chris Date in *InfoDB*, Summer 1993, pp. 2-8.

Third, Date's articles and books about relational matters are much more detailed than the material in this book. Date excels in offering neater examples, less algebra and more interesting discussion than most others writing at the theoretical level.

Fourth, apart from a vague encouragement of simplicity, relational theory contains no rules for determining how to choose between possible candidates for primary key. Commonsense guidelines can be followed but, as the library example shows, dilemmas still arise. Using the record company's number for the CD would break the sensible guideline of not using a field outside your own control as an identifier. But in the library's own internally allocated number the first two characters indicate the type of music: opera, chamber music etc; using that number would contradict the principle of avoiding a meaning-laden field as an identifier. Judgement is needed to decide on the least-bad choice.

6 These steps are from the method described by Barbara von Halle in *Database Programming & Design*, October 1990, pp. 13-16; November 1990, pp. 11-15; December 1990, pp. 11-15.

Zachman's ISA framework for structuring a project is popular with some writers on database. It divides all project work and deliverables over six rows; eg business-oriented modelling comes in row 2; systems-oriented modelling in row 3; technology-constrained modelling in row 4.

Questions flood in, among the most obvious: What counts as a project? Why should six rows (and never five or seven) be the right number for all projects? For more about Zachman's ISA framework, see 'The ISA Lightning Bolt', by Barbara von Halle, *Database Programming & Design*, January 1992, pp. 11-12; and the same column almost every month after that.

7 Another issue may seem to be: Should we make a data model at all — particularly if the database is a simple one? In practice, some form of data model is always a sound investment of effort. A one-page model describing a very simple database can make all subsequent detailed work more efficient and orderly. If the model shows unmis-

takably that the database is built on three main entities, related in certain ways (rather than four entities related in some other ways), it will reinforce people's comprehension of almost every page of system documentation — the report layouts, the input procedures, the enquiries and so on. Moreover, a data model may reveal that an apparently simple, low-volume database actually has some fairly complex data structures.

13. Data Modelling Tools

1 The view that much remains to be done in the I-CASE field is held fairly widely. To gauge the challenge follow this train of thought: computer system design has much in common with engineering design; engineering design is a specialised application, with some striking and very demanding features — version control, logical and physical views, re-usable sub-assemblies etc; see the list in the note below to Briefing 25.

15. Development Tools and Languages

1 Elmasri and Navathe, p28

2 Elmasri and Navathe, p28. Admittedly the text does analyse the notion of the DML further, though not very clearly.

3 4GL is a terrible name because it suggests that a 4GL is a kind of language, with its own syntax and structure. A 4GL is really more like a set of tools than a language. To decide 'We will use a 4GL here rather than a conventional programming language' is *not* like saying 'We will write this consultancy report in French rather than English'. Nor is it like 'We will produce a presentation with overheads instead of a written report'. It is really equivalent to 'We will produce a brief presentation with overheads *and* issue a synoptic management briefing *and* set up a question-and-answer session for middle managers — rather than write a long report'.

The term 4GL is also used in other senses so wide as to be worthless: eg 'any language that is not exclusively used by full-time programmers' or 'any language that differs in any way from languages, such as Cobol or Pascal, normally used to build large-scale systems for mainframes' or 'any language the speaker wishes to praise'.

4 The widely used dBase language is indisputably procedural. It has an instruction LOCATE allowing you to find the *first* record in the database meeting a certain condition; and CONTINUE lets you proceed, accessing records one at a time. Any true non-procedural language shuns the concept of reading records and processing them in any particular order. The non-procedural idea is closely associated with relational theory, since that excludes any notion of the records being stored in a table in any significant order.

On the other hand, you could use dBase (or any other high-level language) in a relatively non-procedural style, by reducing use of certain instructions, or at least keeping them in one fenced-off corner of the program.

5 As given in *PC Magazine*, May 11 1993.

16. Mix, Match, Amend

1 For Codd's rules conveniently summarised, with brief notes on why some are so tricky: Steven J Vaughan-Nichols, 'Relational Databases: the real story', *Byte*, December 1990, pp. 321-5.

2 See the interview with Chris Date in

Interface, a special supplement in *Database Programming & Design*, November 1993, p. 3.

3 Rule 12 is special. It says in effect: the DBMS should *offer* all the features defined in the previous eleven rules, and it should also *prevent* anybody from ignoring those features and doing things some other way (eg by coding integrity constraints in an application program, instead of storing them in the database). Making a DBMS software product that absolutely prevents anybody from getting round Codd's rules in any way, and yet still allows adequate freedom in all those areas that are not covered by the rules, seems quite a tall order.

4 The drawback is that occasionally ensembles of components that ought to fit together and do work correctly most of the time are subject to bugs arising from subtle incompatibilities, that can be the devil's own job to unravel.

5 This important topic is often discussed in a very hazy way, that loses the distinction between an ideal architecture and the features of most current DBMSs. A rare and excellent article explains the issues very clearly: Tom Johnston, 'Cracks in the Foundation', *Database Programming & Design*, October 1991, pp. 50-53. A follow-up article suggests how DBMS suppliers might extend their products to cope with the shortcomings: Tom Johnston, 'Rebuilding the Foundation', *Database Programming & Design*, November 1991, pp. 53-61.

17. Mainstream Software Products

1 Robert Mattison's *Understanding Database Management Systems* (McGraw-Hill, 1993) draws a distinction between the classic network DBMS (eg DEC DBMS) and an 'inverted list' style of DBMS that also supports a network conceptual schema; Adabas and CA-Datacom are given as examples. There is indeed a difference, but only at internal schema level, not at conceptual schema level, which is the more important.

2 This gradations warrant is loosely based on one in a rather good article: Celeste Robinson, 'Databases come to Windows', *PC World*, June 1993, pp. 188-206

18. Untangling Text Systems

1 Two simple approaches deserve mention here lest they slip through an intercategory crack. A mainstream database might have some fixed-length fields containing text, that could be searched for any string of characters. A library might allow titles of books to be searched in this way. There are limitations: a search for books with 'Bali' in the title might also find books on canni*bali*sm and ca*bali*stic signs. Searching on ' bali ' would avoid that problem, but miss titles that included 'Balinese'. Even so, despite its crudeness, this approach could still be the best buy in certain cases.

Again, a library's database might be entirely mainstream, except for the detail that some fields in the schema were named *keyword-1, keyword-2* etc. The trouble is that nobody ever searches for a book with *keyword-1* 'Bali' and *keyword-2* not 'dance'. A real requirement is for a book whose records have *any* out of *keyword-1* through *keyword-8* 'Bali', but *none* of *keyword-1* through *keyword-8* 'dance'. As this example suggests, the approach fits relational conventions only loosely and makes access through SQL or other means very cumbersome. Still, in certain circumstances it could be the best buy.

2 Some people favour information retrieval system (IRS) as the name for this field. Snag: too vague; any database system retrieves information.

3 Sometimes the words used for searching in the content of a document are called keywords — wrongly. A keyword is a word that an indexer has deliberately *attached to* an item to help those who search later to recognise the nature of the item. Searching to see whether a certain word or phrase is contained anywhere *within* a text is quite different; that is a one-off phenomenon, independent of any work by an indexer.

19. Classic Text Systems

1 Of course, distinctions are not always sharp. A book review in a magazine usually has a bibliographic role, but suppose a reviewer indulges in personal opinions and theories, and says little about the book. Then the text is really text-in-itself.

2 The categories and labels suggested here were devised for this book. Text is often called 'full text' or 'free text', but the adjectives are often superfluous, sometimes misleading and best saved for use when they really add meaning.

3 'The key to the situation lay in a heavy, bound volume — *BC Reports*, Vol 34, 1921 — on the judge's desk. It was open at a page headed *Rex* v *Ahmed Singh*. Any individual (the long dead judge had declared in 1921) must be deported to the country whence he came, *and not to any other place*. The deportation order against Henri Duval was therefore unlawful and invalid.' Arthur Hailey, *In High Places*, p. 363 (Pan Books edition, 1970).

4 Sometimes it is worthwhile to carry analysis by role quite far. For example, here are five distinct activities that the text database system of a business school might assist:

Searching — striving to reach some narrow pre-defined goal; eg find a certain article that explains the technique of discounted cash flow;

Browsing — following a path until some broad but firm knowledge goal is achieved; eg read enough to grasp the essentials of JIT and handle questions about it from different angles;

Scanning — covering a relatively large area without depth; eg get familiar with the concepts and issues involved in human resources management, without mastering them enough to handle questions from different angles;

Exploring — finding out the extent of information available; eg survey (without reading) available texts and note down references on the relation of total quality management to business strategy;

Wandering — unstructured dabbling; eg read an article on macroeconomics, feel stimulated to read another one on justifying capital investment, then one on taxation etc.

5 *Conceptual schema* isn't normally found in this context, but is still a good term to use.

6 Some of the techniques and examples here are taken from a handy book: Barbara Newlin, *Answers Online: Your Guide to Informational Databases*, (Osborne McGraw-Hill, 1985)

20. Advanced Text Systems

1 Examples from *Text Retrieval and Document Databases* John Ashford and Peter Willett (Chartwell-Bratt, 1988), p. 25. This is a good book for going deeper into the way text database systems work.

2 Confusion can arise about what SGML is and isn't. It is essentially a standard approach to marking the components of texts with tags. It leaves you to define and name your own tags. If you want to tag the titles of articles, it is up to you whether to call the tag <ARTICLETITLE> or <ARTNAME> or even <FGHJK>. However, if SGML documents are to be exchanged and SGML databases to be used by many people, some standardisation of tagnames and of document structures is desirable. Understandably, groups such as publishers of scientific journals or contractors in the defence industry have agreed standard tagnames and standard meta-files. These remain industry-group standards resting on the foundation of the general SGML standard. Therefore it can't be assumed that any two texts are directly compatible merely because they conform to the general SGML standard.

21. Hypertext Systems

1 Mixed forms are possible too. In particular, you might design a hypertext database structured and accessed in any one of the four styles described, but as an extra resource build in possibilities for access by keyword and text-search of the whole database.

2 This warrant is based on ideas in an article by Jakob Nielsen in *Communications of the ACM*, March 1990.

22. Untangling Hybrid Systems

1 The term 'hybrid' is found sometimes in other quite different senses. A distributed database system may be called hybrid if the data is managed by different DBMSs (or different types of DBMS) at different locations. Also, different again, one DBMS that somehow combines several styles of data organisation (eg relational and network, or relational and object-oriented) may be called a hybrid DBMS.

2 The gradations of hybridity were devised for this book. There is no generally accepted terminology or taxonomy in this area.

3 A hybrid database contains more than one kind of data; eg as with a GIS, mainstream, graphic, spatial. It seems to make no sense to regard one piece of data as hybrid. But on stricter analysis, a piece of spatial data (eg the co-ordinates of a road) might be counted as hybrid itself, since it is at the same time vector graphic data (for map-drawing) and mainstream data (for calculations).

23. Picture Database Systems

1 This is the only place in the book where a real, rather than fabricated, application is described. This database system is a special case: not only is it a fine example, but anyone can go to the National Gallery and use it.

2 This breakdown of structure-styles was devised for this book. As yet, there is no established terminology or taxonomy.

3 Some DBMSs allow you to undermine the neatness of this style by using one

image as the picture field on more than one card. However, there are probably not many cases where that is the best data structure for the application.

4 Much that is published about picture databases gives the impression that the real challenges lie in the technology of capturing images, compressing them, editing them, storing them and so on. This briefing aims to redress the balance. You do need competent people to handle these supply-side issues and you need to encourage them to find sensible tradeoffs so that image quality and other technical aspects are consistent with system purpose. But, as the briefing shows, there are large issues of structure and access to be tackled too; and here it is less appropriate to expect people whose expertise is mainly technical to expose all the options and choose between them.

5 Here are some more technical details. There are 18 powerful Apple Macintosh PCs, each with a 19" (ie large and expensive) colour screen and a WORM disk with a capacity of 1300Mb. Twelve of the PCs have a laser printer too. The software product organising the database is HyperCard. A considerable amount of special software was also written to handle technical matters such as compressing data to minimise disk storage, while optimising the quality of image and text on the screen.

Cognitive Applications Ltd of Brighton, UK was responsible for designing the technology aspects of the system and for software development.

6 The National Gallery database system is also published on CD-ROM as *Microsoft Art Gallery* in versions for Microsoft Windows or Apple Macintosh PCs. Since this system will normally be used by people familiar with a PC rather than casual visitors to the gallery, it can be more powerful on several of the issues of access mentioned in the briefing (eg mouse and keyboard as input device; non-structural searching; tours).

An interesting question for Mountain Blueberry is: Why not distribute the store's picture database as a catalogue on CD-ROM, for wealthy customers to browse on their PCs at home?

24. Document Image Systems

1 As in 'Imaging: the emerging tiger' and 'With imaging, companies are able to do in 30 minutes what it used to take three weeks to accomplish' and much more.

2 Some writers about document-imaging systems seem to suggest that it is worth knowing such things as how the lasers in optical disks actually work. At the other extreme, others offer blind enthusiasm unsullied by recognition of options and constraints. This briefing aims to discuss technology, but only in terms that will assist decision-making.

25. Geographic Information Systems

1 Warning: some people use 'spatial' only in the more restricted sense of *three-dimensional* space, thus excluding most geographic applications (other than specialised cases such as weather forecasting or ecology simulation).

Geographic data might plausibly be used in almost any organisation (a department store, an insurance company, a government ministry etc), but this doesn't apply to engineering design, the next most common type of spatial system. Nevertheless, it is interesting to sketch out briefly some typical features of an engineering design application (in comparison with a mainstream system):

The data is mainly vector graphics

(as opposed to relational mainstream), but the database is hybrid: eg bill of materials data about products, sub-assemblies, components etc is held too.

Data structures are complicated considerably because some parts of one engineering design may be reusable in other designs — a requirement without any real mainstream equivalent.

Multiple versions of design information are required: eg go back to yesterday's version of sub-assembly A, and Friday's of sub-assembly B, while keeping the current design for the rest of the product; or hold one version of the established product and other versions used by groups working to improve its design.

Different views may be needed that are not just different subsets of a whole; eg one view of the logic of a microchip, another of its physical layout.

A special access language may be needed to access data of different levels, versions and views, without tedious formulation of instructions.

There can be frequent changes in the conceptual schema as new designs call for data organised in new ways.

Different pieces of design may be 'linked' to each other in more than just the logical sense of the word. Item A may be literally attached to Item C by means of Item B, a hinge or crank. Database integrity checks may entail seeing that items which ought not to rub against each other in fact do not.

2 Nevertheless, for a splendid feature on GIS and related technology, albeit only on PC, see Robert Kendall, 'Mapping Software: Analyzing a World of Data', *PC Magazine*, July 1991

3 The analysis of demand and supply gradations leaves out three interesting variants, that don't quite count as widely applicable database systems:

Narrow purpose system: makes no claim to be a general-purpose system but is powerful in one kind of problem, eg finding an optimal route along highways, while taking account of speed limits, one way streets, low bridges etc.

Vector mapping system: uses vector graphics, even perhaps with layer management, but primarily to produce maps of high quality on paper or screen, with relatively little attention to processing of spatial or mainstream data.

Bit-mapped mapping system: uses bit-mapped graphics, primarily to produce high-quality and/or very detailed maps, perhaps using some spatial and mainstream data as well, but inevitably in a cumbersome way.

4 Issues such as map-acquisition (or, in other briefings, the image-capture of picture database and the optical storage of document-image systems) don't fit well into the unifying chart of database technology — because they are not usually thought of as specifically *database* issues. Though it would be easy to add another supply-side element to the chart to cover such technical challenges, the drawback is that in the majority of mainstream and non-mainstream database systems few options of any interest arise; you simply use normal disks, normal keyboard and mouse input etc.

5 A more detailed account of GIS would add many nuances. The interplay between the map-acquisition, map-drawing and data-combination elements of a system can be more subtle than the chart suggests.

Suppose twelve bus and tram services all go down the same busy street; how can that be represented without congestion on a map? One approach might be to ensure that during *map-acquisition*, important streets where this problem could arise were stored graphically with a width that was far out of scale. Alternatively, *map-drawing* arrangements could attack the problem; the chosen screen or print technology could be refined enough to squeeze twelve very narrow lines into the width of a road separately and clearly. Or thirdly, ingenious *data-combination* logic might be the answer; eg subtle layer management could avoid clutter by distinguishing only those lines relevant to specific information needs. This is not a simple three-way choice; some mixture of approaches could well be best.

26. Text-with-Mainstream Systems

1 For more on this, see the book by Ashford and Willett, chapter 7.

27. Rules-with-Mainstream Systems

1 Types of knowledge, information, data and so on can be analysed endlessly. Heuristic knowledge (ie facts and rules based on experience and approximations, rather than proved or calculated) is sometimes seen as a separate type of knowledge. But distinction-blurring cases arise. Are the tide-tables in an almanac heuristic? It is best not to wade any further into this intellectual quagmire than you really need to.

2 For example: 'An expert system is generally defined as a computer program that relies on knowledge and reasoning to perform a difficult task usually performed only by a human expert.' Parsaye et alia, p. 162; and 'Typically expert systems require best-guess solutions rather than rigorous mathematical analysis or algorithmic solutions. Heuristics enable the system-builder to use rules-of-thumb or tricks that have been learnt by experience.' Joe Peppard (ed.), *IT Strategy for Business* (Pitman, 1993), p206.

3 This generalisation disguises a formidable challenge. The body of rules data in a knowledgebase needs integrity just as much as any other kind. If there is already a rule (say) that a revolution never triggers a *force majeure* clause, then adding a new rule that a revolution may trigger a *force majeure* clause under some circumstances would set up a contradiction; and a new rule that a revolution led by the army never triggers a *force majeure* clause would be superfluous. Ideally integrity checks should safeguard against such contradiction and superfluity. In practice, it is difficult to program a computer to do this.

4 Even at an intermediate gradation of complexity some vexing difficulties can arise; here is one. The knowledgebase system sends SQL requests across to the database. The nature of SQL is to deliver the whole set of records (whether none, one or 10,000) that meet the defined search criteria. But the knowledgebase system may not want the whole set; its reasoning may only depend on whether there is *at least one* record that meets the criteria. Retrieving the whole set just to find this out can be very wasteful of resources.

5 For an excellent account of the way Prolog can handle facts and rules see William Clocksin, 'A Prolog Primer', *Byte*, August, 1987, pp 147-158

6 '. . the penicillin had been administered shortly before Wyrazik died. Andrew read the rest of the file — including the intern's note about penicillin allergy — in a daze. When he returned the file to a records clerk his hand was shaking, his heart pounding.'

Arthur Hailey, *Strong Medicine*, p. 139 (Pan Books edition, 1984).

7 Medical applications are commonly given as examples of expert systems in enthusiastic management literature. Note that, in this example at least, it isn't true that the hitherto vaguely apprehended skills and knowledge of an expert are translated into automated rules. Here all the facts and rules are already contained, implicitly or explicitly, in a book, published perhaps years ago. In principle, setting up this knowledgebase requires analytical ability but no medical knowledge at all.

In practice, some medical expertise would be present in the team for other reasons. Psychological reassurance is valuable, even if it can't be justified rationally. Also, the reorganisation of the book's knowledge may reveal mistakes, inconsistencies, ambiguities and unstated assumptions that have lain unnoticed, because the material has never before been examined so carefully; once exposed, they need to be resolved.

8 A note on Briefing 2 points out that its arguments about the place of technology knowledge in decision-making have general force. Similarly, here in Briefing 27, the comparison of five strategy options is a generally applicable technique. Its value isn't restricted to debates about rules-with-mainstream systems; it could apply just as well to decisions about hypertext or CASE or any number of other technologies. In fact, most of the decision-making problems and approaches discussed throughout the book have general rather than technology-specific relevance.

29. Object-oriented Topics

1 This briefing omits some of the jargon of the OO field (inheritance, encapsulation, extension, superclasses etc) for a number of reasons: 1, New terms give the impression that everything is new, but you really need to grasp both what is new and what is much the same as in other approaches; 2, In this new field, different authors use the terms differently; 3, Some of the best established terms are not very well-chosen: eg in the briefing's EER model, *Consultant* would be a 'subclass' said to 'inherit' the attributes of the superclass *Fee-earner*. Is this like inheriting an oil painting when an uncle dies, ie at one moment you don't own it and then you do? No. It is more like inheriting blue eyes from a parent, though that isn't an exact analogy either.

2 Mattison's book (chapter 13) complicates matters by presenting *three* distinct methods, called ER modelling, semantic data modelling and object-oriented modelling. But this account seems open to the criticism that it confuses conventions with content. Two modelling techniques may differ in graphic conventions (eg one places dots inside or outside boxes, another uses various arrow shapes), but it doesn't follow that they are recording different content. They may simply be using different notation to convey the same thing.

This is not to deny that there *can* be modelling techniques associated with object-oriented ideas, that do differ in content as well as in conventions.

Semantic modelling is a term used in so many different ways that the only safe advice is: avoid.

3 The diagram uses the ODT conventions for drawing an EER, presented in the extremely useful book by James Rumbaugh, Michael Blaha, William Premeriani, Frederick Eddy and William Lorensen: *Object-Oriented Modeling and Design*, (Prentice Hall, 1991).

4 For an impression of the problems

and the variety of approaches under consideration by computer scientists, see John G Hughes, *Object-Oriented Databases*, (Prentice Hall, 1991)

5 Rumbaugh et al, chapter 16

6 Object-orientation is definitely important, but a great many articles about it fail to reveal the heath for the gorse. Here are two good references: Herb Edelstein, 'Relational vs. Object-oriented', *DBMS*, November 1991, pp. 68-79; and Robert G Brown, 'The Evolution of Domains', *Database Newsletter*, November/December 1993, pp. 3-6.

31. Untangling Database and Wider Issues

1 The field of management that is concerned with all types of planning and decision-making about the use of IT is often referred to as 'information management'. Though inherently vague, this is the least bad term to use, providing everyone understands it to stand for something like 'the management of the organisation's information technology — in a wide sense, not merely the management of IT projects or departments.' This puts it on a very different plane from 'data management' or 'database management'.

2 This book's companion, *Information Management Decisions, Briefings and Critical Thinking*.

Index of Terms and Concepts

Glossaries have two problems. First, many concepts can't be understood in isolation: to grasp what an internal schema is, you really need to know about external schema and conceptual schema too; if you know what concurrency control is, but are unsure how it relates to integrity control, recovery and security — then you can't talk about concurrency control with any confidence.

Second, usage varies; a book may use (say) 4GL in a certain sense, but you also need to be aware whether this is the generally accepted usage or specific to the book.

This index supplies for each technical **term** or concept the numbers of those **briefings** in which the term and others closely associated with it are most clearly defined.

The **usage** is also given:

normal: most people in the field who use terms fastidiously use this term in much the same way as it is used in this book;

tricky: many people do recognise the usage found in this book, but others use it somewhat differently; unfortunately the differences can be quite confusing;

special: the usage in this book is not a generally accepted one, but the chance of confusion is not great (eg because the term is rarely used elsewhere or is normally used quite vaguely).

The list excludes a number of terms mentioned in the text as random examples of things that, for most decision-makers, are not worth knowing about: linear hashing, theta join, Cartesian product, circulating control token etc.

Indirect Index of Software Products

Some representative products are named and classified in two briefings: **17. Mainstream Software Products** and **28. Non-Mainstream Software Products.**

Products mentioned in the other briefings are usually just arbitrary, incidental examples, so it would be misleading to index them.

The magazines *DBMS* and *Database Programming & Design* both produce an annual buyer's guide issue with details of hundreds of products. Either provides a convenient starting-point for any systematic survey of products in the mainstream field. The *DBMS* guide also includes a selection of non-mainstream products.

DBMS is published by Miller Freeman Inc, 411 Borel Ave, Suite 100, San Mateo, CA 94402, USA.

Database Programming & Design is published by Miller Freeman Inc, 600 Harrison St, San Francisco, CA 94107, USA.

If you need to monitor the vibrant market in PC database and related software products really thoroughly, subscribe to *Data Based Advisor*, published by Data Based Solutions Inc, 4010 Moreno Blvd, Suite 200, San Diego, CA 92117, USA.

There are two useful directories for text database and related software products:

Text Retrieval: a Directory of Software, Robert Kimberley (ed.), (3rd ed., Gower, 1990)

European Directory of Software for Libraries and Information Centres, Joanna Wood (ed.), (Ashgate, 1993)

Index of Topics and Themes

The important terms and concepts in database technology are referenced in *Index of Terms and Concepts*. The following is a residual index of topics and themes not included there.